THE INCREDIBLE STORY OF
EPHRAIM NUTE

MW01388291

THE INCREDIBLE STORY OF
EPHRAIM NUTE

❧

Scandal, Bloodshed and Unitarianism
on the American Frontier

Bobbie Groth

Skinner House Books
Boston

Copyright © 2011 by Bobbie Groth. All rights reserved. Published by Skinner House Books, an imprint of the Unitarian Universalist Association of Congregations, a liberal religious organization with more than 1,000 congregations in the U.S. and Canada, 25 Beacon St., Boston, MA 02108-2800.

Printed in the United States

Cover and text design by Suzanne Morgan
Front cover photograph used by permission of the Kansas State Historical Society
Frontispiece cover photograph used by permission of Bobbie Groth

Print ISBN: 978-1-55896-609-3 / eBook ISBN: 978-1-55896-611-6

6 5 4 3 2 1 / 13 12 11

We gratefully acknowledge the following institutions for granting permission to reprint many of the primary-source documents presented here: Andover-Harvard Theological Library, the Kansas State Historical Society, Meadville Lombard Library and Archives, the Ohio Historical Society, the Massachusetts Historical Society, the Harvard University Archives, the American Philosophical Society, Kent State University Libraries, Stackpole Books, and the American Antiquarian Society. For specific information regarding the documents that received permission, and from which institution, see the Notes, pp. 341–80.

The historical documents quoted in this volume, many of which are handwritten letters, are reprinted verbatim to preserve their authenticity. They include grammatical errors, omitted words, and antiquated terminology.

Library of Congress Cataloging-in-Publication Data

Groth, Bobbie.
The incredible story of Ephraim Nute: scandal, bloodshed and Unitarianism on the American frontier / Bobbie Groth.
    p. cm.
  Includes bibliographical references and index.
  ISBN-13: 978-1-55896-609-3 (pbk. : alk. paper)
  ISBN-10: 1-55896-609-9 (pbk. : alk. paper)
  ISBN-13: 978-1-55896-611-6 (ebook)
  1. Nute, Ephraim, d. 1897. 2. American Unitarian Association—Clergy—Biography. 3. Abolitionists—United States—Biography. I. Title.
  BX9869.N88G76 2011
  289.1092—dc22
  [B]
                        2010044812

CONTENTS

God be thanked for ... the bright hope that illumines the prospect for Kansas, ruffian-ridden, oppressed & bleeding thus far. We have sown in tears & all are destined, I am confident, to reach our joy somewhere in the future ... notwithstanding all that unprincipled politicians & their wicked rulers, their toads, can do.

—E. Nute to H. A. Miles, January 12, 1857

PREFACE

This is the story of how the Reverend Ephraim Nute Jr., a young, upright Unitarian minister from New England and my great-great-grandfather, attained a national presence in the 1850s as an abolitionist missionary to the Kansas Territory. His life was a dynamic thread in the tapestry of the fledgling Unitarian movement, pioneer emigration, the Underground Railroad, the Civil War, the soldiers' homes of the Sanitary Commissions, the birth and growth of frontier newspapers, and the origins of higher education in the West.

The years of Nute's active ministry called on Unitarianism's highest moral aspirations and theologies but also revealed turmoil within the American Unitarian Association. While the AUA was forged in the pure values of liberal Christianity, the denomination was divided in its support of abolition. Some of its wealth stemmed from industries that depended on slavery. As a result, Nute was forced to fight for the financial support his denomination had promised him and his church when he set out as a missionary.

By the time of his old age, Ephraim Nute—whose name was a household word in the 1850s and whose adventures had been reported in newspapers all over the United States, Canada, and Europe—was remanded to near obscurity. Despite these obstacles, my family's research, begun for the same reasons any other family explores its genealogy, has turned up substantial writings from Nute's own hands, supported by the writings of contemporaries who knew him. In the correspondence and journals recording Nute's day-to-day life, we find the stuff of legend: a young idealist who was shot at, imprisoned, attacked, and almost lynched as he stood by his parishioners in Kansas. He performed pioneer weddings in cabins with dirt floors. He stood by graves and preached the funeral sermons of family and friends who had been murdered by Border Ruffians. He rode horses across the prairie at night to lead runaway slaves to safety. He opened the foundations of his unfinished church to be used as a fort by men armed to protect the town of Lawrence, Kansas, and their families from attack. Nute's dear friend Edward Everett Hale later wrote of him that he "was a good fighter when the fight was on."

Nute's story is also the story of his parishioners in Kansas—"Bleeding Kansas" as it was known then, in recognition of the enormous violence there in the time leading up to the Civil War. The story of these ordinary folks is different from that of the New England Unitarians enshrined in the annals of Unitarian history. Nute and his companion settlers were not ensconced in the hallowed halls of Harvard and Cambridge, on the quiet streets of Concord, or behind a desk in a newspaper office. They had heard the call to take "true Christianity"—their Unitarian liberal Christianity—to the Kansas Territory to ensure that it would become a free state. They answered that call on the front lines of undeclared civil war, something our most revered forebears only wrote about.

The adventures of Nute and his fellow frontline Unitarians shine a new light on the abolitionist movement leading up to the Civil War. So often this history is told as if the fight against slavery was a discourse on morals and theology, where only slaves, and later soldiers, paid with their lives. But the substance of the movement was found in the daily lives of people who resisted, starved, fought, suffered, and died for abolition. When the grand biographies and histories of the nineteenth century glossed over the stories of these men and women, we remembered the narrators rather than the individuals who made that history.

Ephraim Nute and his parishioners have not been adequately dignified or honored for their sacrifices. Their story reveals the courage of some true martyrs, who emerge as valuable and accessible role models. They will not be forgotten so soon.

A MAN WITH A MISSION

Open any New England classic, biography, or description of a Revolutionary War hero and you will find that the measure of the man or woman is first told through the history of family of origin. Those who came to New England from old England brought family names with them that had borne centuries and generations of legend. Second, third, and fourth sons set sail for the New World for the promise of land that they could not attain in a country with primogeniture. They brought their names and their family connections as one might now bring a professional vitae. As society flourished in the primitive conditions of New England, the surname was an entrée into marriage, business, and the church. A woman left her family, took her husband's name, and so became invisible, as anyone seeking a grandmother in genealogy will remark with frustration. A man, however, wore his family name like a banner that broadcast his past and in many cases all but determined his future.

James Newte[1] emigrated to Portsmouth (now in New Hampshire) in 1631, one of a company of planters settling the Laconia Patent of Captain John Mason. Rev. Ephraim Nute Jr. was a direct descendant, eight generations later, of James, and as he grew up he spent much time in the Portsmouth-Dover area, where the family farms and burial grounds were located.[2] Nute was raised in a Universalist family, which had close ties with the Unitarians of Boston.

Nute's father, Ephraim Sr., left his birthplace in Dover for the Boston area where he was married for the first time to Mary A. Bancroft, a member of the large Unitarian Bancroft family. The couple was married in 1818 at the First Universalist Church rectory by Rev. Paul Dean, a prominent Universalist trinitarian evangelist. Mary gave birth to Ephraim Nute Jr. on September 18, 1819. She died while he was a toddler, and Nute Sr. married again in 1823 to Jane Pratt at the Second Universalist Church rectory. The wedding was officiated by Hosea Ballou, a prominent Universalist minister called "the father of Universalism" and a rival of Paul Dean. Nute's two siblings born of this marriage both died in infancy.

It is likely that Ephraim Nute Jr. had a fairly typical childhood for a boy growing up in the early 1800s. Although it was certainly tragic that he lost his mother and both of his siblings, this was not uncommon in that era. Nute attended one of the Boston Latin Schools, and he prepared to apply for admission to Harvard. He gained entrance to the school of theology by examination, as a scholarship student. There he rubbed shoulders with the wealthy and privileged young men of the Boston Unitarian circles.

Nute married Lucy Ann Fessenden on July 4, 1841, the year before he entered seminary. The Fessenden surname was prominent in abolitionist, Unitarian, and Universalist circles, as were the surnames of Nute's subsequent wives, Skinner and Coffin. The couple was married by Rev. Frederick Gray at the esteemed Bulfinch Street Church in Boston, the Universalist church where Nute was raised and where he served as Sunday school superintendent prior to seminary.

Nute attended Harvard Divinity School between 1842 and 1845. Although on scholarship, he also worked his way through seminary by serving as superintendent of the First Parish of Cambridge Sunday school. Classmates of Nute who figured prominently during the time in which he lived, and to whom Nute went for help when in Kansas, included Joseph Henry Allen, Unitarian minister, scholar, and author; John Pierpont Jr., son of the notable Unitarian abolitionist John Pierpont Sr.; George Frederic Ware, son of the prominent Unitarian minister and theologian Henry Ware; Samuel Longfellow, Unitarian minister and brother of the poet, Henry Wadsworth Longfellow; Frank Parker Appleton and William Orne

White, both of whom achieved long and distinguished careers in Unitarian ministry; Octavius Brooks Frothingham, radical Unitarian Transcendentalist and abolitionist; and Thomas Wentworth Higginson, radical abolitionist, poet, editor, writer, minister, John Brown conspirator, and founding member of the Free Religious Association—the dissenters from the 1866 formation of the National Conference of Unitarian Churches. Small in number, Nute's graduating class comprised a group of men destined to make a mark on the history of the denomination and the country.

Commencement exercises for the class of 1845 involved speeches and other contributions by all members of the class. Throughout the ceremony, the catchwords of the Unitarianism of the time flowed: "truth," "Zion," "Christ," and "duty." Nute preached on "Asceticism in the Church." Given his reputation, it might be supposed that he was highly in favor of asceticism. Nute made perfectly clear in his letters that he was ever attentive to how his soul would be accounted for to God. As a young minister he seemed upright to a fault and stiff with New England Unitarianism; he was described as "pious" by a colleague. His letters abound with New England diligence, parsimony, and some might say, severe honesty. Anyone who fell short of the high standards he set for himself received less than his full admiration.

Upon graduation, Nute was immediately ordained by the Unitarian congregation in Petersham, Massachusetts, where he took up his first call. Frederick Gray, minister of Nute's home church, the Bulfinch Society, had a long and intimate relationship with the fledgling minister. During the ceremony, Gray preached on the text Hebrews 13:17, "For they watch for your souls as they who must give an account, that they may do it with joy and not with grief." The text goes on to declare, "Obey your leaders and submit to them; for they are keeping watch over your souls, as men who will have to give account. Let them do this joyfully, and not sadly, for that would be of no advantage to you."

Such an admonition at Nute's own ordination was ironic, given that later Nute did anything but obey leaders and submit to them. An earlier passage in Hebrews identifies leaders as "those who spoke to you the word of God." In this sense, perhaps the one thing that kept Nute a renegade his whole life was his adherence to his ordinational charge and obedience to the word of God as liberal Christianity first taught it to him. This often put him at odds with political and religious leaders, even those of his own denomination.

Rev. Alonzo Hill, who gave the charge at Nute's ordination, was the minister of the Unitarian congregation in Worcester, Massachusetts, for over forty years. The newspapers reported that his charge had a "power and religious fervor not soon to be forgotten."[3] Nute may very well have emulated the impressive preaching of Hill and Gray as he matured as a preacher, particularly with respect to the extemporaneous preaching style he consciously developed before embarking on his mission to Kansas. He combined the hellfire and brimstone based in the Puritan roots of New England Unitarianism with the spiritual ardor of abolitionist Universalism, and many newspapers testified to his stimulating and confrontational style.

His prophetic preaching caused him trouble at his first parish in Petersham. A major scandal developed after an election in 1846. Nute was a Republican—the antislavery party—and an ardent abolitionist. It became known that the young minister did not vote for one of his own parishioners because he was a Democrat—the proslavery party.

Around Thanksgiving of that year Nute preached an antiwar sermon that raised the ire of a few parishioners who felt he had overstepped the bounds of the pulpit and become too political. Nute was, and always continued to be, adamantly against the consumption of alcohol, which also antagonized some of his congregation, who used and sold liquor freely. It was an affront to their dignity and community stature that their personal wealth and donations to their congregation did not insulate them from sermons on the depravity of alcohol when they went to church on Sunday.

Criticism of and hostility toward Nute from these factions—which, according to his defenders, were all the same people—gained momentum. His detractors manufactured preposterous stories of him dancing in taverns and they insinuated other vague, nefarious misdeeds of his, much at odds with his reputation. When these stories did not immediately drive Nute from the parish, because most of the congregation supported him, some of the detractors chose to leave, but they continued to fan the fires of rumor and scandal in the local papers. By mid-1847 they had taken their scathing accusations regularly to the editorial columns of all the newspapers surrounding Petersham.

Nute wrote a sad letter to a friend at the Petersham congregation in March 1848[4] from Scituate, Massachusetts, where he was filling the pulpit even though his tenure at Petersham had not yet officially ended. From his self-imposed exile, he heard that the parish in Petersham had passed a resolution affirming their admiration for and attachment to him, and he wrote to thank his friend for this news. Nute spoke of how painful his separation from Petersham had been and of plans to go West. Even though the majority of his congregation gave him their vote of confidence, the constant character assassination severely affected Nute's comfort level in the community and caused him to leave Petersham in discouragement.

In May 1848, Nute accepted a permanent call to the Scituate Unitarian congregation, where he served until 1851. During these years he was active with the antislavery movement, publishing antislavery essays in chapbooks like *The Liberty Bell*, one series in the many collections of poetry and prose sold in Boston in the forty years before the Civil War. *The Liberty Bell* was a serious and unpretentious tract that over the years published the works of nearly two hundred contributors, many of them Unitarians. They included such abolitionist notables as William Lloyd Garrison, Unitarian publisher of the prominent abolitionist newspaper, *The Liberator*; Wendell Phillips, Unitarian orator; Theodore Parker, heretical Unitarian preacher and supporter of John Brown; Lydia

Maria Child, Unitarian novelist, editor, journalist, and scholar; Frederick Douglas, African-American abolitionist, women's suffragist, editor of the abolitionist newspaper *The North Star,* orator, author, and statesman; Lucretia Mott, an American Quaker, proponent of women's rights, and social reformer; Harriet Beecher Stowe, founder of the Unitarian literary club and author of *Uncle Tom's Cabin*; Elizabeth Barret Browning, one of the most prominent poets of the Victorian era who moved in Unitarian circles; Ralph Waldo Emerson, Unitarian minister, essayist, and leader in the Transcendentalist movement; James Russell Lowell and Maria White Lowell, socially prominent Unitarian sympathizers; Henry W. Longfellow, the poet and brother of the Unitarian minister Samuel Longfellow; Harriet Martineau, pioneering British journalist, writer, and Unitarian apologist; Margaret Fuller, journalist, critic, and women's rights activist associated with the Unitarians and Transcendentalists; James Freeman Clarke, Unitarian minister, author, orator, and scholar; Thomas Wentworth Higginson, Unitarian minister, social reformer, and author; and John Pierpont, Unitarian minister, teacher, lawyer, and merchant.[5]

Nute's zealous and theological 1849 essay, "The Leaven of Liberty" published in *The Liberty Bell* in 1851, rang with the Harvard prose that was characteristic of his generation, the sentimental passion that was Universalism, and the upright New England Unitarian Christianity that was his youthful style:

> I would appeal to that hope which I trust we all hold dear as friends of the Slave and associates in the sacred cause of justice and freedom; the hope for the abolition of American Slavery; for the universal reign of Liberty. . . . Why do we cherish this hope, so widely accounted as the dream of enthusiasm? Why grows it stronger in our hearts day by day in the face of all opposition, notwithstanding every triumph of oppression? Is it not because we believe in the power of that truth by which all tyranny of man over his brother stands condemned?—because we believe in the spirit of Love which must, in its certain conquest, break

all chains and abolish all oppression?—because we believe in the Liberty for which we contend as, under God, the inalienable birthright of every human being,—the condition necessary for man's highest development, service, and happiness.[6]

He ended his essay with the verse:

They are slaves who dare not be
In the right with two or three.

These closing words from colleague James Russell Lowell (1819–1891), Unitarian poet, critic, editor, and diplomat, are now enshrined in the hymn, "All Whose Boast It Is," in the current Unitarian Universalist hymnal.[7]

Nute carried these words of inspiration in his heart and in his mission to Kansas a few years later. Ironically, he wrote in "The Leaven of Liberty" a warning not to judge harshly those who "exercise of a bitter or tyrannous spirit" in the pursuit of their just goal. Little did he know how the Free-State and antislavery causes in Kansas later would embitter him and bring censure from others. He stood steadfast "in the right with two or three" rather than succumb to the economic temptations that he saw compromising the morals of some of those within his own denomination. These seductions represented a kind of slavery to him, and his own resistance to them destined him to a life of poverty.

Nute cautioned against judging the whole antislavery movement by the frailties of its exhausted saints and their shortcomings. He chided those who would use the human fallibility of the movement as an "excuse for their inaction." These words, ironically, portended his later appeals to the Unitarian establishment for food, money, and clothing to save the Kansas settlers' lives from starvation and attack.

In May 1850 the *Christian Register*, the newspaper of liberal Unitarian Christianity based in Boston, announced that Nute was going to spend some time in missionary service in "the west." The American Unitarian Association (AUA) was sending tentative missions to corners of the earth considered good fertile ground for Unitarian Christianity. During his trip west, Nute visited denominational societies and churches along the way to get a sense of their moral and religious state. His talks were well received and filled the lecture halls.

Nute discovered that mission work agreed with him. He put into practice his habit of working in tandem with religious leaders of other faiths. In this way he garnered a wider acceptance of Unitarianism. He rejoiced that he counted among his listeners the followers of other religious leaders, who willingly received the Unitarian message.

This proved controversial. One Congregational minister, William H. Starr, had invited Nute to preach from his pulpit in Griggsville, Illinois. Starr wrote in his journal that "he visited him [Nute] at his friend's and 'was much pleased; appears evangelical and truly pious.'"[8] Yet, however pious Nute seemed to be, Starr was charged with "unitarianism" by the orthodoxy of his own denomination. Sadly, Starr was soon expelled from that pulpit.

One year after his trip to the West, Nute resigned from his congregation in Scituate to accept a call to the Chicopee, Massachusetts, congregation, where he served from October 1851 until he left for the Kansas mission in 1855. In September 1853, AUA Secretary Henry Adolphus Miles appealed to Nute's congregation for support of the AUA. Subscriptions to the AUA were voluntary memberships from individual Unitarians and congregations to keep the association running. In November 1853, Nute apologized to Miles for the late payment of the subscriptions from his pastorate at Chicopee. His correspondence provides insight into the precarious nature of funding for the AUA, which greatly compromised its ability to respond to the needs of the Kansas mission in the years before the Civil War.

Subscriptions simply did not cover all of the AUA's costs. In an attempt to grow its membership and raise funds, the organization embarked upon a plan to evangelize by selling books and religious tracts authored by its prominent ministers. This paralleled the revolution in publishing during the nineteenth century. Industrializing societies needed better-educated workers to meet the challenges of new technology. At the same time, steam power and new techniques in typesetting and book illustration expanded production and lowered costs.[9] Books had become a growth industry, and the AUA had good reason to expect its book program could help its finances.

In April 1854 Nute accepted Miles's request to participate in the sale of books and pamphlets for the AUA. Now he had a formal venue for bringing liberal Christianity to those outside the denomination. During 1854 he was very active peddling literary materials for the AUA, and he received his congregation's blessing to embark on this aspect of ministry. Nute rhapsodized about the value of this type of "evangelizing." He called the Unitarian books "silent preachers" that made "themselves felt in ever-widening circles to which they have been introduced."[10] He sold books and pamphlets whenever he found a break from his other duties. Nute felt that if people would only have an opportunity to hear the words of liberal Christianity, they would flock to it in impressive numbers. Over time, undoubtedly fed by testimony about the Kansas Territory in the newspapers, Nute's dedication to spreading the liberal Christian message and his interest in mission work together caused him to consider moving to the Kansas Territory.

Meanwhile, Lawrence, Kansas—the town that was to hold Nute's destiny for a significant part of his life—began sending up its first shoots. Charles Branscomb, one of Nute's parishioners in Chicopee, went out with the first group of emigrants to the Kansas Territory. Branscomb later became a neighbor and founding member of both the town of Lawrence and the Lawrence Unitarian Society. He may have been instrumental in persuading Nute that his future lay in the Kansas Territory, too. Branscomb was smitten with the territory, not only for its rich resources but also because of its vital place in deciding whether slavery would move west. His glowing reports hit the Massachusetts newspapers and with them the optimistic belief that the influx of New Englanders would turn the proslavers on their heels.

Out in Lawrence, Branscomb's typical New England dry humor surfaced when confronted with hostile proslavery sorts. Some of them asked whether Branscomb was not the "Eli Thayer of Massachusetts." Thayer was the Republican politician from Massachusetts who, with Unitarian Edward Everett Hale and others, founded the Emigrant Aid Company to move antislavery settlers to Kansas in large numbers. The hostile proslavery sympathizers had heard enough about Thayer and his promotion of Kansas to abolitionist emigrants to put a price on his head. Branscomb indicated that he was not Eli Thayer, but that someone in his company was perfectly willing to impersonate Mr. Thayer if the proslavers would turn over the two-hundred-dollar reward that they had offered for him. This offer was refused, whereupon Branscomb and his company declared that they thought the same way Thayer did and they had come to the Kansas Territory for the same reason.[11]

Early emigrants to the territory wrote back to New England to encourage friends, neighbors, and family to come out, and their letters had become, by 1854, a daily source of news in New England papers. The new immigrants rhapsodized about the truly spectacular landscapes and untapped farmland; lime and other stone for building; riverbank woodlands of oak, hickory, and black walnut; and one-hundred-pound catfish. The vast grassy prairies—which did not have the many large rocks and tree stumps that inhabited New England farmland—must have seemed like heaven to hardscrabble New England immigrant families. Correspondents to Boston newspapers told readers to sell all they had, come to Kansas, and bring as much money with them as possible.

Back in New England, the problem of slavery took a prominent position at the Unitarian annual convention that Nute attended in September 1854 in Deerfield, Massachusetts. The theme of the conference was the promotion of "pure Evangelical Christianity," or Unitarian Christianity. Attendees engaged in animated discussions regarding the importance of strong ties of sympathy and union between neighboring societies. The *Christian Register* reported,

> Rev. Mr. Nute, of Chicopee . . . believed . . . that all such fraternal feeling, and associational union, to be extensively useful and lasting, must be based upon a common deep conviction of the infinite importance of pure Evangelical religion on the part of all who would promote it in their own midst. You cannot expect the fruits without the tree. You cannot expect pure Evangelical Christianity to be promoted in this valley, or any other, unless the agents in the work themselves—those who are to promote it—have a deep interest, not merely in one another, but in the subject.[12]

The Unitarians were told to abandon their negativity, to adhere to principles of growth and action within their own souls so as to embrace "personal holiness and heart-piety" in order to advance pure Evangelical Christianity. Many speakers touted the theology of evangelism and promoted the idea that Christ in the soul was the only adequate way to spread his religion. Others called for the Unitarians to recognize that more had to be done to shore up the conversation between ministers and laity, to extend the pastoral relationship more widely. The first morning ended with a sermon on the church, and after lunch, the conference hurtled immediately toward the issue of slavery.

The agency of the pulpit was identified as instrumental in this project, recalling American Presbyterian theologian Albert Barnes's remarks that "had the American Church . . . done its duty in season, American Slavery would have long since ceased to be."[13] Some ministers intentionally ignored the whole issue in their preaching —underscoring just how much Unitarianism, which called for the reformation of the world, was in need of a reformation itself.

The message of the gospel had to be realized through contemporary models, and according to the voices at this conference, that model was antislavery.

The issue of slavery was still the most discussed topic in the Unitarian congregations and clergy of the time. Some felt that the call to abolish slavery in pursuit of "pure" Christianity eclipsed all other theological questions in importance. Others felt that to dive into the issue of slavery was to leave the other theological issues behind. The controversy was deeply seated in the denomination and its fiercely independent congregations. Many of its most prominent members came from wealthy families whose fortunes were all or in part, either directly or indirectly, dependent upon slavery in the South. Though ministers who preached antislavery were often in grave danger of losing their pulpits, ministers who did not were upbraided by colleagues whose pulpits were safe.

Barely one month after the Deerfield convention, Nute attended the first Unitarian convention in Canada that included the churches of the United States and the newer, smaller Unitarian movement in Canada. The discussion centered on the authority of scripture and whether Unitarians were willing to recognize it. Some felt that "the liberty which [is] given us is not a liberty to destroy or set aside. We may judge for ourselves what is Scripture, and judge what the Scriptures reveal; but to their clear revelation we are to bow in reverence and submission."[14] Others added that "some persons . . . might not recognize in their own positioning the intimation that they reject the authority of Christ, or the Gospel on moral grounds, from unwillingness to accept any authority at all."[15] This may have been an allusion to Theodore Parker, whose progressive —or heretical, depending on where one stood—theology had caused a major scandal and rift in the denomination.

Charles Ansorge, of Dorchester, Massachusetts, voiced one of the primary Unitarian arguments: It was silly to assign so much importance to the authority of scripture since the early church had no Christian scriptures at all. Ansorge maintained, "the two pillars on which Christianity rested were these, a belief in one God and

Savior, and loving our neighbor as ourself."[16] All who subscribed to these simple tenets Ansorge recognized as Christians. To him and many others, to limit "Christian liberty" to a belief in scripture only idolatrized the men who decided what constituted the canon of the scriptures.

Rev. John Pierpont, father of a Harvard Divinity School class-mate of Nute, reflected a progressive spiritual stance that would eventually set Unitarian theology on a course away from Christianity. He encouraged his flock to believe in the Gospel as they, themselves, understood it. Rev. James Freeman Clarke, influential Unitarian social reformer, scholar, secretary to the AUA from 1859 to 1861, and one of Nute's most treasured friends, advocated a tolerance of differing faith perspectives that has shaped modern UU values. He declared this freedom of belief made him love the Unitarian faith.

Thus, through this convention in Canada, one Unitarian controversy then raging in the United States had crossed the border and headed north. Rev. Samuel J. May, author and radical Unitarian reformer of women's rights, education, and slavery, then of Syracuse, New York, believed that "we were opening our minds to a more inlarged view according to which not the letter which killeth, but the spirit which giveth life, is the true test of the Christian.—This is what the Saviour proposed as the true way by which his disciples should be known, that they should have the spirit of truth."[17] With surprising humanism, May compared the Unitarian relationship to scripture as akin to the scientific reverence for Copernicus and Newton. Science had moved on since Copernicus and Newton, but students continued to stand in awe of their accomplishments and research. Such should also be the liberal Christian regard for scripture.

The argument turned to focus on the issue of slavery and the fugitive slaves. Finally, a concern that had been avidly discussed in the wings since the beginning of the conference was given voice. Many Unitarian ministers were involved in the work of the Underground Railroad, which had Canada as its destination. At this point in the convention, the pact was solemnized formally between those clergy of the United States who helped move the fugitives along the road, at much risk to themselves and their passengers, and those clergy of Canada who received them and attempted to settle them in a free country. With this important declaration, the convention came to an end.

It is doubtful that the Canadian convention was Nute's first exposure to the Underground Railroad, although none of his surviving letters speak of his active part in it until he moved to the Kansas Territory. John Brown, the abolitionist, was a resident of Springfield, Massachusetts, during the same time that Nute pastored there, and it is likely that the two were acquainted in some fashion. Nute's activities with the antislavery movement while at Harvard would have put him in direct contact with many who were dedicated to the Underground Railroad movement. The AUA could not have been more fortunate in its choice of a missionary.

In February 1855 Rev. Francis Tiffany, Nute's friend and colleague in Springfield, Massachusetts, suggested to AUA Secretary Henry A. Miles that Nute would be a good candidate for the Kansas mission under discussion in the Executive Committee.[18] Edward Everett Hale, prominent clergyman and future secretary of the AUA, learned of this recommendation and sent his wholehearted support for the idea. The notion of sending settlers, particularly Unitarian settlers, to the Kansas Territory was growing with the formalization and expansion of the Emigrant Aid Company created by Eli Thayer, Edward Everett Hale, and Massachusetts politician Alexander H. Bullock. Hale's extreme enthusiasm for sending Nute was a result of his personal relationship with Nute, but also tied in nicely with his leadership in the Emigrant Aid Company.

The biggest complaint that appeared in the newspapers about Kansas at the time concerned "the heavy winds, which usually blow from one to three days at a time over the prairies, making it rather disagreeable to be exposed out of doors." The anonymous writer continued, "We think the wind and storms are not more violent than in Western Pennsylvania and Eastern Ohio; but it occurs oftener, and is longer protracted."[19] Modern-day Kansans would still resonate with this assessment. The prairie weather and its tornadoes destroyed Nute's personal papers, and later ruined a supply of books the AUA sent him against his directions, causing a controversy between Nute and the organization.

Nute talked to his friends and grew eager for the position of missionary. He wrote directly to Miles of his thoughts on the subject on March 5, 1855:

> You are doubtless apprised of the tide of emigration that is about to set toward the new territory from these parts & appreciate the importance of the movement as deciding the character of the state that is to be & so affecting the welfare of the whole country. . . . As Christian disciples we have an interest in the religious institutions of this region, as those who have received the enlightenment of a doctrine more pure & beneficent than that which generally prevails have we not a solemn charge to let our voice be heard in its behalf in the day of small things, to do our part in giving a right shape to this little twig that is soon to become the stalwart tree. . . . One church of our fellowship planted in that region during the present season would be of great power to decide the fortunes of Liberal Christianity there for generations to come. . . . We are incited & encouraged to make the attempt to found such a church by some circumstances concerning which my mind has been deeply exercised. . . . 1st a considerable number of our household of faith are going to Kanzas, at least 10 from this place & probably twice that number from this neighborhood; Among these from 6 to 8 of my best parishioners,—enough for the nucleus of a society. . . . 2d Efforts are being made by the other denominations to colonise churches of their communion. . . . It will promote the prosperity of the colonies in every respect. Those who will affiliate in religious matters will be most likely to harmonise in their business operations in

the management of schools &c. Then soon this sectarian character of these settlements will be mitigated & shaded down by the coming in of those of other denominations. . . . One society would get a vigorous start at the outset & be a center of influence & operations for establishing & fostering offshoots in other places. . . . We should have the opportunity to distribute our books,—to sew the good seed from which I am sure a rich & abundant harvest must eventually & at no distant day be gathered.[20]

Nute provided his experiences and qualifications for the mission job and warned Miles that the "orthodox" were already out of the starting gate. These orthodox were from the American Reform Tract and Book Society and the Kansas League, which had commissioned two men to explore the Kansas Territory and report on what they found with a view toward disseminating Christian literature and promoting the antislavery cause. This had already produced, in Nute's eyes, a stalwart evangelizer for the orthodox, as the report of these Kansas explorers was being avidly read by the public. It was high time the Unitarians had their own publications about the Kansas Territory to put into the hands of the populace and steer them toward the liberal Christian cause there.

Nute's enthusiasm for the evangelizing potential of a position as missionary in the territory was supported by his wife Lucy's desire to live closer to her own family. The Fessendens had relocated to Alton, Illinois, and other parts near the gateway to the Kansas Territory. Throughout the Nutes' tenure in Kansas, Lucy returned repeatedly, and often, to her family in Illinois, and she spent protracted times with them during the Civil War. Nute was careful to mention to Miles the advantages of having friends and family in the West for support. Members of his own congregation were already there and more would come with him.

In mid-March 1855, the Executive Committee of the AUA voted to pay Nute eight hundred dollars for a one-year mission to Kansas,[21] and Nute accepted.[22] Nute commenced immediately to bring his call with Chicopee to a close, to dispose of or return the books and pamphlets he was selling for the AUA, to close down his house, and to prepare for the trip to Kansas. Nute informed Miles that he was released from his pastorate in Chicopee on April 1 and wanted to dispose of everything in Chicopee before leaving for Boston.[23]

The clash Nute later had with the AUA regarding his possession of or responsibility for AUA books and pamphlets began with his efforts to pack up his belongings in Chicopee. In Nute's letter to Miles on March 24, he mentioned returning two boxes of books to the AUA.[24] It is not known if this represented the entirety of his inventory, but it appeared to be so by the way he wrote the letter. This became an issue in 1859 when he was preparing to leave Lawrence for an extended period and led to a bitter dispute with the AUA about various categories of books that the AUA claimed he should have returned or paid for.

In 1855, however, such eventualities were the farthest thing from Nute's mind. He wrote to Miles to beg him to be part of his installation ceremony. Even as Nute broke down his household in Massachusetts to move to Kansas, letters to the newspapers came in from Lawrence regarding the growing unrest. Large numbers of Missourians had come into the territory with the intent of taking over the ballot boxes and preventing Free-State Kansas residents from voting. The Free-State cause was made up of those with abolitionist beliefs who were emigrating to the Kansas Territory intending to eventually bring it into statehood as a Free State— one without slavery. The Free-State population of the Kansas Territory was growing daily, and so the proslavery Missourians' counter-strategy was to aggressively take control of the voting process. In fact, by seizing the ballot boxes and allowing nonresident Missourians to vote, they had gained control of the Kansas Territory legislature. The U.S. government-appointed Kansas Territorial governor swore that any illegal voting would be rectified, but the Free-Staters rightfully doubted his oath. The Pierce administration was squarely in the camp of the proslavers.

In March 1855 Nute preached his farewell sermon and resigned the Chicopee congregation amid glorious praise from his parishioners. On April 3 he was installed with great ceremony as the AUA missionary to Kansas. The festivities took place at the Chicopee church, with a sermon by Rev. Frederick Dan Huntington, Unitarian author and Boston clergyman. Nute was enjoined by Huntington's sermon to be as proscribed by Romans 6 in reference to Phebe, who was revered because "she had this honorable notice in the records of our holy faith: because she was a servant of the church."[25]

Huntington's sermon described the person who would deserve such praise, a person who "must first recognize a church of the Lord Jesus Christ; secondly, must have his own heart and life converted to be in sympathy with the aim and purpose for which that church was established; and thirdly, must be willing to render any services, according to his situation in life, which the good of that church may require."[26] Nute stood stalwartly by the first of Huntington's conditions. Toward the second he wavered in Kansas, when he felt that the church had abandoned him. By complying with the third, he almost lost his life.

During the prayer of installation, which "commended him to the protection and care of the all present Disposer, and implored success on his labors in gathering souls into the fold of the Redeemer,"[27] the congregation was hushed and silent, a testament to their deep sympathy for Nute's willingness to sacrifice himself to the demands and struggles of a mission that promised only trial and immense labor. No one knew at the time that the mission would demand the martyrdom of many of his parishioners and some family members, and barely spare Nute himself.

The charge to Nute by the secretary of the AUA, Rev. Dr. Henry A. Miles, represented a clear statement of those contemporary purposes and views of the AUA toward its ministers. Miles bade him to bring liberal Christianity to the West, to build the revered institutions of New England civilization—towns, schools, and churches—and to work to make Kansas a free state. The spirit of those charges lived in Nute's actions and echoed in his letters from the moment he set down in Kansas until he left the state nearly fifteen years later.

The Unitarians would be a beacon of religious tolerance, and Nute would be pastor to all who came in need. He would fight slavery with his mission, his words, and his very life. He would be the cornerstone in establishing the social institutions that had provided the foundation of New England's European culture for several centuries and would bring that culture to the West. Miles said that by his word, and even more importantly his deeds, Nute would bring the ministry of Jesus—the lifeworks of compassion—to the West. His own example could only succeed in bringing more to the fold of the liberal Christian church. Nothing in the sincere and fond address by Miles could have predicted the rift that would develop between the two men by the end of Nute's tenure as missionary.

BIBLES AND BREECHLOADERS

In 1855 the Kansas that Nute headed toward was a vast paradise for settlers looking to start anew. They could lay a claim to 160 acres for one dollar and twenty-five cents an acre. Some boasted that the Kansas winters were so mild that settlers could allow their stock to run loose and feed them only on hay, something unheard of in New England. Labor was cheap by modern standards, fifteen to twenty-five dollars a month for men, eight dollars a month for women. But women were scarce, so if settlers needed the labors of a woman, they were advised to bring a few with them.[28] Cows sold for twelve to twenty-five dollars a piece, oxen for fifty to seventy-five dollars, and sheep for one hundred fifty dollars a head—at least the utilitarian kind, good for meat and rough woven fabrics.[29]

Things like furniture and other merchandise that could not be obtained in Kansas had to be shipped from Missouri or farther. The cost of the freight varied seasonally with the depth of the river. In the spring, when the river was high and easy to travel, the cost was thirty to fifty cents per hundred pounds; in the fall, when the river was murky, shallow, and slow, the rate ranged from seventy-five cents to two dollars. Passengers could expect to pay ten to fifteen dollars for first-class transportation and were assured they need not fear the Indians almost anywhere.[30]

The trouble that was already brewing in Kansas in 1855 came from the white man. It grew to threaten the lives of emigrants to Kansas, who sought the security and plenty that they had enjoyed in long-settled New England. Church members in the East were aware of the potential for danger, and Nute received a Colt revolver as a farewell gift before leaving for his mission. Most thought it an extremely necessary article for the frontier in which he would labor. Theodore Parker referred to this in a speech in 1856:

> A noble-hearted Unitarian minister, Rev. Mr. Nute, "felt drawn to Kansas." Of course he carried his Bible: he knew it also by heart. His friends gave him a "repeating rifle" and a "revolver." These also "felt drawn to Kansas." This "minister at large"—very much at large, too, his nearest denominational brother, on one side five hundred miles off, on the other fifteen hundred—trusts in God, and keeps his powder dry.[31]

"VIOLENT CONTROL OF THE KANSAS ELECTION BY MISSOURIANS"[32] screamed the papers as the first assault on the ballot boxes in the Kansas Territory steered the outcome of the elections toward proslavery control. Newspapers across the country noted "some curious facts concerning the recent election in Kansas," where the census recorded twenty-six hundred legal voters, but the election produced proslavery majorities ranging from two hundred to eight hundred votes in all seventeen districts. Investigative reporters did the math and found that the tally included over eight hundred more votes than the number of legal voters in the whole territory. The *Squatter Sovereign*, a staunch proslavery rag, issued to the Border Ruffians—those proslavery thugs from Missouri who were commandeering the ballot boxes in the Kansas Territory —an appalling invitation into Kansas. The Ruffians were bid to bring their guns and ropes for "game" and "horse thieves"—a thinly veiled threat to all the Free-State settlers.[33]

In May 1855, the *New York Herald* reported,

> It is within the limits of possibility that we may have some interesting news from Kansas ere long. There is a determination to fight should the scenes of the late election be attempted again. In order that the settlers may be in a condition to act

effectively . . . a large quantity of arms and ammunition was sent out to them from Boston . . . under the charge of special agents. Among the arms sent out were sixty of the Sharp rifles, which have the reputation of being very effective slaughter weapons. These supplies were paid for with money raised by subscription in Boston. One gentleman of great wealth, and who has occupied a high position in the political world, is said to have given one thousand dollars towards the "arms fund," and very respectable sums were contributed by other gentlemen of known conservative views. There is no difficulty experienced in getting just as much money as is wanted for the purpose contemplated, and some of the contributors gave liberally only on condition that the money should be expended in carrying on the war.[34]

Thus "Beecher's Bibles" came to Kansas on the very boat that brought Nute. Henry Ward Beecher, the celebrated though controversial Congregationalist orator, clergyman, abolitionist, and social reformer, believed there was more "moral power" to end slavery in one Sharps rifle than in a hundred Bibles. From that point on, Sharps repeating rifles, a great leap forward in weapons technology, became known as "Beecher's Bibles." Developed by Christian Sharps and patented in 1848, the rifles were loaded from the breech, or the rear, and used a patented pellet feed that afforded a semiautomatic firing capacity that vastly improved both speed and accuracy for snipers and riders on horseback.

Key wealthy Eastern businessmen—many or most of them Unitarian—began at once to raise money for, contract the production of, and organize the clandestine shipment of arms to Kansas. Despite every effort of President Franklin Pierce's administration and the all-powerful proslavery politics, a constant supply of arms made it west into Kansas. Any connection Nute may have had with the shipment of rifles that came with him that May is not documented. Nute family stories related that he had run guns and money for the antislavery cause without being specific as to where and when.

Guns sent to the Kansas Free-State settlers for their own protection became a huge bone of contention. The proslavery contingent was horrified that the settlers might actually use them in self-defense against the Border Ruffians. Thaddeus Hyatt, inventor, manufacturer, engineer, author, philanthropist, and conspirator with John Brown; W. F. M. Arney, territorial politician and later secretary and governor of New Mexico; and Edward Daniels, fervent abolitionist, were founders of the Emigrant Aid and Kansas Aid companies. They demanded that President Pierce protect the Kansas settlers but were told by the administration that they should have sent Bibles rather than rifles to Kansas. The officers of the Emigrant Aid Company swore on the floor of the Senate that they had never financed or smuggled arms to Kansas through the auspices of that agency. The accuracy of that claim is disputed by the evidence.

Other notables in the argument over Kansas were two men by the name of Douglas. One was Frederick Douglass, African-American abolitionist and journalist. The other, Senator Stephen A. Douglas, was an Illinois Democrat and author of the Kansas-Nebraska Act of 1854, which reopened the spread of slavery and spawned the protest movement that became the Republican Party. His legislation proposed to apply "squatter sovereignty" to the Kansas and Nebraska territories, effectively canceling out the Missouri Compromise.

Eli Thayer immediately chartered the Massachusetts Emigrant Aid Company. He joined forces with Unitarian sympathizers such as Amos A. Lawrence, an abolitionist, businessman, and philanthropist, and Universalist Horace Greeley, editor, reformer, and founder of the Liberal Republican Party; and Unitarians like Edward Everett Hale; Dr. Samuel Cabot, Boston surgeon; George Luther Stearns, industrialist, merchant, and Underground Railroad supporter; and Samuel Gridley Howe, physician, abolitionist, and advocate of education for the blind.

While the company officially gave no direct monetary aid to the settlers, it advertised the promise of the Kansas Territory, organized the emigrants into travel groups for mutual aid and protection, reduced their travel expenses by half, and established town sites in Lawrence, Topeka, Osawatomie, Manhattan, Mapden, and Wabaunsee in advance of the settlers leaving New England. At all these town sites the company established sawmills, gristmills, schoolhouses, and churches, allowing them to become centers for the Free-State cause in the territory. The Massachusetts Emigrant Aid Company joined forces with the New York Emigrant Aid Company in 1855 and was rechartered as the New England Emigrant Aid Company. It organized and directed most of the whole Free-State migration, which drew even more settlers from Ohio, Indiana, Illinois, and Iowa than from New England. But it was the New England Emigrant Aid Company that provided the plan, the inspiration, and—in times of trouble—rescue operations for the westward-bound emigrants.

Dr. Charles Robinson, S. C. Pomeroy, and Charles H. Branscomb became founding members of the town of Lawrence and the Lawrence Unitarian congregation. Eli Thayer had originally employed them to take the Emigrant Aid Company to Kansas. The site for the town of Lawrence was established in August 1854. That fall, seven Emigrant Aid travel groups, called companies, were sent from New England, followed by eleven more by June 1855. Nute's company numbered among them.

Thayer's man, Dr. Charles Robinson, emerged as a great leader, both in his commitment to establish Kansas as a free state and in the people's attraction to him. He was a dignified, intelligent, calmly courageous, and charismatic individual who was also an impeccable gentleman. His energetic wife, Sara, who later published her diaries of the Kansas years, joined him in all his endeavors and opened their home as a haven for Free-State immigrants and political activities. The couple also became two of the Free-State movement's primary historians.

The Robinsons, along with the companies of Emigrant Aid settlers, were a great threat to the proslavery cause. The October 1854 election assault was only the first in an organized and aggressive effort to drive the Free-State settlers back where they came from. In March 1855 another election assault secured both branches of the territorial legislature for proslavery candidates. All told, well over two-thirds of the votes in that election were actually cast by residents of Missouri.

Thus, the Kansas government had become completely controlled by proslavery adherents, through the guerilla work of the Border Ruffians. This was a welcome development to the supporters of slavery in Washington, including the executive branch. But the Free-Staters did not give up very easily. Charles Robinson, along with Free-State militia General James Lane, led the charge to reject what they considered a bogus legislature and organize to arm the legitimate Kansas settlers to defend their citizen rights.

Three days after the stolen election, Robinson wrote to Eli Thayer about the outrages perpetrated by the Missourians and appealed for arms. He followed a few days later with an identical letter to Edward Everett Hale, pleading for the expeditious shipment of two hundred rifles and two field pieces to Lawrence. Fearing the unreliability of mail, Robinson immediately sent George W. Deitzler, a Unitarian, and his clerk at the Emigrant Aid Company, with another letter to Thayer begging for arms. Deitzler, a founding member of Nute's congregation who was later the brigadier general under whom Nute served during the Civil War, described his mission to Worcester and Boston:

> Within an hour after our arrival in Boston, the executive committee of the Emigrant Aid Society held a meeting and delivered to me an order for one hundred Sharps rifles and I started at once for Hartford, arriving there on Saturday evening. The guns were packed on the following Sunday and I started for home on Monday morning. The boxes were marked "Books." I took the precaution to have the (cap) cones removed from the guns and carried them in my carpet sack, which sack would have been missing in the event of the capture of the guns by the enemy.... It was perhaps the first shipment of arms for our

side and it incited a healthy feeling among the unarmed free
state settlers, which permeated and energized them until even
the Quakers were ready to fight.[35]

The Sharps rifle inspired moral controversy in every area
touched by the Kansas project. This weapon proved to be the single
greatest asset to the ability of the Free-State guerillas to prevail in
skirmishes, despite being overwhelmingly outnumbered. The Missouri Border Ruffians, though ruthless in their aggression, were of
a class mostly ill-equipped with clunky old squirrel rifles, buffalo
guns, and antiquated army muskets.

Amos A. Lawrence, a primary backer of all things Kansas and
from whom Lawrence, Kansas, acquired its name, was also a key
investor in arming Kansas with Sharps rifles. In July 1855 he was
so brazen as to write to President Pierce, fiercely proclaiming that
he and others would furnish the settlers in Kansas with the means
to protect themselves since the government had refused to protect
them. Lawrence was joined by other wealthy notables, including
Unitarian sympathizers such as Universalist Horace Greeley, editor of the *New York Tribune,* and Frederick Law Olmsted, founder
of landscape architecture and later leader in the movement to provide medical care to Civil War troops through the U.S. Sanitary
Commission. Through them, Kansas was armed not only with
Sharps repeating rifles, but also with howitzers.

In addition to arms manufactured for Kansas, donations of
clothing and cash for the Free-State cause were gathered through
the New England churches and sent to the territory. The unpopu-
lar criminality of Pierce and his administration, who allowed the
sacking of Lawrence and widespread murder and looting, raised a
passionate ire in the North. One paper announced it would collect
donations of one dollar for the Kansas relief and shortly raised
twenty-two thousand dollars in increments of that paltry sum.

In March 1856 a Thayer-inspired Free-State company set forth
from New Haven, Connecticut, for the Kansas Territory, sent off
with a farewell service from Henry Beecher at North Church.

Beecher presented each colonist, many of whom were Yale graduates, with a Bible and a Sharps rifle. Their spokesman gave thanks for the whole group:

> "We gratefully accept the bibles," said the leader of the colony, "as the only sure foundation on which to erect free institutions.... We ... accept the weapons also, and, like our fathers, we go with the Bible to indicate the peaceful nature of our mission and the harmless character of our company, and a weapon to teach those who may be disposed to molest us (if any such there be) that while we determine to do that which is right we will not submit tamely to that which is wrong." "We will not forget you," said [Mr.] Beecher. . . . "Every morning breeze shall catch the blessings of our prayers and roll them westward to your prairie home."[36]

The sobriquet "Beecher's Bibles" was soon applied to any gun shipped to Kansas. And shipped they were: in barrels of dishes, under bags of clothes, in boxes of books, in false-bottomed wagons, and hidden in ladies' trunks on riverboats.

The difficulties in Kansas originated in Washington. Presidential complicity in the proslavery manipulation of Kansas was largely responsible for the ascendancy of the proslavery territorial legislature and the murder and mayhem visited upon the settlers. Individual Unitarians who were already active in the antislavery movement railed against this insult to the rights of humanity. Young Unitarian men in particular took it as a divine call to go West to seek their fortunes—a fortune they felt patriotic and proud about. Unitarian businessmen were no less committed, although for many, their commitment was greatly inflated by their belief that the territory provided almost unlimited opportunity for land and business speculation and investment.

A FREE-STATE FLOCK

The *Christian Register* lauded the AUA for its "commendable promptness" in deciding "to send a missionary to this field" and called upon "the friends of liberal Christianity [to] at once take measures to erect a church" at Lawrence. Although Nute would not conduct his ministry from a single location for a while yet, "a house erected would be an occupant of the ground, at once important to the success of our cause."[37]

On Thursday, April 19, 1855, Nute left Boston for the Kansas Territory. On June 27, from Lawrence, he wrote at length to the *Christian Register* about the early part of his trip:

> The aspects of nature that were first presented to my view in this territory were pleasant, far beyond my expectations, they seemed to proclaim a goodly land, bountifully fitted by the great Father for the happy abode of his children. Our entrance was by the way of the Kanzas river, by the first trip of the season, and in the second steamboat that ever navigated the river. It was, as you may conceive, a voyage of the keenest interest to all on board, to every one of whom, including the pilot of the boat, it was perfectly new. Our little company of about forty persons were enlivened and bound together by the peculiar animus of an exploring party seeking for new homes in the wilderness. At times, I think, we had a lively appreciation of the sublime feeling that was experienced in the cabin of that little bark which was rocked on the waters of Massa-

chusetts Bay with the germs of our civil and religious liberty two hundred and thirty-five years ago. The thought of that eventful voyage at least arose with impressive power to those of us who came from the land of the Pilgrims, as we united in the social worship of that Sabbath morning on the second day of our trip. The interest awakened by our progress up the river among the dwellers on the banks seemed no less than our own. For the first fifty miles, our appearance was hailed at almost every bend by groups of Indians. . . . Our boat touched at several points and we went ashore, exploring the country for short distances, and mingling with the Indians who came out to meet us. We found the land everywhere fertile, with varied surface, generally well wooded and supplied with springs of cool clear water; the Indians for the most part are intelligent and friendly. . . . One of this class took passage on our boat for some thirty miles. . . . I was much interested by the account which he gave of his first religious experience. . . . By my invitation he took part in our religious service, praying and singing with great fervor in his native tongue. There were also among the passengers several who had come with us up the Missouri who expressed their joyful assent to the doctrine which I presented. Two of these were brought very low in sudden sickness. . . . In a few hours from the time when he had been moving among us . . . he had fallen into the last sleep. . . . At his earnest request I stood by him to the last, and sent his dying messages to the wife and children whom he had left at his home in Ohio but a few weeks before. . . . But I forbear entering farther into the description of scenes in which my conviction of the value of that which is to me the rational faith, has received new confirmation. . . . There are some, perhaps, who will share with me a benefit from this new illustration, of the value of that which we already hold dear.[38]

Modern Unitarian Universalists might be surprised by the overt Christianity of nineteenth-century Unitarianism. Nute's letter reflects the beliefs of his day—that the Unitarian faith was not trying to loosen its ties to its Christian ancestry, but considered itself a greater form of Christianity. It modeled the life and values of Jesus without slavish devotion to orthodoxy.

In his second long narrative from Kansas, Nute described his arrival in Lawrence and the town's very early appearance. He experienced the horrific storms so typical of Kansas and gave his audience a glimpse of the incredible beauty of that unspoiled land. Nute presented the appalling realities of pioneer life and its amazing gifts, side by side:

> The evening shades were just beginning to fall when we came in sight of the settlement called Lawrence city, in which I expected to find the principal scene of my missionary labors. . . . It is on a gentle swell of land of about one square miles in extent, in a beautiful bend of the river where it flows over and through a bed of stratified lime stone, forming a natural levee, spacious and conveniently sloped, above which the bank rises perpendicularly about 20 feet. A mile back to the North and West rise the bluffs some 70 feet. From the top of these the high rolling prairie begins. . . . But I was not favorably impressed in my first acquaintance with the settlement at Lawrence. There was a gathering of several hundred people, who were assembled at the landing to welcome our arrival. I was struck by the look of depression that appeared on the faces of many as we approached, and as they crowded aboard the boat to look for friends and seek intelligence from their far distant homes. In the manner of man there was an unusual brusqueness and abandon that seemed like the effort to banish discontent which had preyed on the mind until it had broken down the spirit of energy and self respect. Bitter complainings were also heard from some, of the want of the conveniences of life. . . . The idea of a large family making their home in a sod cabin, some ten feet square, without floor or chimney, may seem very romantic in the distance, presenting a pleasant picture of

simplicity and humble contentment. But the reality is far from being pleasant. The enchantment of such a view requires a magnificent distance, and gains nothing on acquaintance. . . . In short, if I had not returned to Lawrence after that brief morning visit, my associations with the place would have been unspeakably sad; quite different from those which have been formed by further acquaintance, and the rapid changes for the better which I have witnessed. Some of those who were most uncomfortably lodged are now living in commodious tenements on "claims" in the vicinity, with a cheerful appreciation of their comforts and full of hope for the future. In the village, the tent and the hut of turf are fast giving place to the framed house, or, to what is more likely to be the prevalent style of building, that of stone and concrete.[39]

Nute wrote about how he traveled to Topeka briefly before coming back to Lawrence in the middle of one of those famous Kansas storms. He continued,

The rain came in torrents driven by a high wind; the thunder roared with hardly a moments' cessation; the lightning flashed from one side of the heavens to the other, with every now and then a perpendicular discharge that seemed to make the earth tremble under our feet. It was a sublime scene. How could it fail to have a deep religious significance to us, making it good for us to be there. It was our first hour of worship on the soil of Kansas, our land of promise. How grand and impressive the service by which our minds were awed to feel the presence of Him who "maketh the clouds his chariots, the lightnings his messengers." . . . It was towards evening when we reached the point. The shadows of the high bluffs were thrown for miles across the plain below; and the last rays of the sun lit up the tops of the forest and gave an illusive charm to the uncouth huts in the village. At the first glance we recognized marked improvements in and around the settlement, stone walls of large buildings had risen up in the center of the village, giving it quite a dignified and substantial look; houses of wood had sprung up as if by magic, begun, finished and occupied in a single week. For miles around on the prairie, houses are also being built, fields have been broken up and enclosed, while hundreds of cattle, horses, mules and sheep are grazing in groups or being driven up to their new homes for the night. ... I accepted the proffered hospitality of a family with whom I had made the voyage of the Missouri and the Kansas, and finding them worthy, there abode for several days. There I had some experience of straitened quarters, being one of ten persons who shared the accommodations of a cabin about twelve feet square. But natural congeniality and Christian good will can almost perform miracles in such an emergency, and make the humblest walls seem spacious, as well as find a feast in the most scanty fare. Under this small roof there was room for large hearts and much enjoyment. . . . But more soon, and better I hope. [40]

Nute immediately got down to the business of ministering, which involved preaching in the open air because there was no structure large enough to accommodate more than fifty people. In her journal, Sara Robinson recorded the momentous event in full and gave insight into Nute's public character. She wrote,

Towards evening we heard that Mr. Nute, the clergyman sent out by the Unitarian Association, would preach upon Capitol Hill, and we saw the people already gathering. The scene was impressive. The preacher stood while the audience sat upon rough seats and stones upon the summit of the hill. Earth had never spread out a fairer picture than this lying before us. At one glance the eye rested upon river, forest, mountain, and prairie, miles and miles distant as well as near, and the last rays of the setting sun shed a halo of glory over all. The novel circumstances under which we met were touched upon; our leaving the old homes among the eastern hills to find a new one in the "waiting West," and the hope which actuates one and all of seeing the same institutions flourish here, which make life desirable there. The protecting care and guidance of the same kind Parent are still over and around us. He provides for us this beautiful temple, "not made with hands," in which to worship him; and if from our work here he calls us home, he offers heaven with its "eternal mansions." . . . Mr. N. was for some years the pastor of a dearly loved friend of mine, of whom she often spoke, and in this way he seems to me like an old friend. We are glad he has come among us with his genial sympathies, his heart warmth, his earnest ways, his outspoken words of truth, and his abiding love for freedom and the right. We need such manliness among us, in this new, unsettled state of things; such men, with unwearying confidence in God, and the humanity of men; with whom the love for a distressed brother is more than one's faith in creeds, and whose faith is strong that in doing good to one's fellow we show our love to God. That men are born of the times is an old adage. That men, needed for the times, may arise ready for the work in Kansas, ministers as well as laymen, men of nerve, of principle, "wise as serpents, and harmless as doves," is our continual hope. Most propitious, as well as most disastrous, in its influences upon this territory, will be the effect of the institutions now planted here.[41]

Nute wrote to Miles at the AUA the next day, May 28, concerning his new ministry and first sermon. The letter declared his conviction that liberal Christianity would be a breath of fresh air to the settlers. It read,

Last evening I preached under circumstances novel and peculiarly impressive. All the rooms suitable for public service were occupied, which was but one. In the morning I attended, but not to my edification; heard an old-fashioned, gloomy funeral sermon, calculated to depress the minds of the people, and therefore most inappropriate to the condition and state of feeling in which most of them are placed. The teacher's topic was the probability of sickness and death, and certainty that many of us would be sick and die in the course of a few months; his conclusion was, that we should frequently think of our winding-sheets and coffins and the worms that would soon be eating us in the grave, and should flee from the wrath to come. I have found no one who liked it, and most condemn it in strong terms, among whom are ministers and church-members of several denominations. . . . Several expressed to me a desire to hear a discourse that should present some of the cheerful aspects of our religion adapted to our condition. I made an appointment to meet those so disposed on the top of a hill, a little more than half a mile from the village, at the hour of sunset. More than a hundred (about 150) responded to the invitation, though the notices were given out after four o'clock. One of the most beautiful scenes that I have ever beheld was spread before me and fixed for ever in my mind. From the top of the eminence which I had chosen, an extensive view is presented of the town, the winding rivers, the Kanzas to the north and west, and the Wakarusa to the south, and a panorama of indescribable beauty for more than twenty miles in every direction, and twice that distance in several points;—thousands of acres of the most fertile, undulating prairie, dotted with the tents of the emigrants gleaming in the light of the setting sun, with hundreds of cattle grazing in groups here and there,—the long white wagons drawn by strings of mules and oxen, sometimes to the number of twenty, the prairie-ship of the Santa Fe and California emigrant, slowly crawling over the great sea of grass, unmarked except by the dark brown track on which they are moving;—to the north and west, and beyond the Kanzas, boundless tracts of forest. But I must leave all this for what more particularly belongs to the occasion. Standing on the topmost height, I look down toward the village, (I should say the city) from which are moving the people who are to compose my first congregation in Kanzas, men and women and a few children scattered all the way along the road, some just climbing the hill. I think of the hill-sides of Palestine, of the Great Teacher, and hear him say, as he did when waiting for the people who were coming out from Samaria, "Lift up your eyes and look on the fields, for they are white already to the harvest." ... Soon I am surrounded by a number about the size of that which tarried in Jerusalem for the outpouring of the Spirit by the command and promise of their ascended Lord.... We sing a hymn about the Good Shepherd who leads his flock by the fair pastures and pleasant waters. I read the opening of the Sermon on the Mount and the 17th of Acts, and take for my text, The Unknown God, him I declare unto you.[42]

The splendor of that first sermon out under the broad expanse of prairie sky on Mt. Oread was soon replaced by more awkward circumstances brought on by the realities of the changeable weather. Summer and fall Sunday afternoon services were held at the Robinsons' house on Mt. Oread. In order to have shelter for everyone, the men sat in their buggies in the front yard, the women sat inside, and Nute preached to both by standing in the front door.

Nute continued the narrative of his early days in Lawrence with a letter to Secretary Miles at the AUA on June 4. It read,

I believe I had got as far as the text of my first sermon in Kansas. ... At the close of the service I made an announcement of my mission to the Territory & offered my services to all disposed to receive them, proposing to remain a while among the people of Lawrence & vicinity as a sort of minister at large visiting from house to house during the week & preaching on the Lords day wherever an opportunity could be had. Bro Hutchins who is a preacher of the Christian connection & one of the principal merchants in Lawrence responded & proposed another service of the same kind in the same place for the next Sunday evening to which I consented. During the week I formed the acquaintance of many of the people in the village & visited several cabins of the settlers or claims on the prairie from one to three miles out, at one of which I made an appointment to preach yesterday morning. . . . I have not been able to get a decent lodging place in this neighborhood, not because of a lack of hospitality but bec. of the strictured circumstances of the settlers in regard to shelter & this is owing to the want of lumber with which to build. Theres plenty of timber but no sawmill adequate to supply the demand, hundreds of homes are waiting for the boards to cover them & many families are living in quarters into which a thrifty N. Eng. Farmer would distain to shelter his cattle. For several days I made my abode, an intruder by necessity, in a log cabin of one room 16 feet square the accommodations of which were shared by 12 persons at the same time. This is one of the first class tenements in our infant city, commanding & pleasant compared with some of the turf huts without doors, windows or chimney. But these inconveniences are not occasioned by the poverty of the land or that of the immigrants & are therefore soon to be surmounted. . . . I am now living in a tent about 2 miles South West from Lawrence with my friend & companion of the voyage who has taken a claim in a very charming & desirable situation on a high bluff at the head of a wide ravine an interval of smooth fertile land down which we have an unimpeded view over several miles of beautiful rolling prairie, across the wooded valley of the Wakarusa & the heights beyond to a distance of many miles. In the center of this ravine, extending for several miles & greatly enhancing the beauty of the view is a grove of trees principally elm & oak, through which flows a small stream of the clearest water fed by springs. From one of these about 200 yards distant from our tent we get our supply. In any direction the view is open & presents an aspect of high cultivation making it very difficult to realize that the soil has never been tamed by the ploughshare. Our tent is the work of our hands made & erected on the spot in less than a day. We have found it a comfortable shelter with the exception of one night when a violent thunderstorm which tore our frail habitation from some of its fastenings, exposing us to the rain & threatened to leave us without a shelter, left us in a state of sleepless anxiety for most of the night. Our fare is simple the variety being chiefly of the genus bread. We enjoy our manner of living very much but hope to have more of the comforts of civilization before the charm of its novelty is worn off. . . . I intend to live in the village & have taken a lot for that purpose on wh the frame of a small house is now being built. From present appearances it will be several months before it will be in habitable condition. Yesterday being Sunday we went across the prairie about a mile to fulfil the appointment which I had made to preach at the house of one of the emigrants from Massachusetts. Here we found a gathering of 30 persons who have their homes within a few miles of the place who joined in our service with apparent interest & gave the listening ear to a discourse on "Providence" in which I endeavored to adapt myself to the peculiar circumstances of the occasion.[43]

Many settlers came from the East with no proficiency in farming, carpentry, or any other of the skills necessary for survival. Newspapers, the primary source of public information, ran articles informing would-be emigrants of the prices in Kansas, as well as teaching them some of those needed skills, including how to build a house. These plans allowed the primitive log cabins and A-frame sod huts in Lawrence to give way to substantial wood-frame houses, followed quickly by more civilized municipal structures. In his next letter to Miles, Nute broached the idea of establishing the first church building in Lawrence.[44] In light of the articles in the *Christian Register*—touting the promise for liberal Christianity in the Kansas Territory through the Unitarian emigration to Lawrence and the popularity of the AUA missionary there—his suggestion fell on willing ears.

Nute was not the only religious missionary in the Kansas Territory. Rev. Samuel Young Lum, the "orthodox" Congregationalist missionary, had begun preaching there in October 1854. In a letter to a colleague on June 23, Lum voiced his dismay at the encroachment of Unitarians and other religious liberals into the territory. He focused much on disease and death, and may have been the minister who gave the appalling funeral homily Nute heard on his first day in Lawrence. But Lum had lost a beloved child to disease in Kansas already, and was overwhelmed with having to officiate at three or four funerals a week. It is not surprising that his mood was less than cheerful. Lum's distress at Unitarianism eventually grew into a full-scale personal campaign to sabotage Nute whenever possible. He wrote to his denomination in the East that Nute—and his Unitarian ideas—were a grave threat to the youth of Lawrence.[45]

The two men's denominational competition continued throughout the later 1850s as a quiet race to be the first to construct a church building in Lawrence. Lum resented Nute's success in organizing the Lawrence religious societies. He felt that such a coalition of congregations tipped the balance toward an unacceptable kind of liberalism. At one point, Nute's congregation was even pushed out of access to adequate space and time to provide worship services by the combined machinations of Lum and another group of more orthodox Christians. Nute was annoyed at worst and amused at best by these small town religious politics.

Nute's success at gathering the crowds in Lawrence was reported back to the Executive Committee of the AUA and was published in the *Quarterly Journal*. The article read,

MEETINGS OF THE EXECUTIVE COMMITTEE. . . . Interesting letters were read from Rev. Mr. Nute, our missionary in Kanzas. The Committee were favored by the personal attendance of a gentleman lately returned form that Territory, who bore strong testimony to the great interest there awakened by Mr. Nute's preaching, and who presented facts to show the importance of steps being taken to erect immediately a church in the city of Lawrence. . . . The Secretary was directed to correspond with Mr. Nute in regard to this matter, and to obtain all information within his reach bearing upon the practicableness, expediency, and probable cost of accomplishing this object.[46]

By his July 8 letter to Miles, however, Nute's personal privations began to wear upon his initial missionary zeal. He had been trying to sell his personal effects to survive, but his papers and books were destroyed by the harsh Kansas weather. The desperate nature of Nute's plight was circumspectly edited out of the versions of his letters that appeared in the *Quarterly Journal*. The editors did not want the faithful to know that their man on the ground was suffering, despite the declarations of support and honor bestowed on the whole affair by Boston. One of Nute's letters read,

> Nearly 3 months from Boston & no letter from anybody yet. I have been much straitened, yes actually distressed for the want of funds, wrote to friends in Boston 7 weeks ago to have some property of mine sold for whatever it would bring & the proceeds sent immediately, but no word yet,—wrote another a few days after to one who is able & promised to supply me if I wanted & no word from him either. I must go down to St. Louis & shall start on the 22d inst. Will you send me $100, or even $50, or even 25, yea or peradventure 10 to that place in the form of a certificate of deposit at the Suffolk bank payable to my order if the amount be one of the first named or in bank bills if the latter. I am just to start to fulfil an engagement to preach in the open air on the hill side. Had a congregation of about 100 in the same place last Sunday & about 30 in another place. These long walks under the oppressive heat of the sun are too much for a preacher & no one will let him a horse. If I had the money I should buy a poney. It cost nothing to keep one or one hundred of them have only the rope to tie

them out or time to hunt them up if they are not tied. Money is also wanted to secure the convenience of a roof over our heads which I have not slept under for the last 6 weeks. Most of my books & papers soaked & ruined for the want of this. I have the frame of a house up & partly boarded but cannot go on without money. My habitation will contain one room 15 feet square & has already cost me nearly $300. In fair weather we get along very well in the tent. But in the rains which are frequent just now almost daily & always accompanied with high winds our situation is anything but pleasant. . . . Yours fraternally, Nute. . . . I have sent you 4 letters, have you received any or all? The signs in our political sky betoken a storm. The free state members of the legislature were expelled on the 4th & there is great excitement thereon. It is also said & generally believed in Lawrence that Governor Reeder has proved false to the cause of Freedom, Justice, Law & order & decency. There is to be a mass Convention to repudiate the doings of the legislature & declare it an illegal body—there will be some fighting soon.[47]

The politics that Nute referenced in his letter was a major focus for all the Kansas Territory settlers. They were outraged at the intrusion of the Missourians into Kansas and the corruption of the election process. They had appealed to the U.S. government in general and the U.S. president in particular—only to have him remove the only federal appointee who was their ally. Undaunted, and hearkening to the spirit of the American Revolution, Free-State settlers began to organize. A general meeting in early June set up a convention, for which they solicited the other districts in the territory to send five delegates to discuss the kind of relationship the Free-State settlers would have to the bogus legislature of proslavers convening in Pawnee. At the convention, the Free-State settlers decided that they had no obligation to observe any of the laws passed by the legislature and that they would respond to the threats of war coming from Missouri.

Charles Robinson and other correspondents reported to the newspapers on the meeting of the legal legislature of the territory. The body was empowered by the U.S. government to rule the Kansas citizens whose enfranchisement it had usurped. The Free-Staters decided to call a constitutional convention, frame their own constitution, and apply for admission to the Union at the next Congress. Meanwhile, they organized to defend the ballot boxes themselves.

The *Springfield Republican* published Nute's July 26 letter regarding his trip back to St. Louis to pick up his wife and bring her out to Lawrence:

> "I have fallen in with several persons with whom I became acquainted on the way up. They all exclaim upon my altered appearance, saying they recognize me only by my voice—that I look more like a man than the skin of one stretched on a rail—possessing real flesh and blood, of rather mahogany color." Mr. Nute made the acquaintance of the notorious Stringfellow, familiarly called "String" by his associates, and describes him as gentlemanly in dress, but "a low blackguard in his style of conversation—every sentence well loaded with oaths of the coarsest kind, and frequent intimations of a resort to the knife and revolver." . . . Mr. Nute was assured at Weston, Mo., that Stringfellow and his measures are very unpopular there. A large proportion, if not a majority, of the citizens of that town would rejoice to see Kanzas a free state, and but a small clique sustain the extreme and lawless measures of the invaders of the territory under the lead of Stringfellow.[48]

Benjamin Stringfellow was a notorious proslavery lawyer, politician, and businessman who supported the fraud and violence of the Missourians who stole control of Kansas. The editors went on to describe the noose of tyranny that was being drawn ever tighter around the necks of Kansas citizens.

Events developed so quickly in the territory that most newspapers provided daily updates on Kansas news. There seemed to be a revolving door to the governor's office because those who were appointed in Washington were driven out, summarily dismissed, or fled for their lives. Back East, the Unitarian ministers were urged to become members of the Emigrant Aid Company, as "the people" sought to support the Kansas project, despite the dictates of the government. Almost to a man, the ministers joined the cause and sent money to support freedom in Kansas.

On August 24 Nute wrote a lengthy letter to Miles at the AUA, thanking him for sending emergency cash, reporting on his trip to Illinois to be with Lucy, and describing the deplorable conditions in which the Kansas settlers found themselves. After begging once again to receive his salary, he argued persuasively that the time was ripe to push for a church building. He wrote,

> We have a house, 16 feet square the walls of boards 1/2 inch thick with generous openings through which wind & rain have free passage. Two articles of furniture viz a stove & one chair for the rest we have provisional substitutes hastily made of the roughest boards & slabs. No chimney. Our stove out of doors. In fair weather we can cook our food, but there have been whole weeks when we could not & several other weeks when we had nothing which we could cook, when we have dieted on sea-bread & sometimes milk. . . . The expenses of getting a place of abode just within the limits of decency have been many times greater than I had anticipated at the outset. This has been the real cause of the disappointment & return of many who have come out. . . . I have made diligent inquiries of those here in whose judgment I have most confidence & of those from other places in the territory & find but one opinion in regard to the questions which you propose. . . . 1. The time has fully come, & but just come, for erecting a church. The congregations that meet me on the hill, Sunday evenings, are of respectable size & a large proportion consist of regular attendees. . . . I am induced to believe that I have

made a good impression at the beginning, & I know that I have enjoyed the work both of preaching & of pastoral labor as I never did before, & have been helped to a freedom of speech & facility in approaching people as I have met them during the week beyond all former experience, so much so that it has seemed to come from a source entirely above myself. . . . 2. Have I reason to believe that Lawrence is the place for the contemplated church? Unquestionably it is. It is the best of all the settlements for the center of our operations for many reasons. It is the largest in population. A greater proportion of the people are from the N. Eng. states. We have already awakened some interest here. The eyes of people sympathizing in our views, all over the territory, are turned toward us. Many have addressed me . . . expressing their interest in my mission from what they had learned through friends or through the papers published at Lawrence. Some who live several miles away have declared their purpose to attend my meeting and made enquiries as to the prospect of a church edifice. . . . 3. As to the risk of the investment I think that, for such a house as is needed for the present, it would be as secure as in most new places. If the town goes on to increase as it has for the last 3 months & especially for the last month a small chapel with the lot which we can secure for it without cost, will be worth much more than the cost in a single year. . . . The only ground of apprehension is in the trouble with our neighbors in Missouri. You are probably as well acquainted with the course which they have taken & are taking the legislation of those lawless ruffians at the Shawnee Mission as I am. I have but little fear that Kansas will be a slave state. There are many settlers among us from Missouri & from other slave states who are strongly in favor of excluding slavery. I have talked with several. On the other I have talked with several of the most rabid of the slavery propositionists [*sic*] (Genl Stringfellow among the rest) & they always admit that if slavery be established here it must be by the same overriding of the sovereignty of the actual settlers as was perpetrated at the ballot boxes last spring. . . . If this shall be a free state, Lawrence will be one of the largest cities & real estate will increase in value very rapidly. . . . 4. It will not be advisable to build very large or in expensive style. A chapel that will accommodate from 4 to 5 hundred, built of concrete, to cost from 3 to 4 thousand dollars.[49]

Nute's letter was well received at the AUA. On August 27 he wrote again to Miles regarding his congregation's response to the idea of building a church, noting that some of the orthodox were already abandoning their strict creedalism to stand behind the Unitarian project. The letter read,

Yesterday I gathered my scattered flock on Mt. Oread to the number of about 100. Preached to them on the value of Christian Truth as the security for our prosperity as a colony & especially as the best ally of Civil as well as well as spiritual liberty. "Ye shall know the Truth & the T. shall make you Free." The Truth in its purity is taught & exemplified by Jesus = Liberal Christianity. Exhorted them to maintain their freedom to search the oracles of Truth in the written word & in their own souls & to think for themselves without the fear of spiritual authorities whether it be of those who sat in Moses seat or the popular voice. This is what most are determined to do who have never done it before. This is one of the good results of casting loose from all the old association religious & social if rightly imposed may do much to counteract that which is unfavorable in the change. . . . I have met with several persons who were members of orthodox churches at the East whose sympathies are with us now & are strongly opposed to stronger creeds as the basis of church union. "An assent to the teaching of Christ is all that should be required, all beyond that is inconsistent with the great principle of Protestantism & belongs to Romanism." The people are ready for a church on this broad independent foundation & a large majority of those in Lawrence will favor no other. . . . At the close of our services yesterday I opened the subject of a church edifice & asked for the expression of their opinion in regard thereto.[50]

There exists to this day, under the date of September 2, 1855, a subscription list of the very earliest Lawrence settlers who agreed to help support the building of the Unitarian church and society.[51] It contains some of the oldest surnames of Lawrence—Deitzler, Pomeroy, Woods, Robinson, Tappan, Lykins, Wilder, and Stearns. It also includes Gaius Jenkins, whose later murder, virtually in Nute's backyard, occurred at the hands of another signer, the notorious James Lane, Indiana congressman and commander of the feared Kansas Brigade, one of the Jayhawker militant bands affiliated with the Free-State cause. With donations of cash and city lots in amounts ranging from fifteen to one hundred dollars, the subscribers pledged themselves to the cause of erecting a church building in the newly burgeoning town, duly recorded in what appears to be Nute's own handwriting.

Incidents in the daily life of the Lawrence colony centered around the greater issues of slavery. When Nute wrote to AUA Secretary Miles on September 9 about plans for the church and the ongoing hardships of his mission, he reported on the near-murder of a freedman as well:

The manifestation of interest in our proposed house of worship are more & more encouraging. Several have spoken to me this last week expressing their interest & their purpose to contribute toward it & to attend our services. One young man, with whom I had before a slight acquaintance & with whose appearance I was much pleased, told me that he was a member of a church of the Christian connection in Ohio, that his home was near Antioch where he has a scholarship. He has given up his plan of studying there, desires to unite in forming a church under my pastorate & will cooperate in building the church. Another a carpenter says I don't consider myself a religious man but want to see a church here & that soon. I will give $50 in cash & as much more in labor in the building. The committee are circulating subscription papers for funds to build a church in connection with the A.U.A. on toward the support of public worship & preaching in accordance with the principles of Liberal or Unitarian Christianity. . . . Last Sunday evening our meeting was less than half the usual size owing to the excessive heat & a fracas (expected) about a colored man who claimed to be free but when a party of Missourians here went out to take him armed with rifles & after whom went a party of Yankees also armed to prevent the act. No bloodshed & no seizure. The Yankees marched back just as my services were closing to the tune of Yankee Doodle by a band of expert whistlers. . . . It will be a great thing for the fortunes of Liberal Xty here for us to have the first church in the place. Many will come to hear who would never have gone into one of our churches at the East. It will be a great thing for Lawrence to have a church of any kind do much to retain those who are here & induce others to join us & there help the good work of making K a free state.[52]

On the day a new law came into effect prohibiting speaking against slavery on pain of death, Nute planned to speak his mind anyway in front of the proslavery governor. In the same letter to Miles, he wrote,

Gov. Shannon is at Westport. He has signified his wish to reside at Lawrence & is to have a public reception here next Saturday. Your missionary has been called on for a speech on that occasion. It is the day on which the laws against all speech obnoxious to the ministers of slavery goes into effect. Those laws will be utterly disregarded & so will all the enactments of that quasi legislature including those in regard to election. . . . Will Congress recognize our election which will be based on an independent movement of the people who assume that they are now entirely without law or protection of their rights by the U.S. on the territorial Governments? . . . The country looks charming. The grass in many places above my shoulders waving in the breeze. Fields cut out here & there of from 10 to 50 acres & covered with the haycocks, the great square stacks build on the three sides of a square to some as a kind of barn. The hay is of an excellent quality, so say the farmers, from 1 to 2 tons to the acre, makes thoroughly under this scorching sun in less than a day. It is cut & raked up altogether by machine which make a pleasant music to my ears. . . . Wells have been dug during the past week & good water found at the depth of 24 feet. I know not that I ever drank any better, cool, & pure. One of these is within 5 rods of the location for our church near which our house is also being built.[53]

Nute's letter was followed by his hand-drawn sketch of his plans for the available lots.

The *Herald of Freedom* was Lawrence's Free-State newspaper under the ownership and editing of George Washington Brown, a staunch supporter of Nute and one of his parishioners in the early years. On September 15 the *Herald* announced a meeting to begin plans to build a church based on the principles of liberal Christianity. This came just in time, as the same issue of the paper contained a report on the fate of an old sodded structure known as "the church"—one of the first buildings erected in Lawrence by the Emigrant Aid Company—which had just burned down.[54]

The next day, Nute wrote to Miles about the continuing hardships of the Free-State settlers and about cornering the proslavery governor with embarrassing questions. He reported on the beginning of violent attacks on Free-State settlers by the proslavery Border Ruffians and had the naive belief that the violence would not escalate. The letter read,

Haymaking & Politics absorb the minds of the people just now. We are having much excitement concerning the abominable laws that were to go into affect yesterday. A large mass meeting was held in the village I went in & being loudly called on for the space of 5 minutes essayed a speech & gave notice of the meeting to deliberate about building the church last evening. At 6 o clock Gov Shannon appeared. . . . A public reception was intended & I was deputed to address him on behalf of the citizens but he declined the <u>honor</u>. We should have forced him into a strait corner where he would have been obliged to commit himself for or against the pestilent fellows at the mission. I had an introduction & told him we were looking with great anxiety for some expression from him that would lead us to hope for the reestablishment of that law & order which was now trampled under foot in Kansas. But he plead that he was under the direction of Col Johnson (the judge) in whose carriage he was traveling & that he (Johnson) wished to spend the night in Franklin, a little nest of pro slavery whiskey shops about 7 miles below Lawrence. It is my settled opinion that he has sold himself to the enemy & has come out here to sustain the lawless miscreants. . . . On learning last evening he was saluted with groans which I regret I had left a few moments before & did not hear them. The crowd, I am told, proposed some queries to which he refused an answer & hence their indignation. . . . Pro-slavery men are coming into the ranks of the free state parts daily that is men who uphold slavery a right and joining hands to oppose its introduction into Kanzas, on grounds of expediency & exasperated by the unheard of tyranny of the usurpers at the mission. . . . But what has this to do with my mission & the erection of a church in particular. Much in many ways. The word of Christ is needed & sufficient to still the tempest of human passion & enable men to suffer with patience & without the sacrifice of kindly feelings to any to suffer & do courageously for the right trusting in God in whose omnipotence there is a sure victory at last for the right. I do not think it will be necessary to fight if indeed it ever is necessary nor that there will be any extensive conflict of brute force. Men will generally submit to the officers who attempt to execute the laws, give bonds & appeal to the highest courts. The Missourians will not attempt to ride over the ballot box again. They know the people of the territory are ready & the indignation of those in their own state who have condemned their course is growing wider & deeper day by day.[55]

At this time Nute was living out on his claim, several miles from town. In addition to his constant travel into the village to attend to missionary and civic duties, he also traversed the territory to deliver missionary services at several more remote locations.

In his next letter to Secretary Miles, on September 23, Nute filled the AUA in on the church plans, the desire for a bell, and other territorial happenings. He wrote,

Before this reaches you I trust you will have seen bro. Hutchinson & learned from him the circumstances that should excite us to hasten on the work of building our house of worship. . . . What is peculiarly encouraging to me is the fact that nearly every young man in Lawrence manifests an interest in the movement & they apprise me they intend to become steady church goers. Several have remarked to me that the sound of a church bell would be music to their ears & make the 1st day of the week seem like a Sabbath at home. I need not tell you that I have responded to that desire beyond what words can express. Who of the liberal merchants of my native city will have the honor of sending out the 1st bell that shall call the people to prayer & praise in the territory of Kansas? It will be appreciated here for not one family in a dozen possess a clock & the want of some general time-marker has been in serious interference in getting our out-of-door congregation together. Sometimes 20 come dropping in after the sermon is half through. . . . A few rowdies from Missouri who have been bullying the Yankees for some time with drawn weapons and threats of violence were put to complete route this day by one lone Yankee. He drew his pistol on one who stood with his revolver loaded & cocked & dared him to fire. Another free state man requested the crowd to open and give space for the two combatants to take distance of ten paces which was done. Word was given the Yankee cocked raised his weapon & took deliberate aim at the breast of his opponent who turned pale backed into a door behind him & fled through the building. The Yankee then challenged any pro-slavery man the crowd to fill the place & told some standing by who had threatened his life several times that they were poor bragging cowards. Several others of the free state party who have been aggrieved by similar threats & some by actual violence reechoed the statement & demanded a fight. But no blood was shed, no blow struck & a very important victory was gained for the lovers of law & order in Lawrence by means which your missionary cannot of course approve. How can he refrain from inward joy at the result? . . . I am to preach this evening on Oread & must close this for the meal that is made up to night. Next Sunday means to Washington Creek some 8 miles where I am told about 40 persons will meet me. Sunday after to Coal creek where I have once been to attend a funeral of a young man from a Unitarian family in Charleston, about 12 miles. About the same number can be gathered in that neighborhood. Let me have a letter soon.[56]

With respect to the Kansas Territory *freedom* was a media watchword by now. The *Christian Register* reported on the efforts of Nute in Lawrence, assigning to him, and hence the Unitarians, the responsibility of bringing liberal Christianity and freedom to the territory all at once. The article read,

It is well known to our readers that the American Unitarian Association sent out in April last, as their missionary to Kansas, the Rev. Eph. Nute, Jr., of Chicopee. Mr. Nute, we learn, is doing a good work there; his ministrations are highly accept-

51

able, and the prospect of gathering a flourishing society are most flattering. . . . Mr. Nute has done well to make this the first stand-point to plant the banner of liberal Christianity. . . . Mr. Nute has been preaching to large and interested audiences in the *open air*, and an earnest call comes up for the help to build a house of worship. With such provision a flourishing society will soon be gathered. Never before has there been, and perhaps never again will there occur so favorable an opportunity to establish and extend liberal Christianity.[57]

A few days later, on October 3, Nute wrote to his dear friend, Edward Everett Hale, about his earliest days in Kansas and the first time he put aside his nonviolent beliefs and took up his guns for self-protection. He mentioned having both the Sharps rifle and the revolver given to him before he left the East:

Your word of encouragement to me personally & since for the cause of Freedom & the prosperity of our colony in the wilderness has been appreciated & has given strength to my hands for the work on which I have entered. . . . Hundreds of houses would have been built in & around Lawrence . . . more than have been built should the lumber be had. I began to build a small house 16 x 20 in the village 4 mo. since, the walls of composite. It is now up one story & has waited 6 weeks for the sticks on which to lay the 1st floor & it is now nearly as long since the masons stopped for want of those for the second & weeks of this time I have tented & the rest of the time lived in a small cabin on a "claim" the work of my own hands almost altogether. In the mean time I have been to each of the mills about 4 times a week walking generally a distance of 2 miles & back to get nothing but promises. Do you wonder that I have a keen interest in the subject of logs & saw mills. . . . I am at work about a church i.e. meeting-house, nearly $900 subscribed here, will probably be made up to $1000 good, I think for a pioneer community. . . . All that & what is raised here will be swallowed up in the bare building plans, unadorned & unfurnished. Then we shall want a bell & some other appurtenances for which I must make . . . another effort. . . . This struggle for civil liberty is favorable to the cause of Ecclesiastical freedom just as it was in the struggle of our . . . fathers with Great Britain. It was favorable to the freest Relg. institutions of thought that prevailed then & so it is now. The ground is well broken up in this community for the seed of Free thinking Christianity. . . . The men of Lawrence are wrought up to the fighting pitch. God grant it may not come but there may be something infinitely worse than that. . . . Monday was the day appointed by the sham legislature for election of delegates to Congress. Bands of the invaders began to appear early Sund. morn. About 400 were encamped near Franklin, a pro slavery whiskey drinking settlement some 7 miles below Lawrence. Small parties came up to this place during the day & it was rumored that an attack was meditated on our . . . presses. . . . Hundreds were gathered in Lawrence armed for the defense. Shall I confess that the missionary put his repeating rifle into the hands of a neighbor, took his revolver & went to town & stayed till after dark. 6 mo. since & I could hardly have believed that my trust would ever be put in carnal weakness. But when men behave like wild beasts, what can we do but treat them as such & make men of them as quick as possible. . . . Just what will be done with us is not known. . . . Great excitement prevails in anticipation of the election next Tues. Threats of interference here men arming themselves for resistance, some little skirmishing preparatory to a general fight I fear, one man stabbed by a fellow of the baser sort from Missouri who has been keeping a groggery in the village, but not it is now thought mortally wounded, diverse others assaulted, lives threatened, horses, oxen & cows killed in revenge. But some things will be settled on Tues & we must wait for this vile administration or a Congress but little better to settle the rest.[58]

Less than six months after Nute arrived in the Kansas Territory, ground was broken for the new Unitarian church. On October 7 Nute wrote to Miles about the details surrounding the project's beginning, frontier ministry to the dying, the illegal voting, and the donations coming in for the church building. The letter read, in part,

> On inquiring for one of the builders with whom I had talked on the subject who told that he lay dying at his cabin, called & found him to all appearance at the very point of going. The family were of course in great distress & are as I have since learned in very needy circumstances through the intemperance of the man. They seemed very grateful for my visit & the wife very religiously disposed. As I stood by the bedside she asked me if I knew Mr. Miles of Lowell. "He used to be <u>my</u> minister" (all that emphasis on the—my) "It used to do me good to hear him preach O! That I could hear him now. I never knew the value of public worship & preaching until he came out here, & here I have not been able to attend once." She has since lived in Bolton & attended on bro Edes[59] ministrations of whom she speaks with great regard. Another woman was present whose family here settled over the Wakarusa who have lived in Bolton & also been connected with the Unitarian society there. It is a long time since I have felt myself in a little circle of such deep religious sympathy as that which joined me in the prayer by the bed side of that dying man.[60]

Meanwhile, during October 1855, the Unitarian and Congregational churches in New England—sometimes still one and the same thing—were holding meetings in honor of Nute's mission. One such meeting was covered by the *Daily Mail*, a Boston newspaper. It spread glowing reports of his good character and competence for his mission. Participants at the meetings repeatedly discussed the utmost importance of a church bell to the visibility and spread of the Free-State enterprise. E. B. Whitman, a speaker at some of these early meetings, was soon to become part of the Lawrence project himself. The *Daily Mail* reported,

> The speaker spoke in high terms of the mission, the talents, and the exertions of the Rev. Mr. Nute, the clergyman who preached the first Unitarian sermon in Kansas. Mr. Nute, he said, was stationed at Lawrence, but a short distance from Kansas river, where a year ago there was not white settler, now it had three saw-mills, three newspapers, school-houses physicians and number of lawyers. The town now has from one to two thousand inhabitants. A letter was read from Mr. Nute, who stated that a number of young men had expressed a desire to join a new society and aid in its support; they thought the sound of a church bell would have a tendency to make them commence the new week with better thoughts and resolutions. . . . Mr. Whitman asked who would have the honor of sending a bell to the new church. He said that it was proposed to erect a commodious house, put the Bible upon the pulpits, hymn books in the pews, and a bell to call the people to worship, in the belfry. Many liberal contributions had been made in this city. One gentleman had given one hundred dollars, and others had contributed smaller sums. Money was being received from many surrounding towns. Concord had sent liberally. . . . Remarks were made by the Rev. J. Freeman Clarke, of Boston, who said that if such a man as Mr. Nute was willing to go out to Kansas, surrounded by strange and rude associations, we ought to be willing to send him something to encourage him to stay there. He said, that when Mr. Nute had told him of his intention, he was much gratified. He never hoped to find such a man as brother Nute to undertake the mission; a man of such simple purity, of high and noble purposes, and possessed with all the requisites, mentally and physically, necessary to push forward in such a country. He urged that aid should be immediately raised and sent forthwith. . . . A contribution was taken up. Slips of paper were placed in the boxes for persons to

mark down any amount they were willing to give, and the evidence was that a pretty good sum will be raised to help build up and maintain the first Unitarian Church in Kansas.[61]

Clearly, the most fruitful avenue for collecting the money to build the church came from these fund-raising meetings. Even the children were asked for their help. Whitman launched an appeal to the Sunday school children of Massachusetts through the editor of the *Christian Register* for the resources to establish a Sunday school library in Lawrence. This effort successfully provided books and materials for an ecumenical Sunday school for all the liberal Christian denominations in Lawrence. The appeal read,

A long acquaintance with the feelings and interests of children, leads me to think that the children connected with our Unitarian Sunday Schools would rejoice in an opportunity to do something for the Kanzas Mission. Let me suggest a method to gratify them, and at the same time do a good work. It is proposed to send out, among other things, as an accompaniment of the Church, a Sunday School library, a good one. One gentleman interested in the Sunday School enterprise, has headed the subscription with $20. Will not the children do the rest? . . . Let the Superintendent of each school, give notice on the next Sunday, that on the following Sunday a collection will be taken up in the school for this purpose, and that any little sums, from one cent upwards, as they may have the means, and will freely give, out of their little store, will be gratefully received and appropriated to this object. The aggregate of those small sums would be amply sufficient for the purpose. . . . Should more be received than is required for the library at Lawrence, the balance will be appropriated for the same object in other towns in Kanzas where there is Unitarian preaching. Mr. Nute already has two other stations, and Elder Burgess, of the Meadville school, is gathering a Society at Topeka.[62]

An October 1855 letter from Nute to Miles in response to the supportive efforts in the East is now lost, except for the fragments that were published in the *Quarterly Journal*:

> It is my constant desire and prayer to do something for the credit of our religious character, to make our body felt at this distant outpost as a spiritual power, under the great Head of the Church, for the regeneration of the world. I am oppressed at times by a sense of the magnitude of my undertaking. Such are my feelings, as I read the words of encouragement and commendation which reach me by almost every mail from friends at the East. It would be pleasant to feel that I had done anything to merit the praise. But as yet my work is all prospective. I thank God for the fair prospect, and take heart while I trust that my sufficiency for the work may be of Him. It is a glorious opportunity that is given me. I rejoice with trembling before it, and need the assurance which you and others are giving me of the sympathies and fervent prayers of a large company in our household of faith. . . . Workmen have commenced on the church, literally breaking ground for the foundations. The masons will be ready to begin their work in about ten days. Part of the lumber is bought and paid for by money which I advanced from that just received from you. If the present mild weather should continue for a few weeks longer, we hope to get one of the basement rooms ready for use this winter. At present we have no room in which to meet.[63]

In his next letter to Miles, on October 22, Nute reported at length on the interpersonal violence aimed at individual abolitionists and the continuing government frauds and outrages in the territory. He wrote,

> We are getting the church along as fast as possible, but find many difficulties in the way. On further deliberation and after much counsel we have changed the location from the spot first

selected, but only to the other side of the same street which is considerable higher & a better situation in many respects. . . . My gathering yesterday was again prevented by cold windy weather attended yesterday with some rain. My meeting over the Wakarusa was also prevented by the sickness prevailing just now in that neighborhood & indeed all through this region. Mr. Wilder & his family have all been sick & confined to the bed at the same time with fever. This with the Bro Hutchinson absence to St. Louis has thrown all the labor of the church building as to plans & contracts in my hands but I have had Mr. Wilder's counsel daily & he & his family are now getting up again. Bro Hutchinson has also returned & taken hold of the work with spirit. The lot is surveyed & the stakes set up for excavation the contract about closed for that part of the work & the men set at work on the shingles of which 30 thousand will be needed. Tomorrow I must go about 10 miles to see about some timber for the floor sills & rafters & also in another direction nearly as far to inq at another saw mill to engage flooring. . . . The friends at the East should be fully advised in regard to the brutal out-rages now being perpetrated on the Missouri river. A few weeks since a minister of the Methodist connection by the name of Clark who has preached in Lawrence, an elderly man kind & peaceable to the extreme of non resistance was set upon by a gang of ruffians on the steamboat Polar Star & beaten with fists & a chair until he could hardly stand. He was in that condition put ashore at a wood yard by the orders of the captain & has not been heard from yet by his friends here of whom he has many warmly attached & of long standing. . . . I have made the voyage of the Missouri in that same Polar Star & a viler set of men were never afloat on any waters as the gambling & other vices testified to me. Let her be avoided by all brethren who love righteousness, or decent humility, as the pestilence. If it is not already done I hope you will instigate the public press to give to that boat the fame which it has earned to the warning of all who travel this way.[64]

In late October Nute had to change his worship services on Mt. Oread to mid-afternoon in order to have enough daylight.[65] In addition to the necessities brought about by nature, he was dealing with the imperatives of his mission work and numerous issues outside his control—including finding that letters he had intended as confidential were excerpted in the *Quarterly Journal.* He wrote to Miles,

> It was very far from my thought that I was writing for public print in the first three letters which I gave you & I was sorry to see any of the first & parts of the other in the Quarterly. They were written for the eye of an indulgent friend in the midst of many perplexities & under great fatigue. But if any good is effected by their publication can be resigned to the humiliation & perchance profit thereby. . . . The convention for framing a state constitution is now in session at Topeka & takes away many of our people. There is a strong confidence in this community that the appeal to Congress that we are about to make through the delegate whom we have chosen will be favorably received & that our state organization will be ratified by receiving us into the Union. This confidence gives life to business, more buildings are now wanted than can be erected by the workers on the ground & we are hoping to see a large immigration in time for the spring work. . . . The Missouri rowdies have been very scarce among us of late & our village has consequently enjoyed an unwasted quiet. Some of my neighbors are quarrelling about claims setting fire to hay stacks & firing guns into one another's houses in the night. I was summoned to attend as umpire between two of these belligerents last evening, but was too unwell to go—shall look after them tomorrow if possible. I shall wait anxiously for your approval of our operation toward the church thus far.[66]

In November the *Quarterly Journal* reported that the AUA had hired E. B. Whitman to take over superintendence of the building of the church, relieving Nute of some his burdensome tasks. They hoped that this would hasten the move of the worship services indoors. In his letter of November 4, Nute expressed his whole-hearted relief at Whitman's hiring. He also reported on the night-marish frustrations of a building project on the frontier. Ephraim and Lucy were living in the bare bones of a house structure, buffeted by tornadoes. Nute's letter read,

Mr. Whitman . . . informs me that he is to superintend the building and will be here in the course of two or three weeks from this, at which I greatly rejoice. The perplexity and labor of getting up such a building is too much for your missionary to undertake. I could spend all my time about it profitably. Every body is head and ears in business of their own, and there is a general scramble for building material, workmen, &c. The excavation is nearly, if not quite, finished. . . . My house in town yet awaits the boards for roof and flooring, though I had the promise of two men three months ago that it should be sawed out in one week, and then renewed from week to week down to the present time. Men go in with great logs, and watch their chance to get them rolled to the mill. Do you understand logging? Not political log-rolling, but the management of logs that weight from 500 pounds to a ton,—yes, 3 tons. I have worked at it some here. I had a log of oak 18 feet long, 3 feet in diameter at the but, hauled to the mill to be sawed into joists for my floors, and for rafters; the sawing was promised to be done in two days, but there it laid for a week; then I was told, if I would get it rolled into a certain place, 'it should be sawed to-morrow.' This I did, with the aid of two yoke of oxen, and there it lay another week. Then it must be hauled a little ahead; that done, several larger logs were place on top of it, and 'they must be sawed before we can get at it'; and so three weeks more. After at least ten visits to the mill, two miles distant, and at least one day's work there, the log was sawed; and then I was obliged to team it myself, and lay down the joists and lay up the rafters or they might not have been done to this time. . . . It is Sunday. We are having a cold, driving rain-storm. The water comes in on the side toward the wind, and runs across the floor until it finds a crack through which to reach the ground. It runs down the rusty stove-pipe, which is stuck out of the roof, and across the stove, to swell the currents on the floor. The walls crack and tremble in the wind, as though the house had caught the prevailing disorder and was having a 'right smart chance of the shakes.' The canvas with which part of the roof is covered flaps and snaps as though determined and desperate to get away and leave us entirely open to the storm. I have been at work for hours filling the huge openings under the roof and around windows and door with all the spare garments, rags, &c. that can be mustered for the purpose. . . . The sickness yet prevails. Whole families are down together. Fever and ague, with bilious and typhoid fevers; but the fatality has been less of late than it was for the two or three months previous. . . . The violence of the storm put a stop to my writing for the rest of the day; canvas roof blew off, water came in in torrents, wood all wet, and not a dry corner in the house to retreat to. It is now late in the evening, and the storm has abated. It was a regular tornado for five or six hours, and the wind is higher now than I seldom have seen it in Massachusetts. Nothing is done by halves here. But 'whatsoever you do, do it with all your might,' is the order of the weather. I desire and pray to have grace to act on the same order in the great work for which I have come out into this wilderness. Help me in this prayer.[67]

Nute wrote often of "fever," "ague," and "the shakes" in his letters home. Settlers to the Kansas Territory struggled mightily with illness, malaria in particular. Joanna L. Stratton, in her collection of women's diaries from the Kansas frontier, identified "ague" ailments as malaria and recounted an anecdote about a frontier wife who put the baby in bed with her poor shivering husband so that his shaking could rock the baby to sleep.[68] Many struggled with illness for the rest of their lives. Nute spoke of not having thrown off the illness that beset him in Kansas until 1860, during an ocean voyage to Europe.[69]

In November, Nute's congregation in Chicopee sent seventy-five dollars for the Lawrence church, along with a Bible and hymnbook for the pulpit. The old Bible still resides in the collections of the University of Kansas. The leatherbound, ornate King James pulpit Bible, printed by the Oxford University Press in 1845, is enormous. Inside, it is inscribed by hand, "Presented to the First Unitarian Society in Lawrence, Kanzas, by friends in Chicopee, the late parishioners of its pastor Rev. Ephraim Nute. 1855."[70]

Even as this reminder of the coziness of New England churches arrived in Lawrence, missionary work itself lost none of its risk. Another missionary, a Congregationalist in Leavenworth, sent letters to the U.S. Post Office in the hands of a proslavery neighbor. Instead, the neighbor took the letters to the proslavery newspaper office, where they were opened and searched for antislavery comments, which constituted a hanging offense. When the missionary found out and protested to the neighbor, he was knocked down and beaten, and an attempt was made to gouge out his eyes. Fortunately, some other neighbors came to the rescue before he was blinded or killed.[71]

Nute wrote again to Miles on November 19 of the many hazards of his work and living conditions. The original letter no longer resides in the Harvard collections, although it is excerpted in the *Quarterly Journal*. It read,

Winter is come upon us in good earnest. A cold rain that froze as it fell, encasing every twig and spear of grass in a crystal sheath, ending with a fall of snow some inch or two in depth, fitted up the old brown earth and the leafless trees for a gorgeous morning spectacle when the sun arose in all his glory and looked over us through an atmosphere so pure as to seem the very symbol of the Divine perfection and expression of the Father's love. What a change from the gloomy aspect of yesterday! Our cabin was the perfect picture of discomfort. The rain driving in through the cracks, around the windows, and down the stove-pipe, in streams, our wood, too green to burn well at the best, soaking wet, our slender walls shaking in the wind as though in sympathy with their inmates shivering in the cold. We drew comfort from the thought of how much more favorable these rains would be for the tillers of the soil and for the thirsty cattle than the parched-up condition of the earth a year ago, when for more than eight months the heavens were as brass and nearly every spring failed. The rain continued for the greater part of two days and nights, the third time within as many weeks, so we are delivered from all fear of a drought for this winter. . . . You may readily conceive with what eager expectancy we await the arrival of our excellent brother Whitman, who has been rendering such efficient help in our behalf and in behalf of our common faith at the East. I suppose he is now on the way out. I hope the weather will yet be mild enough to allow the builders to make some progress on the walls of our church. But the true Church, the spouse of Christ, is not to be built of stone and mortar, but of living souls consecrated to him and to the Father, and sanctified by the spirit from the taint of sin. I long to be more widely and efficiently engaged in the building up of his temple. But I will try to wait in patience and faith, believing that the Spirit works ever and in ways hidden from our short-sighted view like the wind which is now sweeping over these wide prairies, bringing to mind the cheering declaration of Jesus, 'So is every one that is born of the Spirit.' Just now I feel more than ever before in my ministerial work the need of all the quickening words of our Lord and the assurances of the Father's presence and help. I feel that I have a peculiar claim to the title 'Minister at Large.' Here, in about the geographical centre of the North American continent, with a field reaching from the Missouri to the Rocky Mountains, my nearest clerical brother of the same household of faith five hundred miles on one side and more than fifteen hundred on the other, if I am not at large I like to know who is. . . . But to come down to particular points where I must concentrate my efforts to labor to any effect,—I have taken some steps for the formation of a Sunday School. A small band meet at our cabin, and we hope soon to make an encouraging report. It is the day of small things; but if we can labor on in the right spirit, we have good ground to hope for great results. 'Fear not, little flock, for it is your Father's good pleasure to give you the kingdom.'[72]

The irony of Nute's sermon on asceticism in the church at his divinity school graduation was echoed in his third major correspondence with the *Christian Register* on November 19. Nute was living with Lucy in their primitive cabin out on their claim. He explained the hardships that had taken him away from his missionary work, but framed his situation with his customary dry humor. His letter describes the reality of the settler life at a time when the town of Lawrence was in a brief peaceful hiatus:

The rapid growth of this infant city in the wilderness and settlement of the country round about has been truly wonderful. A little more than a year ago and from the height instant of the village where my meetings have been held during the summer, not a single habitation of the white man could be seen. To day more than two hundred roofs can be counted from that wide outlook and the walls of many more that have just begun to rise from the foundation. . . . First the sod cabin, with its sharp roof of thatch coming down to within four feet of the ground, the gable ends usually of canvass, through which the light is admitted dim enough to be religious; without floor, the hearthstone outside the walls. Next, the log cabin, with roof of rived boards, and capacious chimney of stone on the outside, with perhaps a window of six panes of the smallest sized glass. Then came the saw mill, and the frame house arose, covered with green cottonwood boards, which have shrunk nearly a quarter of their width, and so warped and twisted as sometimes to be wrenched from their places, the surface at one end standing at right angles with that at the other. The lime kiln and the mason effect the last step and the more stately and substantial structure of "composite" is produced, rising to the height of three stories, with some pretensions to architectural embellishment. . . . Our main business street, called Massachusetts, has quite a metropolitan look, with its long line of stores, with people hurrying to and fro, laden with merchandize and building material. Our largest public house, "The free state Hotel," now nearly completed, is a building of generous dimensions, some 80 feet square, three stories high. . . . For this much credit is due to that admirably conducted enterprise, the N.E. Emigrant Aid Company. I am happy to bear witness to the energy, fidelity and courtesy of the gentlemen who are entrusted with the management of its affairs both here and at the East. . . . Some of those who have made trouble among us have taken themselves off. . . . The revolver and bowie knife are not quite so conspicuous in our streets, as they were a few months since, and I have heard of but one fight for the last three weeks, which used to be an affair of almost daily occurrence. . . . I am obliged to put this little cabin in such condition of defence, against the winter blasts, as I can and here abide until they are passed. Within the walls of boards, not quite half an inch in thickness, we have the space of 15 1/2 square feet, a room which serves in turn the various offices of domestic life, including a workshop for inclosing it more completely against the weather. . . . Our furniture all told is a stove, two chairs, a table and a bedstead, the last two articles of home and quite hasty manufacture. . . . Perhaps, indeed, we should indulge in the effeminate luxury of a thick rug carpet to cover the cracks in our floor if such an article were within reach; but rough boards are a great improvement on the bare ground, and a tight roof on a covering of cotton canvass, and it is not morally wholesome to go too rapidly in this direction.

. . . If we miss many social privileges, with some sadness, we also miss some of the constraints of society, that were irksome, and find a freedom which is good for the health of the soul. . . . No visitor despises us because of uncarpeted floors or goes off offended because asked to sit on a box. During the storm, which lasted for two days last week and was violent, I experienced a feeling of comfort and gratitude, looking around on the rough shelter, which my own hands had raised, fully equal to any that I ever felt in the close ceiled and well furnished houses of the East. . . . My missionary service of late has been of a very irregular and miscellaneous character. . . . Since the cool weather has prevented our meetings in the open air we have been without any place of gathering in the village, and my only preaching has been at neighborhood meetings several miles distant. Many of those who were most regularly with us on the hill are now scattered abroad and will go no where else to join in the Lord's day service. Earnest inquiries are made of me every day as to the prospects of our house of worship. If the spirit of the Master yet lives, in the churches of his name, it cannot be that we shall long have to wait for the answer to our appeal for help in this Christian enterprise. To all in whose fellowship and interest we have a place.[73]

But by December 2, Nute wrote to the AUA of the constant threats from armed Missouri militants, saying,

Our community is thrown into a great ferment and consternation by the prospect of immediate civil war. Several hundred Missourians, armed with rifles and a piece of artillery, are now encamped a few miles below Lawrence, for the avowed purpose of destroying the town as soon as their numbers are large enough by reinforcements now on the road. Our men are under arms, and have been for the last three days and nights, giving our village quite a warlike appearance. To-day men have come in to our aid from Topeka and other places, and a bloody conflict is hourly expected. All work is of course suspended. . . . Since writing the above, one of the company has come in from Topeka to take quarters with us. Several of the most influential men of Westport have come up to the camp of our enemies to counsel peaceable measures, they say, but we distrust them. Governor Shannon has issued a proclamation, requesting the ruffians to return and leave the actual residents of the territory to settle their own difficulties. . . . Morning of the 3d . . . I have just been summoned to be in the village with my repeating rifle. I shall go and use my utmost efforts to prevent bloodshed. But if it comes to a fight, in which we shall be forced to defend our homes and lives against the assault of these border savages (and by the way the Indians are being enlisted on both sides), I shall do my best to keep them off. . . . P.S. By twilight in the village I find between four and five hundred men drawn up in a line just outside the town for battalion drill, ready and thirsting for the fight. At least two hundred more stand ready to join them, if an engagement takes place, your missionary among the number.[74]

The founding Unitarian and other citizens of Lawrence fought desperately for their personal safety, as well as against the encroachment of the illegal politics of the Border Ruffians into their territory. On December 4 the *New York Daily Tribune* published their desperate letter to the rest of country, seeking help for their dreadful plight:

We, the undersigned, Committee of Public Safety, appointed by the citizens of Kansas Territory, assembled at the City of Lawrence, notify you that the said city is beleaguered by a large force of men from a foreign State, arrived with all the implements of war, including several batteries of cannon; and said body of men are perpetrating all manner of outrages upon our harmless, orderly and unoffending citizens—stopping and arresting the persons and seizing the property of travelers, threatening the immediate destruction of this city and the murder of its inhabitants. That said band of lawless men claim that they are acting by and under the authority of the Governor of said Territory; that said Governor has issued a proclamation which, they claim, authorizes their invasion of our Territory and the destruction of our property and lives, which proclamation we declare to be unfounded in fact, and a slander upon the people of this Territory. And, under these extraordinary circumstances, we feel authorized to demand your immediate assistance on our behalf. (Signed) J. MILLER, G. P. LOWERY, J. S. EMORY, M. F. CONWAY, G. M. DUTCH-LER, G. W. HUTCHINSON, ROB. MORROW, C. ROBIN-SON, C. W. BABCOCK, G. W. BROWN[75]

The signatories to this letter were prominent Lawrence men. Martin F. Conway was originally a Douglas Democrat who went to the Kansas Territory and converted to radical Free-State ideas. As a lawyer he became active in politics. "G. M. Dutchler" can only be George Deitzler, who, along with Charles Robinson, C. W. Babcock, and George W. Brown, editor of the Lawrence *Herald of Freedom*, were members of Nute's congregation.

The letter also went directly to President Pierce. Lawrence may have been ignored by the country at large, particularly the politicians, but it was not about to take its fate lying down. Heavy munitions quietly began to arrive in Lawrence, courtesy of the wealthy crew behind the Sharps rifles.[76]

Charles Stearns, a friend and parishioner of Nute and one of Lawrence's earliest Unitarian settlers, wrote to his friend William Lloyd Garrison, editor of the prominent abolitionist newspaper *The Liberator* on December 7. He raised the same issue that Nute faced—giving up the "principles of Jesus Christ" to carry a gun, after grisly firsthand experience with the murder of a neighbor. Many Unitarian settlers confronted this dilemma of belief and morality: They had gone to the territory to bring the peace and nonviolence of antislavery, yet found themselves needing to take up the instruments of war or perish. Stearns wrote,

Little did I think when I wrote you last, that matters would have assumed, by this time, so fearful an aspect. Here we are, a little handful of men, almost completely surrounded by a hideous foe, sworn by the devil to execute such vengeance upon us as Joshua was ordered to upon the heathen of his time. Our enemies swear that neither man, woman nor child shall be spared after the war commences. . . . Our town is in a state of most fearful excitement. About 1000 troops are collected here, and every house, store and tavern is crowded to overflowing. Hardly a man appears in the streets unarmed. The troops are paraded daily, and march through the streets in battle array. It is a fearful sight for a non-resistant. Guards of over a hundred men are on duty all night, and boarding houses have to be kept open to feed them. The Delawares and Wyandotts [Native Americans] have proffered their services, in case of need. . . . Last night, one of our men was shot dead a few miles from here, without the least provocation. Another was fired upon, and his horse taken from him. . . . Yesterday, the long-expected cannon, a twelve-pounder, arrived, and was greeted with tremendous cheers by our people. It came very near falling into the hands of the enemy at Kansas. . . . My non-resistance has at length yielded. For ten days I have kept calm, and withstood all solicitations to enter the ranks; but the cold-blooded murder, last night, of one of our best citizens, has decided me. I am sorry to deny the principles of Jesus Christ, after contending for them so long, but it is not for myself that I am going to fight. It is for God and the slaves. Down with American slavery! will be my watchword. . . . All I have to say is, for God's sake, dear friends, come to our rescue! March straight through Missouri, and proclaim Liberty to the slaves! The war, if once commenced, will not, must not cease until every slave throughout the Union is liberated. Slavery must go down, and, for myself, I am determined to fight for that purpose, if war commences. . . . Yours, for freedom. C. STEARNS . . . P.S. Since writing the above, I have seen the body of the murdered man. He lies within a few rods of where I am now writing, cold and stiff, in Death's icy arms. His wife, mother and sister have just arrived, and their screams can be heard at some distance. Behold the second victim of the demons who are panting for our blood! . . . God never made these fiends—they are the devil's spawn, and are to be killed as you would kill lions and tigers. I have always said I would shoot a wild beast. If I shoot these infernal Missourians, it will be on the same principle.[77]

Due to the frightening siege, Stearns did not get to send his letter. He added to it again on December 9:

The mail is about leaving, and I will add the latest intelligence. Last night, we apprehended an attack, and the soldiers slept on their arms. Two deep trenches were dug, right in front of my store, to guard Massachusetts street, and to place the enemy where our cannon will reach them. I have procured a Sharpe's rifle and a pistol, and mean to die or conquer, as we all do, for we are assured that if we are captured, we shall be butchered. You may be assured, that the danger is the extremest kind, or I should not arm myself. If it were an ordinary foe, I should not do it. But these men are not men; they are wild beasts; and, for God's sake, as well as for man's sake, I must do my duty in killing them, just as I would a wolf. I love all men as ever, but fools and knaves united, and drunk into the bargain, are not men. Christ said, 'If a man smite thee on the one cheek, turn to him the other also.' So say I. But if the devil attacks you, how then? . . . We are outnumbered by the enemy, who have six cannon, and we only one. We have committed no offence whatever. All the demand made upon us is to surrender Sharpe's rifles. Our commanders answer, 'That will not be done, until every man is a corpse.'[78]

A few days later, his narrative grew again:

> I hardly know whether to be glad or sorry as I communicate to
> you the following intelligence. Yesterday, after a day of the most
> intense excitement, an agreement was entered into, between
> Gov. Shannon on the part of the Missouri troops, and Gen.
> Robinson and Col. Lane on the part of our army, by which
> peace is proclaimed throughout this warlike region. This war
> . . . resulted in the loss of one human life only. That life has
> been sacrificed to the bloody demon of Slavery. I helped place
> the body in the coffin, and saw the shrieking wife and mother
> imprint the burning kiss of parting love upon the brave man's
> bloodless lips. Could the Northern people have witnessed that
> sight, and looked upon the garments of the hero, stained with
> blood, they would be ready to swear eternal hostility to slav-
> ery and its infernal allies—Know-Nothingism and National
> Democracy. . . . During the hurried burial, we were hourly
> expecting the enemy, and the corpse was taken hastily through
> the ranks of the soldiers, and deposited within a few feet of
> the fortifications. As I looked upon that form, I reflected that
> probably before night myself and hundreds of others would
> occupy the same position—only that we should lack a coffin
> and shroud. God knows I hate fighting as badly as a human
> being can hate it; and as I snatched my rifle, and buckled on my
> belt, and rushed forward at the news the enemy was coming,
> I certainly trembled. They were armed with splendid swords,
> stolen form the Arsenal at Liberty, Mo., and the thoughts of
> not only being shot, but of having my head severed from my
> body, with one of these swords, were any thing but pleasant.
> . . . When I shouldered my gun, for the first time in my life,
> it was after ten days of prayerful deliberation, and with the
> stern determination never to lay it aside, if the war continued
> until every slave in the Union was liberated. . . . Gov. Shan-
> non,[79] Sheriff Jones,[80] and some of our officers, are now having
> a glorious drunk over the victory. . . . I fear that you Eastern

people will accuse us of cowardice in agreeing to obey the laws; but nobody understands the agreement as any thing of value, because a clause is inserted which says that we express no opinion in regard to the validity of the laws of the Legislature. . . . December 11 . . . Peace reigns triumphant. Our army is disbanded and we feel as though we had been delivered from the jaws of hell. . . . Last night, at our jubilee, considerable excitement was manifested at the presence of Sheriff Jones. Many of the soldiers swore they would shoot him if he entered the room. But, through the influence of General Robinson, peace was restored, and Jones was protected.[81]

Nute's own moral struggle is evident in one of his letters excerpted in the *Quarterly Journal.* On December 10, 1855, he wrote of giving up his avowed pacifism and of the use of the unfinished church foundation as a fort during a proslavery attack on Lawrence. His letter read,

It seems a month since I wrote you last, though it is but a week, lengthened out by days and nights of the most painful excitement. We have been surrounded by enemies on all sides. . . . Our citizens have been shot at, and in two instances murdered, our houses invaded, hay-ricks burnt, corn and other provisions plundered, cattle driven off, all communication cut off between us and the States, wagons on the way to us with provisions stopped and plundered, and the drivers taken prisoners, and we in hourly expectation of an attack. Nearly every man has been in arms in the village. Fortifications have been thrown up by incessant labor night and day. The sound of the drum and the tramp of armed men resounded through our streets, families fleeing with their household goods for safety. Day before yesterday the report of cannon was heard at our house from the direction of Lecompton. Last Thursday one of our neighbors, one of the most peaceable and excellent of men, from Ohio on his way home was set upon by a gang of twelve men on horseback and shot down. Several of the ruffians pursued him some distance after he was shot, and one was seen to push him from his horse and heard to shout to his companions that he was dead. A neighbor reached him just before he breathed his last. I was present when his family came in to see the corpse for the first time at the free state Hotel, a wife, a sister, a brother and an aged mother. It was the most exciting and the most distressing scene that I ever witnessed. Hundreds of our men were in tears as the shrieks and groans of the bereaved women were heard all over the building now used for military barracks. Over eight hundred men are gathered under arms at Lawrence. As yet no act of violence has been perpetrated by those on our side. No blood of retaliation stains our hands. We stand and are ready to act purely in the defence of our homes and lives. I am enrolled in the cavalry, though I have not yet appeared in the ranks, but should there be an attack, I shall be there. I have had some hesitation about the propriety of this course; but some one has said, 'In questions of duty, the first thought is generally the right one.' On that principle I find strong justification. I could feel no self-respect until I had offered my services. . . . These murders, and several other attempts that have been made within the last few days, have been the most heartless, cold-blooded, and cowardly in the whole annals of crime. In both instances the victims were unarmed and going peaceably about their own business. They have fallen martyrs for the cause of Freedom, and not a drop of their blood will be wasted, but weigh more than bullets of lead towards gaining the victory. . . . Day before yesterday we received the timely reinforcement of a twelve pound howitzer, with ammunition therefore, including grape and canister, with forty-bomb-shells. It was sent from New York (made at Chicopee). By a deed of successful daring and cunning it was brought through the country infested by the enemy, a distance of fifty miles, from Kanzas City, but an unfrequented route, boxed up as merchandise. . . . Later.—Sunday morning,

Dec. 9th. The Governor has pledged himself to do all he can to make peace, and we are told that the invaders are beginning to retreat. But we know not what to believe. Our men are to be kept under arms for twenty-four hours longer at least. No religious meetings for the last three weeks. No work done of course. Some of the logs to be sawed for our church were pressed into service to build a fort, of which we have no less than five, and of no mean dimensions or strength. For a time it seemed probable that the foundation-stones for the church would be wet by the blood of the martyrs for liberty. They were piled up on the ground, and with the earth thrown out of the excavation, made quite a fort on the hill-side just outside of the line of entrenchments.[82]

This was the second time that Nute mentioned in a letter the use of the unfinished Unitarian church foundation as a fort. Mt. Oread had another fort at its southern end, erected by Free-State commander James Lane. As the war progressed, the incidents of everyday heroism mounted. The women of Lawrence, no less than their men, were active in the Free-State movement. They hid ammunition in their underwear to smuggle it to their Free-State husbands.[83]

On December 15 Nute wrote to Miles about the growing violence and also reported on the interfaith politics of Lawrence. Rev. Samuel Young Lum was upset that the Unitarians would prove to have the first church. Lum and some of the other more orthodox Christians had monopolized all of the meeting times and spaces and pushed the Unitarians out. However, Nute's congregants prevailed, and the work on the church building went on, navigating around the problems of civil war. Nute heartily reassured Miles that he and Whitman would work together famously and that Miles must fear no conflict between them. No prediction could have proved further from the truth. Nute wrote,

We feel that we have had a narrow escape from a bloody conflict. For several days it needed but a small thing to have brought on a battle. The free state men bore & forbore until forbearance has almost ceased to be a virtue. But peace is now effected & has here gained a great point, our election . . . day on the Constitution will probably be unmolested & in this object at last the result will be a fair expression of the will of the people.[84]

Nute's hopes for election day were not realized. In Leavenworth, the polls were not opened at all in some locations because of fear of violence from the Missourians. Even so, in those places the ballot boxes and poll books were destroyed, and some of the clerks of the election nearly lost their lives.

Nute wrote again to the AUA on December 23 to report on Whitman's arrival and further happenings in the territory. On Christmas Day he continued his letter despite a ferocious cold snap that gripped the territory. His letter read,

We are at last made glad by the coming of brother Whitman. He arrived last Thursday evening. The church-building is at a stand still, and must remain so for some two months to come, on account of the weather; but the preparations for getting lumber, &c., will go on in the mean time. There is some cause of hesitation as to the plan and location. The two do not come together well, and we all think (i.e., Mr. Whitman and Trustees) that one or the other should be changed. . . . I am writing in a room where water freezes rapidly, and a lively breeze flutters my paper, which must excuse my haste and illegibility. . . . Dec. 25. Since writing the above, we have been visited by one of the severest and coldest snow-storms that I ever experienced. We never suffered half so much from cold in our lives. . . . Everything that could freeze froze solid, all our potatoes, apples, &c., hard as so many stones. Water froze within three feet of our stove, in spite of all the fire I could keep up. So much for the mild climate of Kanzas. It is at this moment as cold as ever. Bushels of snow sifted through our frail walls, which will account for the defacement of my paper. This weather is unusual for this part of the country. Missourians say there has been nothing like it for twenty years. Snow about one foot on the level. I have not been able to get to brother Whitman since this was begun. The mail will not probably leave this morning, its usual time. . . . I had an appointment to preach Sunday, but it was next to impossible to get to the place over four miles of prairie. It would have been an actual risk of life to have started, and I should have found no congregation if I had reached the place. . . . Remember (I know you will) that I have been cut off from all ministerial intercourse for nearly nine months. Brother Whitman must fill up the gap as substitute for an Association. My spirit is truly refreshed by his coming. We all appreciate his labors in our behalf, and the noble spirit in which they have been rendered.[85]

Whitman himself wrote to the AUA immediately upon his arrival on December 24, recounting the dangers of his journey through Missouri. Coming into Lawrence in the midst of the election excitement, he tried to emphasize to his correspondents the mounting perils of the territory, referring to the heroics of a group that could only be the abolitionist John Brown and his sons. Whether this was the first time Whitman heard of Brown is not known, but the two men soon worked together. Whitman wrote,

You have learned from my last letter that I had decided upon an overland journey through Missouri. The usual time is four days, but eight had passed ere I saw the borders of the Territory. Such traveling must be seen to be appreciated. Thrice overturned, twice broken down, one horse killed, and drivers pitched from their seats, and the passengers performing half of the journey on foot. Ere my arrival here, the siege had been raised and the farce ended. Mr. Nute can give you the particulars better than I can, as he was not only an eyewitness, but an actor in the scene, having mounted his horse and actually served in the cavalry. We have not, I think, been misinformed as to his popularity here and fitness for the post. He is now shut out from preaching for want of a place, the only suitable accommodation is occupied three times each Sunday by the Orthodox, Methodist, and Baptist. . . . One of the mills here has been blown up, so that we have now but two. . . . Mr. Nute has a yoke of oxen, and I shall probably get the use of a pair of mules for the keeping; if so, we shall be able to collect our materials at a cheap rate, so far as the hauling is concerned. It is a disappointment to me not to be able to push the work along more rapidly, but I see the impossibility of doing any differently. Had I been on the ground a month earlier, it would have made but little difference. In a new country it will take time to accomplish anything besides, the work must have been suspended during the siege. If the work is all ready to go together at once when the early spring opens, it will not occupy more than three months to complete the whole. Should I be unable to stay so long, I hope to get it in such a state of forwardness that Mr. Nute will not find it too laborious to see it through himself. We shall unquestionably be the first on the ground, and the Society will commence under most favorable auspices. The prospect of a bell and clock is most cheering to the people here, and the gift will be duly appreciated. . . . Every move made by the adversaries of freedom seems thus far not only to have been frustrated, but to have worked in favor of freedom. All thanks and honor to the noble band of men who for two weeks slept on their arms, awaiting the attack of their foe, but refrained under the greatest provocation from becoming the actual aggressors in a fight. Had it begun, it would have been most bloody. Women and all were actuated with the same spirit. One old man came sixty miles at the head of a company of eighty men,—among them his four sons,—the father and sons armed from their own arsenal to the extent of being able to fire between them, in the family, ninety shots without reloading, and they would have done it. Women rode in the night across the country and through the enemies' lines to procure powder. The cannon itself was brought here with such cunning, that even Missourians helped it along over the bad places. Once the box was opened by the guards, but when they saw the wheels, they replied that they did not want anything of an old wagon, and let it pass. I hope to hear from you soon, and that the call for a clock has met a response from some noble-hearted man. From the tower it will be seen for miles around.[86]

Six days later, on December 30, Whitman wrote to Calvin Clark, the AUA treasurer from 1855 to 1858. He reported on conflicts over the specifications for the basement of the church and the uncommonly cold temperatures:

I am getting on as well as I expected. . . . The weather for the last eight days has been truly Canadian. Snow 8 inches, Thermometer ranging every morning from 10 above zero to 19 below and a wind that freezes the vitals. . . . Mr. Nute is by everyone well spoken of and I doubt not will take a prominent stand here. We are <u>at peace</u> here and we feel that freedom has gained vastly by this last false move which ~~they have so~~ the Missourians have made. Yet they are desperate fellows and I became convinced ~~that this~~ during my journey through land of friends that there are men among them who mean to rub us out. The safety of the settlers and the <u>peace and preservation of this Union</u> depend more than you at the East are aware of upon their ability to defend themselves. Those 300 Sharps rifles have once saved a Civil war. It was only the fear of them magnified to 1000 that saved such a result. The people of the territory are desperate and had there been a fight it would have been another Bunker Hill contest. Once begun Iowa, Illinois, Indiana & Ohio would have sent in their volunteers to the aid of their friends & neighbors who had emigrated. . . . There is yet great need of arms here and I hardly know which is most desirable <u>arms</u> or a church, both are wanted. I hope the free states will respond to the call for means of defence & that organizations will at once be entered into in all those states within hail by which aid can be promptly sent in, in case of attack. If this is done all will pass off well & peaceably, if not the southern nullifiers will press in to give us a long cherished end through the medium of this Kansas question. The free states are sleeping upon a volcano and heed it not. The forts still know every hour is provided with means of defence, and even the women are ready to fight for their hearths & homes.[87]

In the deep of winter, the violence of the Border Ruffians only slept. Out of sight, it still grew, and come spring, the Free-State settlers would face even more desperate straits.

CRIES FOR HELP

Nute and several others regularly contributed to Eastern newspapers, and their letters were daily fare for those eager for anything about Kansas. An article by "Randolph" appeared in the New York *Daily Advertiser,* reporting on the proslavery-antislavery "war" in Kansas and Governor Robinson's rousing speech dismissing the Free-State troops after their successful protection of Lawrence. "Randolph" was the pen name of William Hutchinson, prominent in Lawrence, a founding subscriber of the Unitarian Church, and the first secretary of the Lawrence Unitarian Society once it was formed. He wrote,

> Today our soldiers were again called out to receive their official dismissal and discharge. Before Governor Shannon left us, he enrolled the volunteers as the regularly organized militia of the United States. So we have been transformed from rebels to United States soldiers, with orders to preserve the peace, and drive the mob—the Governor first called out—to headquarters in Missouri, if necessary. . . . About noon today, colonel Lane arranged his men in a hollow square in the street, and after a few very pleasing remarks, General Robinson was called for. He was loudly cheered on his appearance, and as soon as order was restored, he spoke as follows:—. . . . Fellow Soldiers: In consequence of a misunderstanding on the part of the Executive of this Territory, the people of this vicinity have been menaced by a foreign foe, and our lives and prop-

erty threatened with destruction. The citizens, guilty of no crime, rallied for the defence of their families, their property and their lives. And from all parts of the Territory the true patriots came up, resolved to perish in defence of their most sacred rights rather than submit to foreign dictation. . . . We gained a bloodless victory. . . . Selected as your commander, it becomes my cheerful duty to tender you, fellow soldiers, the meed of praise so justly your due. . . . In behalf of the citizens of Lawrence—in behalf of the ladies of Lawrence—in behalf of the children of Lawrence—in behalf of your fellow soldiers of Lawrence, and in my own behalf, I thank you of the neighboring settlements for your prompt and manly response to our call for aid, and pledge you a like response to your signals of distress. . . . The war is ended, our duties are discharged, and it only remains for me, with the warmest affection for every soldier in this conflict, to bid you adieu, and dismiss you, to go again to the bosom of your families." . . . Amid the most friendly congratulations, and with many expressions of regret, the battalion, composed of ten companies, was discharged, and soon dispersed.[88]

Just like Nute's correspondence with the *Springfield Republican* and the *Christian Register*, Hutchinson's correspondence with the *New York Daily Times* and the *Boston Journal* was picked up by other papers nationwide. The Unitarians' letters gave the Kansas troubles high profile and influenced the hearts and minds of the sympathetic Northeastern public.

At a meeting of the Kansas State Editorial Association in 1900, Nute's friend and fellow officer in the First Kansas Regiment, journalist Richard Hinton, later the author of a seminal John Brown biography, called such man-on-the-ground correspondence from the Kansas Territory "the pens that made Kansas free."[89] Hinton named some of the most prolific of these writers, along with their home papers, and in the case of some, their literary sobriquets. A fair number besides Nute's parishioner Hutchinson were Unitarians. They included William Cullen Bryant of the *New York Evening Post*; George Washington Brown, editor of the Lawrence *Herald of Freedom* and a member of Nute's congregation; Samuel Tappan of the *Boston Journal*, the *New York Times*, and a member of Nute's congregation; and Nute's seminary classmate and John Brown conspirator, Thomas Wentworth Higginson, who wrote under the name of "Worcester" for the *New York Tribune*.

Hinton wrote that the pens of these frontline correspondents were an earlier weapon, and in many cases equally effective, as the Sharps rifles and Colt revolvers that followed. Before the bogus election of March 1855, letters from Kansas were only incidents in the Eastern papers. After that time, "they became 'events' in the history of the land, that rapidly formed their words into epoch-making forces."[90]

Despite the undeclared proslavery-antislavery "war," Lawrence continued to take on the attributes of a settled municipality. The earliest index in existence for real-estate transactions for Douglas County, Kansas, shows Nute heavily involved in buying real estate in 1856. No less than twenty-eight transactions involving lot sales to Nute occurred in that year. In 1857 Nute sold lots fifteen times to someone else. Nute's letters indicate that he bought land in trust for other people expecting to emigrate, as well as for the church. This was one of the peculiar duties of many territorial clergy.

As town development accelerated, lots became harder and more expensive to get, so people were advised not to wait until they arrived in Lawrence to buy. Nute would purchase the lots, and when the intended owners arrived in Kansas and paid him, he would transfer the lots to them. Although the total number of transactions makes it appear as though Nute was wheeling and dealing wildly in real estate, a closer look reveals that several separate transactions were related to each single lot—issuing a bond, a mortgage, and then a deed. Nute began buying for the AUA very early in his tenure in Lawrence, taking responsibility for lots donated for the future Unitarian church and snapping up lots that were convenient to the donated areas. Some of these lots were disposed of once the location of the church was finally determined.

Despite the brief and hopeful periods of quiet in 1855, by January 1, 1856, the violence was raging in earnest once again in Kansas, and attained high national visibility. The troubles escalated throughout that year and through most of 1857 and 1858. In early 1856, however, there was still a debate going on in the East, and especially in the South, about whether the violence was real, who was at fault, and if indeed the Eastern backers were guilty of feeding the fire.

The two sides of opinion regarding the territory were deeply divided. Sending Sharps rifles to the abolitionists was seen either as contributing immorally to the conflict or as a moral imperative to help the Free-State settlers save their own lives. The Pierce administration's complicity with the proslavery side was interpreted either as a grand and glorious maintenance of the Union and protection of the authority of the government or as an evil and wicked erosion of American freedoms guaranteed by the Constitution.

Rumors surfaced regularly that the abolitionists in the East had collected money to buy arms for Kansas and sent the shipments of Sharps rifles that mysteriously appeared in Lawrence. Southern newspapers campaigned sensationally on the national scene to declare that this was proof that the abolitionists were the aggressors. The firearms began to even up the score between the Border Ruffians and the Free-Staters of Lawrence and surrounding towns.

The women of Lawrence were no less important to the military cause. They began to practice pistol shooting in order to properly greet the Border Ruffians when they came in search of the ballot boxes again. According to a January 5, 1856, article identified only as coming from *The Herald,* but not designating the city of origin, "One young girl—a beauty of nineteen years—told me that she dreamt last night of shooting three invaders."[91]

Voting irregularities in the territory continued to capture the nation's attention. Newspapers carried detailed election results that all pointed to fraud. The *Springfield Republican* in Massachusetts echoed the growing national outrage over the complicity of the Pierce administration in creating the Kansas civil war. It carried daily happenings in that war, with Nute himself as their correspondent.

In his January 17, 1856, letter to the *Springfield Republican,* Nute reported the story of the seventeen-year-old wife of Robert Buffum of Lawrence, identified only as "Mrs. Buffum." Her refusal to surrender her husband to the notorious proslavery henchman, Sheriff Jones, was circulated widely for much-needed humorous relief among antislavery readers:

> Of late we have had an abundant crop, and the interest taken in our affairs all over the land, with their bearing on the national weal or woe, will keep many eyes fixed upon us for some time to come. . . . It is no less than WAR AGAIN IN KANZAS! ANOTHER RESCUE!! Sheriff Jones finds himself unable to execute the laws of the late sham legislature in the rebellious town of Lawrence, and more trouble may of course be expected. Yesterday a prisoner was taken out of his hands by the intervention of a woman, the prisoner's wife. The sheriff was taking his captive through the streets, when the wife appeared with a revolver. Coming up to her husband, she took him by the button-hole, saying 'Come with me,' and presenting the pistol to Jones' breast, she said, 'Stir to follow us and I'll shoot you.' And thus she led her lord off to the great amusement of the standers-by, and the no less amazement and mortification of the strong arm of the law. Poor Jones! . . . We shall have another siege of Lawrence, the town will be destroyed, the inhabitants thrown into the river, and the little Mrs. Buffum, who by the way has seen but 17 summers, though too much for Jones, may at last be conquered. If anything monstrous comes of it I will let you know. . . . We live in troublous times, but in hope of final and not long deferred deliverance.[92]

Mrs. Buffum's adventures showed that the women of Lawrence escalated the stakes regarding law and order. In nineteenth-century terms, when women had to take up arms, civilization had truly departed. Robert Buffum's cousin, David C. Buffum, wrote to the family about the incident on January 20, 1856. David was part of the courageous team that smuggled the New-England-made Howitzer cannon on the last leg of its journey to Lawrence in 1855. Sadly, he was murdered by proslavers the following September 12, 1856, when he tried to prevent them from stealing his horses. His letter read,

During the heat of the war, we received the information that there was a brass cannon, at Kanzas City, for us, sent from the East, for our use. Robert and I tackled up our teams and went down right through the enemy's camp, to Kanzas City, got the gun and brought it in safety to Lawrence, the people receiving them with cheers. When we were going down, we met a great many Missourians on the road. We asked them where they were going. They said they were going to Lawrence to kill the damned Yankees. They had several pieces of cannon with them and yet they were afraid to attack us. Robert was arrested the other day by Sheriff Jones, on complaint of a man in this place, and taken before a pro-slavery Justice in Franklin, and ordered to give bonds to appear before another Court for trial. This he refused to do, and the Sheriff proceeded to take him to Leavenworth to jail. In passing through Lawrence, his wife presented a pistol to Jones and took Robert away from him, to the no small amusement of the crowd who were standing by. Afterwards while Robert and his wife were in my room, Jones and another man came in, and the other sprang upon Robert's wife and held her, while Jones seized Robert, and hurried him into the wagon. When the man let go of Robert's wife, she ran after him and fired at Jones three times, one ball just grazing his head; but Robert has returned since that, Jones not being able to find any place to put him in.[93]

Nute's January 21 letter to the AUA appeared, in part, in the spring *Quarterly Journal.* He wrote about the increasing chaos surrounding the Free-State constitution, the continued bloodshed, and the necessity of establishing church and community to bring those issues under control:

> We are still going through a dark place, and are at a stand still. Just now deliberating, 'what step next?' The war is again revived, and all is excitement. The people of Leavenworth made a second attempt to hold an election for officers under the free state constitution. This time they appointed it at Easton, some five miles out, to avoid the threatened collision. A band of armed men went thither, demanded the ballot-boxes, were refused, make an attack, were repulsed with loss of several lives on their side. Afterwards they took prisoners three of the free state men. All but one escaped. Him they brutally murdered after the manner of savages, striking him on the back and horribly mangling him with hatchets. He escaped, and was just able to reach his home, where he breathed but a few moments. The report was brought hither by men who had escaped, throwing us into great excitement. The citizens were again called to arms. But the story was too horrible to be believed. Messengers were sent to Easton to investigate. Through them we learn that the worst is true. . . . These outrages cannot be submitted to much longer. A bloody and general fight cannot be averted. . . . We have reason to believe that a plan is now formed of attacking Lawrence before the river opens. It is thought by the enemy that we shall then be reinforced by men and arms from the East. Nothing but such a help can save us now, it is believed. . . . I have heretofore been slow to believe that anything like an organized attack would be made. But I am now convinced that military companies have been formed and preparations made on a large scale for the purpose. . . . In this state of things of course nothing can be done toward church building or the organization of church and society. . . . Yesterday I went eight

miles across the prairie and over the river to fulfil an appointment. But a fierce snow-squall, with mercury down to zero, came on just before I reached the place, and that, together with the excitement about the outrages at Easton, prevented the people from assembling, and I had to walk back—to ride horse back would have been at the peril of freezing to death, from which I have already had a narrow escape.[94]

Life in a dangerous territory was rough, and it showed in the deteriorating behavior of its men. In 1855 Nute wrote joyfully of the high character of the men he found in early Lawrence, but by 1856 he bemoaned the increase of men who would rather spend their time drinking and drunk than in pursuit of the moral life. Often the bouts of drinking ended in fighting and gunfire. Nute was not alone in his concerns, and he began to form the first territorial interfaith conference. All clergy in the Kansas Territory were invited to gather at a convention in Lawrence to address the men's behavior, among other things.[95]

Then, the ferocity of the violence against the Free-Staters escalated again. The fiendish hatchet murder of a Mr. R. P. Brown that Nute had written about was reported extensively. The murdered man's wife Martha A. Brown's letter of January 25, 1856, to her family back in Michigan appeared in the *Detroit Evening Tribune*. It read,

I never expected to be called to write to you under so great affliction. My dear husband has been very active in the cause of liberty, ever since we came into the Territory. His bold and manly course won the respect and confidence of the friends of a free state, and he was elected a member of the Legislature. On the other hand, the hatred of the pro-slavery party was very strong against him. He was engaged in the defence of the city of Lawrence during the war in that region. He, also, with two or three others, rushed into the midst of a mob, and rescued a free state man they were cruelly beating. On the 17th inst., he, with several others, went two miles to attend an election; an armed mob thought to break up the election, but were repulsed. The next day, my husband and his friends were coming home when they were met by a large band of armed men, who stopped them and made them prisoners. They were all carried back to the place of election, and there the others were let go, but they determined to kill him; and then, some of them fell upon him with a hatchet, and thus in cold blood, murdered him. One blow struck on the eye brow, and another inflicted a deep wound in his left temple. They then put him in a wagon, and brought him home in the night. By this time he was in a dying state; he was not able to tell us much about his cruel treatment. He said they beat him like a dog. He said: "I am not afraid to die; if I have done wrong in any way, I hope God will forgive me; I die in a Good cause. I am sorry to part with you and our little child, but I want you should meet me in heaven!" He breathed his last the same night, and on the next Sabbath was buried. One of the members of the Legislature has told me that he intends to have that body pass a bill to erect a monument over his grave, as a Martyr for Liberty. . . . As soon as winter breaks, and I can settle my business, I intend to start for home. I am not in want by way of necessaries for life. I am living with Mrs. McCrea, whose husband has been obliged to leave the country for life. She will go with me as far as Chicago.[96]

Letters like this, steeped in the sorrow of the settlers, brought the Kansas horror to the hearts of the rest of the nation, whatever side of the slavery controversy they were on. Innocent settlers did not deserve to be mutilated and murdered in cold blood. Thus, the debate about arms only escalated. Eli Thayer, of Massachusetts, long rumored to have funded the shipment of arms to Kansas, reportedly began to manufacture arms specifically for the territory.

In his January 27 letter to Miles, E. B. Whitman reported on the rising violence and detailed his concerns regarding the plans for the church. Unlike his earlier letters, there were no attempts to give reassurance about the violence:

> The war has so disconcerted everything here that I am at a loss to know what to do. . . . Then again the political state of affairs here is such as to discourage one. I do not fear for the cause of freedom here, but it may be through blood that it is to be secured. Daily events are developing a state of things in Missouri & the South that ought to make every lover of his country tremble. Nothing but the fear of our rifles will save our lives & our town and we are not as strong or as well armed for defense as we have been represented. Our backing is becoming known and will invite aggression. Since the <u>brutal savage</u> murder at Easter, of which I gave an account in the transcript, we feel that we are liable to attack at any hour. In truth, so strong is the feeling here that some plot is on foot in Mo to take our town by a coup de main that three companies have been under arms for several days, two forts are manned and a guard occupies the building in which I am located, to guard the magazine. The women are at work casting bullets and making cartridges. The aspect is decidedly warlike and yet I fear our Eastern friends do not see or feel the imminent danger we are in of a <u>civil war</u>. The people here are as conscious of the justness of their cause as were the men who stood at Lexington or Bunker hill and they will fight with equal desperation. The fight once begun will not end here. May God in mercy avert such a result. Full means of defence and ample, <u>will about</u> do it. Arms, Ammunition, Money & men pledged in case of need! Let Missouri know that such is the position of affairs and the principle of self preservation will keep the hotspurs even at bay. But if they think they can rush in a handful by night and destroy a few towns and return with impunity <u>you may rely upon it they will do</u> it. In such a case the contemplated church would not be needed and money had better have been spent for rifles and the bell to have been cast into cannon. The appeal now being

made to the free states to place us in a proper state of defence cannot be unheeded, it <u>must not be</u> and speedily it must be answered.[97]

Even as the war raged and the interfaith coalition began to form, the Lawrence Unitarian Society was born. At a meeting on February 3, 1856, twenty-four of the prominent men and women of Lawrence, including their missionary, signed the charter document. The old church record of the Lawrence Unitarian Society, lost to history, contained a full description of the momentous occasion when "the citizens of Lawrence friendly to the erection of a church assembled at the Free State Hotel to hear the report of Mr. E. B. Whitman respecting aid from the East and to take such further action as might be deemed advisable."[98] Nute's letter describing the event was excerpted by the *Quarterly Journal*. It read,

> It was my hope that long before this I should have been able to report the organization of a Society in this place, and the resuming of our regular Sabbath services. But one thing after another has occurred to postpone our plan, so that it is but just accomplished. For nearly three months, and until within a few days, everything has been kept in abeyance to the extreme cold weather and the expectation of another attack from the enemy on our border. Every room suitable for a public meeting has been occupied for military barracks, and the minds of the people have been engrossed in the preparations for defence. For nearly eight weeks the cold has been severe and incessant, far beyond all that I ever knew for the same length of time in New England. For a great part of the time the thermometer has ranged from zero to 30° below. Of course, with our insufficient shelter, there has been much suffering. I do not know a single family in which some of the members have not frozen their feet, and many so badly as to be unable to walk. In my own family we have all suffered in this way to some extent, but have now regained the use of our limbs, and were never in better

health or spirits. . . . The general tone of the community here just now is hopeful. If it were not for these repeated outrages and threatening demonstrations by our Missouri neighbors, we should be a cheerful and contented people. As it is, we are far from being cast down and paralyzed by despair. The proceedings of the meetings lately held in Lawrence will, I think, convince you that we are not insensible to the kindness of our Eastern friends,—that there are some here who appreciate and desire to profit by the privileges provided for us by the missionary spirit in the churches. . . . The First Unitarian Society at Lawrence, Kanzas, is now fully organized. At the meetings held to confer on the subject much interest was manifested. A large proportion of the most influential men in the city and vicinity have either joined in the Society or signified their wish to do so. Next Sunday we expect to resume our regular public services. The weather has moderated a little, but the snow is very deep, so that it may be some weeks before the people can come in from the country around to attend; but we have every reason to expect a good congregation from those who live in the city. . . . It is my desire that the many friends of this enterprise at the East, whose substantial manifestations of interest have cheered me on in the work, will remember its difficulties and be prepared to hear of reverses, of meager results, or to not hearing any report of good accomplished for some time to come. . . . Remember me to the brethren.[99]

The cause for Unitarianism in the territory was strong, with supporters and backers all over New England and beyond. One Mr. Baker, wanting to promote the spread of liberal Christianity in the territory, gave up his reward of a claim in Kansas from the Department of the Interior for his efforts in the War of 1812.[100] His gift was accepted by the AUA, and he was awarded a lifetime membership in honor of his generosity. Baker communicated his great desire that the land go through Nute's hands and the Lawrence Unitarian church project. Donations like this later contributed to the appearance of impropriety in the AUA's insistence on reimbursement by the Lawrence congregation for the costs of the church project.

The missionary had many duties. On February 10, 1856, Nute joined John Rice, formerly of Roxbury, Massachusetts, and L. J. Ziegler, formerly of New Waterford, Ohio, in holy matrimony. On that same day, he appeared at a meeting of Lawrence citizens called to take action on Whitman's report about the willingness of backers in the East to support the building of the church. At the meeting, the citizens voted unanimously to adopt a letter of appreciation to the contributors, demonstrating that money was coming through the AUA for the mission but not necessarily from the AUA. Nute was one of those who signed on behalf of all the citizens. At the end of the meeting, Nute was lauded for his work as a missionary, and those present pledged their "zealous cooperation" with his cause.

Whitman also wrote to Miles on February 10. He complimented Nute's success in ministry and as a prominent citizen. He told Miles that Nute was drawing young men into the church in good numbers, but at great risk of personal impoverishment. He was obviously a dedicated missionary. Whitman wrote,

> I cannot refrain from congratulating your Association upon the firm prospect here opened. These meetings were no formal affairs attended by a few, but full & earnest the spontaneous meetings and the sentiments expressed are the true indexes of feeling. All that has been said of Mr. Nute at the East is fully substantiated here and more. He is growing to exercise an influence here as a <u>citizen</u> as well as a <u>minister</u> which few ministers at the East possess in their parishes. . . . The young men are much interested in him and many a one will become a church goer who would otherwise have absented themselves entirely from the sanctuary and the places of Christian instruction. My intercourse with brother Nute is of the most pleasant kind, our talks and views harmonize well. . . . He will write

you fully in regard to the modifications made in the church plan. I have assented to the change. The church site could not have been moved but at the loss of some $300 and some loss of confidence in the community. . . . My interest in the movement continually increases and I shall only regret my inability to stay and see it through but the holy writ says that "he who provideth not for his own household is worse than an infidel" and I must at once do something to provide for my children or they must become the objects of charity, and some of them are now, in part. What time in the spring I shall be obliged to return I cannot now determine, but I shall hope to put the matter in regard to the church in such trim that the completion will be without delay or loss. . . . The Society which has been organized consists of some of our best men, young men, many of them & they take hold as tho they were in earnest. . . . Mr. Nute is much encouraged, a place of temporary worship will soon be had and he will resume his services. He seems cheerful and contented as does Mrs N. I feared from some things he has said that he is in some pecuniary embarrassment. No one who has never attempted to pioneer can estimate the expence; everything at double price. He is now living two miles out of town on his claim. If he should be able to secure it, he may save himself in pecuniary matters, but if not, he will have sunk many hundred dollars which he will never see again—so let us have a line from you if it be but a word of cheer and news.[101]

The difficulty Nute and Whitman had getting promised salary out of the AUA and funds delivered to the Kansas Territory was a repeated theme throughout Nute's tenure and during the church project. It was also a concern of the minister who replaced him when he left the territory. A brief note in the AUA *Quarterly Journal* reveals that finally, on April 14, 1856, the Executive Committee voted to send Whitman three hundred dollars for his personal expenses. It was difficult to come by cash in the territory and hazardous trying to send it there. Nute often offered his own belongings to those in need. Such was the code of the territory. Sara Robinson wrote of the repeated flood of houseguests at their abode, which required vast outlays of food and provisions. But there was a territory to be settled in the name of the great Teacher, and what better lesson of His to use than that of giving the coat off one's back.

Birthing a city required many labors. On February 12 the ministers of the territory gathered at the Free State Hotel to discuss intemperance and the religious care of the citizens of Lawrence and the territory. Nute served as secretary to the event and found himself elected to the committee on Bible study and Sunday schools as well as a committee on the clergy relation to slavery. Participants passed resolutions on promoting a proper respect for the Sabbath and addressing intemperance, which itself was probably responsible for much of the desecration of the Sabbath.

A few days later, on February 14, Nute wrote to Miles to relay his desperate need for some kind of contact with his clergy brethren. Earlier, Miles had written to Nute with some very spicy gossip, eliciting from Nute a terrible longing for his peers. Nute reflected that the uncommonly cold winter might be coming to a close, bringing a renewal of free travel to and from the territory. He rejoiced that the end of their long isolation might be in sight. But with increased access to the territory in spring, ominous signs portended renewed violence. Nute wrote,

If you have ever been kept for ten months without seeing the face of a single clerical brother you may form some idea of the joy with which I received your letter of brotherly chat. It filled up one important part of the gap left by the absence of such intercourse & made me feel for a time as though I had just returned from a pleasant visit to the rooms in Brimfield St. for the actual sight of which I have many longings. I was much interested & gratified in the account which you give of parochial moments. . . . Alas, I have no gossip to offer in return for the spicy dish which you have given me. . . . News has just reached us of another intended attack . . . by those savages "the Kickapoo rangers" 12 men from each of our military companies have been drafted & have started with the Sharpes rifles for the defence. I fear there will be dreadful work here before long. But the free state men are determined to be prudent while they are firm. The Legislature will meet on the 4th of March but probably adjourn immediately & await the action of Congress or the administration in our behalf, or against us as hitherto. Our Society has got a far better start than we could have anticipated. Nearly all the men of influence in the place are with us. Some opposition by the "orthodox" missionary has helped us not a little. The other occasional preachers are very coarse & illiterate for the most part, while the people of Lawrence are quite up, yes beyond, the average of New England towns of the same size in intelligence & refinement. . . . To day the weather is probably 25 degrees warmer than it has been for three months. A week of this will devour the snow & unchain the streams. The church will go on, our mails will again be regular. The books for our school will come from St. Louis & the prospect will brighten. We have had some rough times since the first of December. I little thought we had got to encounter such a Polar Winter, or I should have made better preparations against it. My ears & feet have been badly frozen & for weeks we have not known what it was to feel warm. But it is a healthy climate & with close houses & sufficient clothing I should not mind the exposure [accompanied by a picture of a hand pointing to the words "Not a word of this for the 'Secretary.'"][102]

On February 27 the new ministerial alliance met to establish its constitution and pass further resolutions on the religious health of its constituents, declaring how much this depended on the repudiation of slavery. Nute was secretary to the body, which probably put him and every minister in attendance in further jeopardy, as such an appointment would surely violate the territorial laws against the vilification of slavery.

Nute wrote to the *Springfield Republican* on March 1 again describing the murder of Brown and hoping for some tattered remains of Border Ruffian morality. Nute expressed his incredulity at their brutality and how they waved the cross over their murderous ideology:

> The murder of "Brown" was as brutal as can well be conceived of; but the murderers should have the benefit of the least circumstance that can mitigate the enormity of the deed; for at the best we shall find it difficult to feel toward them as we should endeavor to feel toward all who belong to the human family. It appears that we were mistaken in supposing that the murdered man reached his home by flight; but that some of those who stood by when he was cut down by the knives and hatchets of their companions, took him into a wagon, and after carrying him about ten miles, attempted to dress his wounds; when they took him a few miles further to his home. Furthermore, one of the gang remained with him until he died, which was in about one hour. For the honor of humanity, I would believe that there were some in that company not quite so heartless as the deed would indicate, so that, after the cowardly attack on their defenceless prisoner, the better impulses of their natures were awakened, and they were touched with pity and remourse. I could never have believed that civilized men, or men so ranked, could be so deliberately and avowedly inhuman as these have been who shall be forever infamous as the "Border-Ruffians," had I not seen and heard for myself. . . . The rivers have risen, the ice is broken up and nearly all cleared out, the frost is coming out of the ground, and the country is almost impassable. So we may hope for peace for some time to come, as the invaders will be kept at home. For the same causes our mails must be, as for some weeks past they have been, very irregular. . . . No part of the great West has been settled, and improved with the rapidity of Kanzas for the first year. Since that time all progress has been suspended by the machina-

tions of the enemy on our borders aided by the administration and others at the East. The reports of these outrages and the threatening demonstrations made from time to time by the banditti of slavery have for the last three months kept our community in a constant state of agitation, engrossing mind and means in the preparations for defense, interfering with the work of building, the establishing of schools, the services of public worship, and promoting not interest, but that of the whisky shops kept and sustained chiefly by our visitors from Missouri.... If our interests are to be yet further damaged, our peace destroyed, our best citizens brutally murdered and our election rights wrested from us by the hirelings of the slave power, it will be but a poor satisfaction to us to be told in the tone of insolent authority, that all this is only the unavoidable result of the migration of the people of the free states in to the public domain of Kanzas.[103]

Whitman wrote to Miles on March 1 about building delays due to weather and the destruction of the sawmills. He referred to Nute's prominence, his election as secretary to the new interfaith body, and his preaching the first sermon at a new united congregation. The Unitarian church was now meeting in the military barracks amid the pots and pans and sleeping bags. His letter read,

Some report of my progress in church building is doubtless expected by this time. You are doubtless apprised of the existence of some causes which have produced delay. The unheard of severity of the cold, for nine or ten weeks, put an entire veto upon the all human labors, except to keep warm. Then the war excitement, now up now down, but mostly up. One outrage upon another kept our people in constant alarm. There were no thoughts for business, none for the ordinarily concerns of life. To all this, add the accidents to our saw mills, one after another, bursting their boilers, and the only surviving one at length disabled by the breaking of its saw.... Something however has been done in the way of preparing for vigorous work, as soon as the weather and earth will admit of working. . . . A spirit of liberality prevails here that I did not expect to see, and yet it might have been anticipated when the laity throw of[f] the trammels of sectarian bias and think with that freedom peculiar to a new country, the clergy must follow, tho it may be at an humble distance. Some of our Eastern brethren will be surprised to learn of the fraternization of the clergymen of <u>all</u> denominations in the good work of redeeming the world from sin. An "alliance" has recently been formed to promote all good & holy causes, and in a spirit of fraternal sympathy. All ministers of any <u>Christian</u> denomination, in good standing, are eligible. The definition of the word Christian, as applied to Unitarians has been fixed by the election of your missionary as Secretary, and his appointment to preach a first sermon before the <u>United</u> Congregation on the 21st inst. . . . Mr. Nute has resumed his regular services in the barracks of the Artillary Co. now disbanded, but still occupying the room as a boarding association. Sometimes the culinary operations are proceeding during service time and the cooking utensils and sleeping paraphernalia often form the ornaments of the room. . . . I know of no field of labor to be compared in importance and the prospects of usefulness, with the one to which you have here sent your missionary. . . . Young and inexperienced young men are here brought together from all parts with the faults and peculiar habits of their various sections to exert their mutual influence. The restraints of home and of older states of society are removed and the temptations to desert old habits and form new, not always for the better, are strong. The missionary needs all the helps he can have, let him not lack for aid & shall we not have, by the munificence of Unitarian Ladies, a parish library, of such character, that while it attracts the young men, it shall also exert a powerful influence for good upon their minds. . . . We have received no letters to inform us whether those parishes which had promised aid have yet fulfilled their promises. I left, as you know, in the confident expectation that those pledges would be redeemed at an early day. . . . When I arrived in St. Louis, the rumors of wars reached me and the boats had stopped their trips. I was at a loss of knowing my duty, but upon full reflection and by advice of friends there, I decided to push on by land conveyance. Ten days we were in crossing the state of Miss. The road never repaired and at that time in most wretched condition rendered the journey truly hazardous thrice overturned, twice broken down, with delays and vexations innumerable, I at length arrived at my destination alive and in good health. . . . By the goodness of God I have been preserved and blessed in my labors thus far.[104]

Nute wrote to Miles on March 4 regarding the quartering of the army in Lawrence, a brief reprieve from the anticipation of violence, and his personal theology. His characteristic dry humor pointed out the appallingly primitive nature of their accommodations for worship, while remarking how much the harshness improved the likelihood of people paying attention in church. His letter read,

I am glad to have something better to report this time than the obstacles in the way of missionary labor by warlike demonstrations, brutal murders, the engrossment of the minds of the people in preparations for defence against threatened attacks & the extreme cold weather. Just now we are enjoying a respite from all these troubles. . . . We have again taken up the work of establishing churches, schools, temperance society &c where these enterprises were broken off when our difficulties began…. A large upper room is secured for one regular service every Sunday & we have already occupied it twice. It is one in which a large company of men under arms have quartered for the last three months & it is yet occupied as a sort of boarding & lodging hall by an association of about twenty young men. The array of beds, stoves, dishes, cooking utensils & c. give it very much the appearance of a general ward in an extemporaneous hospital. . . . The construction of the building is such as to furnish a good supply of one of the requisites of health viz: a free circulation of air, a circumstance which may be advantage in securing the listening ear & the understanding mind as so much of the drowsiness in better finished sanctuaries has been attributed to the want of this. However this may be, I can testify to an appearance of wide-awake interest in the congregations here very encouraging to the preacher. . . . The meeting of the Legislature & organization of our state government takes place to day at Topeka & has called away many of our citizens. If it were not for this preparations would be made for the organization of our church next Sunday. . . . I am gratified to know already that there are a considerable number here who desire to join us to secure the privileges of a union on the bases which we believe is in accordance with the Truth as it is in Jesus. May we enter into it with believing & praying hearts, that our fellowship may be in the spirit, deep, abiding & life giving, with each & our great HEAD.[105]

Whitman also wrote a letter March 4, his to AUA Secretary Calvin Clark regarding the delays in building the church and the ever-present money troubles in the territory:

This is to notify you that I have this day drawn upon you two drafts of one hundred and fifty dollars each payable to my order. I shall be obliged to draw usually or at present, in small amounts, in consequence of the scarcity of money, but a small amount to be had at any one place. When the navigation opens & emigration flows in or when the contributions from the East to relieve the sufferers by the way arrives we look for improvement. . . . The workmen are completing the excavation for the Church; the sand is hauled and much of the stone, and the masons are only waiting for a little milder weather. I have been delayed some about timber, but it is now being delivered rapidly and will all be ready before the close of this month. I shall be obliged to pay up every body very closely owing to their pressing necessities. The masons as often as weekly I shall only keep back from the contractors sufficient to ensure the fulfillment of contract. . . . My position has been anything but satisfactory here this winter I assure you, but as the seasons open for work I hope to be more contented. . . . We have every encouragement to work and labor in our cause. . . . The subscriptions here are not collected . . . but . . . I have been assured however by respectable men that a large proportion may be relied on some have paid, but the unfortunate state of affairs here since last fall is affecting us sadly. Many have not a cent of ready money.[106]

On March 27, Nute wrote to Henry A. Miles of his enthusiasm regarding the new ministerial alliance based in Lawrence:

Have you seen an account of our alliance of ministers. . . . I assure you it is a real & hearty union, such as I never enjoyed in New England with the brethren of other denominations[.] It is a great point gained that we have the recognition & a respectful, yes a fraternal treatment from the ministers of every denomination with but a single exception (& that has operated thus far greatly to our advantage)[.] [107]

That single exception was, of course, Rev. Lum, Nute's orthodox nemesis.

On March 11 Nute united Amory Wetherbee and Mrs. Mary E. White in marriage.[108] The sicknesses that early settlers faced and the increasing Border Ruffian violence greatly inflated the mortality rate in the territory. Widows with financial means might have the option of returning home to family in the East. But most men had put their all into their travel or their claim, leaving their widows with few liquid assets. Widows often quickly remarried one of the many eligible young men who continued to flood into the territory, making brief, low-key weddings one of the top activities of territorial clergy.

On March 13 Nute wrote to Miles to address the issue of his expired "year for which I was engaged by the AUA" and offered to either remain in the post or seek another, according to the AUA's wishes. He wrote of the continuing challenges of keeping a flock together in the territory and elaborated on his frustration regarding the political machinations of Christian denominations competing for meeting space and members:

By the time that this reaches you the year for which I was engaged by the AUA will have expired. Probably you will have taken some action about the continuance or discontinuance of the work here begun. As it takes so long at this season for letters to pass between us I take the liberty to anticipate yours apprising me of the action of your committee & say I shall be happy to remain at this post if you wish it & as happy to leave it if you can find a laborer who will do the work better as I believe you can. . . . There is every reason to believe that a considerable portion of my support for the next year would be contributed by the people here in the way of pew rents if nothing occurs to prevent the completion of the house of worship by September 1st, which is the earliest days that seem probable to me. . . . I have counted on visiting the East in May all the past year, but do not see my way clear to do so now. Perhaps it is better that I should stay away. . . . I have just heard that we are to lose the place for our meetings of which I wrote on my last. It is to be divided up into small rooms & the carpenters are now at work on it. This is very surprising & vexatious. The building belongs to the Emigrant Aid Co & I have long tried to get it for part of the day. Two & some days three, other societies occupy it. A committee of our society had with some trouble obtained it for one service every Sunday & then been obliged by some very unfair manouvres of the "Evangelicals" to give it up for the 1st Sunday of each month & perhaps for every alternate Sunday & now we have lost it entirely I do not yet understand by whose authority.... What we shall do next I do not know. I have made engagements to preach in other places from 2 to 6 miles out as soon as the roads are passable.... Bro Whitman is much disappointed in not hearing from you.[109]

A few days later, on March 19, Whitman wrote to AUA Secretary Calvin Clark about his need for money, corroborating Nute's complaint in that regard. Whatever the reason for the delays in the AUA support, its inability to provide the funds as promised had a profound effect on both Nute's and Whitman's ability to obtain basic necessities, or even survive at all. Whitmans's letter read,

The masons begin work tomorrow. I have been sadly perplexed about lumber and have not got it all yet. I am driven in every direction at once and the same time. The work for which I came here is not where I expected it would be at this time. Mr. Nute & others assure me that it will stop if I leave and it might need to stop even if I was willing to take the responsibility of defeating the enterprise. I would give much for a few minutes interview with the friends in Boston, but I know they will not in their generosity and sympathy for Kansas permit the burden to fall upon my shoulders.... The present position of affairs is one of those inexplicable cases in which we must draw upon our store of faith in God, over ruling Providence. ... We need, it is true, means of defense. Simply to escape the necessity of it, But over and above all we need gospel conveniences.... I wrote in a letter to Dr. Miles that I saw no way of by which I could remain beyond the spring. But at present I have concluded to stay.... To sustain myself for the summer I am making preparation to cultivate vegetables for the market and shall probably be obliged to peddle milk & beans to eke out my support if I stay.... I have taken a claim two miles from the city where I shall be obliged to stay, coming to town daily to attend to my church. . . . Sometimes I am so much overcome by the responsibility of my position and the difficulty under which I labor that I feel like relinquishing the whole thing, that other and abler hands may be found to take it up. . . . The war has left things so here that I cannot at present collect the subscriptions and the workmen must be paid as they go in. . . . I feel disappointed that I have never received the first line of information or encouragement either from yourself or Dr. Miles. I have written you (3) times and Dr. Miles five times. I know not what the prospects are nor what you wish of me beyond my first instructions. It is probable that some of my letters and all of yours have miscarried. Mr. Nute has heard from you but once since I came. Send by Private conveyance and we shall get them. The mails are unsafe through Mo. I send this to St. Louis by private conveyance and hope it will reach you . . . sheet paper is growing scarce.[110]

The Lawrence *Herald of Freedom* reported on March 22 that a sizeable donation of $514 was sent by the parishioners of Rev. James Freeman Clarke, Nute's good friend and later AUA secretary. The *Herald of Freedom* noted, "This is one of the youngest churches in Boston, and very far from being one of the most wealthy. What makes this act more remarkable is the fact that this church belongs to the despised sect of Unitarians."[111] This touched on the continuing competition between the Christian churches for their stake in the territory and access to its religiously observant citizens. The *Herald of Freedom*'s comment also reflected the belief of many orthodox Christian sects that theologically the Unitarians were already outside the fold of Christianity.

In the spring of 1856, Charles Robinson, James Lane, and Judge Hunt traveled to Washington to correct misunderstandings in Congress. Emigration was at an all-time high. Travelers from Virginia reported that fifteen hundred were on their way; from Kentucky came the report that an even larger number were destined for Kansas; a traveler from Wisconsin reported that two thousand were ready to emigrate. Those in the Free-State cause rejoiced, as these numbers indicated that the territory would be sufficiently populated by the time the next president took his seat to put to rest Senator Stephen Douglas's opposition to its admission to statehood, which was based on the accusation of insufficient population.[112] When newspapers reported on the difficulties surrounding the Kansas Territory's application for statehood, they primarily focused on the Pierce administration as the major blockade to justice and decency in the endeavor.

Aggression toward the Free-State cause was rife. At this time a young man from Washington, D.C., boarded the riverboat *Martha Jewett* in St. Louis bound for Leavenworth. One evening he joined the conversation of "what he supposed a party of gentlemen" and the talk turned, of course, to the ever-inflammatory topics "that are now agitating the public mind," according to reports reprinted in the *Semi-Weekly Times*.[113] The young man offered a wrong opinion and with guards all around was struck in the face, knocked to the floor, and kicked until the ire of his "gentleman" attacker was sated. No one—not the guards, not the other passengers—attempted to help him. Afterward he struggled to his stateroom unassisted. The Free-State and Republican papers were outraged and quickly drew parallels between the unaddressed violence in Kansas and the permission given for that violence in Washington.

Many Free-State sympathizers of the North and East, in response, were already funding, buying, building, and shipping firearms to Kansas. For their part, the Border Ruffians vigilantly attempted to find and appropriate these shipments. Arms smuggling was a dangerous enterprise, for which a number of Free-State men lost their lives. David Starr Hoyt, of Deerfield, Massachusetts, accidentally dropped a letter that implicated him in arms involvement while on board a steamer. He was nearly lynched, the guns were confiscated, and Hoyt was forced to sign a document that he would pay the freight to have the guns shipped to proslavery Kansas Governor Shannon. However, there was no gain from the capture: the slides had been removed from the guns before they were packed and shipped, so that if the guns were seized they would be useless. There was no sense in paying good money for guns that ended up arming the opposition.[114]

On March 20, the cornerstone of the Lawrence Unitarian church was installed. The pride and hope of the large crowd in attendance stood upright in the face of the fear and injustice of the Border Ruffian violence. The Lawrence *Herald of Freedom* reported that the weather was cold, with a typical Midwest high March wind. Reflecting Nute's propensity to work ecumenically, Lawrencians of all denominations stood together for the joyous occasion. The paper reported,

> It argues well for religious freedom and toleration in Kansas, for the existence and manifestation of the great law of "Charity, which is the bond of perfectness," that ministers and people of different sects and doctrinal views, did, on this occasion, meet together and take part in the services. It is hailed as a harbinger of the approach of that period, or that state in the church of the Lord in which a life according to the commandments of the Divine Word is to take precedence of the dogmas of faith, established by human councils, synods and conventions. "Thou shalt love the Lord thy God with all thy heart, and with all thy soul, and with all thy mind, and thou shalt love thy neighbor as thyself. On these two commandments hang all the law and prophets." . . . The address by the Pastor was impressive, elegant and exceedingly appropriate, as were the selections from the Scriptures and prayers by the assisting clergymen of other denominations. A spirit of love and harmony, with an eye single to the promotion of the Lord's Kingdom on the earth, seemed to pervade all. Sectarianism hid its deformed head either in absence or under the cloak of charity.[115]

Sara Robinson later recalled, "In March 1856 the corner stone of the first church building was laid. I placed in the box in that corner stone papers, among which were the *Lawrence Tribune*, a drawing of Lawrence by Mr. Nute and also one drawn by myself."[116] One drawing remains in the Old Unitarian Church collection at the University of Kansas in Lawrence. It supposedly came from the cornerstone, but it is ascribed to Lucy Wilder, Nute's parishioner and later a teacher in the high school in the basement of the Unitarian church. It depicts a windswept Lawrence spreading below the vantage point of the viewer, the rolling prairie and open sky broken by the few dwellings of the nascent city.

The newspaper article described the church completely, which is fortunate because all that now remains of the Lawrence project and the efforts of those stalwart Unitarians is an overgrown side lot next to a residential house. The lot displays a small granite marker reading "Site of Unitarian Church / First Free Public Church in Kansas." In 1856 the laying of the church cornerstone was hailed with great interest throughout the West and all over the Eastern states and New England and viewed as a sign of hope for the peaceful future of Lawrence and the Kansas project.

This moment of glory in Nute's pastoral calling did not overshadow his other duties to bring civilization to the territory in the interest of establishing strong and steady commerce. Sympathy for the Border Ruffians was not shared by all Missourians. The national unpopularity of the proslavery cause began to rob St. Louis of its economic potential, as many began to send trade through Chicago in protest.

In 1856 Nute was a member of a territory committee chosen to travel to Alton, Illinois, to try to establish that city, rather than St. Louis, as the commercial gateway to Kansas. Four of the five on the committee were Lawrence Unitarians. Businessmen and travelers to Lawrence were irate at the failure of officials in St. Louis to police their waterways and prevent the violence and piracy inflicted upon Free-State travelers by the Border Ruffians. In 1856, emigration was estimated at thirty thousand for a six-month period, and it was imperative, in support of the Free-State cause, to make the journey safe.

First, Nute's committee appealed to the St. Louis Chamber of Commerce. They simply wanted St. Louis to reaffirm the U.S. constitutional amendments against illegal search and seizure and to guarantee safe passage. Nute and his committee were summarily dismissed. Officials refused to receive the appeal on the grounds that to do so would divert Southern trade from the city.

Alton, Illinois, was enthusiastic, to say the least, to enter into a commercial agreement with the businessmen of Lawrence. Nute's presence on this committee was no surprise, given that his wife's family in Alton were prominent citizens and businessmen. Lucy had already spent considerable time in Alton visiting her family, so Nute, no doubt, knew how to get connected in the town. Alton's commercial class resolved to assist the emigrants to Kansas by reaffirming the amendments to the Constitution of the United States for their own state, for "such violations demand that the authority of the Federal Government be exercised to prevent them."[117]

The resolutions of Alton's citizens were firm on both constitutional and commercial grounds. They promised to extend assistance to emigrants bound for Kansas and provide the most reasonable rates for travel accommodations they could afford. In addition, they would make a concerted effort to sustain a line of steamers between Alton and Kansas. Amid declarations of gratefulness to the members of the committee, Alton officially entered into an agreement with Lawrence. In a letter to Dr. Thomas Webb, secretary of the Emigrant Aid Company, the representatives from Lawrence and the spokesmen for Alton laid out the benefits to emigrants of the new agreement in an attempt to enlist the Emigrant Aid Company's help in promoting the new arrangement to travelers.

Responding to increasing pressure from angry Easterners, the federal government appointed a committee to investigate the troubles in Kansas. They arrived in Lawrence on April 19, 1856, and their first task was to examine the official records and establish headquarters in Lawrence. Nute later testified to this committee regarding the stolen elections and other matters.

Today the Lawrence Public Library has in its collection a book inscribed "Rev Ephraim Nute, With the wishes and regards of Frank Smith, Boston, Jany 1856." It is known that Nute donated many books to the Lawrence library before he left Kansas. This one, *Report of the Special Committee Appointed to Investigate the Troubles in Kansas with the Views of the Minority of Said Committee*, is the first report of the investigation into the irregularities at the polls and the violence perpetrated upon the Free-State citizens. Of all the books that passed through Nute's hands and into the public library collection, it is ironic that this one—which recounts the great injustices of the early territory—should still survive.

Nute was soon to encounter life-threatening situations as a result of his outspoken preaching and political activism. Nationwide, clergy were sharply divided over slavery, both sides using scripture to justify their stance. Some condemned slavery on the basis of the teachings of Jesus, and some quoted from both the Old Testament and New Testament in supporting slave owners.

The populace was similarly divided about the appropriateness of the pulpit for promulgating such views. There were congregations steeped in loyalty to their abolitionist ministers and congregations that openly split over their pastors' abolitionism. People left some congregations in droves, and many ministers were sent packing. However, as reported in the *Springfield Republican*, one denomination—the Unitarians—took up abolitionism in the majority:

Many pulpits spoke bravely for justice and freedom to Kanzas, on fast day. Rev. Mr. James of Worcester delivered a sound Christian discourse on the subject and a collection of $300 was taken up for the church-building in Kanzas. Theodore Parker of Boston preached a discourse, two hours long, in which he dealt many ringing blows with his sledge-hammer rhetoric against the conspirators who would enslave Kanzas at the price of a chance to pilfer from the public crib. This discourse will be printed. Mr. Parker has also contributed five rifles to the means of self-defense in Kanzas, and thus practiced what he preached.[118]

Theodore Parker stood front and center in the religious controversies over slavery. He had led the resistance to the Fugitive Slave Act in Boston, and he focused his preaching on the sin of slavery and the depravity of those in church and government who would tolerate and even support it. He lived out his theology with both overt and covert resistance against governmental and ecclesiastical support for slavery. He was active in the protection of fugitive slaves, and he later took his place prominently as one of "The Secret Six"[119] who supported John Brown and the arming of Kansas with "Beecher's Bibles."

Back in the territory, the proslavery side was greatly bolstered by the actions of Sheriff Jones, strong arm of the notorious Benjamin Stringfellow and the Border Ruffians, who routinely harassed the Lawrence citizens. The Free-Staters should have been able to take their troubles to him, but he was directly paid by, and therefore under the influence of, the proslavery movement. Not only was he unwilling to acknowledge the Free-Staters' troubles, but often he would arrest and charge them in the very incidents they complained about.

Jones had many enemies and encountered much resistance from the settlers. The enmity with which he was regarded led to attempts on his life, both real and imagined. William Hutchinson, under the pseudonym "Randolph," provided a long letter to the *New York Daily News* regarding one of Jones's more infamous adventures. On April 24, an assassination attempt was made on the sheriff's life during his dragnet for Unitarian S. N. Wood, a man active with Nute on the Underground Railroad and in the political life of Free-State Kansas Territory.

The newspapers picked up the story and were full of accusations and counteraccusations against both Jones and the abolitionists. The Free-Staters maintained that they had cooperated in all aspects with Jones and the U.S. troops who arrived at the request of Jones and Governor Shannon. A correspondent for the *Chicago Daily Tribune* commented that "this interference by the General Government against us would do us more good in the popular feeling of the country than anything else could."[120] The general belief was that the shooting of Jones was the work of one individual at odds with the citizenry's commitment to peace and order.

At the time of the attack, Jones was lounging on the ground in a tent pitched by the federal soldiers, in conversation with his lieutenant. A shot was fired through the tent side from the rear and into the small of his back. A Free-Stater did not commit the crime. It was generally known from the beginning that the shooter was a proslavery man with whom Jones had a claim dispute. Even though Jones had already recovered from his "shot in the arse," as late as May 5, proslavery newspapers continued to attribute the "attempted assassination" to abolitionists and Free-Staters, using the incident to inflame proslavery sentiment against both. Meanwhile, proslavery troops continued to arrest citizens who had refused to assist Jones in arresting other innocents. The scandal surrounding the Jones case complicated the efforts of the federal investigating committee, which was intensely soliciting testimony from citizens in the territory at this time.

Nute and Whitman traveled to Boston during May 1856 to attend the AUA's thirty-first anniversary celebration. They intended to apprise the denomination of territorial happenings firsthand from Lawrence—and to appeal for funds.

During Nute's absence from Lawrence, the troubles continued to escalate. Sara Robinson wrote extensively of the ironic sweetness of the Kansas prairie and the dread of the proslavery activities. One of her letters read,

May, the month of flowers, has come again. Sweet-scented, rose-colored verbenas are blooming side by side with a most delicate straw-colored flower. It grows in heads like the verbena, each separate flower being a little larger, and with serrated edge. The roses and pinks make the air heavy with their perfume. Since the taking of the prisoners to Lecompton, and the ill success of Slaters in arresting any more, there have been a few days of quiet. . . . The outrages of the pro-slavery men are again becoming frequent. Mr. Mace, residing a few miles from Lawrence, the evening after having given in his testimony concerning the ill treatment he received at the hands of the Missourians at the election in the spring, was shot. Hearing his dog bark, he stepped out of his house, and reports of pistols resounded in the air, a ball striking him in the leg. At the same time, he heard one of the assassins say, "There's another d—d abolition wolf-bait!"[121]

Terrorism against the Free-State settlers of Kansas was atrocious. But as in modern warfare that declares the politically sanctioned terrorism inflicted by government forces "collateral damage," the proslavery faction denied the human suffering brought about by the terrorism, projecting the blame onto the abolitionists themselves. Specific Free-State men were identified, targeted, and persecuted. Sara Robinson wrote of her husband's capture on May 10, 1856:

My husband, going upon business to the East, was also taken prisoner on the tenth of May, by a gang of Missourians at Lexington. They declared he was running away from an indictment, and by their whole conversation showed themselves better acquainted with the designs of Judge Lecompte and Gov. Shannon than the people of this territory. They sent word to this tool of theirs, who bears the title of governor of the territory, and he recognized them as his agents and accomplices.[122]

News of Dr. Robinson's capture spread quickly. Not only was he a leading citizen of Lawrence and a founding member of the Lawrence Unitarian Society, he also helped found the Free-State Party—the extra-legal Free State Legislature that invented itself in protest against the appropriation of the ballot boxes by marauding Missourians, and a driving force behind the Free-State Topeka Constitution, ratified in December 1855. To the Free-State settlers, Robinson was denied his office by the appropriation of the ballot boxes, so he was declared governor by the Free-State Party. To the proslavery forces and their newspapers, Robinson was an illegal governor and therefore guilty of treason. When he was captured, Robinson wanted his wife Sara to go on to St. Louis without him, but they were confidentially advised that she should stay with him in his captivity. It was common practice at this time for wives and family members to remain with the imprisoned to feed and comfort them. In addition, Sara's presence might help protect her husband from being lynched.

While the Robinsons were on their harrowing journey to bring testimony about Kansas to Washington, the *Boston Evening Telegraph* reported on May 12 that Nute was preaching brimstone in Boston about Unitarian sloth with regard to the issues in Kansas. The article read,

> The services in Rev. Mr. Fuller's Church, Hanover street, were conducted yesterday afternoon by Rev. Ephraim Nute, pastor of the first Church in Lawrence, Kansas. The new house of worship in Lawrence is being built, the Unitarians at the East having contributed to that end. The troubles inflicted upon the citizens of Kansas by the Border-Ruffians have retarded the work and made it necessary for Mr. Nute to solicit the moderate sum of fifteen hundred dollars, which is needed to complete the work so auspiciously begun. Mr. Nute stated in his report on the success of his ministry in Kansas, that the Unitarians have not been pioneers in the missionary efforts at the West, but have waited until society has resolved itself into

a more settled and definite state. Hence their ill success. Other denominations have laid the foundation of churches previous to them, and when the Unitarians did commence their labors, they had an amount of prejudice to overcome which did not so stand in the way of the first comers. When he first went to Kansas there was no appropriate place in which to hold a meeting. The only substitute obtainable was a small room used by a number of other denominations in succession. On a succeeding Sunday the people were gathered together in the open air to the number of two hundred or more, and his congregation has increased. He had noticed that many people in some of our larger cities were advocating ultra non-resistance, and animadverting upon the practise of the settlers' arming in self-defense. . . . Such persons should witness what he had witnessed. Should see a neighbor and friend, the most peaceful of men, brutally murdered; should witness the grief of the mother, the wife, the sister, all dependent on his arm, and now left alone in the wilderness, and they would then know why the settlers of Kansas took up arms to defend themselves and their families from the worse than savage bands from the borders of Missouri. He had seen timid and refined women, who, at the East, would have shrunk from the presence of an instrument of war, courageously and firmly grasp the implements of death in the days of their siege. Were he to select the most eloquent and decided words in condemnation of the tyranny attempted to be imposed on the settlers, they would be from the lips of men from Virginia and Kentucky who were in the ranks to defend Lawrence. Mr. Nute thought the New England emigration to Kansas an offspring of the religious sentiment, and eloquently urged his hearers to carry fully into practise the glorious theory of their religion, and to make use of the great opportunity opened in the West. The speaker concluded with a desire to carry back to his people in Lawrence hope and comfort from New England.[123]

Even the members of the congressional committee appointed to investigate the troubles in Kansas were not exempt from the intrusions and harassments of the proslavery Border Ruffians. J. Weaver, an assistant sergeant-at-arms of the congressional committee, was returning to Lawrence with a subpoenaed witness and in the company of a U.S. dragoon when they stumbled into a camp of proslavers at the ferry. The Border Ruffians grilled Weaver about where he was going, and when he told them his destination was Lawrence, they proceeded as if he were a "d—d abolitionist." Weaver and the dragoon finally convinced the crowd to look at their papers. The Border Ruffians seemed to be illiterate. With great effort, Weaver and the dragoon eventually assured them that they were in the employ of the U.S. government.[124] Remarkably, they escaped with their lives. Many innocent men had been, and continued to be, murdered for the "crime" of going to Lawrence or being from there.

Another correspondent from Lawrence to the East was Edward Payson Fitch, a young man acquainted with Nute who came to Kansas in 1854 as a representative of the New England Emigrant Aid Company in Boston. He often attended Nute's preaching, and sadly, was later killed in the deadly attack on Lawrence in 1863 by maverick rebel guerilla William Clarke Quantrill and his raiders. During the troubled early days of Lawrence, Fitch wrote extensively to his family in the East regarding the "war on the ground." He described the Ruffian harassment on May 18, 1856, and pled for help from the free states. His father, in fear and horror, passed the letter on to the *Evening Telegraph*. It read,

> We have never been quite so near a war as now. If it begins here, god only knows where it will end. . . . If you lived in such a fever of excitement as we do here, for one week, you would not blame me for not writing more. We are surrounded by an armed mob, and they may attack us at any time. . . . We must have help from the free states. We are not in half as good condition to fight now

as we were last winter—then we were thoroughly organized, now we are not; and we have no man now that we can trust, that is willing to take the helm. . . . Tell every one that feels the least interest in Kansas, that now we want help. Men, money and arms. . . . The blow has been struck! the war has begun! Two of our men have been killed—murdered this day; one within a mile of town, and the other at Blanton's bridge, four miles from here. He was shot about noon (and is now dead) with a U.S. musket, in the back, while going away from the men who shot him. The other man was shot in the head, just over the eye, with a Sharp's rifle I think; he was on the California road and only two or three with him; they snapped their rifles at the man who shot him, but they did not go off, they however wounded one of the pro-slavery men with a revolver, so that he dropped his rifle, and one of our men took it. We are in a bad fix, and no mistake. The enemy have a number of our leading men prisoners, viz. Gov. Robinson, G. W. Brown, (editor of the Herald of Freedom,) Jenkins, one of our good, true and promi- nent men, Judge Schyler, (Secretary of State,) Conway, (Judge of our Supreme Court,) and others of less consequence. . . . I am poorly armed for war—I ought to have a good revolver. . . . Pray for our success, and also help us. Probably men will have to come from Massachusetts even, and fight here.[125]

In the days leading up to the first sack of Lawrence in May 1856, there was a gathering of tension and troops. In Benicia, a town four miles from Lawrence, eleven Free-State men quietly at work on their claims were taken prisoner and terrorized. They were told that they would be lynched if they were caught again and that the party holding them prisoner was going to attack Lawrence and drive out or kill every Free-State man there. The Border Ruffians also barged into the house of a Free-State man to steal his guns, whereupon his wife grabbed one of the guns and was about to fire point blank into the chest of one of the Border Ruffians when another grabbed her from behind and took the gun. The editor of the *Free State* newspaper was dragged from his horse and taken before Stringfellow to be tried on charges of being a South Carolinian abolitionist. He was assigned a proslavery lawyer but was finally released through the intervention of proslavery friends.[126]

General Samuel C. Pomeroy, one of of Nute's parishioners, then arrived in Lawrence amid great cheering. He was one of the leaders of the Free-State provisional government under the extralegal Topeka Constitution, and the people had great confidence in him. Despite Pomeroy's competence and the preparedness of the Free-State militias, Lawrence was sacked for the first time on May 21, 1856.

News was slow from the West, and in lieu of publishing nothing at all about the sacking, newspapers carried correspondence before and up to the day of the attack for weeks after the first telegraphs of the tragedy arrived. Lawrence's citizens made it clear that the danger was mounting, and cried for the help of the free states, in absence of assistance from the federal government. The story of the attack was told best by the Illinois *Daily Democrat* on May 23:

DESTRUCTION OF THE PRINTING PRESS AND THE HOTEL AND PROBABLY THE WHOLE TOWN OF LAWRENCE IN ASHES— WOMEN AND CHILDREN FLEEING IN EVERY DIRECTION. . . .

On Wednesday, May 21, the posse that had assembled at Lecompton, in accordance with the United States Marshal's proclamation, made their appearance on the heights that overlook the town of Lawrence, about sunrise. The first company were mounted on horses and numbered from 87 to 100. They were reinforced until the whole amounted to about 400. They took possession of the roads leading to and from Lawrence, so that the citizens in town could not get any communication with those in the country, and even travelers that wished to pursue their journey, were prohibited from leaving. They marshaled their command in battle array, displaying flags at the same time of various kind and colors. . . . During the forenoon the Committee of Public Safety appointed by the citi-

118

zens of Lawrence, addressed a note to the Marshal, assuring him that the citizens would make no resistance to the serving of any writ, and at the same time, as citizens of the United States and of the Territory of Kansas, asking of him protection of their lives and property, but he (U.S.M.) took no notice of the same. About 11 A.M. the Deputy Marshal, with a posse of nine or ten, made his appearance in the streets. They were unarmed, save small arms. The Deputy Marshal then summoned four of our citizens to assist in making arrests. They went with him and his posse, and made two arrests of our fellow townmen, G. W. Dietzler and G. W. Smith. The posse then took dinner at the free state Hotel. . . . After dinner the two prisoners were conveyed out of town, and sheriff Jones made his appearance with a party of eighteen armed men. He did not attempt to make any arrest but in an insulting manner demanded the arms both private and public, and said that he would give them five minutes to accede to the demand. If they refused to comply he would storm the town. The public arms were given up, and in half an hour after he made the demand he and his whole posse to the number of three hundred and upwards were in the streets with two pieces of artillery, yelling like savages. They commenced their work of destruction immediately by throwing the two printing presses and type in the river. This being done they began to cannonade the hotel and fire by platoons at the same time at the windows; in the mean while the women and children fleeing in every direction, the Sheriff having refused any time to remove them or property to a place of safety, as he said they might have done it before had they wanted to do so. . . . Fifteen miles distant, I could see the flames of what appeared to be a large fire in the direction of Lawrence, and have no doubt but that the town is in ashes, and many of its inhabitants butchered.[127]

The first sack of Lawrence caught the attention of proslavery sympathizers as had no other incident in the Border Ruffian war.

Many papers carried the news in disbelief—some with outright condemnation and fury. However they editorialized about the unworthiness of abolitionists—"As far as we can learn, the Abolitionists failed in their courage, and made but little resistance"[128]— this act of wanton terrorism could not be justified on any level, by anyone. Most of all, the perpetrators violated the code of the West by targeting women, children, and innocent bystanders and shooting men in the back after they had surrendered. Social control was slipping even further in the territory, to the point where proslavery sympathizers with some decency were also in fear and horror of the terrorism.

The indignation over the incident was amplified by the public declaration by Lawrence citizens that they would offer no resistance to the U.S. troops seeking to enforce territorial law that was distinctly injurious to the Free-Staters. It had become illegal to voice any abolitionist sentiments in the Kansas Territory, and armed Border Ruffians had taken to terrorizing innocent citizens as they went about their daily lives. The men were arrested, and if not beaten or killed by the Border Ruffians, were delivered to U.S. troops for imprisonment—for suspicion of sympathizing with the abolitionist cause. In addition, the U.S. troops were often dispatched to round up territorial citizens fingered as suspected abolitionist sympathizers. When attacked by their own government, what were citizens to do—fight back at peril of their lives against their sovereign? Or submit and declare their loyal citizenship, also at the cost of their own lives? This no-win quandary garnered even more public support for Lawrence in the aftermath of the violence.

Nute's house was sacked as part of the attack, as recounted by an unidentified neighbor's letter published in the *Worcester Daily Transcript*:

I saw three of the ruffians around the Rev. Mr. Nute's house (who lives half a mile east of Mr. Whitings) this morning, and after dinner went over to see what they had been doing. Mr.

Nute and his family had gone east, but I found a man there who worked for him. He said that they had broke into the house, and broke everything open and left every thing scattered over the floors. The young man did not know what was in the trunks and could not tell what they had taken but they took his gun, and some clothing, and Mr. Nute's horse and saddle with them.[129]

At the time, Nute was still in Boston briefing the AUA on the situation in Kansas. Lucy, however, was home in Lawrence. With other women of the town, she had hidden in the ravines during the attack. Nute learned about the violence in Lawrence in the most dramatic of ways. Some papers reported that as he stepped to the pulpit to deliver his appeal at the ceremonies for the thirty-first anniversary of the AUA, he was handed a telegram informing him of the situation, with no knowledge of what had become of his wife and friends. The report of the convention published in the *Christian Register* differed slightly on the timing of the telegram, but one can imagine the agony of grief and apprehension that pervaded Nute's address. The article read,

[REV. MR. NUTE] alluded to the telegraphic report this morning of the latest outrages in Kansas, with the probable destruction of Lawrence by a mob of the infuriated defenders of slavery. By request, the speaker read the dispatches in the morning papers and proceeded to speak of the terrible conflict now going on there. The people there had been subjected to innumerable outrages and insults, driven at last from their homes, some savagely murdered within but a few days, among them the most eminent and beloved citizens. Members of his own congregation had been dragged away and probably hung up by a Missouri mob. Those who had gone out from our midst were now engaged at the peril of their lives. Mr. Nute read a letter he had just received from the agent who went out to superintend the erection of the Unitarian Church, confirming the gloomy intelligence up to the 16th inst., and giving him reason to fear that the worst was true. He was utterly astounded at the apathy manifested in this community on this subject even now. He had hoped that every citizen of Boston would fly to the morning papers for further intelligence concerning the attack on that devoted city. . . . Even the administration papers in the city had nothing to say about this last triumph of the pro-slavery mob. He hoped that the people of Boston and of New England, would in some way make their voices heard all over the land in support of the periled, outraged cause of mental and moral freedom. He had received letters from friends in Lawrence, begging him to remain here, and speak for them to plead their cause in this free community. The "laws," which had been his only legal protection during the last year, made it criminal for him to utter a word in behalf of the great principle of freedom. For informing a slave of his right to manly liberty, he was legally liable to be "hung by the neck till he was dead!" Against such outrageous statutes and penalties the people of Lawrence had taken up arms; and now that they had made the last appeal, they were still left without the needed protection, abandoned to the mercy of an armed mob from States even as remote as Georgia. The people of Lawrence had considered the American Unitarian Association as one of the most radical bodies on the face of the earth who had sent a man there to preach FREEDOM! Would this Association sustain him in the position he had taken in their name? Were they really in earnest in so doing? Did they wish him to go on, even unto death? There was a general and hearty response from the audience in sympathy with the speaker.[130]

Nute's report and preaching galvanized the convention as much as a group of Unitarians can be inflamed. As he moved to accept the report, the prominent New York Unitarian minister Rev. Henry Bellows, later mastermind of the U.S. Sanitary Commission during the Civil War, addressed the stunned audience about the necessity for the denomination to come alive to the issue of slavery. His speech addressed all the concerns that captured Unitarian ire toward slavery and revealed the dividedness of the denomination over whether the issue of slavery was appropriate to the business of a religious judicatory.

The slavery controversy had often, to this point, been politely ignored at general meetings of the denomination. The members of the AUA had, as a group, either an oppressive tolerance for opposing views or an unwillingness to challenge the economic complicity with proslavery aims by some of the denomination's most influential contributors. Pastor E. B. Hall, of Providence, Rhode Island, said the AUA should stand by the issue of antislavery as its central mission, offering full support for the Kansas mission. If it did not, the denomination could not call itself Christian, much less Unitarian. He considered "liberty of speech, liberty of opinion, liberty of the slave, liberty throughout the land and throughout the world, as essential points of the Unitarian faith."[131]

Rev. Arthur B. Fuller of Boston then announced that his church had delegated him to present a thirty-dollar gift to the parish library in Lawrence and called on those churches able to do better to do more. The conference responded with more contributions. Rev. Daniel Moncure Conway, Unitarian abolitionist and author, of Washington, D.C., took up the cry and called for money for Lawrence to establish freedom in the first instance and therefore Unitarian freedom in the end. He did not see how Unitarians could pretend to speak of theology without seeing this. "With Lawrence in flames, and our noblest Senator, himself a lover and supporter of Unitarianism, lying prostrate with these bloody gashes upon his head, it is time for us to take a practical stand. Unitarianism must show the world that it is not the old orthodoxy, in allowing man to be so cheap that he should be made a slave."[132]

Conway referred to the attack on Senator Charles Sumner of Massachusetts, another atrocity that almost immediately followed the sack of Lawrence. Sumner was struck down and beaten senseless on the floor of the Senate on May 22, 1856, by Representative

Preston Brooks of South Carolina, who declared Sumner's antislavery sentiments an insult to Southern honor. Brooks planned the attack to coincide with an empty chamber and beat the older man with a cane until it broke to pieces while his victim was trapped by his desk. He had enlisted a compatriot to stave off anyone who might interfere. The public found the cruel and calculated nature of Brooks's attack to be more heinous than his flagrant violation, as a member of the Congress, of another member's constitutionally guaranteed right to free speech.

While some proslavery senators supported Brooks in his protection of the "honor" of the South, much of the country roared with derision at the cowardice of Southern "chivalry"—a cowardice they disdainfully said they expected from a group of people who would defend slavery. In the context of this event, the lack of a moral response by the Pierce administration to the plight of the Free-State citizens of Kansas was even more appalling.

At the AUA gathering, Hon. Albert Fearing, a Boston philanthropist, took up the cry. The *Christian Register* quoted him saying,

We were a very queer denomination, professing to be liberal and enlightened; professing to spread the principles of freedom in theology and freedom in everything else; but when we came to the materials of war, we were madly deficient. How slowly and reluctantly our denomination had moved towards raising the $50,000 fund for the book movement, and we had not accomplished that object yet. The Association had asked for the miserable sum of four or five thousand dollars to enable their missionary to go to Kansas and do his noble work there, and this money should have been raised along ago. We were bound by every principle of love, of justice, of mercy, of philanthropy, to carry out the plan of that church in Lawrence. We have a hundred societies in our denomination, each one of which could have given as much as is contributed by the whole body. One religious society in this city had contributed $17,000 in one year, and we in all our churches had hardly raised that amount. There should have been an immediate response to Mr. Nute's appeal.[133]

Fearing concluded his remarks by offering a resolution:

> *Resolved,* That the members of the American Unitarian Association here gathered, express their strong indignation in the view of the outrage to which the freemen of Kansas have been and are subjected, and likewise our strong sympathy with our brethren in that Territory, in this hour of their oppression and trial.[134]

James Freeman Clarke seconded the resolution and called for a similar expression of sympathy for Senator Sumner. Clarke then proposed another resolution, for Sumner. Both resolutions carried unanimously.

In Brown's Station, Kansas Territory, on June 2, 1856, the abolitionist John Brown wrote to Whitman regarding the Battle of Black Jack.[135] On that day, Brown and his army had attacked an encampment of proslavery troops led by Henry C. Pate because Pate was holding two of Brown's sons prisoner in retaliation for Brown's murder of five proslavery men at Pottawatomie Creek on May 24 and 25. The Pottawatomie massacre itself was in retaliation for the sack of Lawrence on May 21, 1856, by Pate and many others. Whitman acted as an agent of the National Kansas Committee—one of the many groups that raised funds to bring antislavery immigrants into the Kansas Territory—while also working for the AUA to superintend the building of the Lawrence church. At one point in his correspondence with Brown, Whitman referred to himself as a "confidential agent" of the AUA. Influential members of the Unitarian movement, its administration, and its ministry were heavily involved in the conspiracy with John Brown. It is possible that Whitman's position as superintendent of the building of the Lawrence church was part of a strategy to put him in the Kansas Territory as a link between Brown and members of the AUA, along with other influential Boston Unitarians intimately tied, financially and ideologically, to Brown's cause. Whitman's letters certainly support this theory.

Midway through 1856, Nute and Whitman worked together for the greater cause of antislavery. On June 3 Nute appeared at Faneuil Hall in Boston to report on the pillage and suffering in Kansas. In the wake of the sack of Lawrence and the attack on Sumner, the meeting drew Boston Mayor Alexander H. Rice, who presided, and Speaker of the House of Representatives Charles A. Phelps, who spoke. The brightest and most honorable of Boston, also members of the Unitarian intelligentsia circle, were present. Among them were the Hon. Nathan Hale (relative of Edward Everett Hale), Hon. Charles Greeley Loring, Hon. Albert Fearing, Nathaniel I. Bowditch, William R. Lawrence, Samuel Gridley Howe, David Thayer, J. Endicott Peabody, Hon. George Howland Jr., Rev. Edward Everett Hale, Hon. Charles Allen, Hon. Isaac Livermore, and George Russell. The Boston dignitaries waxed poetic about the moral imperatives of freedom. Then those from the territory itself spoke, among them Nute.

One account in the *Boston Patriot and Daily Chronicle* paraphrased Nute's speech in much detail:

Rev. Mr. Nute of Kanzas was next introduced. He said he appeared here, not as a visitor to Kanzas, but as having made his home there, a home which he intends to maintain. He would not attempt to increase the excitement of the hour, but state facts which would show to every one that the citizens of Kanzas deserve the sympathy and support of New England. To this purpose he detailed the circumstances which led to and attended the siege of Lawrence last December, and depicted the sufferings and want which had resulted from the interruption of the labors of peace. The comforts of life might be obtained at the free state Hotel, just burnt, or at a few well kept boarding houses, by paying the price of first-rate Boston Hotels. But the emigrants were too many of them obliged to put up the mud-walled cabins, leaky and floorless—shelters which many a farmer here would not think good enough for his swine. Their only living for weeks had been crushed corn, without butter or anything else to put on it. . . . At the time when they should have been improving their claims and making their houses comfortable, many of them, week after week, were compelled to leave their homes to defend the settlements from ruthless savages from Missouri, who plundered their teams and took every thing they liked. For twelve days many of them stood in the trenches of Lawrence daily expecting an attack. For all this they had nothing to show but scrip issued by the provisional government—issued on the faith that the free state would not allow their cause to fall. Four months of the assaults of ruffianism had made them poor. Six weeks ago, when he left Lawrence, many a farmer who left Massachusetts with $2000 or $8000, could not muster $10 to send to Kanzas city for the seed necessary to plant. Many had lost their teams and could not break up an acre, or even put in crops in what they broke up last year. Now the question is, whether they shall leave all and come back to safety here, or stay there and die. They went there and had stood there because they were told that it was the cause of liberty and it would be sustained. I shall go back to them—even though the perils be multiplied ten fold— but I shall be ashamed to go back to them and say Massachusetts will not sustain them.[136]

The audience then passed resolutions, both philosophical and monetary, in support of the Free-State residents of Kansas. A committee was appointed to raise funds, and Hon. Charles Phelps, speaker of the Massachusetts House of Representatives, remarked, "The difficulties in Kansas were fomented and brought about by Franklin Pierce. . . . We will arraign him before that august tribunal from whose verdict there is no appeal. We will impeach him for high crimes and misdemeanors, for breaking his inaugural vows, outraging justice, violating law, trampling upon liberty."[137] Most of the speakers saw in Brooks's assault on Sumner a metaphor for the governmental backing of the Border Ruffians. They praised the Lawrencians' fighting of fire with fire and called for generous monetary contributions to the cause. By the end of the meeting, money was rolling in.

The next day Whitman appeared before the Executive Committee of the AUA "to ask instructions in regard to the course he should follow in the present distracted state of that Territory."[138] The Executive Committee voted unanimously to proceed with the building of the church and enlisted Whitman to telegraph the decision to Lawrence. Further, "(i)t was also voted, that Mr. Whitman be requested to act as agent of the Association during his stay in New England, in collecting money towards the completion of the church,"[139] a position which would become contentious for the members of the Lawrence Unitarian Society.

Kansas was on everyone's tongue. On June 5, Theodore Parker wrote to Lydia Maria Child, abolitionist, author, and scholar, denying her request for money for a statue—a portrait of Sumner—in favor of sending more munitions to Kansas.

> I thank you for your noble letters with its generous suggestion. I will do what I can about it, but at present I should rather expend $1500 in corn and gunpowder for the men of Lawrence. Were I Sumner, I should count that the better testimonial. By and by when the battle is over, it seems to me it would be better to make a statue. Your design strikes me as classic and beautiful.[140]

The newspapers overflowed with Kansas woes. *The Daily Democrat* in Rochester, New York, published a timeline of the murders and outrages, feeling that the public would be misled by reports coming through proslavery St. Louis. To the raw reports about Kansas murder and mayhem was added the unthinkable— disclosure by the *Boston Evening Telegraph* on June 7 of violence toward the women of the territory during the sack of Lawrence:

Violence to Women in Kansas! ... a party of them (pro-slavery ruffians) went to a claim about four miles from Lawrence, upon which there was only a matronly woman and her two daughters; that they violently abused the mother in her own house, and took her daughters to their tent and kept them during the invasion! ... I hope that the whole North will unite as one man in a War of Extermination upon the barbarous hordes and the dens from which they come forth to commit their depredations.[141]

Madness had descended upon the land. Some thought the entire American democracy project, fought and sacrificed for since Bunker Hill, was at stake. Nute and Whitman began to frequently speak in tandem. When they appeared in Concord, Massachusetts, they addressed a crowd that included Henry David Thoreau, author, naturalist, and philosopher; Franklin Sanborn, activist writer and later John Brown conspirator; and Ralph Waldo Emerson, philosopher. All were active in Concord's antislavery movement, Transcendentalism, and John Brown's efforts.

As the two Kansas men made their way through New England undeterred by the threats of violence, their passionate words and grisly stories continued to inspire a flow of funds to the AUA for the work in Kansas as well as for additional Free-State settlers. But money could only keep the settlers from starving and help build a visible Free-State presence in the territory. It could not quell the powerful backlash from the proslavery faction. The Free-Staters soon found the fight for their lives turn into a struggle against their own president's complicity with proslavery politics. Their self-protective efforts would become treason against their country.

HIGH TREASON AND
LEGAL MARAUDERS

In Kansas, the frontline war of Border Ruffians against Free-State settlers was supported in large measure by the war against the Free-State movement and its leaders by proslavery officials and their courts on the national stage. The first of the Free-Staters arrested on treason charges in May 1856 was Free-State Governor Charles Robinson, ratified in his office by the Free-State people in the extra-legal Topeka Constitution of 1855, but hunted by the proslavery and U.S. troops alike as an insurgent. On May 10 Robinson and his wife, Sara, were traveling East. The governor was taken off the boat and arrested at Lexington, Missouri, removed to Westport, a proslavery camp near Lawrence, and then taken to Kansas City, Leavenworth, and finally to Lecompton.

On May 11 U.S. Marshall Israel B. Donalson issued a proclamation demanding that citizens of Lawrence who had resisted arrest appear at Lecompton so that the law could be executed. The citizens of Lawrence appealed to Governor Shannon for protection, but he wrote back, "There is no force around or approaching Lawrence, except the legally constituted posse of the United States Marshal, and Sheriff of Douglas County, each of whom, I am informed, has a number of writs for execution against persons now in Lawrence."[142]

At a May 13 meeting, the Lawrencians declared that Donalson's proclamation was false and vowed that as law-abiding citizens they would resist an invading mob. On May 14 they made another protest to the governor and the U.S. marshall. They formed a new Committee of Safety, on which Nute had served in the past and whose duty it was to try to plan for Lawrence's protection. More arrests inflamed the anarchy in the territory, and Lawrence, as the Free-State headquarters, was a particular target.

The first district court under Judge Lecompte held its sessions. According to Sara Robinson, Lecompte gave an "extraordinary charge to the Grand Jury":

> This territory was organized by an act of Congress, and so far its authority is from the United States. It has a Legislature elected in pursuance of that organic act. This Legislature, being an instrument of Congress, by which it governs the Territory, has passed laws. These laws, therefore, are of United States authority and making; and all that resist these laws resist the power and authority of the United States, and are, therefore, guilty of high treason. Now, gentlemen, if you find that any person has resisted these laws, then you must, under your oaths, find bills against them for high treason. If you find that no such resistance has been made, but that combinations have been formed for the purpose of resisting them, and individuals of influence and notoriety have been aiding and abetting in such combinations, then must you find bills for constructive treason.[143]

Sara Robinson then continued, "To make the matter so plain that even the dullest of his hearers may not fail to comprehend his meaning, he states that some who are 'dubbed governor, Lieutenant Governor, etc., are such individuals of influence and notoriety.'"[144]

On May 14 Gaius Jenkins, who was later murdered by James Lane, and George Washington Brown, editor of the *Herald of Freedom*, were arrested for treason and appeared before Judge Lecompte in Lecompton on May 22. Soon they were joined by other Free-Staters: Judge G. W. Smith, G. W. Deitzler, John Brown Jr., and H. H. Williams, all arrested "for bearing arms against the

'Government.'"[145] Bail was denied to these "treason prisoners," and the cases were set over until September. All were held at Lecompton. Four of the seven—Robinson, Jenkins, G. W. Brown, and Deitzler—were Unitarians from Nute's congregation.

During this same time period, John Brown's army was on the move. Warned that a group of proslavery men had threatened the lives of his family, Brown and his group massacred the Border Ruffians who had made the threats. Known as the Pottawatomie Massacre, the event became closely intertwined with the trials at Lecompton.

John Brown Jr., upon hearing of his father's violence, announced his resignation from the elder Brown's army and charged the company to find another captain. He later recounted his treason arrest, but he did not touch upon the "madness" that descended upon him in coming to grips with the disillusionment he experienced after his father's violence and as a result of the torturous treatment he received on his forced march to Lecompton. He said,

> During the winter of 1856 I raised a company of riflemen from the free state settlers who had their homes in the vicinity of Osawatomine [sic] and Pottawaomie Creek [sic], and marched with this company to the defense of Lawrence May 1856 but did not reach the later place in time to save it from being burned by the Missourians at that time. On this march I was joined by three other companies, and was chosen to the command of the combined forces. Returning to our homes, we found them burned to the ground by Byford's men from Alabama, who had marched in from Missouri on our rear. Our cattle and horses were driven off and dispersed, there only being three or four which we ultimately recovered. In that distruction of our houses I lost my library, consisting of about four hundred volumes, which I had been accumulating since I was sixteen. Reaching Osawatomie, my brother Jason and I were arrested on the charge of treason against the United States, by the United States troops, acting as a "posse" for the

marshall of the Territory, and taken to Paola, where Judge Cato was to hold a preliminary examination, but he did not hold his court. It was from the later place that I was tied by Captain Wood of the United States cavalry, and driven on foot at the head of a column a distance of nine miles at full trot to Osawatomie. My arms were tied behind me, and so tightly as to check the circulation of blood, especially in the right arm, causing the rope, which remained on me twenty seven hours, to sink into the flesh, leaving a mark upon that arm which I have to this day. . . . From there we were marched, chained two and two, carrying the chain between us, to a camp near Lecompton, where we met with other treason prisoners and were turned over to the custody of Colonel Sacket, who had command of a regiment of United States cavalry. We were held here till September 1856, when we were released on bail; and a few days after I took part in the defence of Lawrence against the third attack.[146]

Daniel W. Wilder, author of *The Annals of Kansas*, said of the Pottawatomie Massacre, "No other act spread such consternation among the Border-Ruffians, or contributed so powerfully to make Kansas free. Hitherto, murder had been an exclusive Southern privilege. The Yankee could 'argue' and make speeches; he did not dare to kill anybody."[147]

Nute mentioned in an 1893 letter to Richard Hinton, a fellow officer during the Civil War and the author of a history of John Brown, that he was away from Lawrence during the Pottawatomie murders but returned soon after. He told Hinton that he heard nothing but support for Brown then, because the Pottawatomie murders put a swift stop to the roughshod stomping of the Free-State Kansans by the Border Ruffians.[148] Nute also complained to Hinton of those who, in 1893, were the "loudest and most bitter to malign the memory of Brown." This was in reference to the national uproar that still persisted at the end of the nineteenth century regarding whether Brown was a murderer or a savior. Many who had supported John Brown in his campaign abandoned him when they believed that he had either ordered or participated in the killings in 1856. This controversy reignited in the 1890s after the publication of several biographies praising Brown. The controversy persists among afficionados of pre-Civil War history even today.

Most of those imprisoned on treason charges were finally released some months later in Lawrence. John Brown Jr., H. H. Williams, and William Partridge were retained in custody and formally charged with treason for alleged involvement in the Pottawatomie Massacre. Brown's house in Lawrence, where he was a prominent citizen, a colleague of Nute, and active in the Free-State legislature, was burned down.

As Kansas burned, the Unitarians in Boston, in traditional Unitarian fashion, were meeting to discuss and pass resolutions featuring their opinions on the matter. Donations for Kansas in the double and triple digits came in to the AUA. Despite the strong sentiments in support of abolitionism and the Kansas project, the denomination continued to balk at making a unilateral declaration against slavery for fear of antagonizing some of its wealthiest members. This was one facet of Theodore Parker's trouble with the denomination and a main issue in ousting other prominent Unitarian ministers, who were forced out of their pulpits for preaching against slavery.

Northern Unitarians did not necessarily own slaves, but many had massive personal investments tied up in industries made profitable by slave labor. Those families' willingness to financially support individual churches would be compromised if the AUA openly vilified slavery or declared on the side of the abolitionists. This culture-war tension in theology, class, and values within the denomination set a palpable mood at conferences and threatened to split the entity in two. These conferences steered their keynote speeches and themes away from slavery. Nevertheless, they discussed this issue at every available turn of conversation and in the groundswell of resolutions from the floor.

The AUA in Boston, with its majority of prominent abolitionists, was at liberty to pass resolutions in support of the settlers in

Kansas and decried the assault on Sumner. The Western Conference, however, was not as willing to do so, to the detriment of some of its own prominent preachers. When ministers such as Rev. William D. Haley of Alton, Illinois, looked into their hearts and to their God for guidance and came out against slavery, internal Unitarian politics deprived them of their pulpits.

The *Quarterly Journal*, reporting on its district agents in the spring of 1856, summarized the conditions affecting Nute's project in Lawrence and gave great credit for Nute's success to the AUA. It read,

Most of the facts about our mission to Kansas are well known. In one work, at least in one field, and that which circumstances have made a very prominent one, Unitarians have been first on the ground, and have taken a bold and successful lead. None of our friends doubt, we believe, that in the character of our missionary we have been fortunate. Mr. Nute has sustained his part well. Should peace be restored to that suffering Territory, we shall soon have a church there, furnished with everything that one of our New England churches has in the service of religion. The bell will soon be placed in the tower, and it is a touching fact, mentioned by Mr. Whitman, that, on the day of its arrival in Lawrence, it so happened that the sewing-circles composed of ladies of all denominations, was then in session; and on hearing the first tones of the bell,—the first ever heard in Kansas,—many could not refrain from tears, at the associations of home awakened in their minds. . . . Mr. Nute's church needs further help. The building of it has cost much more than it would have cost if erected in peaceful times. We have just heard that lumber got out and paid for, and piled up ready for use, has been stolen and lost, and the expense must be incurred again. This is the fact in regard to the flooring of the church. Providence overrules adverse circumstances for good. All that Mr. Nute has gone through has served to identify him with the people of that Territory, and given him a rare hold on their sympathies and regard. He will be a man of command-ing influence in directing the future fortunes of that Territory. Our name, and aims, and wishes, and faith, and works, are not unknown in that region, and we should desert a noble and rare hope of influence were we to desert that mission, or fail to give it a full and adequate support.[149]

In early July 1856, Nute was set to return to Kansas from his New England tour. He wrote from New York to Samuel Gridley Howe, describing the route he would take and suggesting that he and the Howes, who were traveling to Kansas, meet in St. Louis so they could travel on together from there. Nute assured Howe that he and his wife would be safe, but such would not have been the case for Nute himself, who compromised his life every time he traveled back and forth to the East through proslavery territory.

Nute's relationship with the Howes continued through the Civil War and its aftermath, when he visited with them in his own home and in theirs. After the Civil War, Julia Ward Howe was brought to the Unitarian church in Lawrence to speak. In his letter of July 3, 1856, to Samuel Gridley Howe, Nute had a somewhat formal tone, although he clearly held regard for the Howes' company:

I am disappointed in not having the pleasure of your com-pany from this point of my journey on to Saint Louis. I will not go up that detestable Missouri to patronise those floating rendevous of river banditti. You can go with perfect safety as you will be incog. But from Kansas City to Lawrence look out sharp. . . . Can't we meet at St. Louis? I start this afternoon by way of Buffalo, Detroit & Springfield Ill. Because I want to call on Mrs. Nute on the way to St. Louis. I shall be in St. Louis in about 8 days & remain about 2 days thence return for wife in Griggsville Ill. Thence across the country by Iowa City, or pos-sibly by way of Hannibal across Missouri to Fort Leavenworth. . . . The journey through Iowa would be very pleasant & salu-brious. You can go all the way to Iowa City by boat & cars from

St. Louis, thence to Council bluffs by stages—thence down the Missouri to Fort Leavenworth or to Kansas City.[150]

Nute's plan for traveling through Iowa was circumspect for two reasons. The Missouri River was completely blockaded, and any boat that attempted to pass without inspection would be shot with a canon. When nabbed, Free-State emigrants would be sent back and their property confiscated. Meanwhile, the Kansas River was so low that it was completely unfit for navigation.

In a letter excerpted in the *Quarterly Journal,* which is no longer available in its entirety, Nute wrote about this trip back to Kansas from Boston:

In a little over three days from St. Louis we were in Kansas City. Here we were detained two days to procure horses, by which we drove through to within ten miles of home in one day, and one of the hottest I ever experienced. . . . Early next morn our hearts were made glad by a view of the pleasant village of Lawrence, much improved in appearance since we last saw it, notwithstanding the ravages that have been inflicted upon it by the hands of legalized marauders. The amount of building that has been done is, under all the circumstances, truly astonishing. Several of the most conspicuous edifices are missing; but many more have sprung up as by magic within the last few weeks, most of them of stone and two stories in height. Chief above all for our eyes, and making our hearts leap for joy, behold the walls of our sanctuary up to within two feet of the top, and making altogether a better appearance than the plan would lead you to expect. If it had not been for the delay occasioned by the absence of the superintendent, the mason-work would have been completed, ready for the roof. . . . Mr. Whitman has not yet arrived, and I have taken the liberty of deciding the question, with counsel of those here most concerned, for which the work was delayed, and the work will be forwarded immediately. . . . The condition of affairs in the

Territory is on the whole far worse than I expected to find. Up to within two miles of Lawrence the reign of terror is yet complete. . . . Bands of robbers are prowling about, and every night some outrage is committed. Men are fired upon, knocked down, plundered, and left for dead; houses are burned. The night before we arrived at our last halt, a house was burned by a mob at Franklin, the next night another within a few miles of our cabin, and on the same night a man from Lawrence was attacked within two miles of the town by a party of three or four of the Georgian banditti who are yet quartered at Franklin. Several shots were exchanged, from one of which he had a narrow escape, the ball grazing his arm, when the rascals fell upon him, beat him over the head, after the pattern set in Washington, with their pistols until he was senseless, plundered him of his money, and fled. A few days before this, an old man coming from Kansas City with a load of provisions was robbed of everything and driven back. . . . I am astonished to find that, though these things are of almost hourly recurrence, we have no protection from the troops. There are none quartered in or anywhere around Lawrence at the present time. The nearest company of United States Dragoons that I can hear of, is that which guards the prisoners at Lecompte. We are left at the mercy of these guerilla bands, who have been used by the United States Marshall to plunder and destroy and kill, in the hope that we may be forced to rise and fight for our own defence, when we shall be immediately denounced again all over the land as rebels against the government and bloody-minded men, and again subjected to the murderous attacks of more organized bands under the forms of law. . . . I am confident that the worst has not yet come. There is to be a yet darker chapter in the history of these villainies.[151]

On July 24, Nute wrote of his travels back to Lawrence to the *Boston Transcript*. The letter was picked up by the *Hartford Daily Courant*, which also declared, "It is unnecessary for us to say, in this community, where Mr. N. is so well known, that his statements may be relied upon as unadorned facts."[152] The letter read,

I am amazed and horrified at the depths of iniquity to which ruffianism has descended. Up to within two miles of Lawrence the reign of terror is complete. Men are waylaid by guerilla bands every night, and sometimes in broad day-light, shot at, beaten, plundered and left for dead: houses are burned, horses stolen. This is not the report of rumors, but the testimony of what my own eyes have seen—wounded men and smoking ruins. I find my own house was plundered of almost everything of any value except books, and what was not taken was damaged or destroyed—horse, saddle and bridle, blankets and clothing. Three horses were driven off laden with spoils beside my own. Several of my neighbors lost spans of valuable horses, with carriages, harnesses, &c. . . . We had a narrow escape from being robbed if not killed, as we came in. We reached the Wakarusa, at a point about eight miles from Lawrence about an hour after sunset, and hesitated about keeping on home or stopping at a log-cabin hotel to spend the night; decided on the last, and made an early start next morning. When within two miles of home we came up to a party of Lawrence men hunting for deadly weapons in the grass by the road side. . . . It seems that a young man on his way to Lawrence the evening before, had been attacked by one of the robber bands there laying in wait, shot at several times, and finally beaten over the head with a revolver until he became senseless, then robbed and left for dead. He had managed to crawl to the next cabin, and though badly bruised, to get to Lawrence that morning and give the alarm. After discharging his revolver he threw it into the grass, that it might not fall in to the hands of the robbers. In the search for it three bowie knives were found. Night before last the house of a free state settler was burned, some three miles from us, and threats were made that two more would be burned last night and one man shot. . . . In the midst of all this we have no protection from the United States troops. All they do for us is to take away our weapons and guard our prisoners, while the civil officers bring in upon us, or encourage by patronage of public service when they have got here, these very highway robbers. There are no U.S. troops at Lawrence or in the vicinity. Teams have been plundered of provisions, and passengers by the mail coach have had their pockets searched within one week between this and Kansas City. . . . We have just learned that several companies of dragoons have been dispatched to stop the free state men who are on their way towards us through Iowa. Another item is that Gov. Shannon has forbidden admission of the visitors to the prisoners, Robinson, Deitzler, Jenkins and Brown; after this date . . . I am confident that the full enormity of these Kansas outrages is but faintly apprehended at the East, for all that has been said, and that a yet darker chapter is to be written in this shameful and horrible history before the end comes.[153]

Another letter written on August 4 has not survived, except for its extract in the *Quarterly Journal*. Nute was back in Lawrence and reported on the progress of the church. Pastor and populace were gripped in a general anxiety waiting for the next atrocity. Nute wrote of preaching at Lecompton to some of the members of his society who were still held captive as "the treason prisoners":

I have only time for a hasty note. The church building, the disbursement of charities, the building of our cabin, calls &c., with a correspondence about a great diversity of subjects, preclude anything more. . . . Whitman has not arrived, nor do we hear from him. No word reaches us from the party or parties who are said to be on the way to us through Iowa. . . . Yesterday I preached at the camp near Lecompton, where a considerable party of my society are held as prisoners. These, with their friends, the soldiers, and neighbors, made a congregation of over one hundred persons. Services were conducted with order and spirit; good singing, accompanied by an instrument. On my first visit I found the prisoners somewhat depressed, their patience nearly exhausted by the long series of annoyances and the wearing confinement to which they have been subjected. . . . A band of Georgian ruffians are gathered some fifty miles south of this, committing all sorts of depredations. A team, wagon and oxen, was taken from the driver on the way from Westport hither last week, and horses are stolen every night. We keep our horse picketed close to the house, and lie with one eye open, and a loaded rifle within reach, every night. . . . The church building will be resumed to-morrow morning. The caps. for which the masons have been waiting, are now ready. I have about closed the contract for the roof, and about half of the flooring has been hauled up from Kansas City. . . . All freight for this place will in future come by way of Leavenworth City. That large box of books, started from Crosby & Nichols last May, has not yet arrived, nor can we get track of it. It contained those copies of Channing which you gave for distribution, and some thirty dollars' worth of housekeeping stores. Another box of dry goods, started two days before that, is also missing, which cost me about $75. . . . The bell and clock have arrived at Leavenworth, and are probably on the way down to Lawrence today.[154]

There was great interest in Nute's preaching to the treason prisoners, as the nation followed their plight with fury or glee. Sara Robinson was living at the camp in Lecompton along with other wives and families of the prisoners. Here they could be near their husbands to provide for their comfort as they awaited trial. Sara wrote in her diary:

The first Sunday in August we had preaching in camp. Mr. N., and a large number of people, came from Lawrence. As many as possible sat under the pavilion, while others occupied the carriages. The officers and soldiers attended, and all together we made a goodly number. A melodeon was also brought up from town. Major Hoyt brought a large number of beautiful pond lilies, which, at his suggestion, were placed on the table, before the preacher.[155]

The Unitarian church bell, longed for and planned for, was hidden in a barrel of dishes and brought the last leg of its journey past Border Ruffians by a Lawrence man, Billy Hughes. It finally arrived on August 8, when an unidentified newspaper reported that "It was immediately placed on blocks and the first peal of the church going bell awoke the echoes on the plains of Kansas."[156] The bell had taken a circuitous route to its destination, as related by a special Christmas edition of the *Lawrence Daily Journal* in 1890, which finally revealed the name of the anonymous donor who made the purchase of the bell possible:

In the year of 1855 Mr. Wm H. Knight, a retired carpet manufacturer of Saxonville, Mass., who took a deep interest in the Kansas struggle, expressed a desire that the heroic settlers should be cheered by the old familiar sound of the church-going bell, and proposed to donate a bell to cost not over $500, provided a clock to cost an equal amount should be given by someone else. An appeal for the clock was made but up to anniversary week (in May, 1856) no response came. The evening before the public anniversary meeting of the American Unitarian society in Boston Mr. Knight sent for Mr. Nute and told him that he was to sail for Europe that afternoon and that his offer would remain good only up to the time of his leaving. Mr. Nute at once went to the meeting of the association then in session at the Bedford street church where he was called on the platform to make a verbal report of his missionary work in Kansas. As he stepped on the platform someone near the door called out for him to give way, to listen to a report of tragic interest from Lawrence, Kansas, just received by telegraph. The dispatch said the town had been destroyed and many of the

143

citizens killed, and was received with profound emotion, and made an impressive opening to Mr. Nute's account of his work in Kansas. After a glowing tribute to the people who were so heroically contending for liberty in Kansas, mention was made of the offered bell. A collection was taken then and there and the needed sum for a clock raised and by nine o'clock that night the order was given to Mr. Hooper for bell and clock and in a few months they were shipped by way of New Orleans, the vessels in which they were sent was wrecked in the gulf, but the bell and clock were finally recovered, returned to Boston for repairs, and reached Lawrence.[157]

At the fiftieth anniversary of the Lawrence Society in 1900, Sarah A. Brown penned a short history of the church from the old church record. She added some interesting lore to the story of the bell:

From the first the plans for a church building included a school room, and between three and four thousand dollars was pledged for it in the East and one thousand dollars here. Furniture for the school room, a library for the Sunday School, a bible, a bell and a clock were also given by Eastern friends. There being no railroads so far west the bell and clock were shipped by way of New Orleans. The boat was wrecked at the mouth of the Mississippi River and the cargo sunk, and for more than a year the bell and clock reposed quietly at the bottom of the river. When, finally they arrived in Lawrence the clock was found to be much damaged and some parts were lost, so it had to be sent to the machine shop for repairs, where it was kept until the church was ready for it. During this time its striking machinery was connected with the steam whistle, and old settlers recall how the whistle took the place of the bell in sounding the hours of the day. The bell was temporarily hung on a square frame of timbers sox or eight rods west of the old church building just high enough from the ground to swing clear. It was quite near the yard of Gen'l Collamore, whose wife sometimes found it a convenient dinner bell, and often when seeing a funeral procession winding slowly along to the old cemetery, south west of town, she would send her boys to toll the knell for the departed soul. It is a sweet toned bell. There is a tradition that when in the process of making someone threw into the molten mass of metal a bag of silver dollars. The bell bore the inscription, "Proclaim Liberty through out the Land." ... When the church building was completed the city aided the society in raising funds for building the tower where the bell and clock were placed, and where for nearly thirty years they counted the passing hours, summoning the children to their school and laborers to their work. In 1891 when the society moved to their new church building, it was sold to the city and today the familiar and beloved face of the old clock looks out on the passer by from the belfry of the beautiful High School Building, and the silver tones of the bell are still heard calling the children to school morning and noon.[158]

On August 15, 1856, Nute wrote to Edward Everett Hale of the Kansas conflicts.

Again the Missourians are up & pouring over the border, but no odds will deter our people from fighting. They stand fire like veterans of a hundred battles & keep cooler than I had thought possible. But we must be reinforced. The grossest misrepresentations will be made, have been already, of these conflicts & circulated among our enemies. It is understood in Missouri that we are all to be drawn out or exterminated within the next few weeks. Nearly every pro-slavery man has left this vicinity & Franklin intimating as they go that our fate is soon to be sealed. Lane is here & at the head of the military operation. About 500 men are encamped with him tonight between us & the location of the enemy's camp that was broken up this afternoon. But before this reaches you a weeks later report will have reached you by telegraph. . . . I got your letter with the donations of periodicals etc but a few days since have apprized them as much as these troublous times permit me to apprize anything. I assure you that your expressions of interest & good will are of high value to me & though I have had the privilege of a personal interview since the date of your letter yet it comes to me like a fresh greeting upon my heart & strengthens my reliance on you for the future. . . . We are having delightful balmy weather crops promising. With peace we should be sure of prosperity. I am at some loss where to direct this but suffice on the whole you have not left Worchester.[159]

Nute's delight in the balmy weather and wish for peace was not to be. Within a few days, murder came into his own home and family.

August 1856 was a most trying and tragic time for them. Lucy Nute's sister, Nancy, and her husband, William C. Hopps, had come out to Kansas from Alton, Illinois, to visit, with a notion of settling. The Hopps traveled from where they were staying in Leavenworth to Lawrence and William left an ailing Nancy there to be tended by Nute and Lucy. On the morning of August 19, Mr. Hopps set out from Lawrence to return to Leavenworth. The *Kansas Herald* reported what befell him:

Highway Murder . . . On Monday last, the body of a man, which was subsequently recognized as that of a Mr. Hobbs of Illinois, was found about three miles from this place, on the military road. On examining the body it appeared that he had not only been brutally murdered, but had been literally scalped by some unknown fiend. We hope our citizens will take active measures to effect the arrest of the perpetrator of this barbarous and diabolical deed.[160]

Hopps was traveling with his whole life savings. He was met a short distance outside of Leavenworth by a man named Fugit, a notorious Border Ruffian. Fugit murdered and then scalped him. The crime was witnessed by two small children, and word soon reached Lawrence. The very next day, Nute wrote to the *Christian Register*, reeling from the shock:

> Words are wanting to convey to you an idea of the grief and horror that chills our blood. The fiendish doings of our enemies have come so near to me and mine, as to render me incapable of writing a cool narration of the events of the last two weeks. . . . My brother-in-law, Mr. William Hopps, lately from Illinois, and formerly of Somerville, Mass., was murdered yesterday near Leavenworth city. He left our house in the morning to return to Leavenworth, having made us a visit, leaving his wife with us sick. But an hour since, and the sad tidings reached us. He was shot as he was riding in, and then scalped. On the approach of a team from this direction, the murderer fled, went into Leavenworth and exhibited the savage exultation, the scalp, exclaiming, 'I went out for the scalp of a d—d abolitionist, and I have got one.' This new victim was a quiet, kind hearted young man. He had chosen his home in Leavenworth, because of his reluctance to take part in the contest. He was averse to bearing arms, and was utterly defenceless at the time. This is the third man who has gone out from under our roof during the last week, straight to his death, by the hands of these brutal hounds of slavery. . . . I have no heart nor time for comments. I am about to start with a small volunteer company to attempt the recovery of the body of my friend and his property. I have no scruples against borrowing a Sharpe's rifle, and I pray God to give me calmness and skill to use it effectively if we are attacked, notwithstanding the sneers of those who desire that we should be left without any protection against these butcheries. . . . Last night we sent a messenger to the camp of the United States dragoons, near Lecompton, with a request for a detachment to escort a train of our teams over this road to Leavenworth, to bring down provisions and other

goods, and we were refused, and told that all the United States forces in the territory are ordered to repair immediately to that headquarter of all pro-slavery ruffianism, Lecompton.[161]

The fact that the unrelenting horror of Bleeding Kansas had so directly affected Nute electrified the country. He was a well-known and beloved clergyman, whose mission to Kansas had been highly publicized and whose correspondence with several key newspapers in New England was picked up and reprinted in many other major papers. Not only was the murder victim a member of Nute's family, but he was a totally innocent man not connected with the Free-State wars at all. He had recently come into the territory and was murdered solely because he was coming from Lawrence. The national papers reverberated with every unfolding detail of a story that made its way into many early histories of Kansas:

> Mr. Hoppe had landed at Leavenworth and hired a horse and buggy in which to go to Lawrence to visit his brother-in-law, Rev. E. Nute. He was returning the horse and buggy at the time he met Fugit. . . . Fugit had made the bet in a Leavenworth saloon [that he would get the scalp of a "d—d" Yankee]. He started toward the home of his uncle. He met Hoppe on the west side of Three Mile Creek. What was said is not known, but Fugit shot him. The horse ran across the creek, when Hoppe's body fell out of the buggy, his feet entangled in the line, which stopped the horse. Fugit followed him back, and when he came up with the dead body, scalped it. Two children, Jimmie Rhodes, six or seven years old, and his sister, were gathering plums there in a thicket and saw the murder. Fugit returned to town with the scalp and exhibited it and collected his wager. He then went to his uncle's where he also exhibited the scalp. His aunt was horrified and told him he had better leave the country. He went to Texas. In about a year he came back to Leavenworth and was tried before Judge Lecompte. Mrs. Todd was spirited away and not permitted to appear against him.

The court ruled that the evidence of the children could not be admitted, as they were too young. This made it impossible to convict him of the murder. Fugit then went back to Platte County, but his crime was too brutal for even the Missourians of that day. They would have little to do with him, and he dropped out of sight.[162]

Nute next wrote to the AUA of the murder, desperate, no doubt, to tell the story over and over again in his distress. The original letter appears to be lost, but sections of it were excerpted in the *Quarterly Journal*. They read,

We are having horrible work,—our people murdered around us every day, and we denied all protection by those in command of the United States forces. My own house is made a house of mourning. Our brother-in-law, who came out to us but a week since, has fallen a victim to a brutal murder, leaving his broken-hearted widow with us. He was a remarkably quiet man, strongly conservative, averse to bearing arms here, and utterly defenceless at the time of his murder. His scalp was taken off, and exhibited in Leavenworth by a creature in human shape, who declared that he went out for the scalp of a _____ Abolitionist, and he had got one. This makes three men who have gone out of our door within one week straight to a bloody death. In each case the body has been horribly mutilated. . . . The enemy are gathering about us by thousands, and declare through the border prints their purpose of exterminating every free state man in the Territory. Every night I prepare myself for an attack. We have asked and begged the protection of United States troops for an escort over the road to Leavenworth, that our teams might go for provisions,—(it was on this road, and near Leavenworth, that our brother was killed,)—and it has been refused us. We have not a sack of flour nor a bushel of meal for sale in this town or vicinity. We have at least two thousand people to be fed, and this fact is well known by the officers in command of from six to ten companies of dragoons now at Lecompton, some twelve miles from this. The clock, school furniture, books, and several hundred dollars' worth of our household stuff lies in the storehouses at Leavenworth, which is now a rendezvous for the ruffians, and all communication is cut off. I sent a man with a team to Kansas City for some of the material for the church. He has been gone a week, and we have just heard, in a way that leaves us but little ground for hope, that he was taken near Westport, scalped first, and then murdered. I would write more, but must be about other business, and there is but small chance of this ever reaching you. From this apprehension, I refrain from giving more than life and ease, namely, to be faithful unto death, and choosing, above all others, that of heroic martyrdom.[163]

On August 22 Nute wrote to his dear friend Rev. Francis Tiffany at the Springfield, Massachusetts, Unitarian congregation. He was in the throes of the horror around him, and his letter to Tiffany includes some very interesting personal details not in his correspondence with the AUA:

I have tried in vain to raise a company of men to go for the recovery of our brother's remains, to give them a decent burial, and for the effects about his person—all his money, &c. I have taken a rifle, and offered to be one of 50 to go. A sufficient number responded, and were pledged to go the morning after the sad tidings reached us, but it was thought best to delay until we should get an answer from the officer in command of the U.S. dragoons, encamped about 10 miles from this, to whom we had applied for a force to go with us. It came at night, referring us to the superior then on the way with several companies to protect Pierce's bloody officials at Lecompton. Twice we have sent making the request of him for the protection of an escort to go with our teams to Leavenworth for provisions, and twice we have been refused. . . . There is not a single sack of flour or a bushel of meal for sale in this vicinity, and we have at least 2000 men, women and children to be fed. What shall we do—what can we do, but fight our way through, with desperation of men who know themselves surrounded by merciless savages? This we are determined to do. You will have the report of bloody work before this reaches you. It may be that nothing short of a massacre of the suffering people of Kanzas will arouse this nation to a sense of the inconceivable wickedness of the men who are the head of affairs. You may imagine the feelings with which I read the cold-blooded sneers, the diabolical sport, which is made of our sufferings in the Boston Post, which I have just received. Are all the feelings of humanity, is all sense of decency, dead in the souls of the men who uphold this infamous administration? . . . Many of our number have ceased to hope for anything but the foulest injustice from the government. All that seems to be in store for us worth aspiring to is an heroic martyrdom. Plead for our cause with all the might you have, I send this with as many more as I can write before the mail leaves under cover to a friend in St. Louis. The chance that it will reach you seems to me very small. The Missourians are coming over the border and gathering at several points to the number of thousands, we hear. I dare not trust the particulars of our military condition and plans to this for fear it will fall into the hands of the enemy. Only this, we are prepared and determined to strike terrible blows. . . . We are having war in earnest—four fights within the last five days, in all of which the free state men were the assailants, and the victors; four lives lost on our side, and some 8 or 10 badly wounded. To-day the dragoons are in town to effect an exchange of prisoners, and deliver the Chicopee howitzer, taken from us in the sacking of Lawrence. The free state army of about 400 men has passed our cabin twice, half a mile from us on one side, and a mile on the other. Twice we have heard the booming cannon and rattle of muskets and rifles, and seen the flame and smoke of burning forts and cabins. Two nights ago, and my nearest neighbor was visited by a scouting party of the enemy, and two horses stolen. Every night we bring ours (we have two fine ones, I and the man who works for me,) close to the house, keep our Sharps' rifles in readiness, and take turns in standing guard. . . . One night we had four men and a sick woman with us in our little cabin. We have got to the closest place I hope, and I believe, with God's help, we shall force our way through. The fiendishness of these wretches is a tax on credulity. Poor Hoyt went from our house but an hour or two before he was murdered. . . . On taking the strong-hold of the ruffians near which he was killed, a little Negro was found, who said that the day before some men came in from the guard and reported that a prisoner was taken giving his name and asking "what shall be done with him?" The reply of the officer was, "shoot him." But not content with that, they proceeded to pound his head with the breeches of their muskets. Another man of the name of Williams, from Massachusetts, was taken that day, and also shot; both bodies have been recovered. We have taken over 30 of them prisoners, and released all but the 19 who are to be given up today. Do you wonder that our men turned out en masse to rout that fort, and also the den of Col. Titus[164] next day, and that some clamor to-day for the hanging of this wretch Titus? . . . We have gained great advantage within the last week, have now at least 500 men ready for fight in and around Lawrence and two good howitzers. But this is horrible business, and I feel the influence that makes fierce tigers of the mildest men. When I looked on Titus, and thought of his part in the proceedings last May, and the murders of Hoyt and Williams, I came very near joining in the cry "Hang him on the spot." But, on second thought, I gave my voice for mercy. The wretch cowered and plead for his life, promising to leave the territory. Some of his men say they have been engaged in indiscriminate plunder, without any regard to party in some cases, though, under the lead of Titus, they were robbing and murdering only free state men; and this man is the commander of the militia of Kanzas territory, and Gov. Shannon came down to Lawrence yesterday to beg him off. Cry aloud and spare not; raise thy voice like a trumpet, and show this people their sin.[165]

Nute wrote to everyone he could think of, as he never knew how many, if any, letters would make it through the Border Ruffians' censors and actually reach their destination in the East. Settlers were being murdered in cold blood. Their farms had been destroyed by the Border Ruffians, and food shipments were blockaded. Now, everyone in Lawrence was starving.

On August 24 Nute wrote to his dear friend Edward Everett Hale at the New England Emigrant Aid Company and included details about the Free-State army. The first half of the letter survives in the New England Emigrant Aid Company papers at the Kansas State Historical Society; the second half is missing. The extant version reads,

> I wrote you about a week since to apprise you of the storm gathering & about to break in over affairs,—that you might be aroused to put forth every exertion for our reinforcement in this hour of our pressing need. Before this you have some rumor of the first horrors in the renewed contest—so horrible that you will refuse to believe them if they are no worse than the facts. They are probably scowled at & ridiculed as gross fabrications got up for political effect by a large part of the community in New England. But I assure you the worst is true. Nothing more horrible, more devilish, than the truth can behold. . . . I saw a slip from the office of one of these Leavenworth papers summoning the ruffians to this work,—calling on them to exterminate the free state men of Lawrence—or in their own terms "the abolitionist miscreants." . . . The head of poor Hoyt was so battered by clubs or the breech of muskets as to be just recognizable—The body of the last mentioned [Jennison, a Unitarian] has not been found when last seen

he was in the hands of his captors near Westport who had taken off his scalp. This man had never been engaged in any of the political affairs of the territory nor in any of the fighting. He was driving a team from Kansas City whither he had gone for a load of lumber for our church. His only crime was that of being "a Free-State man." & having too much manliness to deny his first conviction to save his life. A companion was taken with him & escaped by pleading his nativity in a slave-holding state. . . . An account of the present position of the forces & the plans of warfare I dare not trust to the mail. You will hear of hot-work soon & have evidence that the free state men can show themselves men. A body of the enemy is not far from here & will be attacked before long.—We are able & determined to keep them at a distance for at least one week longer & though they come at us 3 to 1 they will find no easy conquest. . . . The general muster of the militia throughout Missouri takes place on the 1st day of September & the rumor reaches us of the purpose of a great force over the border on this day.—By that time we hope to have 1000 men armed with Sharps rifles in Lawrence. We can muster that number now with a few hours notice. We have several companies stationed at different points around us from 6 to 10 miles distant & at our most important point have a strong log fort so located & constructed that a small company can repel 10 times their own numbers—We have 500 lbs. of type metal cast into balls for the Howitzer & 100 cast iron balls for the superior field piece taken at Franklin. This last citation of The Herald of Freedom seems more effectual in facing conviction on the march of our enemies than any before issued. Last Saturday morning it made 20 by the weighty arguments in the form of slugs from the cannons mouth.—But this closings too horrible for joking. I am amazed to find myself taking such hearty satisfaction in the success of our people in sending those men whom we [The rest of text is missing.][166]

Nute's August 25 letter to Secretary Miles at the AUA regarding the Hopps murder survived in its entirety, as printed in the *Christian Register*. This letter was also excerpted in the *Quarterly Journal* of 1857. It read,

We are now waiting in readiness to start at a moment's notice for Leavenworth, to recover the body and personal effects of our murdered brother. In fact I have made the proposition, offering myself and a team to go, if a small company will attend us with three other teams. It is thought, or was a few hours since, to be an expedition too dangerous. The widow of this victim, a sister of my wife's is yet with us, and is so far recovered from her illness, that we have communicated the tidings of her bereavement. I need not tell you that under all the horrible circumstances, it is an overwhelming blow. She is left desolate and utterly destitute. Her husband had all his property in the shape of gold about his person at the time of the murder. . . . Three times we have asked for an escort over the road to Leavenworth, of the highest officer in command of the United States troops, now out of the fort, in the territory, and three times been refused. It was plainly no part of Pierce's purpose, that the troops should give any protection to the men whom he has denounced in his message as sectional fanatics. Have we not occasion to feel the deep villainy of slavery as an institution? The smoking ruins, these groans and tears of widows and the fatherless in the wilderness, are its legitimate fruits. Its friends exult over our sufferings, and the men in the highest places of the land, are busy with the malice of demons virtually instigating such deeds as have desolated my cabin during the last week. . . . Of course all church building has ceased. The walls of the church are up ready for the roof, and make a fine appearance. The saw mills are all stopped. If it were not for this, the carpenter who has the contract for the roof would be able to go on at the next breathing place of peace.[167]

But there was to be no breathing place of peace in the near future for anyone connected to the Free-State cause, least of all for Nute himself.

TAKEN PRISONER
AND UNDER SIEGE

As heinous and unbearable as the Hopps murder was for Nute and his loved ones, it was merely the beginning of their terrible trials in the fall of 1856. In the wake of his brother-in-law's death and the loss of Hopps's money, Nute had to somehow convey his sister-in-law safely back East to her family. But this moral imperative towards his wife's sister nearly cost Nute his life.

E. B. Whitman penned an ominous letter to Secretary Miles on August 30:

> I have just time to inform you that your missionary was day before yesterday taken prisoner by the Missourians at Leavenworth. His brother in law Mr. Hopps had been cruelly murdered there and Mr. N went up with the widow to look after his effects. He went in company with a train of wagons for provisions of flour. We have not a sack of flour or meat in town and after appealing to the Military for an escort to bring provisions a few bold spirits started on the errand. The teams are all seized and the men and some women held prisoners. One the drivers of Mr. Nutes carriage was shot. Our church materials are many of them at Leavenworth and must remain there. . . . If Mr. Nute should be released and sent down the river as it is intimated he may be you will soon see him. We are in a state of actual war. Four battles our people have won and a rumor comes of another victory in the south from a

detachment of cavalry sent down a week ago. . . . Where is the north? Bartering her liberties forgotten? I fear so. If Mr. Nute should be murdered and if it is known who he is that now seems likely—will you wake up. His brother's scalp was taken off and exhibited as the scalp of a d—d abolitionist and his may even be sent to your association—as a warning never again to interfere with the barbarism of the peculiar institution nor with the wiles of the Devil. May God give our people wisdom to act with prudence.[168]

Nute had written to Miles at the AUA on August 25, but by the time his letter arrived in Boston, a telegram from someone in Lawrence had already brought the news that he had been taken prisoner. Sara Robinson wrote extensively about the incident in her diary when she mapped out a chronological narrative of the murders that gave Bleeding Kansas its name:

On the twenty-seventh, Mr. Nute, with his widowed sister-in-law, and John Wilder,[169] a merchant of Lawrence, with a number of teams for provisions, started for Leavenworth. They had been advised by the military commanders to attempt this journey. When near Leavenworth the whole party were captured by a band of ruffians under Capt. Emory. The body of Mr. Hopps had been buried, by the troops, in Pilot Knob cemetery, and his widow was denied the consolation of looking upon his grave. After continued refusals by the ruffians, she at last succeeded in getting on board a boat bound down the Missouri. The others were retained as prisoners of war, and untold anxiety was felt for their safety.[170]

As the news leaped from newspaper to newspaper, Nute's imprisonment by the proslavers came into national focus with varying amounts of wrath, disbelief, and accuracy. The Massachusetts *Springfield Republican*, amid its discussion of the politics in the Kansas Territory, headlined the fate of its correspondent:

REV MR. NUTE A PRISONER . . . A letter from Leavenworth, August 29, to the New York Evening Post, says Rev. Mr. Nute came or was brought there a prisoner, the day before, in company with his sister-in-law, Mrs. Hopp, whose husband was so horribly murdered and scalped. Mr. Nute and his sister were just getting upon the steamboat, intending to leave with the property of Mr. Hopp, when Mr. Nute was forcibly "seized by a brutal pro-slavery ruffian named Murphy, and did not get on the steamer. The strong probabilities are that, unless Mr. Nute escapes, he will meet with a violent end, as he was threatened with hanging."[171]

In Cambridge, Harvard's Dean Sibley recorded in his private journals the events of a meeting held on September 10 to address the situation in Kansas and raise funds. The Harvard men were rallying vociferously around one of their own, Rev. Nute.[172] Sibley wrote,

Rev. Dr. Huntington spoke feelingly & eloquently respecting the Rev. Ephraim Nute, who had been seized by the robbers & probably has suffered violence of some kind if not death at their hands. He said he would give $100, $200, $300, of his salary this year, yes $400 or $500 to any body of men who would go to Kansas & bring away from the Border-Ruffians the body of Nute, dead or alive.[173]

Ralph Waldo Emerson spoke at this meeting. As a renowned and eloquent orator against slavery, he had worked alongside Nute and Whitman on their various fund-raising and consciousness-raising trips to New England. George Bancroft, the noted Unitarian historian, wrote,

Emerson as clearly as any one, perhaps more clearly than any one at the time, saw the enormous dangers that were gathering over the Constitution. . . . It would certainly be difficult,

159

perhaps impossible, to find any speech made in the same year that is marked with so much courage and foresight as this of Emerson. . . . Even after the inauguration of Lincoln several months passed away before his Secretary of State or he himself saw the future so clearly as Emerson had foreshadowed it in 1856.[174]

Edward Emerson wrote that his father, "in response to the petitions of the friends of Freedom . . . urged the Legislature of Massachusetts to come to the rescue, [and] a joint committee was appointed by the General Court to consider the petitions for a state appropriation of ten thousand dollars to protect the interests of the North and the rights of her citizens in Kansas, should they be again invaded by Southern marauders."[175] Emerson lost no opportunity to attend speeches and rallies against slavery and for the settlers in Kansas and sent liberal contributions to the cause. On September 10, 1856, Emerson stepped in to speak to the gathering in Concord, as Whitman, the main speaker, had been detained by the recent excitement in Kansas. Outraged by the long list of Unitarians who had been murdered in Kansas, Emerson mentioned each one's home congregation in the East. He said,

There is the peculiarity about the case of Kansas, that all the right is on one side. We hear the screams of hunted wives and children answered by the howl of the butchers. The testimony of the telegraphs from St. Louis and the border confirm the worst details. The printed letters of Border-Ruffians avow the facts. When pressed to look at the cause of the mischief in the Kansas laws, the President falters and declines the discussion. . . . But these details that have come from Kansas are so horrible, that the hostile press have but one word in reply, namely, that it is all exaggeration, 'tis an Abolition lie. Do the Committee of Investigation say that the outrages have been overstated? Does their dismal catalogue of private tragedies show it? Do the private letters? Is it an exaggeration, that Mr. Hopps of Somerville,

Mr. Hoyt of Deerfield, Mr. Jennison of Groton, Mr. Phillips of Berkshire, have been murdered? That Mr. Robinson of Fitchburg has been imprisoned? Rev. Mr. Nute of Springfield seized, and up to this time we have no tidings of his fate? ... In these calamities under which they suffer, and the worst which threaten them, the people of Kansas ask for bread, clothes, arms and men, to save them alive, and enable them to stand against these enemies of the human race. They have a right to be helped, for they have helped themselves. . . . I submit that, in a case like this, where citizens of Massachusetts, legal voters here, have emigrated to national territory under the sanction of every law, and are then set on by highwaymen, driven from their new homes, pillaged, and numbers of them killed and scalped, and the whole world knows that this is no accidental brawl, but a systematic war to the knife, and in defiance of all laws and liberties,—I submit that the governor and legislature should neither slumber nor sleep till they have found out how to send effectual aid and comfort to these poor farmers, or else should resign their seats to those who can.[176]

The next day Susan Lesley, wife of prominent American geologist J. Peter Lesley, attended a meeting in the company of her friend Lucretia Peabody Hale,[177] Edward Everett Hale's sister. She wrote to her husband about it on September 11, 1856:

Lucretia [Hale] came out to spend the night with me. . . . Lucretia, Chauncey and I were quietly taking tea when the Stearnses and Augusta King walked in and told us of the Kansas meeting. . . . We all proceeded in a body to the Hall. I got seated by Dr. Francis, when very soon Theodore Parker came in and sat next to me on the other side, was very cordial and made many inquiries after you. Emerson spoke very well, but was very sad; he evidently feels the wrongs of Kansas to the heart's core. Mr. [Moncure D.] Conway from Washington spoke very finely, and then Huntington in his deep voice made the earnest Chris-

161

tian appeal, and spoke mournfully of the dreadful apathy and indifference even here in the heart of New England. He closed with offering five hundred dollars from his own small salary to any man or body of men, who would go to Kansas, and take the body of Ephraim Nute, whether living or dead out of the hands of his persecutors. Lucretia was deeply moved. She had passed some hours with Nute just before he left for Kansas the last time, and said the last thing she heard him say, in his quiet, gentle tone, as if it were quite a matter of course, was, "I am ready to die for Kansas." Huntington's speech was very noble. He said that God had been trying to rouse us from our luxury, our apathy, our indifference, these many years. First, came the claims of our suffering black brothers and sisters at the South. We slept on.—But now our white brothers and sisters at the West are falling around us, and still we sleep. What will be the end? He and Mr. Emerson thought that no family, no individual, should rest easy, till they have made some great sacrifice for Kansas. We ought not to allow ourselves a single luxury, while there is such suffering there.[178]

Also on September 11, Theodore Parker wrote to a friend. The letter read,

Mr. Nute is in the hands of the ruffians. We fear he is hanged. The accounts are awful from Kansas. Five persons were shot after they had surrendered. Scalping is as common as with other savages. . . . We are now in a civil war. I went to a Kansas meeting at Cambridge last night. RWE was expected, but did not come till near nine; others wasting the time before in idle laughter and jokes. Yet good things were said. E was not happy, but said many good things, as always. He would send out the sergeant at arms to compel all Americans to return forthwith, lest by and by there be no country left for them. I know not what is before us, but augur evil,—evil, and then triumph.[179]

It was not until the end of October that the *Register* finally received the full story from Nute about what happened to him during his capture. Nute reported,

I propose to give an account of my captivity. I give some particulars that have not yet been made public. . . . We entered Leavenworth guarded by a small company of our captors, which we were assured by the captain of the gang, was not to keep us prisoners, but to afford us protection from those of their party who were more lawless than themselves. One of these men rode in the wagon with myself, another of our men and two of the ladies. In a free and quite friendly conversation, he informed me that he was from South Carolina, a physician, was heartily sick of the marauding service in which he had been engaged but a few days, and had got leave to retire; that he intended to return home forthwith. He seemed a young man of superior culture and good feeling, misled by the fiction of Southern chivalry, summoning him to the defence of the peculiar institution. From him and others of the company, I learned that their plan was to cut off all communication between Lawrence and the source of their supply of provisions, and so starve the "abolitionists," until they should be so reduced as to be an easy conquest. From what I afterward learned, I became satisfied that the young doctor gave a truthful account of himself, and of his associates. That afternoon he doffed the ruffian rig, and appeared in the attire of a well disposed citizen. A few days after, he took passage down the river, and I hope before this, has reached the home of his childhood, a wiser and better man, for his short experience in Kansas. . . . On entering the town, the tokens of a general reign of terror were apparent on every side. Most of the stores were closed. A large part of the men in the streets, (no woman or child was to be seen) were dressed in the red or blue shirt uniform of the "ruffians," with pistols and knife belted around the waist, and generally the addition of a musket or rifle on the shoulder. Some were riding too and fro in hot speed on horse-back; others gathered in groups before whiskey dens. Here and there one was to be seen in more civil attire, looking pale and anxious, a "free state man," or one of the more moderate and civilized of the other party. . . . We had been in the hotel but a few moments before we perceived that we were under the strictest surveillance. No free state man dared to be seen in conversation with any of our party; and several assured us of their sympathy and our peril in whispers as they passed us. . . . That afternoon I visited some of the stores on the levee, to make inquiries for the goods we had so long been expecting from the East. Here I found nearly every one professing to be on our side, and learned of the state of alarm in which the pro-slavery men had been kept for several days, by the expectation of an invasion from "Lane's army at Lawrence,"—the violence that had been committed on some of their number during the past few months; the plundering of teams that had started for Lawrence within a few days, laden with provisions and other merchandise; and during this conversation there enters a man with the story of the murder of the young German who had that morning ridden in with me. While we are hesitating to give credit to this new barbarity, there comes in others who witnessed the deed but a few moments before. . . . The reports of several such murders came to us in the course of the next fifteen minutes. The noble Phillips, since enrolled with the martyrs, stands by and remarks: "Our turn may come next, but I shall never be taken again alive." Some time before he had been seized, and after many brutal indignities, tarred and feathered. I was introduced to several others who had suffered for righteousness sake, some shot at, some knocked down with clubs, some cast into the river and warned to leave the territory on pain of death. I could fill many sheets with the well authenticated reports of outrages that were given me that afternoon, but it is needless. . . . Most of the particulars of my re-arrest on attempting to go abroad about next day have been narrated. It was a very peculiar scene. A large crowd was gathered on the levee evidently expecting something unusual. Those nearest the plank were unmistakeably of the ruffian stamp, armed and ferocious. As I came down, I observed an unusual and quite unnatural quiet and silence. No word was spoken by the man who seized me by the breast somewhat roughly as I set foot on the plank. He stood there as a sentinel with rifle and other weapons. On my remonstrating, he commanded "silence"; adding: "You won't be permitted to preach here, and if you attempt it, I'll put you where you won't preach anymore." He also informed me that the citizens of the town knew very well why I was detained, but refused to give me the reason, and ordered me back, to the hotel. It may give you some idea of the manners and spirit of the men into whose hands I had fallen, to have the reply of one of them to an inquiry which I made for the explanation of what I took to be a threat. With imprecations too bad to be written, he hissed through his teeth, "I'll have your scalp yet, though I follow you to blazing hell."[180]

Later in the installment published on November 15, Nute took up the activities in the camp:

Our bivouac for the first night was in and around the rude commencement of a log cabin on the open prairie, within a few rods of the spot where we were captured. A sleeping place was assigned me within the walls, formed by logs laid up in cob-house fashion, through which the openings were wide enough for a spare man to have crawled. The ground,—for floor there was none—was well covered with lodgers when I entered. Finding a vacant corner, I wrapped myself in a blanket, and with my fellow captive, laid down but not to sleep. A very instructive field was opened to our observation that night. The watch-fire was burning on the other side of the open barrier by which we lay, and but a few yards distant. Around this small groups were gathered nearly all the night, conversing on a variety of topics with the freedom of camp life. Among these the events of the war, and the plans and prospects of the future were most prominent. To all of this we were of course curious listeners, and but few words escaped us. We learned the full and horrible stories of murders, which the narrators pronounced barbarous, disgusting, and a disgrace to their cause. Speaking of one of the bands then encamped near them, among whom there had been a fight that day, resulting in the death of one of their number, it was remarked and assented to by several, that if they would keep on until they had all cut one another's throats, it would be a happy deliverance. But one of these men so earnest in virtuous indignation confessed that night to a murder which he had perpetrated within the last twenty-four hours, whose brutality was but a little removed from that of the worst that had been related. It was the killing of young Blimmerton, the German, who had ridden with me to Leavenworth. It came out that the man had formerly lived in Leavenworth, and being recognized by the captain as one who had formerly been counted on their side, he had been immediately released. . . . As he was about to walk off, a second thought occurred to some one, that he might return to Lawrence and report the state of affairs in their camp. He was ordered to stop, gave no heed, but started to run, when this valiant ruffian fired at him with a musket. Missing him, he took a rifle from the hands of a companion, and taking more deliberate aim shot him through the heart. This he said was not his first murder; he had killed several men in California. But none of his deeds had troubled him like this. The image of that man in the death-agony haunted him so that he could not sleep, and had driven him to seek refuge from himself in that circle of midnight watchers. This deed, as I have before narrated, was committed in one of the most public streets in Leavenworth and before many witnesses. Within a week that murderer was promoted to the rank of a major in one of the regiments of the territorial militia. . . . The inference is too plain to need any showing. Another fact concerning this man is instructive. In all that company no one surpassed him in civility to their prisoners. He came to me repeatedly with the warmest expression of kindness, observed my look of illness with apparent anxiety, offered me medicines and other conveniences, pressed upon me the use of his blanket for the night, and early next morning came to me with inquiries about my health and new offers of service. In close connection with these cruelties from others of that company, we were several times reminded, that "they prided themselves in the title of Border-Ruffians." . . . In the course of the talk around that campfire, we heard many expressions of strong dislike to the service in which they were engaged, and of very lively antipathies to the prospect of a pitched battle with the men of Lawrence. "Men who see their wives and their children in danger of starvation," men who have their homes and their all to depend, will fight with desperation, and then those men in Lawrence under Lane have been practicing with Sharpe's rifles for the last six months, and they'll pick us all off before we can get over the river. . . . "Some of those men saw their houses sacked, their press destroyed, and the hotel burned last May; and they'll think of these things when they are taking aim at the men who are storming their town." Another remarked, "I don't like the idea of fighting white men and Americans. I'll never go to make the attack on Lawrence. I'll start for old Kentuck first." . . . Another night we overheard one who had just returned from riding as picket guard with a member from another company, whom they held as disgracefully brutal. He said that his fellow-guard had related to him the killing of the three men who had been taken a few days before on the road to Lawrence, in which he had taken part. His language was, "Boys, it was worse than we heard it. It is too bad to tell."[181]

Nute's final installment, still in existence, was entitled "Another Day of Horrors in the Town of Leavenworth." It read,

Our personal adventures on being taken to Leavenworth the second time have already been related. What we learned while there from our own observation and from the testimony of those who had been there during the time of our absence, is no less significant. . . . We found the reign of ruffian violence and intimidation complete. The whole community was subjected and crushed. All business was suspended, and the larger part of the houses were deserted. More than one half of the people had fled for their lives, leaving all their possessions. Some had been driven on board boats, and compelled to go down the river. Others had taken refuge at the fort. The property in the houses and stores of those who had left was seized, taken off, or destroyed. In several instances the houses had been fired, and two were burned to the ground. The goods in the warehouses of the forwarding merchants, directed to people in Lawrence, was plundered and divided among the marauders. One firm lost over eight thousand dollars worth; another about fifteen hundred. Large companies who had come over from Missouri in filthy rags, were dressed out from head to foot with the clothing taken from our boxes. . . . Many had returned laden with the spoils, and others were continually arriving to get their share. In all of this there was not the slightest attempt at concealment. On every side men were displaying their new apparel, boasting of the fine texture of this garment and the good fit of that. Some of our captors made great show of generosity with their stolen goods, giving notice to new comers where they might supply themselves with a good pair of boots, or a complete suit of clothes. . . . These were not the worst of their villainies. All who refused to arm themselves, and join in the work, were ordered to leave the territory forthwith. Those who refused to go, were attacked with rifle and revolver. Some were fired upon in the streets; others were besieged in their houses, whither they had fled for safety and either murdered or forced to leave. The two brothers Phillips were in this way shot down, after being surrounded in their house. One was swiftly butchered, the other terribly wounded; from which I hear he is likely to recover with only the loss of an arm. After these brutal proceedings, all who remained were armed and enrolled to defend the town against the abolitionists!! . . . We overheard much talk among our enemies of the battle of Ossawotamie, the massacre of the abolitionists, and the burning of the town, which took place a few days before. Plans for the destruction of Lawrence, were also freely discussed. The usual conclusion of all such conferences was, "We mustn't stop until we have killed and driven out every abolitionist in the territory." . . . I conversed with several on the question at issue between the parties. These were, as you might suppose, of the more moderate and civil. The ground invariably taken was, that the attempt to deprive them of the right to hold slaves in the territory by any voting or legislation, was an invasion of their rights. For, was their logic, the constitution recognizes human beings, or rather "niggers," as property, and thus gives its sanction to the claim of the slaveholder. Every citizen of the United States has the right to go into any part of the Union and take his property with him, and all state laws which interfere with that privilege, are therefore unconstitutional. This right is now wrested from them in the Northern States; but the men of Missouri and other slave States, can maintain it in Kansas, and are determined to do so, if they have to wade through blood for it. . . . Such, I believe, is the position taken by those who are now banded together to force slavery, not only on Kansas, but into every foot of our national domain. How long will it be before this doctrine will be openly avowed by the whole party, and in the highest places of the land? . . . If it can be maintained here, and such atrocities perpetrated in its behalf, continued through weeks here, in the eyes of United States officials, and under the very guns of a fort, and no finger raised, how long will it be before this whole country will be as completely crushed down under the iron heel of this insatiable despotism, as is this town of Leavenworth? We await the answer. This persecuted and distressed people await in a fearful suspense, though not without hope, that the next passing breeze from the East may bring us the report, that this American people have arisen in the might of a righteous indignation and declared: It shall be so no more. The reign of this bloody tyranny is ended, the era of FREEDOM is begun.[182]

Nute provided other details of the jail later, in an article printed in the *Herald of Freedom*:

We were locked up with thirteen others in a foul dungeon—a place which deserved commemoration with the Bastille and the Black Hole of Calcutta. For the credit of the community by whom it was built, it should have a faithful description. Its walls are of stone, two feet thick, inclosing a space 10 feet by 15 and about 10 feet high. The door is of solid iron. The light and ventilation furnished by 4 apertures near the top, 5 inches by 18, in which are set iron bars so as to fill up about three quarters of the space. The stone floor was covered with rubbish and offal of the filthiest kind.—The foulness of the air in such a place during one of the most sultry of dog days may be conceived of without further description. On inquiry, we found that most of our fellow-prisoners had been taken the day before, from their homes near town, without any charge or pretext. Several were arrested on their way from different parts of the Territory, intending to go down the river.[183]

Sara Robinson's diaries explored the events from her particular perspective as the wife of the Free-State governor. She described how her husband was finally released from captivity by the proslavers, but Nute and his young parishioner, John Wilder, were not found among them:

When the fourteen prisoners at Lecompton were released, Rev. Mr. Nute, and Mr. Wilder, about whom great anxiety had been felt, were discovered not to be among them. Col. Cook provided Mr. Whitman, Mr. Sutherland, and Mr. Wilder, father of young Wilder, an escort, in Sergeant Cary, to go to Leavenworth to attempt their release, if they were there. Within a short distance of the town, after passing several picket guards, they were taken prisoners by Capt. Emory's band. After a little consultation, the leaders concluded it was advisable to release Sergeant Cary. Riding post-haste, he reached the fort and stated the facts. Soon there was a bustle among the soldiers, and two hundred of them marched to Leavenworth. Two hours later, they returned, bringing in Capt. Emory's band of thirty horsemen, with the three gentlemen last taken prisoners in the rear. . . . Mr. Nute and Mr. Wilder had been released that morning. They had been, for a part of the time, imprisoned in a seven-by-nine stone building with grated windows. There was not an article of furniture in the room. . . . In such a place, without ventilation, with thirteen others, they were kept one day, without anything to eat from early morning until five o'clock, p.m. Then, some dry bread and coffee were brought in. The prisoners said they could not eat without going into the fresh air; and, on being taken out doors, were scarcely able to stand from faintness. . . . Rev. Mr. Nute and friends reached Lawrence on the evening of the 10th. . . . The prisoner was admitted to bail in the sum of five hundred dollars. . . . The other cases were then called,—"The United States against Charles Robinson and others,"—and continued. The prisoners were released on bail of five thousand dollars each. . . . Judge Lecompte accepted the bail offered, and seemed anxious to get the cases off his hands. . . . John Brown, Jr., and H. H. Williams, who had never been indicted, were also released on one thousand dollars bail. . . . On the afternoon of the 10th September, just four months from the day my husband was taken prisoner, and nearly four months since the arrest of the others, the tents on "Traitor Avenue" were struck. Three wagons were filled with the furniture and valuables of the prisoners. . . . With two carriages of gentlemen, which came from Lawrence in the morning to attend the court, the ambulance, and two others under military escort, we left for Lawrence. Within a mile of the town, the "Stubs" [the free state militia] were waiting to welcome us. Soon after, we were met by Gen. Lane and his staff, who led the way into Massachusetts-street, where crowd of people had gathered to greet their long-absent townsmen. . . . My husband made them a short speech. In the evening the people had a jubilee of rejoicing, and short speeches from several of the prisoners. The arrival of Mr. Nute and fellow-prisoners, the same evening, added not a little to the enthusiasm of the hour.[184]

The 1893 story in the Lawrence paper about Nute and his church bell recalled the joy the bell had brought to Nute as one of the returning prisoners. It read,

In that month Mr. Nute and Mr. John Wilder, had been imprisoned by the pro-slavery men under Capt. Fred Emery. Mr. E. B. Whitman went to Leavenworth to secure their release. As the party were fording the Kansas river late in the evening, they heard for the first time the welcome sound of the bell. Governor Robinson and others who had been confined at Lecompton had been released and returned to Lawrence, and the "boys" in their enthusiasm had improvised a mounting for the bell, of two dry goods boxes, and were "ringing out the old" and "ringing in the new," for times had taken a turn for the better and the Kansas troubles were virtually at an end.[185]

In September, Nute had been out of prison for some time before news of his release reached the East. However, Nute's high-ranking Harvard fan club sent a letter to Governor William White Geary, the latest of the Kansas revolving-door governors, asking for his intercession on behalf of Nute. Whether Geary did anything is doubtful, but when the governor replied to the Harvard men, Nute was already free. Geary's response read,

Executive Department, . . . Lecompton, KT, Sept. 23, 1856, . . .
REV. HENRY A. MILES, Sec. Amer. Unitarian Association:— . . .
Sir,—I have received your esteemed favor of the 10th inst.,
informing me of the 'arrest of Rev. Ephraim Nute, Jr. of Law-
rence, Kansas Territory, by some persons who have carried
him into Missouri.' . . . In reply, I have the pleasure to state that
I met the gentleman in question on the 9th of this month, at
Fort Leavenworth, in the enjoyment of his health and liberty.
. . . Very truly, your obedient servant, . . . JNO. W. GEARY, . . .
Governor of Kansas Territory.[186]

The Unitarian *Quarterly Journal* stood behind its man and
waxed eloquent with relief at his release. It printed his next letter
to them, a recount of his captivity in which for the first time Nute
addressed the psychological toll the war in Kansas had taken on his
parishioners, no less on himself. Not only had they been diverted
from the survival tasks of building town and church, but a violent
vengefulness had taken hold of them. He thanked the East for the
profound healing of their expressions of support and prayers and
let them know that those expressions were all that was keeping the
Kansans from the abyss. Nute wrote,

The most serious evil of the melancholy condition of affairs in
our Territory for the last eight months, I have not yet touched
upon. This, to my mind, has been the influence of the spirit
of war, and the feelings awakened by the depredations, murders, and outrages of every kind that have been inflicted on
this people. That these have been adverse and powerful against
the prosperity of our religious institutions, no one can need
be told. While our homes were being destroyed, our neighbors and nearest friends murdered, and all of us threatened
with death by bands of men who had invaded our Territory,
and were besieging our towns with the bearing of infuriated
savages, our people could have but little heart for organizing
churches and Sunday schools, and but little time or interest to

give to the services of God's house. Nor was that the worst. It would have been strange if the spirit of our holy religion had not suffered, the spirit of meekness, of forgiveness, and love to all men giving way to a burning indignation rising beyond what is righteous into bitter resentment and thirst for revenge. Tried in such a fiery furnace, it was natural that some of the refinements and gentle charities of civilization should suffer damage. The manners of our community became for the time like those of the camp. Men living together in crowded quarters, with the rudest and most scanty accommodations, without the influences of domestic life, handling the weapons of war, preparing for deadly contest with murderous enemies, and the greater part of the number from time to time engaged in such conflicts,—bringing back the wounded, and sometimes the mangled remains of those who had fallen in the fight,—in such circumstances could we expect men to maintain their highest tone of Christian sentiment, to escape altogether unperverted by these barbarizing influences, to be peculiarly susceptible to Christian impressions? I should be surprised that so little injury has resulted to the morals of our people, if I did not take into account the righteousness, the moral grandeur, of the cause for which we have been made to do and suffer these things. In view of this, we may hope that all our experiences will yet work the peaceable fruits of righteousness, affording the discipline through which we shall be trained up into an eminently Christian community.[187]

On September 4 Theodore Parker wrote to a friend about Nute and the work in Kansas. Heavily involved in the plans of the co-conspirators backing John Brown, in this letter Parker relayed the information that Higginson, another of the conspirators and a seminary classmate of Nute, had gone to Kansas:

Congress passed the Army bill without the proviso: so the President can use his money to push slavery in at the point of the bayonet. There is continual fighting in Kansas. You remember Rev. Mr. Nute from Kansas. His brother-in-law, Mr. Hipps, came from Leavenworth to Lawrence, staid a day or two at Nute's, left his sick wife, and started for home without weapons. A ruffian shot him dead, scalped him, and then exhibited the scalp in Leavenworth, and said, "I went out for the scalp of a d—d abolitionist, and I have got one." Of course, the government likes this; "The Post" likes it; and the respectability of Boston must say, "Served him right!" You will hear of yet bloodier work in Kansas. Higginson has gone there. But for your visit to Europe I should have spent my vacation in Kansas. Next summer will probably find me there.[188]

Clinton C. Hutchinson, a founding member of Nute's congregation in Lawrence, wrote a firsthand account of Lawrence in a state of siege in the fall of 1856. Everywhere around the town men were dying, men known and loved as family members and friends. Governor Shannon was preparing to flee the territory, as the proslavery Border Ruffians had turned on him, too. Hutchinson wrote,

> We found the road to Lawrence blockaded, and, disguising my companion, who would not meet with good usage in their hands, we engaged a team to take us around through Topeka, making a journey of 100 miles to get 30. . . . The Border-Ruffians were taking advantage of the lull in affairs, to erect forts and concentrate provisions and munitions of war. Our men saw how things were going, and nipped it in the bud. They would have taken Lecompton, had not there been U.S. troops there. All the forces in the territory are now concentrated there, and it is thought that they will not interfere between the warlike parties, but stay there to protect the Government. Shannon . . . is now deposed, and the dotard is begging for an escort of troops to guard him out of the Territory.—He wishes to be saved from his former friends. . . . In this town is a company of

fighting men, well officered, and all under Gen. Lane, a terror to the Missourians as well he may be. . . . Several thousand dollars in funds from the East has come, and is being disbursed as most needed. Our men are healthy and in good spirits. A large and excellent fort is being made of the stones which composed the walls of the free state Hotel. The whole Territory is awakening, and we can rally three thousand fighting men of the right stamp, and if we had arms many more. . . . A Council of War was held last night, and to-day a party of sixty or seventy of our mounted men went back to Leavenworth, accompanied by six wagons, to draw flour, as we are about out of that article. . . . But . . . you must not infer that we are entirely safe. Our enemy have already gathered to the amount of between one and two thousand, and are using every means to bring all Missouri against us. . . . Had it not been for the help rendered by the North since the sacking of Lawrence our people would now be entirely at the mercy of the foe. Our men must be supported, and Kansas must be free, but the North must continue in the good work, or we fail.[189]

Concurrent with Nute's troubles surrounding the Hopps murder were the movements of John Brown's army in the Kansas Territory. Brown and his army were well outfitted with Sharps repeating rifles, far superior to the Ruffians' arms brought from the South. The *Daily Democrat* reported,

Old Ossawatomie Brown is maintaining his ground south of Kaw river. His force consists of about two hundred men. It is reported that he has had an engagement with the invading forces, as they have entered that portion of the territory. News was received at Westport, that in the collision between Brown's men and the pro-slavery party, some eighty of the latter, out of a company of three hundred were killed and wounded. . . . Brown's loss is stated as much less. Capt. Wilke's Company of fifty Carolinians arrived at Leavenworth a day or two since. . . .

They 'pressed' a sufficient number of horses in the neighborhood to mount themselves. . . . The pro-slavery force, consisting of Georgians, Carolinians, and other late emigrants from the south, are encamped some eight or ten miles from this city, in the interior. Some 800 of Lane's men are between this and Lawrence.[190]

Theodore Parker wrote to Nute during Nute's capture and incarceration, but attempts to find a copy of that letter have been unsuccessful. On September 14, after his release, Nute wrote back to Parker. Parker then read Nute's letter aloud in Faneuil Hall to rouse his own followers against slavery. Nute was recovering from his ordeal and "means to be heard from." In his letter, Nute mentioned that "Theological differences have kept us apart & I feel shame for it," but did not say what those differences were. They likely stemmed from Parker's "heresies" that led to his estrangement from the Unitarian denomination and the pulpits of Boston —except his own—or perhaps from his support of John Brown's violence. Nute's letter read,

Never did a word of good cheer come to a mortal man more opportunely and with warmer welcome than that contained in your note of the 3d. I had just escaped from the hands of my enemies, the enemies of Government and Freedom, with whom I had suffered a fortnight of the most harassing captivity. . . . I fled first to Fort Leavenworth and claimed protection from the officials there, both civil and military, and was in both instances denied. The officer of the day at the fort, Lieut Drum, referred to by Reeder in his speech at the NY Tabernacle, told me he could give us no harbor, and ordered me with hundreds of others with women and children who had sought refuge at the fort to leave the Government preserve before 5 o'clock of the next day. Some of these refugees had fled from blazing homes—women and children having husbands and fathers weltering in their blood—their homes and their all perished in the flames. Still this officer said there was no alternative; he must compel all to submit to the inhuman order which had been issued and repeated by Gen Smith. . . . Gov. Geary told me that I must submit to the banditti who had me then in their power, and whose captain then stood before us though they demanded me to be hung (I was then a prisoner on parole) because that banditti was the regularly constituted militia of the territory and all those murders and house burnings and outrages of every kind had been committed by the authority of the creature then acting as Governor of the Territory, and that until he, Geary, could get to Woodson and supercede him, that authority would be valid and paramount. . . . I then mounted a Government horse, and rode amuck through the enemies going around 50 miles by unfrequented ways, and reached Lawrence that night, last Wednesday the 10th. . . . I find myself nearly broken down in health but am fast recruiting and mean to be heard from, as far and wide as I can, soon. For the greater part of the time I have been forced to sleep on the bare ground without wholesome or regular food, sometimes in a close, crowded, filthy dungeon into which I was thrown when so sick that I could hardly stand. Three times I have had every reason to suppose that my last hour had come both from the intimations of enemies and the warnings of friends. Once I was saved only by a quarrel and a scuffle in which the weapon with which I was to be shot was wrested from the hands of one infuriated ruffian but enough. I am yet alive and more alive than ever before, and with a keen sense of the value of Freedom, for whose cause I do count all persecutions as an unspeakable gain, and myself truly blessed in being permitted to endure them. I assure you the confidence that this cause is of the Almighty has sustained me through it all and my heart has not for a moment failed me. . . . I am not indifferent to the commendation and God speed of good and brave men. I have often thought of you and the little band of brethren in Massachusetts, alas that it is so small, who have been here to bear this witness against the iniquities of the times, when so to speak brought on you a greater obloquy than it ever can again. ... Theological differences have kept us apart, and I feel shame for it—The Gospel of Humanity of Freedom is the Gospel for which our fellow men are perishing today. With all who serve that in word or deed, I must have common lot and be one. Yours is the first word that I have received from one of the brethren since I left the East, though I have written at least 20 letters to different ones. Until I got yours, I supposed that all my letters must have been waylaid, and others to me have been intercepted. ... I do get the Boston Post regularly. My father is a custom House, pro-slavery democrat and sends it. ... It is well to know what the Devil is up to. I feel just as you do about any abuse from that quarter. I should rejoice in it, and as soon think of being angry with the driveling of one of Pierce's drunken imbeciles here in Kansas. ... What I learned of the plans and brutal works of the ruffians while in their hands, will be worth much to the cause—by night lying awake while they sat around the camp fires and stood guard and thought the ears of their prisoners were dulled in sleep. They are a pack of mean, sneaking cowards. One hundred of our men with Lane at their head, or with the report that he was there, would have driven a thousand of them howling into the Missouri. I have the confession of several of them to the most brutal and cowardly butcheries. ... A young man who rode with me, was shot dead in the most public street in Leavenworth a few hours after we were taken, and the body lay there for the rest of the day. Another noble hearted man Phillips was hunted like a wolf, and beset at last in his house when he fell pierced by a dozen balls, fighting to the last—another his brother was shot down, and terribly mutilated, and is probably dead before this. The mangled bodies of many have been found between this and Leavenworth during the last two weeks, and buried by the dragoons who went at the call of the Indians to afford them the protection which they have not been permitted to give us.

. . . It is estimated that over 60 families have been burned out of home, many of them losing their all—in some instances all the males of the family butchered. I found my wife had been suffering the bitterest anguish during the whole time of my absence, hearing no definite word from me, in hourly expectation of an attack on the cabin, for several were within 3 miles of her. At one time she had all our effects hid in a ravine, and fled to a neighbor, but returned after a few days, thinking a woman's presence might be some protection to the house. . . . I hoped to have had a comfortable shelter for the winter but here we are in much worse plight than we were last fall, my house having been sacked of every article of warm clothing or bedding, and the structure more rickety than ever before because of my having torn away to make preparations to build. Now I have spent my salary three times over since I first started on this Kansas mission, spent all that I had or could raise—less than $200—to be prepared for a Winter anything like the last, I must borrow or beg. . . . But what is my case to that of hundreds of others who have lost their all. Aid must be raised for them, or there will be sore distress. There are men who have been in arms away from their homes in the hardest service for 3 or 4 weeks, repelling those who have been threatening us with utter extermination. . . . Some of these return and find in the place of their homes but a heap of ashes and their families racked with terror living on the charity of neighbors. . . . Here, at 5 PM I am interrupted by an express rider bringing the report that 100 of the enemy are on the march toward Lawrence and already within 5 miles of the town. to arms! to arms! . . . Lane and 200 of our men are away to the west. No United States troops nearer than Lecompton 12 miles. We are likely to have horrible doings before tomorrow morning. I will try to add a PS in the morning. . . . Yours as ever . . . E. Nute. . . . The force at Franklin 5 miles from Lawrence is at least 2500—400 tents have been counted—and there are others hidden in the timber. . . . Postscript. Monday Morn Sept 15 a little after sunrise. We have had a night of alarms. The enemy came within half a mile of town with their skirmishing parties, and were repulsed by our skirmishers, with loss of several men, none killed on our side. The main body numbering between 2 & 3 thousand are posted about 2 miles from us. The principal part of our forces are away to engage a force of the enemy several hundred strong to the North and West. A messenger was dispatched to the governor for U.S. troops, they arrived here about midnight—400 dragoons and are now stationed at several fronts around the town. Just now I hear the sound of firing —a dozen rifle shots, now skirmishing—our company of dragoons moving towards the enemy. 3 hours later. The enemy retreat—*I see the governor's carriage entering town*—the smoke of burning cabins is rising from several points in the direction of the enemy. The men who were at work for me have just returned from town where they spent the night on guard. One of them was stationed with a squad of about 20 in the walls of our church which have been awaiting the roof for some weeks, all the night. Those marauders should be driven howling over the border before the sun sets. I'm off to town. . . . Monday night. 150 of our men taken prisoners by United States forces at the West. Two companies of dragoons to be permanently stationed at Lawrence. But the telegraph will give you intelligence to later date.[191]

On September 19 Theodore Parker wrote to a friend that Nute had been released, but Parker knew nothing more of Nute's fate. In his letter, his deep involvement in the running of guns is evident. Parker wrote,

Things look better in Kansas. The ruffians have been worsted in some fights. Lawrence is well fortified now; has a fort that will hold a thousand men. Dr. Howe and others raised five thousand dollars one day last week to buy Sharpe's rifles. We want a thousand rifles, and got two hundred in one day. Nute is now at large; but the particulars I know not. . . . Geary's inaugural speech is just telegraphed to us. He demands obedience to the Territorial legislature till its laws are repealed (repudiation by the people is no repeal of the Border-Ruffian "laws," I suppose); but promises to protect all, without respect of party, and calls on armed bands to disperse, or quit the Territory. He has dignified with the title of "militia" the companies of Southern marauders whom Shannon had furnished with arms, banners, protection, and whiskey, and set to scalp the peaceful inhabitants of Kansas. Things look much better for Kansas. The Emigrant Aid Society has forever prevented it from becoming a slave State; for, if this company had not been at work the Missourians and others would have flocked in, and made its institutions to suit the South. Now I have no fears for its future.[192]

Parker regularly read from Nute's letters during his services, finding in Nute's long and descriptive narratives exactly the tone and content to stir his audiences. From the impact of these letters, Parker was able to garner monetary support from his listeners for the Kansas church. Other ministers in the East did the same. Parker wrote in his journal on September 21,

Yesterday I omitted the chapter of St. James as morning lesson and introductory to a sermon on Franklin, and instead, read from a new epistle of St. Ephraim [Nute] written a fortnight before in Kansas, and telling of his captivity and cruel treatment. There was an immense audience, seats all full, and men leaning against the wall. Dr. Bowditch came and suggested that contribution should be taken up at the door. I mention it; and now three hundred dollars are in my drawer for Mr. Nute and his fellow-apostles. It was not ten cents apiece for the audience, but a pretty sum for him and them.[193]

And many of these "pretty sums" were needed to sustain the

settlers and build up the Unitarian church against the destructive attacks of the proslavers. Records reveal that a substantial amount of money flowed from the East to Kansas. If the settlers and the church still struggled, where was all that money going? The media on both sides rightly begged that question—but scandal mongers among proslavery journalists ended up catching many innocents in their spurious dragnet. Their attempts to cripple Free-State fund-raising almost succeeded, and Nute soon found himself in the line of fire.

SCANDAL, MISSING FUNDS
AND A SHAM ELECTION

Although campaigning strongly on the side of pacifism, Nute always had the reputation of acting boldly and decisively in the face of danger, without undue fear of the high offices of government. His independence was alternately praised as courageous and criticized as blunt or impolitic. On the front lines, however, he had the admiration of his chroniclers. He was an unswerving man of action, even in the worst of times.

John Gihon, Kansas Governor John White Geary's secretary, wrote in his 1857 history of Kansas an anecdote about Nute's recovery of the horses stolen from him in the aftermath of his brother-in-law's murder:

> Soon after the troops left the fort to arrest Emory, a scene occurred there strongly illustrative of the times. Rev. E. Nute, a Unitarian clergyman, had several times been arrested and imprisoned on the grave charge of being an abolitionist. He had also been robbed, almost starved, and otherwise cruelly abused, and had just made his escape from his persecutors and fled for safety to the fort. Whilst relating his adventures to an admiring company of his associates and friends, who like himself were refugees from oppression, he espied a wagon passing along the road towards Leavenworth, drawn by two horses, and containing beside the driver, two women and a good supply of household furniture and other moveables. The

reverend gentleman immediately recognized the horses as a favorite pair that had been pressed from him when last taken prisoner. Without waiting for a legal process, he summoned to his assistance a half-dozen friends, and demanded the driver of the wagon to halt. He then deliberately unhitched the horses and drove them away in triumph, amid the congratulations and shouts of the bystanders, leaving the driver and his female companions in their wagon in the middle of the road in mute state of consternation. Chief Justice Lecompte and associate justice Cato, would have pronounced this act unlawful and unwarrantable, and all the judge and lawyers in the land would have agreed in the decision. Mr. Nute should have appealed to a court, or some judicial functionary—made affidavit in regard to his stolen horses—obtained a warrant for the arrest of the thief and the restoration of his property—placed it in the hands of the marshal or sheriff, and waited patiently for its executions. Such would have been the process in ordinary communities, where the laws are made for the protection of the people—where courts are occasionally held—where judges deal out even-handed justice—and where officers of the law can be induced to execute writs against culprits of their own political faith. But such was not the condition of things in Kansas. There the balance of legal justice had but one scale, and Mr. Nute occupied the opposite side of the beam. Had he asked the courts or the judges, the marshals or the sheriffs, for the restoration of his horses, he might have been regarded as a madman, or at least been ridiculed for his presumption. And had he waited until they reached Leavenworth city to recover them, he could only have made the attempt at the hazard if not the sacrifice of his life.[194]

This Nute was a far cry from the pious young man who ped-dled books door-to-door for the AUA in Massachusetts, and who rhapsodized about the promise liberal Christianity held for the Kansas Territory—as if it would win over by love and reason the

Border Ruffians who were already doing their dirty work when Nute landed in Kansas in the spring of 1855. It is a different Nute than the man who criss-crossed the country to raise money in New England with alarming reports on the woes of Kansas, and then took that money back to Kansas, somehow avoiding during his travels the dangers his notoriety had put him in. This Nute was the man of action, who even in the grips of life-threatening terror refused to be defeated. He thought on his feet and grabbed whatever opportunity he could to balance the terror with justice and safety, however small that justice or short-lived that safety.

And this Nute would change again. He would soon stand at the heart of scandal, struggling to live without funds he needed to make a success of his Kansas project, while being accused of nefarious use of those funds. His trials would bring him to a crisis of faith in his denomination, and forever change his path towards the future.

News and correspondence were generally slow to reach the East from Kansas. The proslavers were waiting at every turn to abscond with the mail and prevent eyewitness accounts from getting through. The federal post was hung up by rivers, livestock, drought, and the other challenges of prairie pioneer life. Nute undertook a frenzy of writing of his capture to friends in the East, both to spread the word of the outrage and to try to correct some of the inaccuracies in the stories that found their way back to Kansas.

Nute's October 1 letter got through to Daniel H. Haskell, the editor of the *Boston Transcript*, "one of the first of the Boston papers to realize, in the [eighteen] fifties, that a grave crisis in the country's affairs impended," according to one historian of the paper.[195] Letters from anyone in the territory were a precious commodity to those back home trying to get the latest news on the conflagration there, but letters from Pastor Nute directed to the editor were printed in full and often contained details that didn't appear in other reports. Nute closed his letter to Haskell with the following note: "One more correction I must add, which to me is by far the most important. It is not my purpose or wish to leave Kansas for the East."[196]

This was the second time that Nute denied to a correspondent that he wanted to leave Kansas for the East. Many in the East were calling for those in danger in Kansas to come home. At the same time, if proslavers knew that prominent abolitionists like Nute were getting ready to travel, they would be on high alert to capture them. Nute's denial that he was leaving the territory may have been an attempt, at least in part, to derail any efforts to take him prisoner again.

Joseph Henry Allen, Nute's Harvard classmate, was the pastor at the Unitarian church in Bangor, Maine. Nute had gone to Allen's congregation while on his fund-raising tours of New England. Nute managed to get an October 2 letter to Allen, in which he told Allen more details of his capture. He wrote,

A word of good cheer is worth something here, coming from the far away old congenial brotherhood. Yours of Sept. 7 reached me only two days since, and made my heart feel stronger. I wanted to answer without the delay of a single mail, but that was out of the question. Our Mail arrives every other night, and leaves very early next morning, and we live two miles from the Post Office. I fear now it will be too late for my word to reach "the brethren" in convention at your place. But I am glad to believe that they need no stirring up on Kansas matters. In this death struggle of Slavery I am sure their interest will not be permitted to wane. A man must be dead beyond the hope of any resurrection in this life, who professing to preach the Gospel, in these times, feels no glow of righteous indignation against the deep working systematic iniquity by which the sons of Belial are seeking to secure and extend the reign of Tyranny. You cannot need any more stories of the butcheries and other outrages in these parts to make you alive to the diabolical spirit of the peculiar institution, or inlist your sympathies for the suffering people of Kansas; or I could give you a new batch of whose truth I have the most trustworthy evidence. Almost every hour of the day for the last three or four weeks has brought some new instance to my knowledge. . . . Yesterday I heard of three murders for the first time and learned the horrible particulars. One from the widow of the murdered man who was in her house while for an hour her husband was being pursued round it and through the corn-fields vainly endeavoring to escape from a large gang who were firing upon him at every opportunity, while he true to the charge of protection to his family still circled close to his home until he fell and perished pierced by a dozen balls. Two were men taken out of the mail stage between this and Kansas city and hung, & c. . . . The first procedure after our capture was a general search for our weapons. My carriage was nearly the last in the train after we turned back at the bidding of our captors. I had an excellent "Sharpes" under my feet, but no carnal weapons about my person. I jumped out when the search commenced at the first carriage, and went forward. Have you any weapons about you? I said nothing but threw open my coat. Of course, replied a young Kentuckian, and a man of some culture, and quite gentlemanly deportment, "we don't find a minister going armed," others standing around echoed the magnanimous Christian sentiment, some adding "we would like to get hold of one of the Sharpe's Bible minister—we'd like a chance to hang rifle Beecher and some others of that kind." I improved the first opportunity to get that shooter out of my wagon, and into the hands of one through whom it went into the keeping of a good Free Soiler from Kentucky. Several circumstances which appeared like so many interpositions of Providence enabled me to do this, though in less than an hour from that time I and those in that wagon were transferred to other conveyances, and wagon, horses and all driven off to the head quarters of the division of Woodson's militia, situation a few miles from Leavenworth. The time has not come for telling how this was done. . . . Before this reaches you, we may all be fleeing for our lives, leaving our homes in ashes. Lawrence is certainly doomed to destruction. This has been my settled conviction for the last month with hardly a hope to the contrary, and yet I must go on with my house-building, for it may be a siege of Winter instead of an attack from Missourians that we must be prepared for. Do contradict the report that I am coming East, for it will cut us off from all letters and remittances, as we suppose it has for the last two weeks, and what we are to do, unless we get help from the East I do not know.[197]

In the last two lines of this letter, Nute revealed the main reason he was so adamant to state that he was not leaving Kansas—he was assuring the East that he was not abandoning Kansas, nor should they. He feared that if they believed otherwise, they would stop sending letters and funds for the people in Lawrence. Then, the settlers would starve.

Nute wrote to Edward Everett Hale on October 13. The horrors of August and September had faded into helpless acceptance. He focused instead on the disbursement of donated goods and the plight of the settlers as the winter weather approached. He wrote,

Many suffer of undoubted & extreme distress here come to my knowledge & I hastened to respond to some of them in anticipation of the rect of the funds which you and others have placed at my disposal. Let me give the account of several that I have provided for this morning—1st comes a man whose crop of oats were taken for public service to feed the free state horses. He has worked hard since . . . to get some land ready for a wheat crop & . . . to pay for the seed & get some things necessary for his family—I gave him an order on one of our merchants who agreed to advance for the wheat & he went his way. Next comes No 2 a young man with one foot frozen off . . . the poor man for eight weeks unable to do any work & unable to get home to his father in Nebraska. I gave about ten dollars in provisions to the man who has been giving him a home & shall consider further about helping him on his way home. It will cost $20. I have offered to provide one half of the amt if others will make up the balance. No 3. A family of three persons all of whom have been down with "the shakes" more or less for the last three months in want of flour . . . & medicines, to them a sack of flour & about 8 dollars in other articles. These last were former parishioners of Dr. Ware of Cambridge[198] who has written me about them & Mr. Henry Learned. . . . No. 4 A Methodist preacher with a wife & 4 children living in a little sod cabin without any floor, some of the family shaking all of the time, out of flour, went to sow three bushels of oats, no boots or shoes to his feet, children scantily clad, no sugar or molasses & diverse other articles wanted wishes he could get boards enough for a floor & I have given him in all about $20 having known him by reputation for more than a year. . . . There are many others to whom I must give but in smaller sums—as the cold weather comes in there will be cases here without some help there will be great suffering —& yet the prospects for the settlers for the next year are good. Some of the most needy at this time have from 10 to 40 acres of wheat sown & crops of several hundred bushels of corn to be harvested. Of course there are others who are stripped of everything they possessed by the marauders. If we are let alone for a year we shall be able to repay the benefits we are now receiving by assistance to the immense immigration which we confidently expect will pour into the territory should Fremont be elected.[199]

Someone other than Nute wrote his name at the bottom of the page, and here the letter ends in the collection of the New England Emigrant Aid Company Papers at the Kansas State Historical Society. Another two pages of a letter in that collection, labeled "Undated to Unknown Person," are filed under undated correspondence but are undoubtedly the end of the preceding letter:

Now I would like to go down to Bangor tomorrow. Methinks the fires of Freedom will flame up there somewhat. I received a long letter from Allen a few days since requesting one from me that he could read to the convention. I acceded with all possible dispatch hope it will reach him in time for an infliction on the brethren. . . . Write me as often as you can. I assure you it is a great treat for me to get now a line from you in these trying times. It is the great compensation for the trials & deprivation of this Kansas life that it seems to have given us a deeper hold on the sympathies of those whose friendship I most desire & whose approval I most value among men. In Massachusetts we might have lived without exchanging a word for a year & never have felt each other's heart-throbs as now. I have never experienced the feeling of loneliness in this wilderness & for the greater part of the time have lived in the fullest enjoyment of the society of souls that I have ever known. These common perils & fellowship of noble purposes in the struggle for Freedom makes us feel very near to one another here, & add, to our community, some of the noblest & strongest of spirit of the ages, yes and of every age. The images of heroic men & women of whom I have read rise to mind in these circumstances every day & with peculiar distinctness. God makes & keeps us worthy of such society.[200]

That this passage was the end of Nute's October 13 letter to Hale is borne out by the first statement: "Now I would like to go down to Bangor tomorrow." On October 14 a Unitarian convention was held in Bangor, Maine. Nute told Hale in his letter that Allen (the Bangor Unitarian minister) had requested a letter of him to read at the conference, which he sent in all due haste. In fact, that letter did reach Allen in time and, according to the *Christian Register*, was read out at the conference:

The REV. MR. ALLEN, of Bangor, wished to say to the Convention that he had received a letter from Rev. Mr. Nute, of

Kansas, addressed to the brethren, and with their permission he would now read it. This was granted. . . . The reading of the above letter was listened to with breathless interest.[201]

When Nute wrote to Miles again on October 27, his letter contained the first indications that his relationship with E. B. Whitman was beginning to break down. The building of the church had come to a standstill as a result of Whitman's long absence. Nute wrote,

No letter yet from Whitman, I am tired of repeating this item. The timbers of the church roof are about on & all goes on well. I go hoping to find letters by the mail which reaches us this evening. The young men prisoners at Lecompton are having their trial. No arrests of the other party that we hear of. The peace state continues. God grant it may not be broken but we have fearful apprehensions which will be augmented if Buchanan is elected.[202]

The city of Lawrence was not to be kept down. The people had weathered each of the Border Ruffian invasions and protested mightily to the rest of the country. Their newspaper, the Lawrence *Herald of Freedom*, declared that what had been happening to them was outside the pale, unacceptable, outrageous, beyond redemption:

Monument to Border-Ruffians . . . We have erected the heavy iron frames of the two hand presses belonging to the *Herald of Freedom* office, on pieces of New England granite, of which our imposing stone was made, and which was broken by Border-Ruffians, in front of our new office, in scribing on one side of the largest, "Destroyed by Border-Ruffians, May 21st, 1856." On the opposite side, "Revived Nov. 1st, 1856." These presses shall remain as lasting monuments of the infamy of Border-Ruffianism. The day will come when those who were afraid of the truth, and who sought to smother it, would willingly give all their earthly possessions to erase that dark crime from their memory, but the "d—d spot" won't "out." . . . The friends of Freedom visiting this Territory, are expected to look upon the ruins of that press, ere they return East. If they do so, they will have ocular demonstration that the advocates of slavery were in the wrong, and dared not tolerate a free and untrammeled press. By subscribing for the *Herald of Freedom*, they will have weekly proof that the press in Kansas is not yet enslaved![203]

Nute wrote to Miles on November 4, answering a previous letter from Miles that called Nute on the carpet for his not-so-subtle complaints about Whitman. Nute had developed a reputation for brutal honesty, calling things as he saw them with no apologies and none of the romantic evasions of speech that were the norm of courtesy in his age. Some applauded him in this, for he refused to dignify that which deserved no dignity. Others found him crass and harsh and pulled away from him. This was the first time Nute's direct tone surfaced in his letters to the AUA, but his tendency for blunt speech grew with the mounting violence of the Kansas experience. Modern counselors would recognize symptoms of post-traumatic stress. Gone were the superfluities of polite conversation; the raw realities of terror and violence held him in their grip, without relief or escape.

But Nute was no fool. He knew he had to step gently around Miles, for not only was his own salary—meager and sporadic as it was—coming from the AUA, but funds for his community, church, and parishioners often funneled through the organization as well. And certainly, the media picked up much of the Kansas story from the Unitarian newspapers. It is clear that Miles had little understanding or sympathy for the extreme life-threatening trauma that Nute and the Unitarians of Lawrence were undergoing. Nute denied his "quarrelsome" attitude toward Whitman, probably in an attempt to avoid making things worse for himself and the Lawrence colony. But his annoyance with Whitman became impossible to dismiss as time passed. In a November 4 letter to Miles, Nute said,

> Two letters reached me by the last mail at which I am much surprised & a little grieved. One from you the other from Mr. Whitman. You reprimand me for the quarrelsome tone of my last two or three letters & reprimand my complaining to you that he had left the church work uncared for. What an unhappy way I must have of expressing myself. For the spirit of complaint against the people of the East for neglecting us & against our excellent & faithful brother for any neglect of his duty was the furtherest from my heart. I beg of you to give those obnoxious epistles one more careful perusal & if still they seem to breathe a quarrelous spirit destroy them & [set them aside] all over again which indeed I will in this endeavor to do. . . . And first, concerning my apprehension that enough would not be done for us at the East to carry us through this struggle victorious. I did not mean to complain of those who have done & are yet doing so much for us, but to express my idea of the urgent, desparate emergency of the case. . . . The one feeling that has been uppermost in my heart towards our friends at the East has been & yet is that of gratitude. It has weighed upon me as a burdensome load especially with reference to the expressions of sympathy & offers of benefits which have come to us by every mail. I should be insensible to all the influences of kindness to indulge in a complaining tone under all this. But will this save us from a bloody civil war? Will it save us from the attack of our enemies by overpowering preponderance of numbers? I still fear not. You speak of the peace which has finally come for us. Alas we here do not consider this cessation of hostility as settled peace. . . . We are yet in a state of War & both parties are preparing for a more desperate conflict than we have yet had. There is nothing but this new governors high-sounding egotistical talk to the contrary & his authority will be but as a spiders web to either party under certain provocations that

were almost inevitable. Every day it looks more imminent. . . . I pass to my alleged complaint of bro Whitmans leaving—I find myself in great perplexity about many matters connected with the church building. Mr. Perry is unable to effect anything with the other contractors & comes to me every day with a long list of difficulties. Then I have been embarrassed for want of funds but am now relieved temporarily by the recall of several hundred dollars to be used for the relief of the needy which together with my quarters salary I am using for the church expecting that the money for that use will soon come. I will not go into the particulars of my perplexity as Mr. Whitman writes me that he intends to be here before this can reach you. I am very sorry that I have written a word about them & did not mean to complain of him. In future I will try to make less of my difficulties & say nothing doing the best I can under the circumstance which can never be understood at the East. . . . I have not the slightest feeling of regret that I undertook this mission. I rejoice in it. But had I foreseen a half of the difficulties, hardships & perils that laid in my path, I fear I should have shrank from the work. Something has sustained me through thus far & I assure you however quarrelous my letters may have seemed to you & others the dominant tone of my spirit has been that of cheerfulness & gratitude to the many friends who have manifested themselves to me since we came out here & above all to that kind Providence which has preserved sustained & blessed us on the way. My trust that God called me to this service & would be with me in it has not failed me from the outset & is stronger now than ever before. . . . This I have not written for the Journal or for publication in any way but to correct a misapprobation in your mind. Let it be a matter between us & those who have read the letters of which you speak & received the same impression from them as yourself.[204]

A correspondent identified only as "Marion" wrote to the *Herald of Freedom* about the distribution of donated goods with which

Nute was so active.[205] Marion's letter testified to the resilience of the townsfolk: While coping with the history of violence against them and under constant threat of more coming, they nevertheless rallied and wrote letters expressing profound gratitude for the donations they received. Thanksgiving was not enough, though; they also had the constant task of reassuring their benefactors that the gifts were going to the truly needy. How like the character of modern-day American charity: Generosity of spirit that gives materially in times of need is linked to victim-blaming that demands proof that the recipients mightily deserve the charity.

The proslavery media's attention to this issue maligned Nute bitterly at this time. Proslavery sympathizers in Democrat newspapers constantly cast aspersions on the agents who distributed the donations, accusing them of living high by pilfering the charity and preying on the sympathies of the American people. This was true in some cases. But Nute was blindsided by his father, who—to curry favor with the Democrats responsible for reappointing him to his position in the Customs House in Boston—released to the proslavery *Boston Post* parts of a private letter that Nute wrote to his stepmother. Taken out of context, the passages were used to accuse Nute of living high on the hog in Kansas at the expense of donors.

The right-wing newspapers were in a feeding frenzy. They used Nute's assurances to his stepmother about his well-being to disillusion the American public about the "deserving" nature of the Kansans and to slow or stop the flow of goods to them. Nute's relationship with his father had never been warm, but this incident of sabotage was particularly bitter. On November 13 Nute wrote to Haskell at the *Boston Transcript* about the incident, with a full disclosure of his "affluence" couched in his customary dry humor. His explanation was reprinted in the *Christian Register*:

LETTER FROM REV. E. NUTE, JR. .... The mail of this morning brought to hand the following letter from the Rev. Mr. Nute, pastor of the Unitarian church in Lawrence, Kansas. It has been elicited by the publication of an extract from one of his letters to his mother, in which he endeavored to allay the fears of his parent for his safety, alike from hunger and murder. Mr. Nute's father is an officer in the Boston Custom House. This statement will probably explain how extracts from the letters of the son to the mother, came to be published in the Post had the whole of the letter been given to the public, so that its spirit and aim might have been seen, it is not probable the writer would have made serious objection. . . . We shall not despair of Kansas, while men of the stamp of our friend remain within its borders. They have the true elements of that Christian heroism so much needed in the founders of a state. They will stamp their impress upon its character, and thus become its benefactors in the highest sense. All honor to them, for their privations and sacrifices in behalf of free institutions. [Transcript of Saturday.]

Friend Haskell . . . I see by your latest issue that has reached me that some of my most private affairs are dragged forth to public notice, and in view of all the circumstances and the spirit in which this has been done, to my great regret. You will understand me as referring to the extract from a familiar letter to my nearest relative, which has lately appeared in the Boston Post. But the injury is only in intention. Indeed, I am confident that it will result in some good to the cause nearest to my heart. My personal reputation I leave to take care of itself, by the help of my friends, thanking them, and you especially, for the ample vindication made in this case from the malicious sneers of enemies. . . . My present purpose is to turn this very small matter to some benefit above all merely personal considerations. I am not a whit ashamed of the extent of my investments in Kansas, nor of their successful result thus far. On the contrary, I wish to make a fuller confession on this point, in order to bring out the facts on which my improvement is to be founded. . . . It is true, I have a good claim within two miles of the center of

Lawrence, on which I am the first settler, the quarter section on which I pitched a tent on my first arrival in the territory, nearly eighteen months since, and where, from that time to this, has been my home. . . . Here I have a cabin nearly sixteen feet square, to which I have lately added a room, built of rough boards, 18x16. It is true that I am meditating the luxury of closing the larger room by a coat of plaster, though I have not yet been able to get as far as the lathing preparatory thereto, and the two snow storms of last week made their free passage, as usual, through the walls. Another week of pleasant weather, and we may be in a better state of defence against the wintry blasts. . . . The depredations and murders that have been perpetrated around us from time to time, with but little cessation, for the last eleven months, the recent house-burnings in our neighborhood, the murder of my brother-in-law, who, with his family, were then staying with us, my own captivity and subsequent illness, have thus far prevented me from providing a more comfortable shelter. . . . It is true, I have nearly twenty acres of land broken, and wheat springing up thickly over about a half of it. Moreover, on two sides of the same I have an excellent stone wall, over 100 rods. This wall has been built by hired help, and cost but little over one dollar per rod, paying wages of one dollar a day and board. . . . It is true, I have harvested nearly eight acres of sod corn, and it has yielded well for the first year's planting. Several of my neighbors have raised fine crops on land that has been broken a year. The usual calculation for the first year, is "half a crop," and of a quality unfit for bread or for feeding out to horses. Mine has turned out better in quantity and quality than I expected. . . . It is true, I have two horses, and they were in good condition when I drove them into the territory last August, and until stolen from me, or, perhaps I should say, pressed into service, by authority of the officials of the administration, when on my way to Leavenworth with my sister-in-law, to recover the body and effects of her murdered husband. . . . When I recovered them after my release, by forcible seizure from an officer in the territorial militia, they were so jaded and run down by their ill usage in the public service, that I came near failing to recognize them, and some of my neighbors, more versed in horse matters than myself, predict my inability to winter them. . . . But I hope that good care and gentle usage will save them from further decline, and that I shall be able yet to report them restored to their wonted vigor and fullness of flesh. . . . My three yoke of oxen are all in good order, thought they have been worked hard for the greater part of the summer and fall, and fed only on the wild grass of the prairie. They would furnish to-day as good beef as the average of that offered in Quincy market.[206] One yoke I bought but a few weeks since, to relieve the pressing need of a man whose cabin had been recently burned, and his brother butchered near Ossawatamie, and who was then fleeing from the territory, hunted like a wild beast. Those hundred hens, or more strictly speaking, fowl of the hen kind, are no common poultry, but mostly full-blooded shanghais of the black variety. Their progenitors, five hens and a rooster, I brought all the way from Illinois a year ago last summer, at an expense that would startle one of the most infatuated of the fanciers at the East in the height of the hen fever. But I have never repented that investment. The birds promise to pay their way. The cost of their keeping is small. Every square yard of the prairie is populous with grasshoppers, bugs and grubs, and the ungainly limbs of the Asiatic fowl do good service in stalking about among the tall grass; so that through the greater part of the year they cater for their own crops. Many a dozen fresh eggs have the elder biddies furnished for our table, and some of their descendants are rapidly approaching the size and plumpness which will render them meat for the dinner-table. Meat, by the way, has always been the cheapest article of provisions in Kansas; flour and groceries the dearest in comparison with the cost with you. . . . A year ago last June I began to build a small store house in town. It is not yet completed, or far enough advanced to be occupied. This long delay has been occasioned chiefly by the trouble from invaders. Workmen on whom I have relied have been called off to defend their homes, driven out of the territory, and in one instance murdered. Saw mills have been stopped, and one destroyed by the marauders who were enrolled as territorial militia. By the same causes the cost of building has been increased nearly twofold, so that now I shall be forced to rent the house when completed, in order to repay the loans which I have been compelled to make to carry on the work, while we continue to live in this cabin, which has been built mostly by the labor of my own hands. . . . I think I have given enough of my experience to show that the natural advantages of our fair territory offer great inducement to the farmers of New England to come out and engage in the cultivation of our millions of acres yet unbroken. The great hope to my mind for the final success of Freedom in this struggle lies in the fact of the great superiority of the free labor system over that of slavery in this the noblest of human avocations. Let the two systems be put in operation side by side, and the advantage is too manifest to be denied. Though hundreds of the most enterprising and thrifty farmers have been driven from the territory, if we can have but a few years peace, protected in our rights, the success of this experiment would convert every supporter of the slave system who is an actual settler in the territory, as it has several to my knowledge already. I purposed to point out a yet more immediate and practical use to be made of those conclusions by our friends at the East. This must be deferred to another letter.[207]

Nute wrote to Hale on November 15 of his trials in Kansas: the weather, prices, and the constant vigilance required for survival. He couched this in the ironies of the fallout from his father's betrayal of him in the proslavery *Post*. Nute reiterated to Hale the reality of his small holdings and desperate life in Kansas, feeling the jab of his father's character assault all the way out there. Despite his high profile in mission work for well over a year, the scandal threatened to damage his credibility with those he didn't know intimately. He was grateful for Hale's coming to his defense in the *Advertiser*. He wrote,

I suppose it was you that came to the rescue in the Advertiser when some two weeks since I was betrayed in the family (unkindest cut of all) & disjointed extracts from my private familiar letter were forwarded with low sneers in that vilest of all sheets the Post. I thank you for the friendly service. I wish you could have known all the facts in the case. Some of them I have given in a communication to the Transcript. There are others which might with more propriety & effect be made public by appearing as extracts from a private letter. Consider yourself at liberty to use anything in this as you think best. . . . My hens have acquired a dangerous notoriety. It may surprise you that so much is made of them since their first introduction to public life. In New England I think it would not be considered a very noteworthy item that some poor country parson had reared a large flock of chickens or that he mentioned the fact of his success in that line in a letter to the "old folks at home." But I assure you it is a quite remarkable achievement for the last season in Kansas and those among you in closest sympathy with the marauders here will of course be first to perceive it. It has been an occasion of surprise to my neighbors who have been less fortunate in this respect. Almost the first remark of one who called on me within the last two days was "How have you raised such a fine lot of fowl. The ruffians long ago stole all mine." The fact is their security thus far has been quite excessive. Every night they have been closely confined in coop & my hired man has slept near an open window with a Sharpes rifle at his side for the protection of this & more valuable stock. Three horses have been taken from me during the last eight months one by the U.S. marshal's posse & two by an officer of the militia under the authority of a U.S. official with the latter a wagon & valuable harness which cost $175.

My nearest neighbor has also lost two horses in the same way, another within a mile of us has received yet more attention in this way having no less than six (6) excellent horses & a good wagon stolen from him by the marauders since the sack of Lawrence last May. I can enumerate losses of this kind in this immediate vicinity amounting to over ten thousand dollars. The whole amount taken from the territory over into Missouri on the three general invasions has probably exceeded ten times that sum. The whole loss to our people occasioned by this marauding has been more than three times that i.e. $300,000. Hundreds of acres of corn have been destroyed by the cattle who range the prairies, for the want of fencing which the settlers were prevented from building by the necessity of being in arms & away from their homes to repel these invasions. Much of the crops will be lost for the want of the means of securing them. About one half of my potatoes are frozen in the ground because my cellar was not in readiness to receive them until within the last 24 hours. The balance may be lost before I can secure them. If I had not been kept for two weeks a prisoner in the Ruffian camp this would not have occurred. Many families are to night shivering in half built houses who have been hindered in their work of building by the same cause (The thermometer has indicated 6 degrees for two days already.) . . . My room was finally plastered day before yesterday, but we fear the mortar will freeze for all we can do & in the mean time we are in the most uncomfortable quarters we have yet had in Kansas in a sort of back shed built of green lumber through which the gusts of north wind sweep flaring my candle so that I have difficulty to see the writing left by my pen. I write this, bundled up with coat & shawl as though in a sled-ride & shivering at that. Alas for those who must be in no better quarters the whole winter long. If our plastering ever gets dry we shall have one room comparatively comfortable & will be resigned to the ridicule of such printing as the Post on . . . our luxurious living.[208]

Even Edward Fitch, the young Emigrant Aid Company employee in Lawrence, was affected by the gossip and wrote home about it. In his November 21 letter to his parents regarding the happenings in Lawrence, he directed that they should send donated articles directly to him instead of to Nute for fear that Nute would favor other Unitarians in their distribution, though he admitted that this was hearsay. For Nute, who had struggled, lost family members, given money out of his own pocket, lived in near squalor for over a year, and almost lost his own life, this threat to credibility brought about by his father's treachery must have burned in the extreme.

Fitch mentioned in his letter the rumor that Governor John White Geary had been arrested. Geary began his term as governor desiring to support neither the abolitionist nor proslavery side. Eventually, however, he developed a close friendship with Charles Robinson and Samuel Pomeroy, the two Unitarians who led the Free-State cause, and planned a democratic government for the territory. Shortly after his private secretary, Dr. John Gihon, later a historian of Bleeding Kansas, was beaten by Border Ruffians, Geary submitted his resignation to the newly elected President James Buchanan, who promptly fired him. According to some versions of Kansas history, Geary was not in fact arrested by the proslavery judge Lecompte, but fled the territory armed and under the cover of darkness. Fitch wrote to his parents,

I have not seen Mr. Nute and do not know exactly how we shall manage that that was sent to us but think if you had sent it to me alone it would have been better as Mr. Nute, being a Unitarian is a little more apt to look for that kind of men to help. At least so I have heard and I only say it as a report. . . . Three of the bdls of things sent by you have arrived and I have distributed quite a number of things for which I have recd many thanks and for which I in my turn thank the givers. . . . Gov Geary appointed yester the 20th as a day of Thanksgiving and the ladies of Lawrence got up a dinner to which they invited him, the proceeds of which were to be used to give a dinner to the free state Prisoners at Lecompton. The dinner took place yesterday about 5 P.M. Gov. Robinson was here but Geary was not. The reason for his not being here we understand this morning was that he was arrested by order of Judge Lecompton while on his way home. This is said to be fact but of its truth I am not certain. . . . The Dinner was quite a good affair, about 100 sat down to the tables. A blessing was asked by Rev. G. W. Hutchinson after which all ate a genteel sufficiency of roast Turkey, baked pig, Chicken pie & such like fixings. We then adjourned to the hall where we had speeches & toasts and a good time generally until between nine & ten when the floor was given up to those who wished to dance, while the sober staid portion of us went home.[209]

In mid-November boxes of items sent to Nute and another frontier pastor, C. J. (Charles) Lovejoy, husband of Julia Louisa Lovejoy, were stolen. The *Herald of Freedom* reported on the misdeed and reminded the community that both pastors had lost their all to the marauders, so the culprits should return the items—even if for no other reason than both shipments were personal items and would be known if used. George Washington Brown, the editor and owner of the *Herald of Freedom* and a founding member of Nute's congregation, was deeply involved with the Free-State cause. He did not dignify the rumors about Nute pilfering donations by mentioning them at all in his article. He wrote instead,

Three boxes of goods, two directed to the Rev. Mr. NUTE, the other to Rev. Mr. LOVEJOY, were stolen from the Committee Room in this city, on Friday night, the 14th inst. They contained clothing and bedding, forwarded by the friends of those reverend gentlemen in the East, to relieve their necessities. No person, with a particle of the attributes of a man about him, could steal from these gentlemen. Mr. Nute's dwelling was pillaged by the marauders from Missouri, and stripped of his bedding, and all his valuables during the summer; while Mr. Lovejoy has also suffered from the same cause, and, in addition has been sick for several months, and unable to look after his affairs. The person who took those goods can never enjoy them. The contents of the boxes are known, and wherever used will be recognized. To escape the stings of a guilty conscience, he cannot do else than restore them to their proper owners.[210]

The rumors of graft in the Unitarian mission in Lawrence were taken seriously throughout the denomination and its media arms. Not only was the integrity of their poster-boy clergyman at stake, but the veracity of the entire Emigrant Aid project and the Unitarians in the Kansas support network could be called into question. Nute's friend Rev. Francis Tiffany in Springfield, Massachusetts, wrote to the *Christian Register* to disarm any suspicions about the accusations, stating for the public record the motives behind the rumor. Tiffany wrote,

> Rev. Mr. Tiffany, of the Unitarian Church, happily and ably defends his friend Mr. Nute, from the misrepresentations of the Democratic press and the grosser assaults that have had an industrious private circulation. The defence was hardly necessary in this community, where all parties are too well known— the one as worthy confidence, the other as unworthy it,—to require any explanation. It was Mr. Nute's father, an officer in the Boston Custom House, who hastened to furnish the grubbers for the Border-Ruffian party, with this partial extract from one of his son's letters, whereby he and his cause might be misrepresented and maligned. The father has probably thus purchased the right to hold his office for another four years.[211]

In Lawrence the Free-Staters refused to be cowed and held a rousing Thanksgiving festival attended by many of the prominent Unitarians in town. This was the party previously mentioned in Edward Fitch's letter to his parents, attended by the likes of John

Brown Jr., Free-State Governor Robinson, Thaddeus Hyatt, chair of the National Kansas Committee, and Richard Realf, the infamous abolitionist reporter. Samuel C. Smith, a correspondent of the *New York Times*, toasted Nute, who though feted, was not in attendance:

> Rev. Ephraim Nute—The fearless and faithful minister of the Gospel, and the honest man. He is able, by bitter experience, to give a real South side view of slavery. Mr. Nute not being present, Rev. Geo. W. Hutchinson was called upon, who responded in a happy style.[212]

The rousing support of Nute by this rowdy bunch was a great vote of confidence. Nute was no stranger to the quirky social displays of frontier life, as evidenced by the following *Lawrence Daily Journal* report on an unorthodox wedding he performed during a church service. The groom was his beloved young friend, fellow prisoner John Wilder. The account read,

> On Sunday, November 30, '56, great interest was added to the afternoon service by an event of rare occurrence here at the time. The service opened and proceeded as usual till about the second singing, when at a signal from the minister, much to the astonishment of the audience, the chorister and leading alto left the choir and passed out of the room to the Emigrant Aid office in front. Returning speedily however, they ushered in the contracting parties to a marriage ceremony, which was at once performed by the Rev. Mr. Nute. Whether the happy couple took their accustomed seats with the choir or with the audience while the service proceeded is not here stated. At the close of the meeting, however, having received the hearty congratulations of their friends, (which embraced the entire audience) Mr. and Mrs. John H. Wilder were escorted by relatives and a few favored ones to the home of his parents in the Meadow, where the wedding feast had been prepared.[213]

The work on the church proceeded in fits and starts and at a snail's pace. The *Herald of Freedom* announced, "The schoolroom in the basement of the Unitarian Church, in this city, will be completed within three weeks.—Patent seats manufactured in Boston, have been received for seating the room."[214] During the fall of 1856, the church building was so far advanced that arrangements were made for opening a school in the basement rooms. A six months' engagement was made with a teacher, and Nute and Whitman agreed to pay the teacher's salary out of their own pockets. It was expected that the rooms would be ready and the school opened in December or January. But various disappointments related to plastering delayed the work, so that the rooms were not ready for the new Boston desks and seats and books until the last of March 1857.

A letter from one of Nute's parishioners appeared in the *Herald of Freedom* on December 1, 1856, admonishing the public to support its ministers, for the ample presence of churches in Lawrence would be a calming element pushing it to the side of lawfulness:

Last Sunday, I attended public worship in Lawrence. After the sermon in the morning, a brother arose, and proposed a collection; and said we have no other way to support preaching, than by the free will offerings of the people. He said the minister was in a strait where two ways meet; the first was a command to "Go and preach the gospel to every creature"—he felt that "Woe is me, if I preach not the gospel." In the other way stood his family, claiming their daily support; and the words came sounding in his ears: "He that provideth not for his own household, has denied the faith, and is worse than an infidel." Now, while the preacher was filling up the first way, the people should fill up the second, by taking care of his family, so that he can look well after their spiritual interests. . . . I was well pleased with the remarks, for I believe that a man is as much in duty bound to pay for the food for the mind, as he is for food for the body; that he has no moral right to borrow his neighbor's newspaper, unless he takes on which he allows others to read. And he is equally bound to support the pulpit, provided he be able; but not if he be poor, for our Savior said: "The poor have the gospel preached unto them." . . . Kansas is acknowledged to be the home of the brave. Let us give a liberal support to free churches, free schools, and a free press; and thus make it the land of the free.[215]

Whether the letter referred to Nute is unknown, but it would seem so—certainly Nute struggled to maintain his family when his salary from the AUA did not come through, or was inadequate to meet the demands of the frontier and the results of pillage. Nute was surely not the only minister in Lawrence in this position. But in the wake of his father's sabotage, he must have been heartened by a public call for confidence and funds.

In the midst of all the turmoil about donations, Lawrence busily consolidated itself as a town with the amenities of New England civilization. According to the *Herald of Freedom*, work on the church progressed, "notwithstanding the cold weather. The roof is already completed, and the fine room in the basement, that is designed for a high school, is ready for the plasterers. We shall soon have the pleasure of chronicling its completion."[216] The *Herald of Freedom* also reported that the clock for the tower was making progress from New England toward Lawrence:

The clock, given for the tower of the Unitarian Church, in this city, has arrived safely in New Orleans. Apprehensions were felt for its safety, as the vessel on which it was shipped, was wrecked on the route, but the clock arrived safely in Havana, and has since arrived at New Orleans, as stated above. The clock is a fine specimen of mechanical skill, costing $500 in Boston. It will be a valuable addition to the improvements in Lawrence.[217]

While the church was still incomplete, Nute preached in the "school-room" over the stove store in Lawrence on Sunday afternoons at one o'clock. Nute, as a pistol-packing preacher, was in good company in the Kansas Territory. He was fortunate—unlike some others, he had been placed in his pulpit specifically to assist the Free-State cause and to spread the antislavery message, so his abolitionist preaching at least did not put him at risk of his job. But his calling was still fraught with danger: Anyone preaching against slavery did so at the risk of his life, and not a few of the territorial ministers had to dodge more bullets than theological questions.

At this time Nute served on a committee to form a public school system and championed that cause both in Lawrence and in the East. The committee also met in the stove store. A subcommittee of mostly Unitarians was elected to appoint a board of trustees for the school system. When the whole group met again on December 2, the committee appointed Nute, James Blood, treasurer of the New England Emigrant Aid Company, and C. Hornsby, a Lawrence merchant, as the first school board members in Lawrence. The school was to be located in the basement of the Unitarian church.

From the beginning the new school system was focused not only on the elementary grades, but all the way through the secondary level and on to a university. On December 16, 1856, Boston philanthropist Amos A. Lawrence first wrote to Nute concerning his desire to support both a preparatory high school and a college. He wrote,

> Some time ago I requested Governor Robinson to spend some money for me in laying the foundation of a "preparatory school" in Lawrence, but the title to the land was imperfect, and the thing was not done. The plan of a preparatory department must be adopted before you can have a college; unless there should be a classical school established by the town. Nevertheless, I wish to see the plan adopted, and to help along its completion. I have thought it over much and it is briefly this,

viz.: You shall have a college, which shall be a school of learning, and at the same time a monument to perpetuate the memory of those martyrs of liberty who fell during the recent struggle. Beneath it their dust shall rest. In it shall burn the light of liberty, which shall never be extinguished till it illumine the whole continent. It shall be called the "free state College," and all the friends of freedom shall be invited to lend it a helping hand. ... Will you oblige me by conversing with Governor Robinson in regard to this, and with any other whom you would consult, but without publicity. I cannot furnish cash for building, but I can give what will be as good for paying expenses after it is up. For instance, having advanced $10,000 to the university in Appleton, Wis., last year, I hold their notes on interest. This is a good institution, and owes little or nothing except this. They have about two hundred thousand dollars' worth of property, and 450 students on their catalogue. I wish I had money, but fear the time is distant when I shall have more than enough to carry along my plans begun long ago.[218]

The end of 1856 was spent not in the violent terrors of the earlier part of the year but attending to the daily matters of a young growing town. The mass meeting of citizens interested in establishing a university met on Christmas Day, 1856—proof that establishing the noble institutions of New England in Lawrence was more important at this time than the actual practice of honoring the traditions of New England. In the East, Christmas Day was a time of religious and family gathering; holding a meeting of this kind would have been unthinkable. But in the territory, a day of work was a day of work, and the time and place for it stood aside for no man (or religious holiday).

Nute addressed this Christmas meeting. As part of his mission to establish institutions of education in the territory, he had already engaged in personal correspondence with Amos Lawrence regarding funding for a college or university. The meeting aired the opinions of all Kansas Territory movers and shakers on how to accomplish this. Nute was chosen to stand on the first board of trustees for the projected college—which eventually became the University of Kansas, still in Lawrence today.

S. Cabot Jr., of the Massachusetts State Kansas Committee in Boston, wrote to James Blood in Lawrence on December 28 about the distribution of clothing for Kansas that was coming through his committee. Donated clothing was not arriving in Lawrence, and the general opinion of these men seemed to be that the National Kansas Committee in Chicago was stealing it. A later letter between Whitman and John Brown confirms that, indeed, articles donated to the national committee had been sold to provide Whitman, and therefore Brown, with money.[219] Cabot's letter to Blood read,

> Yours of 6th inst has been recd. I already knew that most of the clothing sent to yourself & Rev. Mr. Nute since I ceased sending through Chicago, had been stopped at St. Louis by the closure of navigation. At the time I wrote I asked you to either distribute them in your individual capacity or as a member of the Disembarking committee, I have reason now to wish that you should not let them go through the Committee but to advise with Pomeroy & Rev. Mr. Nute in regard to the distribution. I hope you will be able thus to supply some of those who have been too proud to be willing, that their name should be published & have preferred rather to suffer want. This supply is not a mere charity but a contribution of the North toward the support of her free state soldiers who have been bravely battling for the cause of freedom & in defense of our common rights against the slave Oligarchy. The names of the recipients should be kept secretly to yourselves & all that I want is a proof that I have taken proper precautions to secure the proper distribution of the clothing is a statement to that effect signed by yourself & Messrs Nute & Pomeroy with an enumeration in gross of the amt distributed. I shall send more soon by the way of N. Orleans to arrive at St. Louis in time for the opening of navigation & shall probably direct that they be delivered to the

charge of yourself & the above named gentlemen. I send you herewith my report to the State Kansas Committee & also the report of the Boson Kansas Clothing soc who have been my most efficient coadjutors in this work.[220]

The letter contained correspondence from the Massachusetts State Kansas Committee, detailing the donations being sent from Massachusetts—who they were from, and in what amount. Each was carefully numbered and accounted for. Obviously, the theft of donations was a serious concern, and by the end of 1856, eyes were trained on the National Kansas Committee in Chicago.

In his old age, Nute preached about and praised John Brown to audiences at the Grand Army of the Republic, an organization of veterans of the Civil War. In 1893 he wrote to his friend Richard Hinton, who was working on a biography of John Brown. He told Hinton,

I am Chaplain of Post 92 G.A.R. and let no opportunity slip to give them a touch of Old J.B. which is always rec'd with applause. In visiting other posts the first question asked is Did you know Old J.B. At one in Dorchester I gave a discourse on Him & they chanted the "Glory Hallelujah" with vim at the close. "Wasn't he a fanatic?" asked one—"Yes A God intoxicated Fanatic would to God there had been & ever may be more such.—They are the salt of the earth." . . . "You Unitarians claim to recognize the manifestation of Divinity in Jesus on the cross the great majority of professed (we say Confessed) Christians say the proper Deity—But if we cannot see this in John Brown on the gallows tree our confession is an empty thing." This is substance I said in my last sermon preached the Sunday before Memorial Day a year ago in Brighton. I preach but seldom now. Who would care to hear the old fanatic in sacred synagogue? Such irreverence! But Emerson & Theodore Parker would say Amen! . . . From a prudential point of view perhaps the raid on Harper's Ferry was a seeming mistake. But Providence was in it for a wise end. And as Adrea said—"J. B. was right." Posterity is sure to do him honor.[221]

But in 1857, Nute was hampered by some who secretly supported Brown. Whitman was entrusted with money from the AUA and the Lawrence congregation, and at certain points, evidence in his own letters suggests that he funneled it to John Brown. The National Kansas Committee received donations from charitable Easterners, and some of these were sold to give money to Brown. All this is known in retrospect. In 1857, Nute thought he was simply struggling with the fallout of suspicions about donations that did not arrive to the needy settlers in Lawrence. Anyone connected with the Kansas project was painted with the same scandalous brush when these breaches of honesty were discovered.

Nute wrote to his friend Samuel Gridley Howe on January 2, 1857, expressing his own concerns about the misuse of funds and goods by the Chicago branch of the National Kansas Committee:

I have just recd. a letter from a Miss E. A. Livermore of Milford N.H. requesting me to give her an acknowledgement for the recei't of $180 sent to me for distribution through you. . . . This is the first I have heard of it. She says she sent a draft to you for the am't Oct 24. . . . A few days since I gave a sort of letter of confidence in our Central Kansas Committee to Col. Eldridge & after stating that I had the fullest confidence in the integrity & discretion of those gentleman on the committee with whom I was personally acquainted, Mr. J. Blood & Mr. Wm Hutchinson. I added that I had heard no charges against the other gentleman of that committee. The very next day I did hear some loud & grievous charges & learned that such had been made public by a gentleman formerly of the committee in a letter in the Herald of Freedom of last week which in the press of business had missed my sight. If these charges are true, & I find that many believe them, I have no further confidence in that committee.

If they have charged for the work of distribution (exclusive of the expenses of room, rent etc) . . . $50 per diem beside helping themselves freely to the best of the articles & the fact be proved I fear that my recommendations will not be of much use to anybody's reputation in future. But I do hope this & other charges may be disproved. Everybody here knows that the members of the committee have spent but a small part of their time on the public services. . . . I make this statement to you believing you are a member of The National Committee between whom & our Kansas Comm. there may be some controversy. . . . I am convinced that there has been great misuse of the funds through the Chicago operation . . . of your committee. But I do not wish to make any public statements on that point.[222]

Nute wrote to Amos Lawrence on January 5 to bring him up-to-date concerning the schools in Lawrence to which he was contributing, including a free school in the basement of the Unitarian church:

The subject of a college has been of late much before our people. On the 25th Dec, auspicious day, a meeting was held in this place to deliberate upon the matter together with the interests of Education in general & to take some preliminary steps toward the establishment of institutions of learning. It was not a large meeting, but considering all the circumstances,—the short notice, the scattered location of the people & the inclemency of the season, the attendance & interest was quite encouraging. About 40 of our most influential citizens were present. . . . Your liberal offer is the first step toward the realization of the project fraught with the deepest interest to our friend of Freedom of Humanity & the welfare of our common Country. . . . In the basement of the church now being built for the society under my charge by funds contributed chiefly at the East we have a fine school-room nearly completed. It is provided with furniture of the most approved model, built in Boston & given by one of the religious societies there. When completed it will be probably the best appointed school-room west of the Mississippi. In this room it is proposed to have a High school free to all. Two excellent teachers are engaged & here on the spot & nothing but the extreme cold weather has prevented the completion of the room & the commencement of the school.[223]

On January 11 Nute wrote to Thaddeus Hyatt to express his dismay over the controversy surrounding the Central Kansas Committee (Blood and Hutchinson) and its relationship to the National Kansas Committee. Nute was worried. Should this matter become public, it would jeopardize the whole project. The settlers in Lawrence needed the donations from the East for their survival. If evidence surfaced showing that these items were being siphoned off to benefit those entrusted to distribute them, not only would the flow of goods stop, but those, like Nute, who had been working to promote this cause, would have their own integrity seriously compromised in the public eye. Nute wrote,

I have been much surprised . . . of late to hear the complaints that are made of the Central Kansas Committee in regard to their course in the disbursement of the relief with which they have been entrusted.—Surprised because I supposed until quite recently that the gentlemen serving that comm. enjoyed the confidence & approbation of our people as they have certainly my own. . . . I expressed my confidence in those members with whom I had the honor of a personal acquaintance (Mr. Blood & Mr. W. Hutch) in a note to Eldridge some ten days since & am yet unwilling to give up my strong regard & respect for those gentlemen because of the charges that are made against their honor & integrity. . . . But I also added in the note referred to that such I believed was the confidence felt by the people of Kansas in general & that I had never heard anything alleged against the integrity or discretion of that committee in relation to their management of their trust—

or something to this purport. I wish you to understand that I had not then seen or heard of the letter of one of their number published in the Herald of Freedom & further that had I known as I now do charges against them that have been in circulation in this community I could not have written what I did. I am unspeakably sorry to hear of the unhappy conflict between the committee here & the agents of the National committee. I hope an early explanation of some dark things may be made leading to reconciliation & that the affair may not be brought before the public.[224]

W. F. Arny, general agent of the National Kansas Committee based in Chicago, traveled to Kansas to replace the Central Kansas Committee there because of suspicions regarding their distribution or theft of donations. He appointed Nute to a committee of clergymen to fill the dismissed committee members' places. Clearly, Nute's father's stab in the back had not raised doubt in those who knew the younger Nute personally. While in Kansas, Arny also assessed the needs of the settlers for tools, farming implements, and especially seeds and trees, perhaps a calculated face-saving strategy for the organization at large.

On February 9 Nute wrote a touching letter to Caroline Wells Healy Dall thanking her children for the three pennies they had collected for the Kansas immigrants. Caroline Dall[225] was active with the Transcendentalists, and in 1845 she was instrumental in influencing her father, a multimillionaire, to rent Boston's Music Hall for Theodore Parker to preach to supporters and to provide part of Parker's salary when controversy caused him to be banned from most Unitarian pulpits.

Caroline Dall was married to Charles Appleton Dall, the AUA minister who embarked on a mission to India near the same time that Nute took up his mission to Kansas. Her husband was plagued with physical and mental illness that eventually destroyed his ministry. After he went to India, he returned home barely a handful of times in the next several decades. This forced Caroline to raise her children on her own while she worked to establish herself as a formidable social activist and feminist intellectual and writer.[226]

Nute was well acquainted with the Dalls. He had been a guest in their home, knew of and offered condolences on Caroline's virtual abandonment, and was very fond of her children. He took particular care in his warm letter to tell her how he used the pennies her children gave to the cause and how that small donation served an important purpose. He quoted in Latin the phrase, "He who brings forth through others, brings forth for himself," a reflection of liberal Christianity. Nute wrote,

> Your kind letter was recd. with pleasure. You have certainly had a hard time of it, but I trust have got around onto the bright side & have not lost sight of it in your severest of trials. The interest of little Willie moves me very much & I rejoice to hear of his escape from his perils. I was much impressed with his affectionate spirit & winning ways while at your house. I don't know when a child fixed itself so strongly on my mind by so short intercourse. I have often thought I would like to tell them what became of their three cent pieces. I carried them for a long while wrapped up in paper in my vest pocket, or rather in diverse pockets of vests, & as I changed them from time to time I felt my heart warmed by the recollection of the warm little hearts that made the donation. So they did some good in that way, comforted me & sustained my spirit for labors of love. Then I laid them in a little box in my desk in which I keep postage stamps & finally considered them metamorphosed into such stamps or exchanged for them. In that form they made the journey back to New England to carry tidings of young men sick and in prison & of others recovered to their parents who had written me in great anxiety for their fate. So by the rule *Qui facit per alici facit per se,* the children served to carry messages of great comfort to those fathers, mothers, brothers & sisters. . . . Now I am to send off to day three letters to so many places in Kansas, Manhattan, Ogden & Shannon (hateful name) con-

taining money for the relief of persons in each of those places of whose great destitution & distress I heard last week. In one instance a family of which the father is an old man of 80 without flour or in fact any other food but corn & without shoes to their feet. Another where the head is disabled by lameness & other members have frozen their feet very badly so that they are unable to leave the cabin to work & are shivering for the want of clothes. Another, the little colony of Ogden where two are very sick & all deprived of things necessary to their comfort, have been without butter etc since they came late last fall & without flour for much of the time, their minister wrote to Mr. Sanborn of The State Kansas Aid Com. in Boston & he to me before they could get help as they did not know of the money in my hands. How their hearts will leap with joy to get $100 & the promise of more if their need & of clothing, good warm bedding etc as soon as we can get it to them. It is 100 miles from this. These last stamps from the kind little souls in Connecticut shall prevail on our old uncle Samuel take the letters along in the bag that he carries their way tomorrow morning. What better service could I put the love of the children to? . . . I regret say that I have no Sunday School to get the benefit of the lesson to encourage them in usefulness. We have but one place for all our services those of three societies & the Sun. School of the Orthodox which got ahead of ours. But a few weeks of mild weather will see our vestry ready for occupation & then we will start, God willing, & all these things will keep. Give my warmest love to the children & believe me.[227]

Nute wrote again to Amos Lawrence on March 4 regarding land prospects for the college, and the continuing political situation. The mail was cut off this time of year by the condition of the rivers, but it was obviously not preventing the plans for the Free-State college and Lawrence schools from going forward. The letter read,

Yours of the 11th ult. reached me only by the last mail. For the last month we have been almost entirely cut off from postal communication with the East, a small part of the mail only being brought through about once in two weeks. You are certainly right in your preference for the location of the college in the broad table land on Mt. Oread or Capitol hill (the limits of the two are rather undefined). But I had understood that the question concerning the title had hitherto prevented the building of the preparatory school-house or academy for which the excavation was made on that tract. I have not hesitated to locate our church & a house for myself[228] on the side or lower table of the hill about which a similar question is mounted. The spot of which I wrote is very similar in fact a continuation of the same table, a little further round on the edge of the great basin in which the city is located & in plain sight from every part of the same. These the land would be had without cost & with a clear undisputed tittle, after the present claimants have preempted. . . . If a flout laid by Ex Gov. Robinson should hold, of which there seems some doubt there will be no difficulty in securing the more eligible spot. Until that question is decided there need perhaps be nothing done. . . . I feel deeply with you the importance of establishing a good system of common schools at an early day. But in the present state of our political affairs I see not how anything can be effected toward it. All the legislative power & with the exception of Governor, all execution offices are in the hands of the usurpers. They have just perfected a system of villainy by which, without help from Congress, or civil war, their power is made perpetual, I apprehend troublous time for the next six months. Our people will not submit to the collection of taxes without resistance. The blood of 76 will be up at the first attempt. The counsels of prudence will not always be heeded. Both parties are too ready to fight at the slightest provocation. Only one life now stands between us & the reopening of civil war & that is daily threatened & has already been once attempted. I believe that attempt was part of a deep laid plot which is not yet abandoned. If Geary had fallen we should have had another invasion called over by another proclamation from Woodson summoning "the militia" to put down rebellion. . . . Perhaps I magnify the danger, God grant it may prove so. Just now all sorts of alarms are hushed for fear of deterring immigration for the spring in which lies our chief hope of deliverance from bondage. If this should be very large it may serve to intimidate our enemies. We have also a first hope that Congress has done something for us before the adjournment. . . . The preparation for our two schools in Lawrence are about completed & we shall try to put them in operating two weeks from next Monday.[229]

Nute also penned a hasty letter to Miles telling him that Whitman had finally written and was soon expected back in Lawrence. Nute had written to Miles and others about how to get the work done on the church without Whitman. Nute now suspected that this would bring him additional accusations of contentiousness, so he asked for Miles's discretion on that account. Nute's frustration with Whitman had become palpable. He was suspended between his great desire to get the church built, as per his own charge, and Whitman's caprice.

Meanwhile, Whitman's involvement with John Brown and his project had deepened. This undercover operation, whose public face was the National Kansas Committee and the Emigrant Aid Company, shared many members with the inner circles of Unitarianism in Boston. Those men considered it a higher calling in the interest of ending slavery. Nute wrote as if he had no knowledge of this and merely suspected Whitman of being a slacker.

On March 19 the ministerial alliance that Nute had a hand in forming held a special meeting in Lawrence. Nute acted as secretary. Committee reports detailed the alliance's stance on various inflammatory issues: slavery, temperance, swearing, tobacco, and breaking the Sabbath. It addressed the issue of Sunday schools, and the meeting ended by appointing a committee to draft bylaws for a temperance society, always dear to Nute's heart.

Amid the routine calls to perform marriages and other pastoral duties, Nute wrote to Edward Everett Hale on April 6 to request a list of book titles that were bestsellers in Unitarian circles, so he could focus on establishing a parish library. A new flood of emigrants was coming in, and donations were being stored in anticipation of their needs. Nute sold his claim to Rev. John Stillman Brown, the Unitarian minister who eventually replaced him in Lawrence's pulpit. Nute was finally relocating into town, a move that was probably quite a relief in terms of the amount of time he must have spent away from home on business, and the resultant hours dedicated to getting back and forth from the claim. In this letter Nute campaigned for John Stillman Brown to be paid by the AUA for his heretofore voluntary ministerial services.

Nute fulfilled the role of missionary, minister, public servant, education promoter, ad hoc building supervisor, chaplain to the legislature, and all around social worker in Lawrence—all of which took priority over his labors to build a home and provide for his family. Any support from the AUA for another minister-type would have been a dream come true. Nute invited Hale to the dedication of the new church, which he expected to happen in July. He wrote,

Yours of March 19 enclosing one to Gov. Robinson came by the last mail. I handed it to Mrs. R. immediately. He is at Quindaro. . . . As to the books our benefactress at Portsmouth I wish she would bestow them on our Parish Library for in this way they will be in the way of doing the most good if not too late. I advise none of the good Unitarian books, publications of A.U.A. etc for in that article we are well stocked. . . . Rev. Brown stands by me as I write & says "tell Hale I am here settled down for life planted in Kansas forever." He has taken my "claim" house & improvements & bought me out. He will have light work to get on with his limited means for a few years. I wish he could have some employ with us as a missionary by our people at the East. He might preach at such places as Bloomington,

Topeka, Big Springs & other new settlements every Sunday & start societies. Perhaps the A.U.A. will allow him a support of a few hundred per annum or perhaps some church in Boston will be glad to operate in this way with some others—Can anything be done? You ask my mind on the proposition to send a "brother" out with a colony. I say if there be a brother who has it in his heart to come let him do so. By all means in God's name. The fields are very white here & laborers exceeding few to reap a harvest for what we call Liberal Christianity. But encourage no one to come who is not prepared to rough it for a while & work in small ways to go into some incipient places & stick to grow up with it—ready to turn his hand to many kinds of work to do anything by which he can be useful. . . . Since receiving your letter I have found the valuable box of clothing sent by The South Cong. Society. It was one of 39 that came up the Kansas last week. They were stored in a building occupied by Mr. Whitman as agent for The National K. Comm. & this box opened to search for bedding for a man who sleeps therein (the building, not the box) when your note turned up. The goods will not be given out for some time, but will be timely help to some persons between this & another winter, especially that fine lot of pantaloons & those superior woolen socks. I have no room yet in which the boxes can be offered so as to fully expose the contents. . . . We are about moving into town. The church-building, starting schools etc etc give me but little time to write or attend to anything else. I must therefore sign myself yours as ever. . . . in haste E. Nute, Jr. . . . Postscript—N. B. The Kaw is navigable.—boats are running daily & well-loaded to this place. Immigration comes in like a flood. Hundreds enter Lawrence daily & thousands into the territory. Nothing but the best of material for building is on the way of a large city here straightaways. . . . Postscript No. 2—The time of our dedication is very uncertain. About July 1 I think. But you shall be notified in time & I hope you will be with us.[230]

On April 17 in Lecompton, acting governor Fred P. Stanton—who replaced John White Geary—addressed the people of Lawrence.[231] His appointment was interim; the new governor, Robert J. Walker, could not leave Washington for nearly a month. The Kansas Territory had already earned the reputation of having a "governor of the hour." In the seven years of its existence it had endured a whirlwind succession of six governors, the first three of whom fled the proslavers under cover. Stanton would prove every bit as untrustworthy a gubernatorial ally for the Free-Staters as the previous governors appointed by the Pierce administration. In his first address he told the Lawrencians he would "uphold the law," with the unpoken implication, however unjust it may be.

On April 25 the *Herald of Freedom* reported that the building of the Unitarian church was finally at a point that Nute could preach regularly in the basement. The citizens were eager for their church and all the comforts of a New England community. The paper waxed poetic about the Unitarian bell, which had been hung in a temporary frame until the tower was finished. It was already a much-beloved comfort for the citizens of Lawrence. The article read,

> The Church-Going Bell. . . . For those of us who have "lived where bells have tolled to church" the pleasant sound seems a voice of civilization and indispensable to make Sabbath on the prairies. To such the first ringing of the fine toned ball of the Unitarian church was a glad occasion. It is hung for the present in a temporary belfry, near the church, to admit the completion of the tower. Besides its service in summoning to the Sabbath worship, it daily calls our young folks to school and gives noon time at which all rally with cheerful zeal to the support of the important institution of dinner. . . . Blessing on the liberal hearted man, one of the merchant princes of Boston, to whom we are indebted for this humanizing sound. It makes us feel a whole generation ahead of where we are without it.[232]

Also on April 25 Nute and many other leaders of Lawrence signed a letter responding to Stanton's speech declaring his intention to "uphold the law." This meant that he would require the Free-State settlers to abide by the bogus legislature's antiabolitionist laws, which would, in many cases, put their own lives in peril. Nute and his compatriots' primary complaint concerned the governor's intentions regarding the election of delegates to the state convention:

> In your address to the people of Lawrence last evening, we understood you to say in substance, that you would enforce the laws enacted by a legislature elected by the people of an adjoining state until they should be repealed; also, if the laws are unjust or distasteful, our remedy is the ballot box. . . . History has indelibly recorded the fact . . . that the ballot-box was taken from the people of Kansas territory, on the 30th March, 1855, and has not to this day been returned. From that time until the present the people have had no voice whatever in making laws or in selecting officers to administer them, notwithstanding the worldwide declaration by the administration at Washington, and its friends elsewhere, that the people should be perfectly free to regulate their institutions in their own way, subject only to the Constitution of the United States. . . . We are now invited to participate in an election of delegates to a constitutional convention to meet in September next, to frame a constitution and state government. We are told that the election law is a good one; that the voice of the actual settlers can be heard at the polls, and that justice will be meted out to all parties. We regret that the past conduct of the officers to superintend this election has not been such as to permit us to believe that they will secure a fair vote of the people; and the fact that many well known citizens in Kansas are omitted from the registry list, and that as well known citizens and residents of Missouri are registered, is conclusive proof to us that a fair election is not intended and will not be permitted

by the officers who have thus far had the matter in charge. Very respectfully, Your obedient servants,

C. Robinson, G. W. Smith, Wm. Hutchinson, Geo. F. Earle, Edward Clark, Joseph Cracklin, Ephraim Nute, Jr., G. Jenkins, John Hutchinson, S. S. Emory, G. C. Brackett, John D. Wakefield, E. D. Ladd, J. A. Finley, C. W. Babcock[233]

Of the fifteen signers, at least five are documented Unitarians: Robinson, the two Hutchinsons, Nute, and Jenkins.

Nute wrote to Edward Everett Hale on April 28 concerning a German religious party who asked for help. He also told Hale of the scandalous state of the Emigrant Aid Company in Lawrence. Nute's opinions about the company in this letter differed from his firm vote of confidence when aspersions were first cast upon the gentlemen in question. Nute was now very disillusioned and tired of the tainted politics on both sides. He wrote,

I enclose to you a note from Miss Hansen [sic] acknowledging the package of books rec'd by the Serenbetz. These books will do a good work here I believe. . . . The Serenbetz & his party are about starting out to take possession of a tract chosen by their tribe "down south" on the Acosho—to build a town to be called Humboldt I think. If they stick to it they will do well. But I fear they will be rather lacking in self-reliance. They seem to be entirely without funds & in trouble because of finding some in the hands of Pomeroy or others.—I have lent them $100. Whitman became responsible for their board at the public house to the amount of $140. Brass and for a bill of provisions to amount of $100 & Whitman filled them out with seeds & as agent of the Nat. K. A. Comm. . . . Parson S. preached to his people in der Feusche sprache [sic] in our vestry at which they seemed much interested as well as those to whom it was all Dutch. . . . The immigration continues to increase. Hundreds come into this place daily & at the lowest computation a thousand per day into the territory, probably three thousand. They are of the right kind to stay—families from the Western states with their teams stock furniture farming tools etc. Provisions are at enormous prices. . . . This comes hard on the people for everything must be bought in Missouri. But one year more & no fighting will bring all right. Yes, next harvest will do it. . . . I am now convinced that more aid will be required to feed the people during the next three months. That $20,000 from Vermont should be forth coming & some more in the shape of loans. What an empty farce The Emigrant Aid Co has made of the business in Saw mills, grist-mills &c &c &c. At this moment they have absolutely nothing in Lawrence but some agents drawing large salaries; nor anywhere else that I can learn. . . . Not a bushel of grain can be ground here— nor within 40 miles of this—not a log sawed at all at one little wheezy crippled mill owned & managed by men who are disposed to take full advantage of their monopoly. Every foot of lumber costs us from 40 to 90 dollars per thousand & one must watch at the mill for that & scramble for it, & so he must spend another winter in open sheds. Brother Hale I would give more for one live yankee lumberer from Maine with the thousand dollars to invest for himself in a mill than for all any company managed in N. Eng. can do for us with all the . . . raised for The E. A. Co. Everybody in Lawrence if not throughout the territory considers this company total failure as far as doing anything in Kansas is concerned. It has done a good work in N. Eng. I know & so indirectly we have rec'd the benefits. If it had not been so I should have exposed its humbugging inefficiency here long ago. As it has been I have said nothing except here among ourselves where it is the standing object of ridicule & this must be strictly inter nos. Of political matters I know but little definite & care less. We are full of plans & speculations. My confidence is in The Immigration. Our thought is to sit still for a while. For a while longer we are destined to be under the management of usurpers, but our people cannot be kept under & led about by the pro-slavery pack like the people of

Indiana & Illinois. The people who come to us from those states are of the class who desire a more Free soil atmosphere than prevails of late in those regions.[234]

A few days later, acting Governor Stanton answered the letter of the citizens of Lawrence, denying any need for a change in anything regarding the upcoming election. The blatant stonewalling of his ponderously long speech sat bitterly with the outraged citizens of Lawrence. They had been abandoned by all higher authorities to whom they could appeal. Thereafter, the Free-State voters became nearly unanimous in their decision to take no part in the election, eliminating hope of anything short of a civil war to settle the Kansas question.

DEEPENING RIFTS

Though spring might be said to ever hold promise, life weighed heavily on Nute in May 1857. His somber mood would prove unrelenting in the coming year as his dissatisfaction grew. It was a cold spring, and the resulting severe flare-up of rheumatism interfered with his ability to keep up his correspondence. Nute wrote to Miles on May 18 about the overwhelming stress of his job and, perhaps as a measure of his weariness, told Miles that it was time for the Unitarian congregation to stand on its own feet in Lawrence. He suggested that the congregation give bonds or notes to the AUA for anything owed on the building.

This statement came back to haunt Nute. In the time between writing this letter and the AUA's action following his advice, the violence exploded again, and there was no way the Lawrence congregation could even support itself, much less pay sums to the AUA. Despite the news about the escalating violence and the pleadings of Nute, Whitman, and others in Lawrence, the AUA persisted in declaring their mission accomplished in Kansas. They pulled up stakes there and demanded payment far exceeeding what the struggling little church could muster. Nute wrote to Miles,

> I have been for the last month & am now more pressed than ever before with business that cannot be deferred—people calling on me for all kinds of service, advise, introductions & c. & most of them strangers, with letters from organizations at the East, the schools, the church society, S. School getting a

house in the village [in order] to live in something like a civilized manner. Then to cover all I have though a rugged bodily health otherwise been generally tormented with rheumatism or Neuralgia in my hips & legs which has made it impossible for me to sit & write when at all fatigued. From day to day I have been hoping to be better & so—well enough of excuse—.... I have nothing new to report. Our meetings are fully attended. The meeting room is crowded at service. Work on the church stopped for want of funds. Everybody is [so] busy with their town building, farming & land speculation that nothing can be effected towards getting on again. I am strongly opposed to any attempt to raise more funds abroad. The people here are able to finish the building in good style & it will be no help but a serious injury to them to relieve them entirely of the work. We shall have a society meeting as soon as possible & I hope some proposition will be made to take the building off the hands of the A.U.A. giving bonds or notes for what they here expended & then go on to complete & henceforth support their own minister. . . . Our Union S. School will soon be divided by the drawing off of the Orthodox to the new house of worship—the minister Rev. Mr. Lum has shown himself bitterly opposed to the union & did all he could to prevent it. A few sympathise with him. This circumstance of course operates unfavorably to the harmony & success of the school, but I hope for good to come of it nevertheless—The Immigration continues to come in fast & several of the liberal thinking have lately pitched their tents in Lawrence & promise to be of much help to us. Time will favor them—& many other things yet in uncertainty relating to our affairs here.[235]

The next day, May 19, Nute wrote to Amos Lawrence to discuss support of the Lawrence schools, having made the executive decision with Whitman to use some of Amos Lawrence's contributions to that effect. He wrote to Lawrence because Charles Robinson was too busy with other matters to attend to it. His letter read,

Some few weeks since I conferred with Dr. Robinson concerning the support of our High School & he agreed with me that it would be a good use to make of the fund which you have designated for the support of schools, "or a system of common schools in the territory"—that perhaps no better appropriation could be made of that amount ($425. I understood him) I suggested that he should make the suggestion to you. He assented proposing first to visit the school & to make of course his satisfaction with the appearance of things there a condition of his nominating it to your patronage. Now as I hear nothing further of the matter I fear that in the multiplicity of Mr R's engagements it has been neglected & as the first term is about half through & no provision is yet made for the support of this school I must venture to command it to your notice. Thus far Mr. Whitman & myself have taken the responsibility advising the funds for its support. The people of Lawrence subscribed some $400 for the support of the primary school which is now in operation in another room in the basement story of our church on condition that we would establish the High School & look to the friends of Education at the East for its support. Occupying this position in regard to this institution I have some delicacy in speaking in its behalf & would much prefer that some other person would bear witness for its success. To my mind it has succeeded thus far to the highest of my anticipations. The teachers are both of the best Massachusetts manufacture graduates of a normal school & prove themselves fully competent for their work or as near to that as any in has ever been my good fortune to find. Forty-four scholars are connected & the attendance has been on the whole regular. This school has already done much for the cause of Education in Kansas by provoking emulation & by setting a pattern worthy of imitation. For some time to come I believe it will occupy the position of a model school. But I care not how soon it shall be superseded by those much better. It would certainly be a bitter disappointment to me & I think some others, it would be a calamity to this people to have it fail for the want of funds. I will make a long pilgrimage & many appeals rather than suffer this to come to pass. But I trust such efforts will not be required.[236]

The citizens of Lawrence finally met in person with Governor Walker on May 27. The Kansans would not be intimidated; they stood strong on their Free-State politics and called the governor's and the Washington administration's policies toward Kansas on the carpet. In 1890 Nute wrote a piece for the *Lawrence Daily Journal* that described the events of that fall and the first service in the Unitarian church. With shocking forthrightness, he adapted his sermon that day to throw a barbed bouquet at Governor Walker and his gang who, anticipating a handy publicity opportunity, had shown up unexpectedly at the event. The article read,

That fall and again early the next spring the work on the building was pushed forward, and on March 29th, '57, the first meeting was held in the basement, which had been fitted up and furnished with the most modern appliances for a school, including text books, globes and maps. There was established the first free school in the territory with 170 pupils in two departments. The first meeting in the main room above was held on the evening of May 26th. For speakers that evening we had the gifted poet and prophet of freedom, John Pierpont. Hon. Henry Wilson, and Doctor Howe, of Boston, and Governor Walker were also present. To the eloquent utterances on that occasion, it may be, we were indebted for the enlightenment and conversion of that benighted official. . . . That occasion I have ever considered as the real dedication of the house to the service of humanity and practical religion. . . . On the Sunday after, May 31st, regular services were begun in the main room, and continued through the summer. It was yet very much in the rough. The congregation was seated on rude slabs, among the tall cottonwood poles of the staging; the walls unplastered, the windows without casing, the massive oak timbers over head. But all this was in keeping with the general rudeness and simplicity of our new settlement. It amazed no one, but rather added to the impressiveness of the place, bearing witness to the privations and perils among which those walls had been reared. . . . No pictures hung in the chambers of my memory stand out more distinctly to this hour or are more impressive than those of some of the assemblies in that rude house of worship: especially that of our first meeting there. Just before the hour for service, I was notified of the arrival of Governor Walker with a party of officials who had come down from Lecompton to attend our meeting. Agreeable to the suggestion of my informants, I tried to adapt a part of my discourse to the special need of our visitors. Taking for my subject the bearing of our great leader to the publicans of his day, I proposed that following his example we should kindly welcome these representatives of an obnoxious administration and advocates of an iniquitous institution to the privileges of our house and extend to them our religious sympathies and fellowship, though with him we should run the risk of being called the friends of publicans and sinners. To these remarks I had a respectful hearing and no offence seemed to be taken, only the governor afterword called my attention to the fact that the people of Massachusetts had shown themselves as ready as any slave holder to avail themselves of the profit of the institution, to which I fully assented.[237]

On June 1, 1857, Nute wrote to Miles at the AUA about that first service held in the Unitarian church and conjectured about the completion of the structure. The original of this letter seems to have been lost, and its contents are excerpted from the *Quarterly Journal*:

Yesterday for the first time we met for worship in the principal room of our church. That in the basement proves much too small to accommodate the congregation which assembles. The

233

work on the upper room has been for some time suspended for the want of funds, and, for all that we can see, must so remain for a while longer. We have therefore decided to occupy it in its rude, unfinished condition, until the work shall be resumed. So by dint of borrowing and contriving with rough lumber, as new settlers best understand, sittings were speedily provided for a house full, and we had the satisfaction of seeing it completely filled. . . . It was the largest worshipping congregation that I have yet seen in Kansas, gathered from nearly every State in the Union. Some had ridden long distances that cool breezy morning to be present. Among these were our newly-arrived governor and attending dignitaries, who, to their credit be it told, came all the way from Lecompton to place themselves under the influence of Christian institutions. God grant them abundant profit from the visit. . . . Two other services were held in the same room, by the Congregationalists (Orthodox) and the Methodists. The former will hereafter occupy their own house, which is in about the same stage of forwardness as ours. This will divide our Union Sunday School, a painful separation to some on each side. As the other meeting is to be held at the same hour with ours, we may expect a serious diminution in our numbers. Our Methodist friends will probably continue to share our accommodations. . . . What shall we do about the completion of our house of worship? I have delayed writing for weeks, in hopes of saying something definite on this point; but as yet all is uncertain. It is a critical period in our missionary enterprise. Thus far we have been held up and helped on by the hands of our liberal friends at the East. Our life as a society has depended too much on their missionary spirit,—too much for our independent vitality. The time has come when this should be otherwise. We have outgrown the need of guardianship, and should begin to shift for ourselves. We should at least take the management of our external affairs, if we must be to some extent yet further dependent. Our 531 people will not take much interest in an institution in whose support and management they have no agency. This house of worship will not be to them a home until they have it in their own right and charge. We must do or die. I hope that you will soon have a report of action, and that the Association will receive a proposition for a transfer of their title to the building, and of responsibility for the support of a minister. . . . We have been lately much strengthened and refreshed by the accession of kindred spirits. Several men of substance and energy, formerly connected with societies and churches of our fellowship in the States have cast in their lot with us, manifesting a deep interest in the prosperity of our religious and educational affairs. Some have left us for other parts of the Territory, whose loss we deplore. But on the whole we have gained in numbers and strength. . . . I am summoned away on a painful business,—to be present at the trial of the man arrested for the murder of my brother-in-law, Mr. Hopps. It is to take place at Leavenworth, and commences to-day. I must therefore dispatch this hasty letter this morning.[238]

At this time, Fugit, the man who killed Nute's brother-in-law, was finally captured. Ironically, he was kept in the same jail that had housed Nute during his imprisonment by the proslavers. Eventually, Fugit was acquitted and released by a proslavery judiciary, even though it was common knowledge that the Hopps murder was not the only incident in which he had killed someone and taken a scalp for the proslavery cause.

On June 30 Whitman wrote to Miles that he thought others were badmouthing him and implying that he had held up the progress of building the church. Whitman clearly meant Nute, despite his meek denials that he was accusing Nute. Nute was no longer guarded in speaking about his suspicions that Whitman diverted church donations to other purposes.

Other sources document that during this time Whitman ran money for John Brown through the Emigrant Aid Company. In

1859 a letter to John Brown from fellow conspirator Gerrit Smith, the politician and philanthropist, was recovered from belongings left behind at the Kennedy farmhouse, headquarters for Brown's army near Harper's Ferry. In the letter, Smith told Brown, "I suppose you put the E. B. Whitman note in Mr. Kearney's hands. It will be a great shame if Mr. E. B. Whitman does not pay it. What a noble man is Mr. Kearney, and how liberally he has contributed to keep you in your Kansas work."[239] Whitman was obviously known for his financial shell game. If he was employed by the Emigrant Aid Company and the AUA and skimming the Lawrence church for the cause of John Brown, then he was apparently also borrowing from Brown's cause for monies due and owing to others.

On July 1 Nute wrote to Miles concerning the transfer of church property. Nute diplomatically tried to tell Miles that in Whitman's prolonged absences he had to raise money on his own to pay for the church building expenses. On top of that he also had to supervise the work that Whitman was paid by the AUA to supervise. This seemed to be the cause of the deep anger that grew in Nute as the mission drew to a close and fed his resentment about the mortgage note the AUA demanded of the Lawrence congregation. In this letter he carefully assured the AUA that the church could be viable on its own with just a little more help, while he presented Miles with the society's plans for how it would become independent of the AUA. The Lawrence Society's plan, however, was far from what the AUA intended, and Nute knew it. One can almost see him tiptoeing on eggshells as he wrote,

I am commissioned as chairman of a committee chosen by the Society for the purpose to "correspond with this Association through their authorized agents" upon the subject [transfer of the church property to Lawrence society]. . . . Mr. Whitman was absent at this time and we have waited some three weeks for his return hoping that he would be able to state pretty nearly what were the expectations of your Executive Comm in the matter. On conferring with him we find that no distinct understanding exists between him & you on the subject. . . . He is engaged to confer with you & that is perhaps all that is necessary. But I am moved to add my word that you may have a full understanding of the position in which we stand—that you may see the importance both of immediate & of liberal action. . . . The church has remained in about its present condition for the last eight months. All the work that has been done upon the building during this time has been that in the vestry & the tower. This work I have been obliged to superintend in person. . . . All the funds expended during this time I have had to raise or to furnish out of my own scanty treasury. . . . But yet the work is far from completion & beside I am responsible for about $400 for work that has been done at my request—which I am utterly unable to pay. . . . I have urged the society to come forward, take the building into their own hands & complete the work. . . . But in the midst of the excitement about our political affairs & the eager speculations on lands &c. it has until quite recently been impossible to get the people to move in the business. . . . About (I believe a little over) two thousand dollars are now subscribed toward finishing the building on condition that the property be transferred to the society, that the society conduct the work & manage the property according to their own judgment. . . . Our society now consists of 23 members. We might have many more, several times that number, but I have felt it of the utmost importance that the property should pass into the hands of those only of undoubted liberal or Unitarian suasion & no one has been yet admitted without my consent (fortunately given). . . . I mention this that your committee may feel some assurety that the property shall not be wrested for other uses than . . . in accordance with what I understand to be the intention of the contributors & of your Association. . . . I learn from Mr. Whitman that the intentions of your committee has been from the beginning to transfer the church to the society when the building should be completed taking their obligation to refund the sum expended by the Association in aid of other societies in the territory more feeble than themselves. Whether this amount was four or five thousand dollars Mr. Whitman is in doubt. Now the society proposes to take the building incomplete no part but the room appropriated for a school being perfectly finished—to raise the $2000 for its completion & then to take responsibility for the support of their own minister. After the building is finished I believe they will be able to support themselves with but little, perhaps without any assistance. . . . To encourage them in making the effort I think it will be good policy to relieve them of all other burdens leaving the debt to the Assoc without interest and making it no larger than for other considerations, it may be expedient. . . . This effect toward the completion of the building has increased the interest. . . . I believe a people cannot be brought to take interest in the services of public worship & the prosperity of a religious society until they are made to feel individually responsible for the right management of both. As long therefore as this people look upon the temple of their worship as the property of an Association foreign to themselves, & listen to the preacher as the Authority sent & supported by that Assoc but little can be done toward building up a church or religious society. . . . But thus far all other religious societies have been in the same condition and of this you may be well assured we have got the start of them all. . . . Thanks to your early and your generous action we have got the vantage ground of a manifestation of existence & I think I may add of an honorable name thus far. . . . In this new movement for our self support we have also taken the start of all others, I do most earnestly hope and pray that we may succeed in the effort.[240]

As the election loomed, the citizens of the territory, particularly those who formed their own Free-State legislature of which Nute was chaplain, declared their own plans for protecting the ballot boxes against a repetition of the outrages of the past few elections.

"General Order #1" had the audacity of the people's will behind it. Signed by James Lane, it indicated that he was given populist permission to raise militias and organize the people's resistance. Whitman signed as quartermaster general, fulfilling his charge from the National Kansas Committee, another cause which took him from his labors for the AUA.

The Unitarian church, as the hub of a growing Lawrence, received a lot of coverage in the *Herald of Freedom,* the Free-State Lawrence newspaper, during this time. Both the Episcopals and the Methodist Episcopals met within its walls. The political caucus to nominate candidates for the Free-State legislature met there as well.

Not all the media attention was positive, however. One anonymous correspondent of the *Boston Herald* cast great aspersions on the goings-on at the Unitarian church. This writer claimed personal witness that good faith donations to Kansas from the East were being hoarded in great quantity at the Unitarian church and that several men had grown fabulously wealthy from those donations and the provisions of the Emigrant Aid Company—while the settlers languished in poverty, cold, and illness. This probably referred to Hutchinson's and Blood's chicanery with the National Kansas Committee and the fact that numerous donations to the Emigrant Aid Company were stored in the Unitarian church basement. But Nute also had reason to stockpile a certain portion of the goods.

Prior to his trip to the polls on August 3, Nute wrote to Edward Everett Hale to offer excuses for not forwarding Hale material for an article to bring him up-to-date on the schools project and to beat the dead horse of Whitman's failures:

> You have doubtless set me down as an ungrateful wretch for giving you no material for that Examiner article, but I am confident that if you know of one half of the perplexities & engagements with which I am pressed you would reconsider the verdict or at least recommend me to mercy. Of the Educa-

tional and other . . . affairs of the Territory in general I know but little—but of Lawrence in fact about nothing but vague rumors. Every body who has town share or lots to sell has a story of a great college or University which is established near by . . . somebody else. Many of these stories have for basis only that someone has remarked "this would be a good place for such an institution," or perhaps "I will go to work and get one up." In some cases a close investigation would bring to light something more tangible but amid all this stuff & dust raised by land speculators it is hard to get a distinct view of anything. . . . In Lawrence we have had . . . a high school for a term of 14 weeks for the effort of which the sum of $150 has been contributed by A. A. Lawrence. The balance of the current expenses hither to have been paid by Mr. Whitman & myself out of our own pockets. We have not the first cent toward its future support. The principal & assistant teacher of last term are now on a visit to their homes in Massachusetts & await some movement for the support of their school as the signal for their return—Mr. Whitman in going East last Fall undertook to raise funds for the purpose on condition that we here should raise enough to sustain the primary school for one year. We have accomplished our part but he has not raised the first dollar. He came back with the report that Mr. Quincy (x prex) had promised $500 & called it the Quincy School but that turns out all a mistake. I wrote to Mr. Lawrence urging him to designate some part of a fund which he had placed in the hands of Pomeroy & Robinson for this object & he named the $150 mentioned above. . . . You probably know all about the fine school room in the church basement with its furniture & books and globes etc. It will be a shame if it remains unoccupied & if nothing should be done for it at the East. I hope the citizens will be able & disposed to keep it in operation. . . . The "free state College" towards which Mr. Lawrence donated $11,000 remains just there. The gift in the shape of notes against the Lawrence University in Appleton Wis. are in the hands of Pomeroy & Robinson as trustees to be used for the college however the right time has come. . . . To day is our election under the Topeka Constitution. Walker has taken himself off this morning with his dragoons & artillery after the Cheyennes who as the report goes are at Fort Riley threatening an attack. We believe . . . he is glad to so cover his retreat, we shall probably manage to keep the peace without his help. . . . That Serenbetz should be looked after. I entreat you devise some way to head him off from raising money & coming back to Kansas. His people . . . will do much better without him. He's an uncivilized humbug & nuisance, too lazy to do anything but smoke, sleep and eat. . . . Is it right that such men should come out here to consume the little funds we have in reserve against the times of distress next Winter? Send us no more men who can't or who won't work their way & who have no means to support themselves in their lazy shiftlessness. If funds should be raised . . . it should not be entrusted to Serenbetz. This I say advisedly and as the result of careful observation & much injury.[241]

In this letter Nute repeated his rationale for holding back seed or other donations, in response to claims in the media about hoarding and the aspersions cast by whomever had complained to Hale about it. Nute wanted to be sure that there were ample supplies to last the harsh winters, when the rivers were closed to travel. Nute knew that the means to put in a crop had to be conserved if travel conditions held up the early spring flow of supplies. Nute had a reputation for his stubborn refusal to be swayed from a path he thought was correct, regardless of outside pressure.

The first annual meeting of the ministerial alliance was held on August 19. In one year, the alliance had met exclusively in Lawrence, but Nute's secretarial pieces in the *Herald of Freedom* consistently called for "ministers of every denomination, in good standing" to "urgently" attend. Nute maintained that meetings would be taken to other parts of the territory on invitation. The Lawrence movers and shakers had birthed the thing, but clearly they also meant to expand its reach.

Miles had apparently proposed what Nute felt was an outrageous money-making scheme with respect to the building of the church. Nute's incredulous response indicates that Miles proposed that the Lawrence church purchase the building back from the AUA at a much inflated rate, reflecting what Boston thought should be the increase in land and property values in Lawrence. Speculators were selling the idea in the East that Lawrence property values had skyrocketed as settlers poured into a thriving town and bought up the choicest lots available. The AUA Executive Committee supposed the church building was worth more than the money they had put into it and saw this as their opportunity to cash in on the land speculation in Kansas that had enriched many individuals in the East. Nute felt that this was a direct affront to their philanthropic and moral duty to support the mission they had created, and to which he had been called—to say nothing of the fact that the congregation and Nute had raised a major part of the capital for the church project themselves.

Miles proposed that one option was for the congregation in Lawrence to sell off the church building to reimburse the AUA for funds expended on it. They should then build another church at their own independent expense. The AUA expected the Lawrence Society to pay them for the church building but intended for the schoolroom to remain under AUA control, for the exclusive purpose of serving the free public schools in Lawrence. This would have effectively tied the hands of the Lawrence Society with respect to anything requiring changes to their building.

Nute and others at the church were angry and flabbergasted. In Nute's mind, which he had little inhibition about speaking, the AUA's public declaration of support for a liberal Christian mission in Kansas had perhaps finally been revealed as truly motivated by undisguised financial speculation. He no doubt felt this money grab was at the expense of those who, like himself, had done the expensive, backbreaking, and life-threatening duty of surviving the territorial violence in order to bring liberal Christianity there. Nute and many others in the congregation had put up a great deal of their own money to get the church building where it was by that time, and the AUA would be making a profit off their blood, sweat equity, and tears.

In addition, funds and land donations had been raised by the efforts of Nute and other Free-Staters—and a certain number of those gifts appeared to have gone to the AUA administration instead of the Lawrence church. Nute also placed a great deal of responsibility for wasted money on the shoulders of Whitman, whom he considered not only inexperienced as a building superintendent but remiss in his attention to his duties, thereby contributing much to the overages in expenses on the project. On August 18, Nute wrote to Miles,

> Yours of the 6th is just received and with much surprise. I am utterly unprepared for such a view as you present and such a proposition. Is the A.U.A. also possessed with this mania of speculation? Have we to deal with a money-making corporation trading on the missionary spirit in the churches? If such be the purpose & expectation of your committee then are they doomed to a bitter disappointment as great as mine at the present moment. You shall be quickly undeceived. . . . I will get the estimate which you request. In the meantime as you wish "to hear from me at once" I will give a few facts bearing on the case. . . . I. The building is not worth what it cost, not more than half as much. . . . Between the Association, the architect, the superintendent, & the trustees the business of building has been . . . mismanaged. . . . It was certainly unfortunate that we had for a superintendent one who had no practical knowledge of building who came an entire stranger to the way of doing things in Kansas who was absent a great part of the time when from the necessity of the case, perhaps, I say not from any fault of his, the business was left at loose ends and our

hands completely tied from the want of the funds, of the plans & of the contracts. . . . Then at least $1000 was lost by plunder during the troublous times. Several hundred more (probably 800) by change of plans:—in the first instance through severe misunderstanding between the Assoc., the superintendent & the architect. I know not exactly how. The other and principal change was in the roof to save the building from great disfigurement & to secure a covering that should not leak. The trustees are not responsible for this change. They devised it but our superintendent came before the contract was signed he reconsidered the whole subject keeping the workmen in waiting several weeks & finally gave our plan his approval and signature to the contract. There is but one opinion here as to the wisdom of that change. If the lumber ordered for the first . . . had not been stolen there would have been little cost in the changes. The building is worth at least $1000 more for it. . . . II. The land on which the building stands has risen in valuation. But one lot was given to the society by a citizen of this place. He knew nothing of any A.U.A. until we came to make the deed. The cost of the other lot, as you will find by reference to a letter of mine I pledged myself to give, if I remained here another year, which is past. I wish the $45 to be deducted from my present quarters salary. Can you justly expect the society here to pay for the rise on land given for their benefit when they are unable to complete the building without more help from abroad? . . . Buildings have risen in value in Lawrence that is to say above their actual cost. If it were not for the great rise in valuation of land they would not sell for what they have cost—For—[242]

The rest of the letter is missing, but Nute laid out to Miles the stark realities of why the expenses of the church exceeded what was predicted and implied that this made preposterous the prospect of the church as a moneymaking scheme for the AUA. Whitman's inadequacy as a superintendent and his long disappearances that held up the building of the church had been items of contention for which Nute had received more than a little censure from Miles. Especially infuriating to Nute was the implication that the Lawrence Society would be charged for a rise in value on land initially donated by Nute and others. Property values in Lawrence increased because common people like Nute and his parishioners had paid with sweat equity and their lives to make that happen. From this point, Nute's relationship with the AUA limped along, damaged, and his loyalty to them slowly turned to disillusionment.

In its report for its thirty-second anniversary, the AUA boasted about the success of the Kansas mission. Every New England Unitarian knew the association had channeled a great deal of money to the mission through its auspices. The report put a positive spin on the proposal that Nute had found so insulting to the Lawrence Unitarians, completely ignoring the issues Nute raised regarding the AUA's financial affront to their own mission. The report read,

We have to report a similar success attending our mission to Kansas. It will soon outgrow the necessity of any further aid from the Association. On every Sunday morning the first church-going bell ever heard in that Territory summons a large congregation to the neat and substantial stone edifice that overlooks the city of Lawrence. At present, only the basement room is occupied. A formal dedication of the church will take place this summer. By an act of Christian courtesy, which will meet with a hearty approval from this body, the Orthodox Society occupy the room in the afternoon of each Sabbath; and by an act of Christian fellowship, reflecting the highest credit upon both Unitarian and Orthodox Societies, the Sunday schools of both meet together for instruction at the feet of Jesus. May the act be prophetic of Christian union and co-operation in a Territory well-nigh blasted at first by wrath and rage inhuman. Through the growth of Lawrence, and the rise of property in that city, the church owned by the Association will become valuable, and can be sold to the Society there worshipping, for many thousand dollars. The proceeds will be sacredly appropriated, to repeat in other places in Kansas the work done in Lawrence.[243]

In the next volume of the *Quarterly Journal*, an extract of one of Nute's letters was published without a date on it. The original letter appears to be missing from the Harvard collection and does not show up in the Kansas collection either. The tone of the letter published was different from the letters that Nute wrote to Miles in early fall of 1857. In it, Nute conveyed the idea that if the AUA was serious about promoting Unitarianism in the territory, now was the time to secure property in a few key towns. The AUA's plan to "sell" the Lawrence church to its members was paraded again before the readers of the *Quarterly Journal* with no hint of its bitter taste to those it affected:

> We give below a short extract from a late letter from Mr. Nute, conveying an intimation of his hope of useful action in other places than in Lawrence. We will only add, that measures have been matured for the sale of the church in Lawrence to the Society there worshipping, which will soon become, it is believed, a self-sustaining body. Should it attain to this independent position, it must become an important center of influence throughout the neighboring region.

> There are opportunities now opened to us in several of the most promising of the embryo cities of this Territory to secure desirable building lots for Unitarian churches. . . . I have been invited to visit two of these, Wyandotte and Sumner, to make the selection and secure the land. I shall avail myself of these openings as soon as possible. Will it not be well to have deeds made to the American Unitarian Association, or to trustees in their behalf, to hold until such time as a Society of our views may be ready to build? This plan would secure the land from being appropriated by other denominations. . . . There is a

very general expectation of more trouble here in the fall. It is the opinion of many that we shall not get out of our house of bondage without more bloodshed. Governor Walker's army is yet encamped near us, and we hear that warrants are out for the arrest of our leading men, to the number of one hundred and fifty, and that attempts are soon to be made to collect the taxes. The general counsel is quiet submission in both contingencies, under protest; but there is not much security for infallible prudence and patience under such a long series of outrages, and the rash deed of one man may lead to a general outbreak. If it should come to that, it will be a more serious affair than we have had before. I pray we may be saved from such scenes, and get our rights, so long wrested from us, in some more peaceable way.[244]

The opening of the school in the Unitarian basement rooms in early September 1857 was a momentous event in Lawrence. Mr. C. L. Edwards, one of the teachers, recalled the event when he spoke at the closing of the old Unitarian church in 1891:

The fall term opened on the 7th of September. Total attendance 67 in May 1857 the rear basement room having been completed, the emigrant aid building was abandoned on the Sabbath and church services for a time were held in this west basement room. Rev. Mr. Nute preaching in the morning service, the Sunday school was held at noon, and on the first Sabbath a brief but sharp discussion arose between the two pastors as to the manner of the organization—the one fearing to lose the precedent of having the oldest Sunday School in Kansas, and the other, as would be natural in coming into his own church building, desiring a larger recognition of his own congregation in the Sabbath School organization. The matter was finally settled at the suggestion of Mr. Whitman, the superintendent (against whom personally there was no contest), by the election of Mr. Nute as assistant superintendent.

Rev. Lum did not hold services here for any length of time as his health failing he gave up preaching. . . . The Congregationalists, however, continued to attend Mr. Nute's services in this room, and the singers joined with your own reorganized choir. Many of my pleasantest recollections are of the church and choir services in this building with its bare walls and staging holes and scaffolding.[245]

Nute's duties as a territorial minister and missionary were ever changing. On September 13, 1857, he delivered the first sermon in the new Methodist church building in what is now the town of Quindaro, Kansas. Despite the resentment of Rev. S. Y. Lum, there was a great deal of cooperation between many of the frontier churches. The church was later finished and dedicated in 1858 by the Methodist bishop, with Nute listed as pastor.

While Nute was preaching the first sermon in the Methodist church in Quindaro, Rev. John Stillman Brown took his place in Lawrence's pulpit for the day. Brown would replace him permanently in that pulpit when Nute left Kansas.

On September 14 Brown's daughter Sallie wrote to her brother Willie, who was left behind at Phillips Exeter Academy to continue his education in New England while the family pioneered in the Kansas Territory. Amid gossip about the family, Sallie dropped tidbits about the political situation around Lawrence. The terrorism seemed far away from a teenage girl's world. Nute's eternal rival among the orthodox, Rev. Lum, wrote to his church sponsors that Nute's influence was an obvious danger to the youth of Lawrence, as he was "making special efforts to draw off the young to their eternal destruction."[246] Other documents laud Nute's inspirational powers for young and old alike. But Sallie Brown thought he was not very motivating of attendance at the Sunday school. Besides her loyalty to her father, she may not have appreciated the many other things—crops, livestock, terrorism, illness, and the weather—that might have been more of a deterrent of crowds at the Sunday school than the pastor's charms. She wrote,

Father preached for Mr. Nute, who went to Quindaro—Gov Robinson's city—& to Wyandott in which places he preached morning & afternoon respectively. He intends taking up lots in those places for churches & forming societies there. Also he is interested in forming a society in Bloomington & I hope father will find preaching on some of those places. It is pleasant to hear him preach again. The Sunday School here does not flourish surprisingly Mr. Nute is not exactly the man to interest teachers & scholars & they are very irregular in their attendance. After Sabbath School we walked home in the hot sun & by that time I was pretty tired. In the afternoon we feasted on a forty pound watermelon which our neighbor Mr. Heywood brought from Lawrence the day before. It was a very nice one but notwithstanding such a monster the people left it unsatisfied & in the evening May & I walked over to Mr. Heywood's & he gave us another.[247]

In his next surviving letter to Miles, on September 24, Nute divulged the difficult financial position that his mission work put him in. In the context of an annual salary that was only eight hundred dollars to begin with and the many times he had put up his own money to provide for the church or his flock, it is clear that his mission work was dipping into his personal estate, meager as it was. He felt it was time to cut through the third-party delays in his negotiations with the AUA, come to Boston, and take matters into his own hands. He wrote,

Mr. Blood presented the enclosed bill to me a few days since. I am unable to pay it, having already paid some nearly three hundred dollars for church bills and am in need of the same. Mr. Whitman took as he offered all the accounts against the Association with him but this bill was forgotten. . . . It is I believe a just bill & I expect it will soon be paid. . . . I sent you a long letter ten days since & . . . hoping to receive . . . an answer to some of mine, to learn your proposition concerning

249

the transfer of the church property & get the funds which I have advanced. . . . I want very much to spend a few months in the East to counteract . . . my Kansas life, get that clock for the church &c. I have a plan thus: Rev. Brown can fill my place here and take the salary. It would be a help to him. I can earn my expenses to & fro & while there by lecturing on Kansas and preaching. Now tell me candidly & practically what you think of the plan? [248]

A clandestine letter on October 5, 1857, from Whitman to abolitionist John Brown confirms that Whitman worked to raise funds for Brown:

I have just returned from Boston where I have been for the last five weeks. On my return from Chicago in June I sent Mr R to you as I agreed. He was there on the appointed day with some additional funds making near $400 in all. I was in hopes that would enable you to get in here, but he failed to see you. The letter which I sent by him, I think, stated that I could do anything in the way of teams. Of course the only alternative was for you to come on with the teams you had. He returned with the word that you had been detained by sickness. I could learn nothing more of you and could find no one who had heard a word from you until I reached Boston. Then I saw a letter saying you been waiting for teams. Before I left another one came to Mr S—asking for funds—The letter of his which I forward with this will explain matters in part. After considerable exertion I succeeded in getting funds into my hand to such an amount as would justify me in advancing for your use $500 and wait for it to be raised. This I was to send on to you at once. As ill luck would have it the financial panic had risen to such a pitch in St. Louis that it was impossible to negotiate Mr S's draft and I was most reluctantly forced to send it back for collection and come in here pennyless. . . . Your messenger I found here, sick. He is now desirous of returning and as the funds may not arrive for a week I am unwilling to let you remain so long in suspense and therefore I shall pay his expenses and start him back with this message. As soon as the funds arrive I will send on a special messenger with teams if they can be procured or without them if they cannot. In the latter case you must do the best you can with your furniture. I shall send direct to Tabor by the Loveland route probably. . . . How matters are to turn today I do not know. I shall not be surprised to learn of collisions, if they do occur the difficulty will spread; at any rate the end is not yet. Fortunate indeed shall we be if we lose nothing by this move. . . . Your friends will welcome you home and I hope we shall see you here soon. I understand that you have written to me but I have received not a line. . . . If you cannot bring all the furniture I think you had better bring the 190 telescopic tubes and the fillings.[249]

"Furniture," no doubt, referred to guns, "telescopic tubes" were the rifle barrels, and "fillings" were the slides ordinarily removed before shipping in order to prevent the enemy from using the guns if they confiscated them.

On October 15 Whitman wrote to Miles that Nute and the other parishioners disagreed with him about taking monetary responsibility for the costs of the school and giving the general citizenry control over that part of the church. Whitman implied that he was hurt that Nute and the others believed that he had obstructed the building of the church. Whitman declared he was going to resign when he got to Boston. He felt he was unjustly blamed for the problems with building the church and the fact that it was not yet complete. However, in this letter, he did not address the complaints by Nute and others that he had been absent from Lawrence for long periods of time, even though he was on the AUA payroll to superintend the building of the church.

The conflict between Nute and Whitman was in full swing. The proposal of the AUA had been rejected. It seemed that although the AUA wanted to charge the Lawrence Society more for the church building than it cost, they also expected the society to maintain the school room but lend it free of charge to the general citizenry. To Nute and others who had sacrificed personally and borne the brunt of unreimbursed expenses and gross building overages due to terrorism beyond their control, this was unthinkable.

Nute was now in direct opposition to the dictates of the AUA, so Whitman naturally presented himself as their ally. He maintained that his reputation had been martyred to the cause of the AUA and he could not understand Nute's and the other parishioners' accusations and animosity toward him. The conflicting loyalties and monetary boundaries between the two groups for which Whitman was an agent—the AUA and the Emigrant Aid Company—seem to have been blurred by Whitman. This created the rift between Whitman and Nute and others in the Lawrence congregation. Things would come to a head in Boston soon. In his October 15 letter, Whitman told Miles,

Enclosed you will find an official copy of the proceedings of our society at a meeting recently held to consider the proposals for a transfer of the church. . . . The meeting was quite thinly attended and as you see the proposal of your Association was declined. The chief obstacle to its acceptance seemed to be the reservation of the use of the school room for the benefit of the citizens generally free of expense. I explained as fully as I could the original design and the understanding that so much was to be for general use. I argued that it was not right for us as a society to charge rent—and control the room. That if we had the right, it would neither be for the benefit of Education nor for the good of a society to be so linked with it. If as a society we felt that we were called upon to pay for the room and did not feel able or willing to do so we should say that and ask for a reduction in price on that account. Mr. Nute much to my surprise took active ground against the reservation and has not hesitated openly to charge the hard terms upon me personally. I think in this case he both shapes and utters the opinions of the society. What his motive is in leading off in this matter I know not. He will see you and can argue his own case. . . . I spoke freely and frankly to those present and defended the liberality and good intentions of the Association and assured them that there was no opposition of interests. The good of the cause was your sole object but you must act in good faith to all parties. . . . I suggested that if it should appear that the society did no[t] have to pay for the school room they could not object to its being held for the use of the citizens. This did not however meet the difficulty and I am compelled to feel that something more than the mere control of the room is sought. . . . I am sorry to be compelled to take a position apparently antagonistic. Certainly it is not agreeable to be looked upon with suspicion by those whom you would serve. . . . One would sometimes think from remarks made here and publickly in parish meeting, that but for me they would have had a church long ago. . . . I will resign my position as Agent as I proposed to do while in Boston. . . . I will see to the payment of the outstanding debts as far as the money for which I am authorized to draw will enable me. Some additional bills of which I knew nothing have been sent in and a lot of fine lumber which I left locked in the church has been abstracted during my absence. You will hear from me more in detail about the cost and value of the church and the expense of replacing it. That however need have no bearing on the transfer but is important to me in regard to a certain letter in your possession.[250]

The next day Whitman included an addendum to the letter, concerning money owed to Nute. Whitman had "missed" Mr. Nute, to whom he expected to give the October 15 letter to deliver to Boston in person. Nute maintained that Whitman intentionally missed their meeting. The two men were locked in bitter battle. One believed he was acting on his loyalty to the AUA, and the other believed he was acting on his loyalty to his call, which the AUA was now betraying.

253

In Boston, the Executive Committee met on November 11 and voted to have Nute look into buying land in Quindaro for the purpose of erecting another church. Despite the conflict with Whitman, Nute must still have had the confidence of that body.

Back in Lawrence, the Unitarian church continued as the seat of all activity in that part of the territory. Rev. John Stillman Brown filled the pulpit and Unitarian services continued under his ministry until Nute returned from the East. The quarterly meeting of the Methodist Episcopal church was held at the Unitarian facility. A huge rally of the Lawrence citizenry for the purpose of crystallizing community resistance to the Ruffian politics and terrorism took place there as well.

On December 15 Nute wrote to Rev. John Stillman Brown from Boston. He divulged details of his own troubles with Whitman, which Brown was experiencing himself. Whitman was helping himself to money that came for Kansas relief or was supposed to go to the building of the church. He had also borrowed Nute's personal funds and had not returned them.

Nute related that Whitman's behavior had almost cost them the clock, and Nute had to put up serious money from his own pocket to save it from an abandoned freight sale. This letter cuts to the heart of all the difficulty between Nute and Whitman and fully reveals the difficulty that Nute had with the AUA on Whitman's account. Nute's letter to Brown reflected his relief that someone else was experiencing the side of Whitman that he had struggled with for so long. The letter read,

> I console with you from a vivid recollection of like trial for the gross delinquencies of that great self-sufficient E.B.W. I might sug I share with you painfully in the results of it. . . . I am on the whole encouraged by your account of the missionary operations. The prosperity of our society must be very much dependent on the political & business prospects. . . . I am now on full blast lecturing on the Kansas struggle & my experiences therein. . . . I am amazed & indignant beyond the power of

words to express at Whitmans meanness. Do tell me at once if he has paid on anything to Adams & how much. I want you to know the facts of his dealing with me: I advanced about $480 a large part of it over ten months since for paying bills on the church building. Whitman took the vouchers & examined the accounts when he left for the East last August, promising to get the funds for me from the Treasurer of the A.U.A. Instead of that he got some $400 for himself & came back to Lawrence saying he had got authority to draw for my pay & had been unable to get the draft cashed in St. Louis & that he would soon . . . get funds from St. Louis for me. When he found I was coming East he proposed to let me take a draft & get the money here, he promised to call at my house for that purpose the night before I was to start. He didn't come. I waited another day. Found on inquiring for him that he had gone to Lecompton & that he would be back before night, didn't come & was obliged to leave without seeing him. I wrote him from Jeff City saying I expected to get the draft in Boston, but no word has yet reached me from him. I hear from Adams that on the 15 of November he had not sent the draft but had been trying to get it cashed there & said he was going to send it to me the next day. . . . Now beside the 480 dollars which are due me from AUA he owes me $59.75 borrowed money & has owed from that sum to $500 for the last 6 months. I found a letter here to Dr. Miles in which he had endeavored to injure my standing with the Association & prevent the acceptance of the terms of the society for the transfer of the church property. I sent the due-bill for the 59.75 to G. W. Hutchinson for collection some month since asking him to collect the same & pay to Adams if he had not recd his $200 from Whitman or in case he had send it to me as I was short of funds. Though on that disagreeable subject, I am also troubled about that letter from Mr. Little with $40. Mr. L. informs me that he had written to Whitman informing him that he had sent the money to be disbursed to his sons wife. Now I suspect W. has taken the lib-

crty to lay hands on that to reimburse himself. . . . Postscript.
. . . There is another matter that must be attended to. . . . That
clock of our church-tower. As I suspected I found on reaching
St. Louis that Whitman had done nothing abut it. It had since
been opened (you remember his statement at our peevish
meeting how he had it opened & examined by a clock maker
had got the charges abated &c). . . . I found the commission
merchant had advertised it for sale, had refused & still refused
to have the boxes opened & declared it out of his power to
abate the charges. After much entreaty & by the intervention
of some friends in St. Louis I got his consent to an examination opened it myself & found it to all appearances in good
order—The charges are nearly $300 I have got the consent of
some who sent me funds for relief to appropriate some of it
to this purpose—& I must commission you to request G. W.
Hutchinson to transmit to me two hundred dollars for this
purpose from the funds which I left in his hands. . . . The time
for the sale of the clock has already passed but I trust in some
friends in St. Louis to see that it was not sacrificed. But it must
be attended to soon.[251]

Nute's lecture tour was going gangbusters according to a *Boston Journal* story picked up by the *Herald of Freedom*. Apparently, he made an entertaining evening for his listeners:

It was our pleasure last evening to listen to a lecture from Rev.
Ephraim Nute, delivered before the citizens of South Reading,
in which he gave a vivid picture of his experience in Kansas.
. . . He began his lecture by giving a description of his passage
from St. Louis up the Missouri River; which account, though
brief, was rich in important information, and afforded not a
little food for indignation, and now and then, for mirth. Arriving at Lawrence he gave a very clear statement of its situation,
appearance, the kind of people he met, and the welcome he
received. Then followed an account of Kansas life; turning

mainly upon the difficulties by which that virgin Territory was beset, and its honest, liberty-loving citizens robbed of peace, property, all political rights, and, often, of life itself. We were particularly impressed with his picture of the first meeting of the citizens of Lawrence, when they learned that the city had been doomed to destruction. It was no holiday gathering; it was a meeting where men must devise means to protect themselves, their wives, and children, their all, from the most imminent danger. There was not much said; they looked into each other's faces, feeling that deeds, not words, were now wanted. Portraits of Lane, and others of the leaders, were drawn to the life, and let us into the very heart of their characters and aims. . . . He then passed to an account of his own arrest and imprisonment; told us whom and what he saw while a prisoner; what conversations he had with the enemy, and what he overheard, which revealed their dispositions, purposes, and daily transactions. This portion of the narration was intensely interesting as the personal narration of an intelligent, active man must always be, when he has himself played so conspicuous a part, and been so deeply involved in the events he portrays. . . . He closed with touching tributes to the memory of several of the prominent persons who early fell in the struggle, and who, in a coming day, will be looked upon as martyrs to liberty. . . . Mr. Nute is a very pleasant speaker, fluent, yet concise, eminently fair and candid, and we hope may be induced to repeat his lecture in many of our New England villages. He imparts a clearer idea of the real state of things as they are and were in Kansas than we have been able to gain from other sources.[252]

Nute was born and raised in Boston. With his eyes set on the ministry from youth, as the son of a merchant, Harvard was a goal he undoubtedly worked hard for. His trip back to Boston and his alma mater in the fall of 1857 lasted into the new year, as he tried to set things straight with the AUA. Whitman, back in Lawrence, must have become concerned by Nute's long absence. It wasn't lost on him that part of the reason that Nute had gone East concerned his own behavior.

Whitman wrote to Calvin Clark, the AUA treasurer, on January 1, 1858, to inform Clark that he had drawn another draft for funds.[253] His apologies to Clark leave the clear impression that he was not supposed to do this. Whitman said he was trying to pay debts on the church. He mentioned that Nute, now in the East, was angry at him for neglecting his duties. His defense was that his papers were with Nute when he left for the East. Nute's previous letters belie this defense, as Whitman had never shown up to convey those papers to Nute in the first place.

A few days later Whitman wrote to Miles[254] that Nute had cast him out of the Lawrence Unitarian Society. He wrote with regret about the damage in his relationship with Nute and stated that his work as a confidential agent of the Emigrant Aid Company and the AUA had put him in a "terrible position with [his] own pastor." Now he must "seek a new denomination."[255]

Whitman felt that some things had to be kept secret—for example, the complicity with John Brown's abolitionist cause. From Whitman's point of view, Nute's persistence in bringing these things to light jeopardized Whitman's and, by extension, the Emigrant Aid Company's and the AUA's "confidential work." Whitman's business for the AUA clearly encompassed much more than the supervision of the building of the church. He also served as the point person to distribute funds among the three organizations, although this had to be done in a clandestine manner.

Although Whitman sounded sincere, it is difficult to imagine how his position as a confidential agent in a worthy cause justified siphoning off funds legitimately donated to another part of the cause. All sides had been burned by Whitman's financial dealings at some point.

Whitman conveyed little animosity toward Nute in his letters to Miles in spite of Nute's anger toward him. He told Miles that Nute was well thought of, except for questions about why he left so precipitously on his current trip to Boston. Whitman felt that it would be best if Nute returned to Lawrence to resume full-time pastoring. Although Rev. John Stillman Brown's sermons would suffice, Rev. Brown was not pastoring and seemed to have little interest in doing so. This was quite a vote of confidence from a man in such an adversarial relationship with Nute and most likely was an attempt to retrieve the good graces of Miles.

Despite its precarious political situation, Lawrence continued to flourish. There were now two hundred students between the ages of six and twenty-six enrolled in the Quincy High School in the basement of the Unitarian church. Their teacher, Mr. C. L. Edwards, was assisted by the Misses Wilder, Brown, Bouton, and Oakley. Many students were the sons and daughters of prominent local families. The troubles continued, however, particularly with respect to communication with the East. Nute and others constantly wrote that the mail was unreliable, and many letters inexplicably disappeared. These allegations were borne out by the later discovery of a cache of hidden mail, dumped in a well in Westport, Kansas Territory, that contained a large number of letters addressed for Lawrence in June and August of 1856.[256]

Whitman wrote to Miles later in January about the increasing unrest in the Lawrence Society over whether it would be Unitarian, Universalist, ecumenical, or some other religion.[257] Whitman implied that Nute garnered donations without telling anyone the church would be Unitarian. Whitman's accusation is not supported by all the newspaper articles in Lawrence regarding the progress of the "Unitarian Society" and the "Unitarian church building" or by Nute's anecdotal comments in his own letters. This raises the question of whether Whitman was trying to create a belief at the AUA that Nute put them in danger of losing the society in Lawrence to another denomination.

Whitman wrote that Nute left in haste and everything was in disarray, but this could be interpreted as things being out of Whitman's control. Nute's deputies carried on in his absence by notifying the rest of the Lawrence Unitarian Society of Whitman's attempts to sell the church building to the AUA. Additionally, they were vigilant in trying to keep anyone from giving Whitman any more money.

Whitman also told the AUA that the society was in a "crude" state, perhaps best taken to mean that it was too independent and that its loyalty to the AUA was unreliable. The AUA was enamored of the idea that the Kansas enterprise could become a financial investment. The society in Lawrence, however, believed that the AUA was there to support its existence, not the other way around. Whitman tried to say that Nute left a lot of confusion about whether he would return to Lawrence at all, believing that Nute would come back and settle in Quindaro instead. Nute had already been providing ministerial services to Quindaro and assisting the Methodists in starting a church there. The AUA's instructions to Nute to look into the possibility of purchasing property to begin a Unitarian church in Quindaro might not have been known to Whitman.

The *Quarterly Journal* published extracts from a letter from Rev. John Stillman Brown written on January 23.[258] It covered Rev. Brown's experience replacing Nute in the pulpit of the Lawrence church while Nute was in the East. In between Rev. Brown's not-so-subtle hints at fishing for a job like Nute's, he stood strongly behind Nute's reputation as a hardworking, beloved, and respected citizen and minister.

Whitman wrote to Miles on February 18.[259] The Lawrence Society had embraced the terms of the AUA's proposal on the deed for the church except for one provision: The ownership of the church would return to the AUA if it ceased to be used as a Unitarian church. In that case, the Lawrence Society wanted the option to sell the property and invest the money in another building at another site. This conflict had afforded Rev. George W. Hutchinson—a founding member of the Lawrence Society, a mover and shaker in the Free State cause, and at this time, Nute's trusted ally in the management of the church and building project—a reason to divorce himself from the process. Whitman alleged that all thought that he really wanted to take over the society, and when he couldn't, this was his way out. Whitman thought Nute should not have confided in Hutchinson because Whitman thought Hutchinson was lying about what Nute had said to him. Whitman believed those conflicts had divided the society and blamed Nute for trusting in Hutchinson, who was now leaving in a huff since he had not gotten his own way. Whitman hinted that the society needed a pastor to bring it back together, and despite his previous vote of confidence in Nute, in this letter he recommended Rev. John Stillman Brown in that regard.

Nute had a different take on these events. He wrote to Miles from Boston on February 22 that he wanted to meet with the Executive Committee on March 1 to discuss the church plans in Quindaro and to "answer the charges" of Whitman.[260] Nute's anger was evident in the formality and abruptness with which he addressed Miles, a man whom he previously referred to as "my dear Miles."

Rev. John Stillman Brown wrote to Edward Everett Hale on May 2 of his experience substituting for Nute while Nute was lecturing in the East for the preceding six months.[261] Brown campaigned again for a steady pulpit. He wrote that he would rather be back in his profession than hampered by the homesteading that was taking up all of his time, and he asked Hale for money to support his missionary work. Clearly, those who wanted to minister in liberal Christianity in the territory were all competing for the support of the Emigrant Aid Company, the AUA, and the public.

Nute's lecturing and fund-raising tours in the East raised a lot of money for the church and the Free-State settlers in Kansas and should have situated everything well. However, there were expensive destructions and thefts by both the Border Ruffians and the less-than-scrupulous supporters of the Free-State cause. These factors sent Nute back again and again for more aid. It is clear from AUA financial records and newspaper articles that many contributions for Kansas were sent to the AUA, but it is unknown how many of them, beyond those promised to Nute in salary and for building the church were in fact forwarded to Kansas. It appears from Nute's letters that some of those funds were never sent along to Kansas by the AUA. Additionally, more than a little money sent from Boston to the territory was stolen on the way.

The Kansas cause also provided a chaotic smokescreen for carpetbaggers. Men with secure support, like Nute, were rare. Men of integrity, like Nute and John Stillman Brown, who were homesteading rather than siphoning funds from the East for their own support, struggled mightily to provide for the actual ministry needs of the territory. These needs far exceeded the reach of the formal efforts of the AUA.

Nute wrote to Hale on May 10 that he had returned to Lawrence from his trip to the East and regretted not having had the chance while in Boston to fully fill in Hale on the situation in Kansas.[262] He related the results of his audience with the Executive Committee regarding the Lawrence congregation's obligation to pay them back for funds expended for the church. Nute had prevailed upon them to abandon their pursuit of an inflated rate of return on the church and to release the basement to the society so that they might collect rent for it.

Nute asked Hale for advice about whom to approach to obtain a loan large enough to finally complete the church. He was embarrassed by the amount it would still cost to finish the building, which he said was only worth about half what it had cost thus far because of territorial setbacks. So much had obstructed the completion of the church and so many expenses had been compounded by the terror campaign, the martyrdom of society members to the violence, the sacking of Lawrence, and the dire poverty of the subscribing populace. Unspoken were Nute's previous suspicions of Whitman, undoubtedly because of Hale's leadership in both the AUA and the Emigrant Aid Company.

Nute remained committed, but he navigated a difficult territory regarding the church building. He still felt that the accomplishment of securing a New England-type church would provide a beacon of liberal Christianity to a population torn apart by violence and poverty. At the same time, he didn't know how to navigate how much should be provided by donations from the East and how much should be expected from the society, with its meager resources. To acquire such a building only by charity would not give the populace a proper stake in it, but to try to pull any more blood out of the ragged and abused society might cause the whole project to fail. Other denominations supported their missions in full. Nute wrote to Hale,

> I write now and enlist your interest in a plan we have for the completion of our church building. Our people do not ask or expect any further gratuitous help, but we must make a loan at a reasonable rate of interest 6 or even 10 per cent would be a great favor to us in the present condition of money affairs. . . . Here we could not raise it for ten times that rate. Everybody is getting ready for the land sales the new act in our long drama of oppression from this infamous administration. Besides we are now just experiencing the full effects of the financial panic of last Fall. From the same causes is now a favorable time to build. Material & labor are much cheaper than ever before. If the house were completed we could rent the seats for some good sums. . . . The rent of the basement will pay our interest to the A. U. A. & nearly meet the two first payments of the principal i.e. $1,000 in two years. We can give the best of security. Our trustees will sign the notes & three of our wealthiest men will endorse. Mayor Babcock who has a large amount of property here in lands & buildings, the late Mayor James Blood who is also a man of means & some one of our Society who has property enough to secure the whole amount. We want $2000. The church & land when the building is completed will be worth at least one half what it has cost, I think over two thirds now & more than the cost in one years time. It will have cost when finished twelve thousand dollars. We are to give a mortgage for five thousand to the A.U. A. which will be paid off in two years. We rent the basement for $500. We pay interest on but three thousand of the sum due . . . at 6 per cent. . . . Now you know, as I do not, who to ask for this loan & have influence with such

persons. Perhaps you could persuade several persons to take shares in the loan & let it lie for several years. I am confident it will be perfectly safe. We will give a mortgage on the property; the value is certainly sufficient to cover that & the sum due to the Assoc. Our church should be the first completed & it will be if we can make this loan but meetings are now held in the principal room, rudely fitted up but unsightly, inconvenient & untidy. The congregations are large but would be much larger if we had a suitable place.[263]

At the end of May, Richard Realf, author and John Brown conspirator, wrote from Canada and used Nute as a reference to get the other wealthy John Brown backers to send him funds to go to England to see his parents and perhaps raise even more money for Brown's cause there. The letter was addressed to the members of what came to be called "The Secret Six"—the clandestine backers of abolitionist John Brown's militant cause.[264] George Luther Stearns was a merchant industrialist, one of the chief financers of the Emigrant Aid Company and a Unitarian. Franklin B. Sanborn was a journalist and Transcendentalist, and ran in Unitarian circles. Theodore Parker was the radical Unitarian minister. Unitarian Samuel Gridley Howe was a physician, advocate for the blind, and husband of Julia Ward Howe. Thomas Wentworth Higginson was a Unitarian minister and Harvard classmate of Nute. Gerrit Smith was a leading philanthropist and politician who unsuccessfully ran for U.S. president in 1848, 1852, and 1856.

In his letter Realf mentioned a "certain enterprise" that had to be postponed for six to nine months before "active measures can be taken." Realf cryptically referred to the attack on Harper's Ferry, which was to pull Nute into its sphere of influence when it finally went forward in October 1859.

In early June 1858, the infamous James Lane—Free-State general, ruthless warrior against the Border Ruffians, and a founding member of Nute's congregation—shot and killed another Unitarian society founding member, Gaius Jenkins, over disputed rights to a well situated almost in Nute's backyard. Nute had to testify at the trial, as he overheard the violence.

Rev. John Stillman Brown wrote to his son Willie at Phillips Exeter Academy and mentioned that after the shooting Nute put up handbills all over town announcing the text of his next sermon: "Thou Shalt Not Kill."[265] His letter provides insight into Brown's extremely upright, puritanical Unitarianism. He was very critical of his son and scolded him about drinking tea, which he felt was too much of a stimulant.

Nute wrote another unhappy letter to Miles on June 15 regarding the transfer of the church property. Whitman had been remiss in notifying the congregation that Boston had done it already. Nute and the Lawrence Society were angry with the AUA—so angry, in fact, that Nute addressed his letter "To the Secretary of the American Unitarian Association, Dear Sir" instead of his customary "My dear Miles." They felt that the AUA's year-long delay in settling matters had eroded the fund-raising necessary to finish the church. Nute's descriptions of the state of mind of the people of Lawrence revealed a community deeply wounded by trauma. He mentioned the Jenkins murder, and as he wrote, his ire cooled and he expressed undiminished faith in the good that Unitarianism was doing for liberal Christianity in Lawrence and the Kansas Territory. Clearly, Nute was suffering post-traumatic stress as well. The letter read,

> Today is the anniversary of our meeting when we voted to accept what your agent had repeatedly informed us was the offer of the Association. A year has passed and yet the transfer remains to be made. . . . This morning at 10 o'clock when calling on your agent to urge the execution of the business, he informed me that it was effected and that he had written you to that effect. But none of us have yet seen the deed or signed the notes. If I understand the business aright we now await some document from your body which being received will enable

your agent to conclude the matter. I assure you this years delay has been to our great vexation & damage. In the mean time two other church buildings have been commenced and one of them will be completed in a few weeks. A year ago the funds needed for the completion of the building was subscribed and could have been readily collected. Now it will be impossible to raise the amount here, men are paying from 5 to 10 per cent per month for money and nearly every one is distressed for want of enough to carry on their farming or other kind of business, and many for what is needed to feed their families. . . . Last Sunday the room was quite full. In the afternoon I met a small congregation in a school house at Bloomington a village about 8 miles from Lawrence in the other side of the Wakarusa. I have been there once before & am encouraged by the numbers that gather & the readiness manifested to give a hearing to the liberal word. I made an appointment for my fellow laborer, brother Brown to preach there a week from next Sunday, the place being otherwise occupied on every alternate Sunday. Next Sunday I preach in the afternoon at Lecompton, Providence permitting. . . . We have a new Superintendent & several new teachers who by their zeal and efficiency have infused new life into the school. I have a bible-class number about 25 adults. The teachers meet at my house every Wednesday evening when we spend a couple of hours in social conference upon the interests of the school and kindred topics. So, you will see, a considerable part of my work has become like the ordinary routine of a settled pastor in New England. It is pleasant thus to renew the memories of our old civilized life after our long experience of the rudeness of the wilderness. But there is yet enough to remind us daily and painfully that we live in an unsettled, & must I not say, grossly unchristian, state of society. These terrible wholesale butcheries which have lately taken place in the Southern part of our territory & this more recent killing (the time has not come to give the deed its fitting name) of my next door neighbor; these things have shocked us beyond all former atrocities here in blood stained Kansas. That our community is capable of a deep thrill of horror before such deeds after all we have passed through leaves some ground for hope almost for surprise; for as the natural result of what we have experienced the spirit of War, of Murder,—the disregard of human life & the bitter intolerance of all opposition is rife among us. Many of our people are too ready to talk of resorting to violence to seek justice or rather retaliation for injuries received. So many robbers & house-burners & murderers have gone unpunished (indeed I know of none that have met punishment through the law) that men despair of getting any legal protection or of seeing the worst criminals brought to justice or arrested in their career of crime & hence become impatient, violent, vindictive. Evil passions are too little restrained, anger breaks out in threats of killing & frequently to a display of murderous weapons on our streets. These tendencies are aggravated by the use of intoxicating drinks that prevail to a frightful extent in our larger towns.... These things admonish us that we have here a great work to do in the use of the Gospel & there are some signs to encourage us in such efforts.[266]

Later that fall the Unitarian *Quarterly Journal* published the treasurer's report for the thirty-third anniversary of the AUA. The report stated that the Lawrence church would be sold to the Lawrence Society, the proposal had been received and accepted by the Executive Committee, and the board had only to receive the legal papers. The statement gave no clue to any of the ill feeling in the Lawrence Society and in the AUA's missionary regarding negotiations for these transactions.

By promoting donations to the denomination for a missionary program in Kansas, the AUA tacitly implied to the giving public that they were going to fully fund that program, when in fact they had no intention of doing so. The AUA's acceptance of donations of land and money toward the Lawrence church, when they planned to charge the Lawrence Society for that church, smacked of withholding information, or worse. Nute became disillusioned with the AUA for intending to require the Lawrence Society buy those donated lands and building back at a property value inflated in great part by the society's own hard work. It shook his faith in the AUA's integrity.

On June 22 a letter from John Brown to "Dear Friend" provided further evidence that he was using Whitman as an intermediary. He wrote, "Write E. B. Whitman, Lawrence, enclosing an inside Envelope to me; all the news you get; till I advise you further."[267] Whitman's connection to John Brown was thus made explicit, and in it lay an explanation for Whitman's unreliable behavior and the grounds for Nute's suspicions.

Also on June 22 Nute testified on the eighth day of the trial of James Lane for the murder of Gaius Jenkins. Lane was known for his ruthless character, but he had attained a larger-than-life image in Lawrence because of his heroic military actions for the Free-State cause. During the attacks on Lawrence by Border Ruffians, he led a local volunteer army to successfully defend Lawrence and the surrounding area, routing many bands of Border Ruffians.

Gaius Jenkins was also well known and figured prominently in the building of early Lawrence. Throughout the trial testimony, Nute was mentioned, since his hencoop, garden, fence, and house had center stage in the crime scene, and he was in close proximity to the event when it happened. Nute had long been aware of the trouble between the two families over rights to the well, which could not supply the water needs of both, and he had attempted to run interference before.

This was a very stressful experience for Nute. Both men were neighbors, original subscribers to the building of the Unitarian church, and had fought bravely to protect the lives of the citizens of Lawrence. Now, one had lost his life to the other in a dispute that should have been handled with the same spirit of cooperation with which they had approached the protection of their neighbors' lives. As their colleague and pastor, Nute must have been furious as well as saddened. No one can say whether Lane's actions could have been predicted, though it is interesting to note that, after a very checkered life, Lane committed suicide in 1866.

Miss Maria Felt, a young friend of Thomas Wentworth Higginson—Nute's Harvard classmate and a John Brown conspirator—arrived right around this time in Lawrence from Massachusetts to teach at the high school in the Unitarian church. She spent her first days in Lawrence becoming acquainted with prominent citizens. In due course she paid a visit to Nute, whom she did not care for at all. She wrote to Higginson that he and Lucy "sat up like two icicles" during their visit and barely spoke.[268]

Felt arrived in Lawrence on June 21, during the Jenkins murder trial. The Nutes were probably in a less than sociable frame of mind, and perhaps even annoyed, if Felt was as glib as she appeared to be in her letters. She also met James Lane, who must have been feeling the stress of his trial as well, for she described him as looking "sickly."

At the conclusion of the trial, Lane was acquitted. On July 3 the *Herald of Freedom* printed an editorial denouncing the verdict.[269] Publisher George Washington Brown was incensed that a mere justice of the peace had tried a man for murder, apparently with a premeditated design to secure Lane's acquittal in time for him to campaign for a seat in the Free-State legislature. Brown called for the Free-State party to distance itself from Lane for its own integrity. This may have initiated the schism that developed between George Washington Brown—with his newspaper, the torch and banner of the Free-State cause—and the rest of the movement, in which Lane grew to have legendary influence.

Two days later, in the wake of Lane's acquittal, the Lawrence Unitarian Society adopted its constitution. Nute and Lucy numbered among the original fifty-five signers. Lane, who had signed the subscription in 1855, was absent, and Jenkins was dead. Many of the original signers also appear prominently in the history of early Lawrence, a testament to the Unitarian nature of the Lawrence colony.

Nute wrote to Amos A. Lawrence on July 24 regarding the foundation of what would become the University of Kansas. He did not like how the Free-State college was in danger of becoming a Presbyterian institution, and he felt that it should be nonsectarian in the interest of being more liberal leaning in perpetuity. However, Nute felt it would be better to have a Presbyterian college in Lawrence than none at all. He wrote,

> I cannot, as my associates well know, say that I am perfectly satisfied with the shape in which the affair now stands. I am opposed to any sectarian trammel or reservations. Let the field be open for the friends of the cause, of every denomination; Let none be excluded nor included because of denominational bias from having a voice in the management of the institution. As near as practicable the contest should be in the hands of those who contribute the funds. Let persons, or organizations of any sect endow professorship under such conditions as they may severally nominate. . . . Here therefore is the place too big by the experiment of an institution of learning Free in the largest sense of the word. To the support of such an institution I have hoped that the friends of Learning & Freedom all over our land would rally with generous gifts. From the tenor of the communications with which you have honored me I hoped that such was your conception of "The free state college" for which you have taken the initiatory steps. Of the final success of your plan I have never had a doubt. It is only a question of time.[270]

On August 5 Amos Lawrence replied to Nute, saying that although Nute's ideas were better in theory, in practice it was necessary to appeal to both the liberal Free-State populace and a more conservative religious populace.[271] Amos Lawrence felt that nonsectarian institutions had not met with adequate success. Nute keenly understood the need to interface with other religious traditions. He wrote back to Amos Lawrence on August 27, asking him to approve the appropriation of his previous donation for the Free-State college for a prep school; the free high school had been closed for two months.[272]

In September Nute wrote again to ask Lawrence for a loan to finish the church.[273] The AUA *Quarterly Journal* had already reported the AUA's "success" in building the Lawrence church and proclaimed that the society was purchasing the completed building from the AUA. But the sanctuary of the church was in fact not yet completed, and the Unitarian society was holding its services at the Methodist chapel, although its Sunday school met in the finished basement of the Unitarian building. Nute still had to approach known philanthropists for donations to actually finish building the church, which in its present state would not be ready for winter.

Nute's September 17 letter to Miles appeared in the *Christian Register* on October 30, with a note from Miles in his capacity as AUA secretary to the effect that it had been "received too late" for the *Quarterly Journal*. It was published because Nute had insisted on it in another letter to Miles. Miles had suggested bringing Nute's tenure as the AUA missionary to a close, and Nute had answered that proposition affirmatively, since he had approached Miles regarding that issue himself some months earlier.

The society struggled with the financial separation from the AUA, especially since they had to buy the church building back. Nute did not want to continue in his position with the Lawrence Society, even after having birthed and nurtured and protected its life through the violence of the early days there. He was sick with the fall influenza that gripped Lawrence. Tired, discouraged, and disillusioned with the AUA, Nute withdrew emotionally from his investment on their behalf. He seemed ready for a change:

> The sickness of Mr. Whitman, and the absence of his attorney, to whom the business of transferring the church building was committed, and the absence of different members of our Board of Trustees, have long delayed the final change of

papers. . . . Just as this was effected, I was taken down with the fever, and have been a close prisoner to my bed for the last two weeks, until within two days. I am now just able to sit up for a few hours at a time. . . . It is a general time of sickness in Kansas. There is but little fatality, as yet, but people are slow in getting up. As they come out from the sick rooms, the chills, the "shakes" pounces on them, and drags them down at regular intervals. There is hardly a family in which some members are not sick. . . . The Transfer is, I believe, effected. A few days before I was taken sick, three of us trustees signed the notes and the mortgage. . . . And now comes the struggle to get the building finished, and be prepared to meet the payments. Unless the main auditory can be so far completed that it can be made comfortable for the coming winter, it will be impossible for us to be ready for the first instalment. . . . We must get a loan of about $1000, OR ALL MUST BE ABANDONED. . . . As to your proposition for making my position independent of the Association, it strikes me favorably. Of course it must be for the Society to say who they have for their own minister. But until the building is completed, or rather a room in which services can be held, no step will or can be taken about it. It will be perfectly easy then. My interests must not stand in the way. And now if you deem it best for the cause of Christianity here and elsewhere, that I be no longer sustained as a missionary at this post, do not hesitate, from any regard for my thrift, so to decide and act. . . . I see a great missionary work to be done all around me, as well as in this city, and should you decide to sever the connection between us, and should this Society not choose me for their pastor, I shall labor on for a while, as far as strength will permit. I never loved the work so well, nor saw greater encouragements in it than now. . . . Though the society here is but this mere handful, I have had from the start a wide circle of influence here. I have preached to and had religious conversations with hundreds of young men whose faces I shall never see again—young men with minds open and all alive, some of whom have gone further out into the wilderness, where for months at a time no voice of a preacher will reach them. To some of these I have given copies of that selection from Channing with which you so bountifully supplied me. Then during the time when all denominations worshiped in one room, I had many rare opportunities to scatter the seed of what we call "liberal Christianity" in places where it had never fallen before. . . . I have never received any but the kindest treatment from those of every fold, being everywhere recognized as a minister of the Gospel, and called upon to officiate as such by both ministers and laymen of the other modes of faith. . . . I am confident our people do all they can. Remember we have now seven other societies in Lawrence, and all struggling in the same way. Only we, by the liberal and timely aid of the churches and your Association, are far astart of them all. Do not permit us to lose this vantage ground. . . . As you will at once see, the interests of the Association hang upon this appeal. It will be to its great damage if we suffer the building here to remain unfinished through another season. But I have said enough. The urgency of our case, and of your interest in having this work completed, so that we may begin to refund what you have expended, must be apparent to you, and I shall be surprised as well as grieved if you fail to respond to this appeal. . . . So may the light spread from the rising even unto the setting sun, eve prays.[274]

Nute wrote to Amos Lawrence again on September 21, explaining the present free status of the school, and asked again for a loan for the church. Whitman had implied to the Executive Committee that Nute was adamant about wanting a nonsectarian school that would charge a fee, but in his letter to Lawrence, Nute indicated otherwise. He had tempered his wishes to his donor's advice:

Yours of the 8th is recd. Since I wrote you the city authorities, startled by the prospect of our high school coming under sectarian control, have made liberal provisions for its support, as well as for the other schools, keeping them all free. . . . They are now in operation. Five teachers are recg. a salary of $3000 in the aggregate. The college "Preparatory" will therefore be deferred for the present. . . . Will you now consent that the unappropriated half of the income of your donation for the current year shall be loaned to our society to help us complete the building? . . . The use of at least $1500 of our funds in finishing & letting up the basement story of our church for the use of the schools is what has crippled us and now hinders us from completing the main room above. . . . Then, supposing that our funds would be ample for the completing the church, I appropriated $500 sent me by Francis G. Shaw Esq, with discretion to use as I thought best for the good of Kansas & the cause of Freedom here, to the support of the High, or, as we then called it, "The Model School." These considerations embolden me to ask you this favor and make me hope that you will accede to the request.[275]

On October 15 Nute wrote to Miles in great irritation. He was angry at Miles for blaming him for delays and irregularities obstructing the transfer of the church property when he felt they were caused by the AUA's continued use of Whitman as their agent, against Nute's advice. Nute felt that Whitman was making everything ponderously difficult when all that was required was a standard blank deed. Nute called into question the complicated deed that Whitman presented them with, which contained clauses that appeared irregular to Nute. He wrote,

Yesterday I learned that your agent has gone East without the papers. It seems they now lack acknowledgement before a Justice of the Peace. The reason why they are not so acknowledged is that on signing them we found a form of acknowledgement appended which required it to be made before a specified justice & he was at that time & for several weeks succeeding absent from the territory & beside all this time the deed was in his possession. . . . My conception of the business capacity of your agent has not risen since I conferred with you on the subject. . . . We must again wait his return before the papers can be exchanged & then of course it is for him to take the papers that belong to the association. I cannot see how I can do anything towards having them forwarded to you & I protest at your holding me responsible for this shameful delay. . . . Now I am desirous that my letter of Sept 17 should be published as early as possible as a sort of entering wedge for the appeals that I must make to keep up this society & enable them to meet their liabilities to the Assoc. . . . Will you have the kindness to send it to the Register remarking by way of preface that it was recd too late for insertion in the Quarterly.[276]

Nute wrote to Miles again in early November.[277] Adding insult to injury, the AUA had billed him personally for $450 worth of books, some of which he had dispensed with according to AUA orders prior to coming to Kansas and some of which were sent to him to disperse as part of his missionary duties. He was outraged by this, as he was being charged for book orders placed during the time when he was en route to Kansas on a river boat. He could not have made those orders himself. He had specifically instructed the AUA not to send books before he had secure living quarters in Kansas in which to put them, fearing they would be ruined. The AUA sent them anyway, and subsequently, they were damaged and destroyed. This conflict over book charges lasted quite a while, and Nute's indignation considerably widened his rift with the AUA.

Whitman wrote to Calvin Clark from St. Louis a few days later explaining why he had not left the deed for the Unitarian church at the AUA as promised: It was somehow mislaid among his papers.[278] Nute's perception of Whitman's manipulations and skullduggery surrounding the signing and conveyance of the Unitarian church deed seems to be supported by Whitman's correspondence. Whitman was incensed that Nute submitted seventeen pages of charges against him with the AUA, after Whitman felt secure that the AUA sided with him against Nute.

Nute prevailed with the Executive Committee regarding his complaints against Whitman, and Whitman wrote that he had decided to leave his post. He posed some questions regarding Nute's allegations, stated they were unjust, and then declared that he would leave well enough alone and withdraw. The heated conflict was over, but at the expense of both men's relationship with the AUA. Although Nute had prevailed with the AUA regarding his complaints about Whitman, he ended his tenure as missionary with considerable bitterness. Despite everything, Whitman eventually returned to Lawrence and became the Sunday school superintendent for the Unitarian society during the pastorate of John Stillman Brown.

The Executive Committee of the AUA voted on November 15, 1858, to terminate the missionary position and end the mission in Lawrence. This was a natural end to the project, given that Nute's original charge of starting a society and a church had been declared completed.

The AUA's self-reported "present embarrassed state of our treasury" could have been their reason for trying to squeeze money out of the Kansas mission, charge Nute personally for books sent to his mission, and terminate the Kansas mission—although the church building remained unfinished and the society not sufficiently stable and solvent to stand on its own. Nute verified in a letter in 1859 that his mission contract ended on December 16, 1858. Interestingly, this statement appears in a letter from Nute to the AUA business office while he was still trying to settle the contested book charges. At the end of 1858, the church building still unfinished, Nute was preaching at the Masonic Hall in Lawrence.

Despite his alleged release from his duties as missionary, Nute wrote to Miles on December 21 to inform him that the Lawrence Society had still not received the deed to the church and Whitman said he did not have it. Lack of a deed further obstructed the society's ability to get another loan to finish the church building. There seems to have been some irregularity in the AUA's dealings regarding the deed, as the society had been forced to sign a mortgage to the AUA without first seeing the deed. The Masonic room where they met was large and commodious, but Nute felt the inability to meet in their own sanctuary could have a negative effect on the society's numbers in a time when the other religious organizations in Lawrence, still supported in full by their denominations, were growing by leaps and bounds. Nute explained,

Mr. Whitman refers me to you for the deed we have so long been trying to get through him as the agent of the Association. ...We now hope that this long deferred business of transfer will be effected. Our Trustees would have preferred to see the deed before making the mortgage & it would seem proper that both that & the mortgage should be of even date, or at least that the date of the deed should be prior to that of the mortgage. But I suppose it is not essential to the solidity of either document. Please send the deed on receipt of this as we want to make another mortgage to secure the loan which we have effected for completing the building & it is important that the deed be first deeded. . . . The appeal of my letter published in the Register was immediately responded to. Mr. Thomas Suffield of Boston whom you doubtless know as one of the noble spirits among the laymen of our body, zealous in all good marks, and who from the first has been a valued friend & effectual helper of our missionary work in Kansas and whom I rejoice, & count it an honor, to number among the most esteemed of my personal friends from our early youth wrote me as soon as he learned our want pledging himself to our relief. The work upon the church has accordingly been urged on as rapidly as possible. A few days of extreme cold weather coming just at a most unfortunate juncture, as the mortar for the plastering was being mixed & congealing it to stubborn solidity, delayed the work for a time. But two weeks of milder temperatures since has subdued the frost & the first coat of plastering is now spread upon the walls. If this weather continues a few days longer the plastering will be finished & the rest of the work in the main room will probably be done in a few weeks more. . . . On the whole our prospects look more encouraging than they have for some time back. Some have left us whose loss we shall severely feel; but others come in to fill the vacancies & on the whole our number (I mean of the regular congregation) suffers no diminution. . . . The Sectarian lines are more closely drawn with the multiplication of religious societies & as each society has it own place of meeting so that many services are held at the same hour (no less than six societies hold services in our city & more are forming). We cannot expect our congregation to increase at even pace with the growth of the city. If we hold our own we must be gaining strength and this I think is our present condition. And yet, it should be borne in mind, the number of decided Unitarians or liberals who appear in earnest for anything positive in religion, faith & effort is exceeding small, not twice a "handful."[279]

A few days later, Nute wrote to Miles in a much more conciliatory mood regarding the books in question.[280] He tried to remind Miles that he was given books and tracts for the parish library and they were distributed in a missionary sense to those too poor to buy food and clothing, much less AUA publications. He also reminded Miles that Miles himself directed Nute to keep a copy of each publication for the parish library. Nute continued to try to make Miles understand that books sent to the territory often arrived damaged, moldy, and unusable, implying that the AUA was remiss in packaging and could not expect to be paid for damaged goods that were their own fault.

Thus, the man once called "The Lion of Lawrence" set about tidying loose ends in preparation for bringing to a close his tenure as the missionary to the great Unitarian mission in the Kansas Territory.

There is a photographic portrait of Nute with his wife, Lucy, taken in New Orleans in 1855, when they were on their way to the Kansas mission by riverboat up the Mississippi. Lucy is a petite woman, sitting at the feet of her scarecrow-thin husband, staring up at him devotedly. He holds a book. After all, before and after the ministry, his life was devoted to scholarly pursuits, and such things were immortalized in nineteenth-century portraits.

Nute and Lucy posed in the golden days of hope and promise of 1855, when Kansas seemed like a vast blank book for the writing of true Unitarian liberal Christianity upon the West. Only four years later, Nute was battered and bruised, and his denomination was desperately trying to shed the Kansas mission. But the AUA was also trying to assume an appearance of success there—even though the church was unfinished, the settlers still hungry, and its missionary bridling at what he considered the betrayal of their promise to him and his flock.

In 1859 the *Quarterly Journal* published a number of articles regarding the "embarrassed state" of the AUA's finances. The report "Meetings of the Executive Committee" recorded that they had provide eight hundred dollars in the coming year for the Kansas mission.[281] This is a little mystifying as Nute's tenure as missionary had ended on December 16, 1858, and he expected no pay from the AUA beginning that winter. No one had replaced Nute in the Lawrence pulpit. The AUA also published a circular regarding the role of the Kansas mission in its overspending. They blamed their fiscal problems on the Kansas church and the war, which had made the construction of the church much more expensive than anticipated. Indeed, the war had doubled and tripled costs, but the AUA did not fund the project alone—many individual donations had been given to help cover the cost overages. Some of that money went directly to Kansas, but much of it seemed to fall into a black hole in Boston. The AUA would also receive mortgage monies from the Lawrence Society, as it persisted in requiring the society to purchase the church building from the AUA.

Elsewhere in that issue of the *Quarterly Journal*, under "Results of Association Action," the AUA declared its success: "A stone church has been erected in Kansas, and a missionary sustained there, till the Society to which he ministers grew into a self-sustaining position."[282] The "Minutes of the Executive Committee" recorded that the Lawrence Unitarian Society had sent a mortgage note secured with insurance to the AUA for the amount of five thousand dollars. This item of business was referred to the business committee in order to convey the deed for the church to the society. This note must have helped quite a bit with the AUA's attempts to right their finances. Their debt, which amounted to $7,727.64,[283] was blamed on the Kansas mission, but it should have been mostly offset by the mortgage. No mention was made of the considerable amounts of money reported in the newspapers and letters as having been sent directly to the AUA for Kansas but seem never to have found their way there. Further, this "embarrassed state," however curious and mysterious its origin, may also have been responsible for the AUA's attempts to collect the much-disputed book money from Nute.

It is difficult to ascertain from the record if the AUA was simply financially inept and attempted to squeeze payment for its fiscal debts out of the murky money pit of Kansas. Considering that influential Unitarians were involved with the AUA as well as the National Kansas Committee and John Brown, it is possible that they blurred the financial boundaries between the organizations—borrowing from one to fund the other, thus contributing to the debt. That would explain why the Executive Committee turned a deaf ear toward Nute's outcries about the unreliability of Whitman and the money and supplies that disappeared under Whitman's care. Or perhaps major donors had simply withheld unrestricted contributions to AUA appeals because their money was invested otherwise in the Kansas cause—including John Brown, Beecher's Bibles, and the Emigrant Aid Company. In any case, the record does not fully explain how the AUA could have courted financial insolvency by its involvement in Kansas when so much money was coming its way under the auspices of the mission there.

THE UNDERGROUND RAILROAD
AND HARPER'S FERRY

Even as Nute ended his stint as AUA missionary, he remained very much embroiled in the abolitionist causes in which he had been active since his arrival. Rev. John Stillman Brown's daughter, Mary Ann, wrote to her brother Willie on January 30, 1859, mentioning Nute and the capture of Free-Stater John Doy while on an Underground Railroad mission aiding fugitive slaves:

> There has been a great excitement in Lawrence this last week, about some fugitive slaves. I will tell you all about it.... Fourteen slaves, who had escaped from Missouri, started from Lawrence for Canada. Dr. Doy and son, and a Mr. Clough, went with them and were going as far as Iowa city ~~with them~~ they had only got about ten miles from here, when, as they were going over a little rise of ground through the woods, a band of Missourians sprang out suddenly from the trees and took them all prisoners as the colored people were in a close covered wagon they had no chance to fight there Border-Ruffians took them to Western in Missouri there they took Clough and made him swear all kinds of oaths that he would not betray them and sent him back to Lawrence with the teams. They kept Doy and son as prisoners and night before last a man came from Western and he said "the Border-Ruffians have decided to punish Doy and son" the people think they will hang them; if they do it will cause a disturbance here. I pity them and the slaves too, it

is outrageous. There were only ten men who knew when these people were to start, and one of those ten must have told the Missourians all about their plans. Mr. Nute <u>knows</u> who is the traitor so does Mr. Robles but they will not tell till Doy's fate is decided for they are afraid if they do it will go harder with them and now they may possibly get away. It is queer how the Missourians knew every thing about it as soon as any change was made they knew it instantly. There are as many spies all around. ~~West~~ Wade, the man who owns the claim joining us, is one of the worst kind but enough of this I have said a great deal about it—but everyone is talking of it. It is a beautiful day, Father has gone to Bloomington to preach and Charlie and Edward have gone to hear Mr. Nute preach.[284]

In a fragmentary letter, probably to Brown conspirator Franklin Sanborn, Nute related that he had heard from Dr. Samuel Gridley Howe. Howe was about to leave New York to accompany the dying Theodore Parker to Italy in search of a better climate for his tuberculosis. An upcoming festival was mentioned in the letter that other sources reveal occurred on February 16, indicating that this letter must have been written before that time. The first part of the letter is missing from the Kansas Historical Society's John Brown Collection, but the postscript indicates it was written to Franklin Sanborn. Sanborn's attached note indicates that he was passing Nute's letter on to the other conspirators because it contained news from John Brown and the Underground Railroad. In his letter, Nute acknowledged that he received money from Samuel Gridley Howe to use for the defense of Dr. Doy. Sanborn's note must be addressed to George Luther Stearns, as Sanborn asked his correspondent to give regards to Mrs. Stearns. Nute was obviously well acquainted with all of the Eastern abolitionists who were funding John Brown in the time leading up to the assault on Harper's Ferry. This part of the Nute family story passed down by his daughter Mary is thereby documented:

Yesterday we heard from "Old Brown" at Mt. Tabor Iowa. But you will have later news & the plot thickens. . . . I have just rec^d a letter from Doct. Howe [Samuel Gridley Howe] about to sail from New York with our noble brother Theodore [Theodore Parker]. God grant him restoration to health. But he has lived already to a glorious result & whether he is to abide longer in the flesh or not his life will be an immortal power on Earth to hasten the coming of the Heavenly Kingdom. . . . Dr. Howe writes me that $25 is at my disposal for the cause of the oppressed & it will be immediately used to enable Mrs. Doy to go to her husband & make preparations for his defence & if possible for his comfort in that wretched Platte City jail. . . . We are right in the midst of a Festival & Exhibition of Tableaux for the completion of our church or I would give you more full account of recent doings here. But will try to write again soon. Sincerely yours, for Humanity . . . E. Nute Jr. [ATTACHED NOTE]: Concord, March 1st '59 . . . Dear Friend. . . . Please read and share this as you have occasion and return it to me by the boys on Friday together with Brown's last letter. The affair seems to have been badly managed— while Brown has proved his skill once more by marching his party safe thro—Success to the old brave—Give Mrs. Stearns my thanks for her note, and believe me . . . Ever yours, F.B.S. [Franklin Sanborn][285]

Another Nute letter fragment from February 14, 1859, relays news of John Brown, the Underground Railroad, and the ill-fated Doy capture.[286] Doy was leading a group of fugitive slaves from Lawrence to Oskaloosa, Iowa, when he was captured and taken to Missouri. The "colored people, both free and slaves" were sent on to New Orleans to the slave market, and Doy and his son were jailed in Platte City, Missouri. As mentioned in a letter written by Mary Ann Brown,[287] Nute believed this operation was betrayed from within. He was one of the group who planned the mission, although he did not accompany it. This fragment seems as though it was addressed to Samuel Gridley Howe, as Nute's letter to Howe of February 24 fits nicely as a follow-up to this letter. It read,

Yours of Jan 27th & that of Feb 2 enclosing $10 are rec^d & with much thankfulness—Before this can reach you you will have learned something of the disaster that befell the last expedition from this place with fugitives, But you are not likely to get the facts just as they were & I will give you those of most importance. The party consisted of 13 col^d people (11 fugitives & 2 free by birth) with 3 of our citizens, with two teams (horses & wagons). The col^d people were put across the river some 4 miles above this place about 2 o clock on the morning, the teams crossed the ferry about 2 hours later & took the river road, after taking in the passengers they took the road toward Oscaloosa & about an hour after on entering a sort of defile between the bluffs & the timber found themselves surrounded by a party of armed & mounted men. They surrendered without a blow & were taken over into Missouri, the col^d people, both free & slaves, have been shipped for the New Orleans market. One of the white men was released & returned to Lawrence the others, Dr. John Doy & son, are now in close confinement in Platte city Jail awaiting their trial on charge of stealing a slave from Westin (one of the 13). . . . This party of kidnappers consisted mostly of men from Westin Mo. but no less than 5 of our own citizens were among them. One of them the Postmaster of Lawrence <u>Doct Garvin.</u> It is certain that the movement was betrayed by a professed friend. Our suspicion is strongly fixed on several persons. The whole affair was managed perhaps as well as it could be with the obstacles in the way. The great trouble was the want of funds. This hindered us from sending them forward as fast as they arrived, as before has been done, & so permitted such a large number to accumulate here; then too many persons were admitted to the councils & applied to for funds & other aid—wagons, horses, provisions, drivers for the teams, men to cut away the ice & get a skiff across the river &c &c. Great rewards were offered, spies sent out & men holed in this place to watch & aid in recovering the run away property. We find that every movement was known to the enemy who were gathered at Lecompton the evening before the starting of the train. . . . The conclusion to be drawn from the whole occurrence is that this business must either be done in quite another way or abandoned. This last expedition has cost a few persons over $200 & there is further expense yet to be met. . . . Brown started about the same time as the other party & with about the same number of "chattels." He went via Topeka was surrounded by pursuers & beseiged in a log cabin near Holton three days afterward—A party went from Topeka & a few persons from this place to his relief—By a strategem he made his escape with the live stock just as the enemy here about to inforce the sieze & the U.S. troops were moving to their aid. Of his subsequent movement we are yet ignorant & in great anxiety, though confident that he will ultimately succeed. . . . Feb. 17 Well three days of intense excitement here passed. Two U.S. Marshalls have been seized in our city & their posse about 50 strong each have been disarmed & the chains broken from the limbs of their prisoners free state men of Lum & Bourbon Co—the Legislature having passed a bill of gen¹ amnesty peace is now expected.[288]

Also on February 24 Nute wrote to Samuel Gridley Howe again about the Underground Railroad, the Doy rescue, and John Brown. Nute's involvement in the Underground Railroad was deep and personal. He received fugitives in his home, helped plan their escape, and accompanied them on the next leg of their journey. Nute reported, "The X which you sent me has gone for that cause being spent to get Mrs. Doy & daughter & other witnesses from this place to Platte City."[289] Although the recipient is unidentified in the collection that holds this letter, this passage indicates that the letter was written to Samuel Gridley Howe, who had promised to send Nute an amount of money for this express purpose. If this letter was indeed to Howe, then Nute's unidentified letter of February 14 was addressed to him also.

Although Nute denied his sympathies with John Brown in other letters, in this one he reported on a compatriot taking Brown to safety in Iowa and seemed sympathetic. This indicates that he had much firsthand knowledge of the Brown project at this time and much sympathy for Brown's cause, despite the violence. Perhaps in the wake of his disillusionment with the AUA, Nute's sympathies changed toward Brown, although he did not seem to change his disapproval of Brown's methods. The letter read,

> Last night one of the captured fugitives of whom I wrote you in my last arrived at this place. As no one appeared to claim him he was lodged for safe keeping in the jail at Platte city with some ten or twelve other slaves, most of whom had been recently bought up to be taken South. He broke jail by burning out the bars from the window; he walked 10 miles to the Missouri river & crossed on the floating cakes of ice; got 1st on to an island or sand-bar in the middle of the river where he spent two days & nights hid in the young cottonwoods; then on again over the running ice to the Kansas side & walked the 35 or 40 miles to this place in one night. He is a resolute fellow right in the prime of life (35 years old) has a wife who has lived with him here in Lawrence since last September up to the time of their attempted migration to a freer soil in British dominion & their capture by the human blood hounds but 10 miles from this place (He thinks she is now in Lexington Mo, where she is owned). We have him now hid & are to day making arrangements to have him set forward tomorrow 30 miles to another depot. I think they (there are 2 others to go) will not be taken again without bloodshed. You have perhaps seen some account of the Charley Fisher affair in Leavenworth. But three persons know of his present locus; you may be the 4th. He came to our house in a coach from Leavenworth disguised in female attire. We kept him 2 days. I then took him

by night & afoot across lots through an 80 acre corn field in which the stalks are standing & to another hiding place from this he has in the same way been moved on from house to house until he is about 8 miles on his way & will be started in the small hours tomorrow morning for Canada. . . . I suppose you have heard of "John Brown's" heroic success through Kansas Nebraska & Iowa. Before this his band of chattels . . . are probably safe off this cursed U.S. soil. . . . Dr. Doy & son are yet in jail at Platte city, locked up in an iron cell 8 feet square without fire, light or pure air. We are now making every effort in our power for their defence. The X which you sent me has gone for that cause being spent to get Mrs Doy & daughter & other witnesses from this place to Platte City. . . . You need not be surprised if you hear of an invasion into Missouri & a forcible delivery of our kidnapped citizens out of that vile iron box—about the time that this reaches you. . . . One of our people went with John Brown as far as Mt. Tabor Iowa where deeming him out of harm's way he returned & has just reached Lawrence. He reports Brown a "perfect daredevil." The pursuers are glad to keep out of his path—The pro-slavers consider him a wild demoniac who will never be taken alive. This I have from a man who lives among them in the Western part of Jefferson county & who spent two days at our house this week. . . . He informs me that several of his neighbors went out on the Brown hunt but came back and saved their credit for discretion by reporting that they kept a respectful distance from the "old maniac"—& one man lost his horse saddle & bridle being surprised by a party of Browns guards one of whom happened to be afoot. The end is not yet.[290]

On March 12 Nute wrote to Miles thanking him for the deed to the church and responding positively to a solution for the book charges. Nute was feeling a little better as he severed his ties with the AUA as missionary. He also reported on the status of the Lawrence congregation:

Perhaps you will like to have some account of the condition of our society affairs and the prospects before us. Under this head I regret to say I have nothing very encouraging to communicate. ... The workmen promise to have all finished about April 1 but I have not the faintest hope of seeing the house ready for occupation before May 1 and consider June 1 the more probable time. ... We continue to worship in the house of the Orthodox Congregationalists by their courteous invitation; but we cannot have the room long enough to hold a session of our Sunday School, & it is consequently suspended. Our Society cannot keep up a very spirited existence in the present posture of affairs. We now wait for the time when we shall get into our own house for renewing our zeal and activity. Then I hope since movement will be made toward the settlement of a pastor; but I have my misgivings as to any action being taken as long as I continue to labor on without any support. This of course I cannot long do and yet I am loathe to sever the tie which binds me here and to withdraw from this field of labor. I have no plan of action in regard to the matter, but await the leading of Providence in the course of future events & try to possess my soul in Patience. ... Your kind words called out by the occasion of sundering the relation in which we have stood to each other during the nearly four years of my Kansas mission are gratefully received. I do heartily reciprocate your friendly assurances and good wishes. The small cloud of coldness and misunderstanding that has come between us for a short time during our connection under the Association is to my mind entirely dispelled. I dismiss all feelings of distrust as to your good-will toward me & remember only the pleasant part of that connection; the many words & deeds in which the kindness of your heart toward me, far beyond any merit on my part, was most unmistakably manifest. May never anything occur to disturb these pleasant remembrances in your heart or mine and may you somewhere in the blessed hereafter have some assurance that your labors of love were not altogether wasted on ... Your ever thankful brother.[291]

Martin F. Conway came to the Kansas Territory in 1854 originally as a correspondent of the *Baltimore Sun*. Though a Douglas Democrat at that time, he soon became embroiled in Free-State politics and was elected to several different positions and finally to the U.S. Congress in 1859. Interestingly, Conway wrote to George Stearns, organizer of the Massachusetts State Kansas Committee and one of the underground supporters of John Brown, on March 16, trying to secure a loan for some unstated investment opportunity, perhaps backing for his political campaign.[292] He mentioned giving Nute twenty-five dollars for Mrs. Doy. This is the twenty-five dollars about which Howe wrote to Nute and Nute reported to Sanborn, who then passed the information on to Stearns, who then paid Nute through Conway. Passing money to the Kansas Territory was a risky and convoluted business. Not only was it often difficult to get it there safely, but the factionalism of the Free-State and abolitionist causes required that where the money came from and to whom it was going often had to be concealed.

On March 5 the *Herald of Freedom* reported that Conway tried to physically assault Dr. Robinson, and that Nute had been the recipient of Conway's ire as well, although Nute was quick to correct the editor that in his case the assault was verbal, not physical.[293] It is curious that Conway lashed out at Nute when they were tied together in this work. Author Richard Hinton, in a letter addressed to the Kansas Historical Society, later intimated that Conway must have struggled with some sort of mental health disorder that affected his behavior.[294] At the end of his March 16, 1859, letter, Conway stated in a cursory manner that they were about to organize a chapter of the Republican Party in Kansas, which was the antislavery party at that time.[295]

Nute wrote to Sanborn on March 22 about the Underground Railroad. He talked of his actions on behalf of fugitives, including the notorious Charley Fisher, a fugitive slave who had been captured and rescued several times. Fisher was from Kentucky and worked as a barber at the Planters' Hotel in Leavenworth. A proslavery customer had recognized him and notified his owner, who came to collect him. There followed a standoff between proslavery sympathizers and abolitionists on Fisher's behalf. The next day, at Fisher's hearing, the judge was distracted, and Fisher was spirited away by abolitionists, never to be captured again.

Nute's house was one station on Fisher's journey out of Kansas, and it appears Nute took considerable risks. Nute also wrote in this letter about the bounty hunters in and around Lawrence and about needing more money for the Doy defense, which was to start the next day in St. Joseph:

Day before yesterday we (ie about half a dozen who have had the management of the Doy expedition) were almost in despair for the want of funds to meet the pressing emergency for his defence. His trial is to come off at St. Joseph tomorrow & it was necessary to send 6 witnesses over by which an alibi can be formed & some other facts bearing on the case. We had contracted debts in the preparation for the trial. . . . But here are 4 more fugitives who must be forwarded immediately 1st Charly Fisher who has twice kidnapped & of whom you here before read. 2d Bill Riley one who was taken with Dr. Doy & who escaped from Platte city jail by burning out an iron bar from the logs in which it was fastened across the window (Dr. Doy was shut up in an iron cage within the general enclosure & so could not escape with Riley) 3d a woman with a child who has been here some three months, 4th a smart young fellow who walked into our house one day last week. He escaped from masters in Tenn Co KT & had walked hither in 3 or 4 nights. I directed him to the next depot 7 miles west telling him to make inquiries at a friends a mile from this. He had been gone but a quarter of an hour or so when a young man rode over from the main street (our house is on the western border) & after inquiring about the fugitive informed me that the hunters were on his track—that they had reached Lawrence but a short time after the fugitive the evening before & had put up at the public house in which or in the outhouse of which the "property" had found shelter,—that they had got sight of their game in the morning, had engaged the base helpers who, I am pained to confess, are not few here in Lawrence to be in the watch & they had tracked him to my house & were proposing to make a descent on us that night. In the mean time his further progress through the corn-field back of our house had escaped their vigilence. It not being according to the usual method they had been mislead supposing he would not move again before night. I mounted & rode "across lots" to intercept the hunted one to have him take a hiding place through the day & then get him convoyed under cover of darkness by an unfrequented rout. In this I succeeded. That night he was taken horse-back & safely conducted to a good place 7 miles on the road & last night 25 miles further I expect. On returning to town & going into the main street I found the alarm had been well grounded. The leading man among the man hunters had conferred with the landlord in great trouble about the escape of "his uncle's" chattel—said he was authorized to offer $600 for his delivery in Lum Co & offered 200 for information that would lead to his capture, this he also did in several stores. He was very anxious to know if it would be possible to take him in Lawrence & get off with him, or safe to make the attempt, but the replies which he got were not very encouraging & he pretended to give up the hunt. But some of the underlings are doubtless on the watch. I give these particulars to help you to a clear idea of the business & the desirableness of dispatch in our operations. I must close abruptly & hope to write more soon, as ever yours.[296]

Nute wrote to Miles in April regarding yet another glitch in his "book debt" to the AUA.[297] The AUA had charged Nute for books transferred to another person. With accounting, Nute's "debt" to the AUA had been whittled down to something that he no longer found infuriating. In fact, Nute was eventually found to be *owed* something by the AUA, which he graciously remitted as a donation. Nute informed them of another thirty dollars due from the AUA to a builder, which sum was contracted by E. B. Whitman but never paid.

Nute also asked what had "become of the land warrant that was donated to our society," which he felt could be used to settle some more of the building expenses and bills.[298] Clearly, these were embarrassing questions and Nute seems to have been ignored. Nute was disillusioned with Kansas. He wrote that he could not swear that they would have the church done and occupied by the end of the month, as hoped. He had not heard anything about the society coming to the support of a minister—himself, or anyone else, for that matter. In spite of Nute's cynicism, the Lawrence *Herald of Freedom* reported on April 30, "The Unitarian Society in this place have just finished the work on the main room of their church building. Services next Sunday at 10½ o'clock A.M. and thereafter at this hour."[299]

At the end of May, the thirty-fourth anniversary report of the AUA took a great deal of credit for the Kansas mission, neglecting to mention that unlike other denominations they did not offer their support of the project in free will, as was probably assumed by their friends and donors, but had made the society in Lawrence pay for it. Additionally, they did not see fit to mention that they had placed the blame for their own financial difficulties on the mission, which blame appears to be at least somewhat exaggerated, or deliberately misplaced.

By May 9 the AUA's former missionary was not sure how long he could continue to work for nothing in Lawrence—he had ill health and a recurring fever. Nute was obviously despondent, so much so that the editors of the *Christian Register* felt the necessity of stating, "The following letter is quite interesting, but allowance must be made for the depressing influence of ill health, as plainly causing its desponding tone."[300] They lamented Nute's health as a casualty of Kansas but felt that should he vacate his post for any reason, another energetic individual might jump up to fill his place. How strangely callous an attitude toward a missionary who had lost his health to the cause and, several times, almost lost his life. Further, how curious that Nute's input as the AUA missionary was still sought by an AUA newspaper, when his position and salary had ended many months before.

Nute was, however, grateful for his correspondent's inquiry about the Lawrence Society, for although the problems in Kansas continued to buffet the settlers, the country as a whole had lost interest, and now the labors and struggles of the Kansas settlers were ignored. The Lawrence Society made do with finishing the church on a loan of one thousand dollars, far less than Nute had tried to get. The society moved worship services to the church sanctuary, but the number of subscribing members was not predictable, as they were not the only game in town anymore. Lawrence, a town of twenty-five hundred in 1859, had nine different religious denominations, seven of which met at the same time. Nute realized that if he continued to volunteer his services as a minister, the Lawrence Society would not have any motivation to pay him, and so his last unpaid sermon would be delivered on the following Sunday. He wrote,

> There is no self-supporting society here yet. I am surprised at the statement which I have seen repeated in public print to the contrary. The only part of our religious institution that has thus far reached the position of self-support is the minister. Since January 1, my services have been voluntary, and with the exception of a quantity of books, the publications of the A.U.A. from which thus far I have derived only the satisfaction of gratuitous distribution, I have been entirely without support or the expectation of any. That this society will be able to support a minister for the next year is quite improbable. Next Sunday will close my volunteer services. A meeting of the society is called for the day after, and I trust action will be taken to do something for the support of a regular ministry.... I think the time has come when this people should be left to take charge of their own religious institutions. They may need

help, but when they make some effort to do for themselves they cannot decently urge a plea for further help from abroad. . . . My future field of labor is, as you will see, quite uncertain. I see no prospect of a support in the field of ministry here. I cannot ask it from the East, unless I labor in places where people are less able to sustain themselves than they are here in Lawrence. Certain it is, I cannot much longer stand in the position which I have occupied for the past four months. . . . But I would not have you think that I am disheartened by this uncertainty. Far from that. For the present, the intermittent fever, which has returned upon me with the warm season, prostrates me for half the time, and renders all active exertion of mind or body impossible for the other half. With returning health I am confident that some field of service will present itself in which I can work and live, here or elsewhere.[301]

If there was a lessening of the Border Ruffian violence in Lawrence, it did not mean that there were no risks living in the territory. In early June 1859, the *Herald of Freedom* reported that Nute and his wife, Lucy, had a close call while sitting in their own parlor:

Almost a Serious Accident. . . . As Rev. Mr. Nute and his lady were sitting at the tea table a few evenings since, a bullet passed through the window in a line with the heads of both, and just missed them. It was shot by a careless boy. When will those, who handle instruments of death, cease to be thoughtless?[302]

Nute promised to preach on "Womanhood" in mid-July,[303] but the lecture was postponed when he became involved in the rescue of Dr. John Doy.[304] In the aftermath of the capture in January of Dr. Doy and his son and their impending trial under the Fugitive Slave Act, Nute and Charles Stearns, who had engaged Doy, were overcome with remorse and a feeling of culpability. They took public criticism from those who, in hindsight, declared Doy lacking the kind of common sense that was necessary to lead the fugitive slaves. But it is questionable whether there would have been anyone else to send in Doy's place.

Regardless, feeling responsible and fearing that unless Doy was rescued soon, he would go to the penitentiary for five more years, Nute and Stearns approached James B. Abbot of Blanton, Kansas Territory, who worked for the Lawrence *Herald of Freedom,* to rescue Dr. Doy from the jail in St. Joseph, Missouri.[305] Nute and Stearns declared that fifty men with Sharps rifles would do the deed well. But since nine men and thirty dollars were all that was available for the effort, they decided to send a posse to St. Joseph in the middle of the night under the ruse that they had a prisoner for the jail.

Abbot and his band of nine, through an elaborate plot planned at least in part by Nute, Stearns, and others, deceived the jailer at St. Joseph, sprung Doy and his son from the jail, replaced them in the cells with the jailer himself, and hightailed it back to Lawrence. By June 6 their co-conspirators had been revealed, and the town of St. Joseph, Missouri, less than politely asked the editor of the abolitionist newspaper to leave town because of his role in the rescue.[306]

One of the earliest family stories I remember about my great-great-grandfather Nute was that he traveled to Harper's Ferry, Virginia, when he found out that John Brown, a longtime friend, was about to stage an attack. He went to try to dissuade Brown from violence. My great-grandmother, Nute's daughter Mary, told my mother that he had related the whole story in the manuscripts that she had sold after his death.

This was an elusive bit of family lore to try to track down and either substantiate or disprove. Attempts to find the missing manuscripts have so far come to naught, and nothing that I could find that was written about the Harper's Ferry incident seemed to mention Nute by name. I pursued a detailed study of the Harper's Ferry incident through the letters of John Brown's family and both the state and federal investigations and court proceedings. I also gathered evidence regarding Nute's whereabouts during that time period. Although no words from Nute's pen verify the family story, I found a number of "smoking guns" that lead me to the conclusion that it was probably true.

I believe Nute did ride to Harper's Ferry to attempt to see John Brown at his headquarters at the Kennedy farm during the days immediately preceding Brown's historical assault on the armory. Nute's purpose, according to his daughter Mary, was to attempt to dissuade Brown from attacking the armory. Although Nute may not have been successful in seeing John Brown in person to make his case, it seems that his attempt placed him in Harper's Ferry right at the time of the attack.

In August 1859, Nute wrote to his dear friend and then AUA Secretary James Freeman Clarke, saying that he would be gone from the territory for about a year, starting October 1.[307] The date of the attack on Harper's Ferry had not yet been set at that time, but Brown and his conspirators were already planning it for the late fall of that year. Nute may have intended merely to go back East and to go abroad. As a correspondent with newspapers throughout his time in Kansas, he would finance his travels by lecturing and writing. Whatever his original intentions upon leaving Lawrence, the year that followed his departure was key in the annals of the antislavery cause, during which Nute may have been an eyewitness to important events at Harper's Ferry.

In his August 10 letter to Clarke, Nute wrote,

I have on hand a large lot of the Quarterly for July 58. Anything else can be disposed of to good effect during the coming Fall & Winter. I expect to be absent from the territory for a year from Oct 1. But brother J. S. Brown will be glad to distribute the documents & for fear the package might not reach here before I leave it will be well to direct [it] to him.[308]

In mid-September Rev. John Stillman Brown, struggling to perform some ministerial duties to keep the Lawrence Unitarian Society alive, wrote to the AUA about the hardships of being a Unitarian missionary and minister.[309] He needed some support from the AUA if they wanted him to do missionary work. He was so busy on his farm that it was too much for him to do anything more than preach occasionally—but if he was to build a congregation, he would need to.

In his letter Rev. Brown wrote an amusing description of a claimholder's Sunday. In addition to preaching, he must drive cows out of the cornfield, repair the fence, run into town for a business transaction, eat dinner, trudge for a half mile to get two buckets of water, drive six piglets and their mother out of the vegetable garden, start plowing, stop plowing to fix the plow, send his son two miles to the blacksmith for parts for the plow, milk the cows, discover that two cows and two oxen are missing and go to look for them.[310] Brown echoed everything Nute had written to the AUA about the burdens territorial living placed on any one human being who sought to support himself and his family. Against those obstacles, doing the work of liberal Christianity seemed impossible. Brown also documented the many obstacles still in the way of a self-supporting Unitarian congregation in Lawrence.

Nute was said to have left Lawrence, but the exact date of his departure is unclear, which continues to obscure whether he could have been at Harper's Ferry. Nute reportedly performed the wedding of Brinton Woodward, Free-Stater and secretary of the first territorial convention, to Lucy Wilder of Lawrence, on October 9, 1859,[311] but it is unknown if Nute's name or the date are accurate —the details of wedding announcements in territorial newspapers are often incorrect.

On October 11 Rev. Brown wrote to the AUA that he had taken over for Nute, whom Brown said had already given "his farewell sermon," although he did not mention whether Nute had actually left.[312] Brown begged some support from the AUA, given the desperation of life in the territory and the lack of money that limited his ability to contribute to his children's schooling. Certainly Brown's experience with the AUA validated Nute's struggles with them to be compensated for his appointed mission work.

Rev. Brown next wrote to George Hosmer at the AUA on October 17.[313] He said he needed to be paid if he was going to put more time into the Lawrence Society. He talked about his hard work on the farm and his fears for Unitarianism in Kansas. He reiterated that Nute had already left, and he blamed Nute for the failure of the society. However, he seemed unaware that Nute had not been under the employ of the AUA for close to a year.

Brown discovered firsthand exactly the same thing Nute had found. Given the ongoing trouble and strife of a territory in civil war, and despite the AUA's declarations in the *Quarterly Journal* about the Lawrence Society's independence, the Lawrence Society still needed the full support of mission status to survive.

Brown began his letter very critical of Nute, claiming that Nute did not follow through and had enthusiasm only in fits and starts. And yet, alongside that criticism, Brown begged for more support from the AUA and implied that if it did not come, he could work only sporadically. Brown also said that Nute had given offense with his brusque attitude, yet Brown bemoaned the frustration of carrying the society forward under the present conditions—exactly the conditions that led to Nute's frustration and despondence.

In any case, Nute had definitely left Lawrence by Brown's October 17 letter, either by October 1 as he had planned or perhaps as late as October 9, after the Wilder-Woodward wedding. He headed East. The Nute family story maintains that he had heard of John Brown's plans to attack the arsenal at Harper's Ferry and so took a detour there to try to stop him. Brown's plans were not a well-kept secret among his intimate sympathizers. Nute's acquaintance with Brown and his sons and Nute's role in passing information to "The Secret Six"[314] would certainly have provided ready access to the information.

Brown's plans for the attack on the armory were in fact changed abruptly the day before it was scheduled to start. They were altered so quickly that members of his small army were not even aware that they would be called into action until that very evening. If Nute went to Brown's headquarters at the Kennedy farmhouse on his way back East, trying to get an audience with Brown to reason him out of the attack, the date of the attack could have coincidentally, or purposefully, been moved up precipitously while he was there. If Nute, who was not a member of the inner sanctum of Brown's army, knew enough about the plans to show up at their secret headquarters, there might have been concerns about who else knew, jeopardizing the whole effort. This might account for the abrupt change in the timing of the attack. It began weeks ahead of the time originally planned.

Richard J. Hinton was a longtime friend of Nute from Lawrence, and as adjutant to the First Kansas Regiment, he was a compatriot during the Civil War. In 1893 Nute assisted Hinton with information about John Brown when Hinton was writing his book on Harper's Ferry. Hinton's *John Brown and His Men* reported:

> One hand from Kansas reported to Captain Brown himself, between the 10th and 14th, while the latter was absent from the farm. This Western man was sent to Hagerstown and Chambersburg, receiving a distinct impression that a week would elapse before positive action. He managed to remain from the 15th to the 18th in the neighborhood; and then, finding it impossible to assist in any direct way the party headed by Owen Brown who had escaped into the laurel hills of southern Pennsylvania, successfully made his way to Cincinnati, returning immediately to the border counties of Pennsylvania. As a newspaper correspondent, being recognized or suspected of being, moreover, a "Kansas" man—not a safe designation in those days—he soon left for Harrisburg and Cleveland, and finally went to Boston.[315]

Initially, it seemed that this unnamed man might be James Redpath, notorious abolitionist sympathizer and Kansas territorial newspaper reporter, who was directly connected with John Brown and his guerilla fighting in Kansas and elsewhere. But in 1859 Redpath penned a letter himself hotly denying his presence in the days leading up to the Harper's Ferry attack.[316]

Neither did it seem that the unnamed man was Richard Realf, who, according to one history of Kansas, was "charged with treason in connection with the Brown raid at Harper's Ferry, but was discharged by the United States senate investigating committee."[317] Realf's testimony to the Senate committee revealed that although he was elected secretary of state to Brown's army during the convention at Chatham, Canada, on May 8, 1858, he had no contact with Brown or the others after the date he left for England in 1858.[318]

Perhaps this "western" man was Nute, as the actions of this figure paralleled the Nute family story closely—specifically, that Nute traveled to Harper's Ferry to stop John Brown, was not able to, and so telegraphed news of the event as it broke, and then fled. Going through Harrisburg, Cleveland, and finally to Boston would certainly have taken Nute along a track familiar to him in his previous travels back and forth to Kansas.

The first news of the Harper's Ferry incident came to the newspapers by telegraph, although it is impossible to know if Nute participated in this. In his book about Harper's Ferry, John C. Malin noted, "Brief telegraphic notices of events arrived from Kansas within a few days, while the full accounts by mail did not arrive for two weeks to two months."[319] Certainly, this is the dynamic observed in the reporting of crises in Kansas—first reports coming by telegraph and then more detailed accounts of the events written by the Unitarian correspondents.

The Lawrence *Herald of Freedom* acknowledged in its October 29 edition, "On our first page will be found the detail of news from Harper's Ferry, Va., relative to Brown's attempt at Negro insurrection. We are indebted, chiefly, to the *Leavenworth Herald* for the dispatches which we have clipped from its columns."[320] The Nute family story indicates that Nute had telegraphed "the *Herald*" without being specific about which "*Herald*" it was. Perhaps it was the *Leavenworth Herald* that Nute had telegraphed, a Kansas paper from which other smaller Kansas papers typically took their news. Although the newspaper reports do not verify the family story, they do not disprove it either.

One of the challenges presented by the family story is trying to reconstruct how Nute could have gotten to Harper's Ferry from Lawrence between the time he was last known to have been in Lawrence and October 16, when the Harper's Ferry incident began. If Nute was the figure in Hinton's book, his arrival time "between the 10th and the 14th" was not very precise, but neither is it clear whether Nute left Lawrence closer to October 1, when he planned, or October 9, if the date listed for the Wilder-Woodward wedding is actually correct. Many newspaper accounts of weddings reflected the date on which the wedding was finally registered, which could be days, weeks, or even months after the date on which it actually occurred.

A timetable for Nute traveling from Kansas to Virginia between October 9 and October 16 would be very tight but not impossible. Even in the 1840s, steamboats were a preferred mode of travel because they could attain up to "a remarkable sixteen miles per hour."[321] Most of the trip between Lawrence and Harper's Ferry would have been made by steamboat. The 1,085 miles from Lawrence to Harper's Ferry theoretically could have been traversed in less than three days if done continuously at sixteen miles per hour. If Nute was indeed the mystery man from Kansas, he could very well have traveled from Lawrence to Harper's Ferry between October 1 and October 10 and certainly between October 1 and October 14.

The other piece of circumstantial evidence supporting Nute's presence at Harper's Ferry includes Hinton's consultation with Nute when he wrote his book about Harper's Ferry. There must have been some reason for his doing so. Hinton's book told the story of the one unidentified white man coming to the Kennedy farmhouse, failing to make contact with John Brown, leaving briefly, and then returning just before the attack.[322] This man is mentioned in the court records, although without the detail of his activities that Hinton wrote about.

The Harper's Ferry saga gripped the media and the public for months and even years. The trial of John Brown made history in the struggle between state and federal legal jurisdiction, and its verdict would have been appealed if the state of Virginia had not summarily and illegally executed Brown. The country was hopping mad, both at Brown and on his behalf. Many abolitionists thought him a criminal; proslavery sympathizers were all of one stripe and rejoiced at his execution. Some faction of abolitionists, though they did not agree with his actions, mightily protested his trial and execution. The Unitarians, in particular, were shaken by this event, both publicly and privately. The denomination was as split over the John Brown debacle as it was over abolitionism in general. For the group of influential Unitarians like Hale, Howe, Higginson, and Parker—who had all been clandestinely supporting and financially backing Brown—the fear of being charged with treason was palpable, and several fled the country.

All across the nation, but particularly in New England, masses of protestors gathered to cry out and mourn Brown's hanging. On December 8, 1859, in Faneuil Hall in Boston, one of the signers on the roll of a Union meeting of protest regarding the execution of John Brown on December 2 was none other than one "Ephm Nute." Although this could have been Nute's father, whom the census placed in Boston at this time, it is more likely that it was Nute himself, as his father's politics would not have made him a John Brown sympathizer.

After Harper's Ferry, Nute departed the country in mid-January 1860 and arrived in England to spend about ten days sightseeing. On the day before he planned to go to Paris, the heavy mantle of his Kansas experiences began to leave him. He wrote,

> To one thing I must confess a change of opinion. I believe from experience in the benefit of a sea voyage with the protracted infliction of sea-sickness. I believe I took leave of the Kansas intermittent about midway of the Atlantic, hoping never again to renew the acquaintance and, with the exception of a fashionable London cold, am happy to report myself in vigorous health.[323]

Between February and May 1860, Nute corresponded with the *Christian Register* from Switzerland, en route from England to Italy, where he planned to see Theodore Parker. As he took in the sights of old Switzerland, the dungeon at Chillon[324] made him reflect on his captivity and the other sadness of Kansas. He was starting to heal, and it turned his thoughts back to the theology that sustained him:

> In what a narrow circle the world revolves, repeating from century to century its most stupid follies and its darkest barbarities, ever denying in deed its loudest pretences of honor for the good and true. Such was my sad reflection as in the dungeon of Chillon I stood by the pillar to which for six long years was chained the noble Bonnivard, and marked the deep path worn by his feet in the solid rock at its base, as he paced two and fro in his narrow limits. The light reflected from the water came through the narrow grated windows more cheerfully than I had expected to see it, and the shimmering of the waves against the walls had a pleasant, friendly sound. But how wearisome almost to madness must this sight and sound have become to the captive in his long, monotonous solitude. What could have sustained him through those lonesome hours, days, years, to possess his soul in patient endurance unto the end? What but that thought on which all souls must to-day rely, who labor and wait amid sorrow and suffering for the coming of the reign of Justice and Humanity, namely, that the kingdom for which they wait is of the ever-living, omnipotent God, and that, therefore, by His favor it surely cometh and shall come until the victory be complete.[325]

Theodore Parker's health took a turn for the worse in 1857, and in January 1859 he quit preaching when tuberculosis brought on a collapse. In February of that year he left Boston with his wife and friends for the kinder climate of the Caribbean. On Santa Cruz (the contemporary St. Croix) he wrote a confession of faith to his beloved congregation that was published as "Theodore Parker's Experience as a Minister." Parker then traveled to England, Switzerland, and Italy. He recorded in his own journals that he and his family arrived in Rome in October 1859. It was there that Parker heard of the events at Harper's Ferry.[326] Parker's condition worsened in the winter, and he died on May 10, 1860, in Florence.

In October 1860, just after the publication of his travel diary in the *Christian Register*, Nute accepted a speaking engagement in Theodore Parker's former pulpit. He planned to talk about his visits with Parker before his death.[327] Although in 1856 Nute lamented in a letter to Parker that he had let theology come between them, their shared concern for abolitionism and Kansas built a sympathy between them, so much so that Nute shaped his trip abroad for one more contact with Parker.

In May 1860, Rev. John Stillman Brown wrote to the new AUA secretary, James Freeman Clarke, regarding the progress of the Lawrence Unitarian Society.[328] The congregation seemed to be stabilizing as the population of the town stabilized. Brown needed an income to continue as a missionary and sang Nute's refrain in trying to get sufficient money out of the AUA for that purpose. Although he was not in the throes of the bloody civil war that Nute had weathered during his tenure as missionary, life in territorial Lawrence was still a struggle.

In mid-June, Rev. Brown wrote to Clarke again and told him that the congregation had stayed at around fifty members.[329] Much of Nute's work was unraveling. The Sunday school association was cancelled because the orthodox Congregationalists—Rev. S. Y. Lum's faction—and the Baptists did not want to be joined with the Unitarians. The Unitarians planned to start another Sunday school association with those denominations that didn't mind working with them.

The money Brown needed was not forthcoming from the AUA. Brown continued to run his farm, tried to feed his family, and spent what time he could on ministry and missionary work in

Lawrence and Kanwaka. At the end of June, the clerk of the Lawrence Unitarian Society wrote to Miles, saying that they very much needed financial assistance and a full-time minister.[330] All the other churches in Lawrence were getting help from their judicatories—why couldn't the AUA help them?

Soon after, in early July, Rev. John Stillman Brown wrote again for the society to Clarke.[331] They desperately needed support from the AUA to continue, as the locals were barely able to feed themselves with the crops, which were not good because of the year's drought. Brown at first blamed Nute for the society's falling apart, but he then said Nute was not at fault for he had done all he could.

Nute had spent five years under war-zone conditions and endured the deaths of family and friends he held dear. He had been captured, jailed, and almost hung more than once. He undoubtedly had to navigate family sentiments over the murder of his brother-in-law, something for which his wife's family may have held him responsible. Additionally, he had been on the move constantly, traveling back and forth to the East to speak and raise money and to attempt to bring enlightenment to the AUA regarding his struggles with E. B. Whitman. In the end, Nute felt that his denomination deserted him. It would be no wonder if, in the wake of the trauma of his years in bloody Lawrence, he no longer had the conciliatory and patient demeanor that a practicing minister must assume toward the public.

Nute also weathered disapproval from his community. John S. Brown contended in his July 7, 1860, letter to Secretary Clarke that Nute had tried to survive for the last two years he was in Lawrence "on business transactions"[332] in a town where money and supplies were hard to come by. During that time, many in the church, including Rev. John Stillman Brown, seemed to assume that Nute was still being paid by the AUA. They looked askance at his dabbling in business, which Brown reported had alienated the congregation. This must have been difficult for Nute to bear without a great measure of impatience, given the desperation of his financial circumstances during those years.

By 1860 E. B. Whitman was back in Lawrence permanently, serving as John Stillman Brown's Sunday school superintendent. Brown seemed to have high regard for a man who had wooed the trust of many but had a reputation with all of them for not paying up.

Brown had coveted Nute's position as missionary for a long time, and he dreamed often of taking the job and doing it right. Now he was confronted with the same difficulties Nute had faced and tried to blame Nute for his own inability to deal with them. Nute, with a mixture of bitterness and relief, had finally thrown up his hands and gone on with his life. Whatever his role at Harper's Ferry, or however it had bent the trajectory of his life briefly, he had intended to leave the Territory for a year, including a trip to Europe, and that is exactly what he did. Brown, upon shouldering the impossible yoke, alternated between blaming Nute and the AUA for the state of the Lawrence Unitarian Society.

In early August, Rev. Brown wrote to Clarke again regarding some visiting preachers.[333] He wanted Unitarian books and tracts to distribute. However, he must have learned his lesson from Nute's difficulties with the AUA's books program, for he was clear that he did not feel that he could sell them. Brown thought he should "start a church" and said he would keep Clarke apprised of both his successes and failures.

In mid-October 1860 Nute was back in the country, and back in Boston. He attended the Nineteenth Autumnal Unitarian Convention in New Bedford on October 9. Samuel Gridley Howe presented the keynote speech, "Unitarianism in the West," and Nute spoke in response to it, coming out in support of AUA efforts and John Stillman Brown in Lawrence.[334] It might be supposed from this that he knew nothing of Brown's complaints about him to the AUA. Perhaps he had reached a place of peace after nearly a year away from the Lawrence mission, that allowed him to come out in support of the AUA once again.

Howe's address was more than a little controversial, as he spoke out against the same Unitarian "machine religion" that blacklisted

Theodore Parker in Boston. He was referring to the well-heeled segment of the denomination whose investments, though not in slavery itself, were in industries that depended for their profits on the fruits of slavery and the other burning culture-war issue of the time: alcohol. This faction was affronted by Parker's or anyone else's abolitionist or temperance activism, and had separated many Unitarian abolitionist and temperance preachers from their pulpits. John Pierpont later responded to Howe's speech. He had also been relieved of his pulpit when he alienated the more wealthy members of his congregation by preaching abolitionism and temperance and for giving Theodore Parker a place to preach.[335] The convention's focus on Unitarianism in the West exhibited a touch of irony, considering that the AUA had already withdrawn support for the Kansas mission.

On October 23 Nute wrote to Charles Wesley Slack, saying that he would accept the speaking engagement in Theodore Parker's former pulpit:

> Of all places the pulpit of the late Mr. Parker is that in which I would choose to give my reminiscences of Italy and especially of Rome where it was my good fortune to enjoy something of his society and of Florence his last resting place. . . . I therefore gladly accept your invitation to speak in Music Hall next Sunday morning.[336]

In November of 1860, Edward Fitch wrote home and urged his mother to attend one of Nute's lectures in the East and advised her to try to get Nute to stay with her if she could, because she would so much enjoy his company.[337] Some time between that date and April 1861, Nute returned to Lawrence, where he caused Rev. John S. Brown much consternation because he could no longer be persuaded to preach at the Lawrence Unitarian Society for free. What Nute planned to do to earn a living at that point is unknown, but no matter—the Civil War, poised on the horizon, would have changed it anyway.

CIVIL WAR

During the Civil War period the activism of Unitarians and Universalists came to the fore once more. When the persuasions of abolitionism failed and war became inevitable, those who wrote and fought for the antislavery movement got caught up in support of the Union troops and the civilian war refugees, both black and white. Nute and many other men in Lawrence enlisted in the Kansas regiments and left for active duty. The officers took their wives with them. The war should have brought an end to Bleeding Kansas. But those who stayed behind in Lawrence were to suffer martyrdom once more before it was over.

Although the AUA *Monthly Journal* listed Nute as residing in Medford, Massachusetts, in 1861, according to the letters of parishioners he was actually back in Lawrence by sometime that spring. In April 1861 he wrote to G. W. Fox, assistant secretary at the AUA, still trying to settle his book account with the AUA.[338] He sent Fox a large book inventory, and although he had already settled his account with the AUA, he had just succeeded in getting the records all together after his year abroad and in the East.

A few days later, Rev. John Stillman Brown wrote to James Freeman Clarke, AUA secretary, saying once again that he needed money from the AUA if he was to continue as a missionary in Kansas.[339] Brown related that Nute had been back in town for about a month and was very troubled, which seemed to mean that Brown wasn't able to get Nute to preach *pro bono* anymore. Brown said he didn't think Nute wanted to preach at all. Whether Nute was only troubled because he had to resist Brown's attempts to get him to preach for free is not known. Brown's letter does suggest that Nute's return to Lawrence was difficult. He still had a wife and household to support but no visible means of doing so aside from his paid lectures. In the grips of post-traumatic stress from the Bleeding Kansas years, newly back in Lawrence in early 1861 after his year abroad and protracted visit to New England, Nute was discontented as the nation slipped into the Civil War.

The men of Lawrence enlisted in the First Kansas Regiment when it formed in early May 1861; Nute enlisted as its chaplain. In this war the chaplain was persona non grata in most military life and ritual. Individual regiments might use him for the flag service or to offer a prayer or two at a holiday,[340] but by and large, chaplains waited at the beck and call of officers and enlisted men who didn't know what to do with them.[341] They bore ever-present criticism for their "uselessness" while being taken advantage of for any kindness, small or large, that was asked of them.[342]

The conflict within the military over the role and usefulness of the chaplain was not the only thing contributing to the negative regard in which most enlisted men held them. Civil war historians John Brinsfield and William Davis note,

> A purposeful smear campaign aimed at army chaplains by the U.S. Christian Commission during 1861–62 did considerable damage as Evangelicals behind the Young Men's Christian Association tried to use the Christian Commission as a means to establish a strong influence in the Northern armies. . . . There came thereafter a steady stream of defamation about military chaplains that found its way into orations or newspapers. These incessant aspersions nurtured a suspicion in the public mind that decades thereafter would equate "chaplain" with "legendary rogue."[343]

The U.S. Christian Commission was trying to wrest power

from the U.S. Sanitary Commission, which handled much of the pastoral and personal support of the soldiers, working through the military's chaplains. The Sanitary Commission was huge, well organized, and replete with women and Unitarians. The motivation to displace it arose from orthodox Christian religious contempt for the Unitarians and Universalists who figured prominently in the Sanitary Commission works:

> During the last week of November 1861, the New York Times reported on a "convention of army chaplains" at Trinity Church in Washington, D.C. It was held under the auspices of fifteen Northern chapters of the Young Men's Christian Association, which had just met in New York City to organize a "national mission for the temporal and religious relief of Union soldiers." Their "mission took the shape of a relief agency run by Evangelical Christians called the U.S. Christian Commission (USCC). The chaplain-delegates demonstrated their enthusiastic support for the USCC as a source of religious relief to Union soldiers and as a disdainful answer to the "Godless Christianity of the Universalists," who were prominent in the competing U.S. Sanitary Commission (USSC) organization.[344]

This religious war between the orthodox Christians and the Unitarian and Universalist liberal Christians persisted for the duration of the military action, with aspersions of incompetence cast from both sides. These brought a predictable increase in interfactional conflicts among the troops and of course prompted even more disregard for the chaplains. However, "[w]hen the war ended, both the Christian Commission and the Sanitary Commission voluntarily dissolved amid thunderous self-congratulation."[345] Perhaps the enlisted men's cynical view toward religion was not misplaced.

During the war, the frontline chaplains could not get the unqualified respect of the enlisted men—they did not have the collegiality of the other officers, they did not have a strong infrastructure from the military, and the Sanitary Commission and the Christian Commission were at war with each other. And so, to put their shoulders to the impossible tasks before them, individual chaplains had to make their allegiances with, and cement support for, each other despite their denominational diversity—38 percent were Methodist, 17 percent were Presbyterian, 12 percent were Baptist, 10 percent were Episcopal, 9 percent were Congregational, 3 percent were Catholic, 2 percent were Lutheran, and all other religious groups accounted for 1 percent or less. In spite of the denomination's leadership in the Sanitary Commission, only 4 percent of all chaplains were Unitarian or Universalist.[346] Despite their differences, the denominations managed to work together in a remarkable fashion on the front lines, and the chaplains who met the challenges there were a hardy, loyal, and diverse bunch who survived the same grueling conditions as their flock.[347]

Leigh R. Webber was a young private in Nute's regiment who was also a very close friend of Rev. John Stillman Brown's family in Lawrence. It is not documented that Webber was a member of the Unitarian congregation in Lawrence, but given his intimacy with the Brown family and familiarity with Nute and other Unitarians, and Nute's special kindnesses to him, it is likely. His rigid Christian rectitude put him in good stead with the upright, conservative Brown and his family, and Webber carried on a prolific correspondence with all of them during his time with the First Kansas Regiment. His letters give great insight into the day-to-day activities, culture, and politics of the regiment. Because to this date so few of Nute's papers and letters from the Civil War period have been recovered, and none of them are personal letters home, Webber's letters to the Brown family that mention Nute's whereabouts help create a picture of Nute's military experience in a way his official military record cannot.

Webber complained often that officers like Nute had all the benefits and breaks denied to the enlisted men. However, Webber had no problem seeking out Nute whenever possible to take advantage of his and Lucy's attentions. As has been noted, this was a common relationship between enlisted men and chaplains during the Civil War, initially due to the amorphous role of chaplains within the army.[348] The dynamic was later fed by the smear campaign perpetrated by the Young Men's Christian Association in its attempts to leverage itself into taking over the chaplaincy in the Union army.[349]

On October 29, 1861, Nute wrote to G. W. Fox at the AUA from Tipton, Missouri, to request music books for the soldiers. He also wrote about the great losses the regiment suffered during the battle of Wilson's Creek:

> I see by the "Inquirer" that "Army Melodies" are sometimes furnished by the A.U.A. to our troops. Could you send me two or three hundred for the use of our regiment. . . . If you can, send by express to St. Louis notifying me of the manner of sending. Direct letter to me officially at this place. We are liable to move away any hour, but letters are forwarded to the regiment as they go from place to place. The books I must order again from St. Louis. . . . We have been changing about so much ever since we have been in the field that we have been cut off from the regular publications. This copy of the Inquirer is dated Sept 28 & reached me only a few days since. . . . If you have any other publications specially adapted to the soldiers I would be glad to get a small quantity. Nearly one half of my regiment are either Roman Catholics or German unable to read English. Beside we are reduced to about one half our original numbers by losses incident to the battle of Willson's Creek. Not more than one hundred copies of any one publication could be used in our regiment. The singing books will be in more demand especially if they have music notes. . . . The struggle in Missouri is not yet over nor do I see any prospect of its termination for this year to come.[350]

In fact, most soldiers wanted no reminder of what the chaplains represented: the disapproval of jaunts into alcohol, prostitution, and other sins helpful to assuage the trials of combat. Webber himself was a teetotaler, but his mood was dark and critical of Nute and the entire regiment. Though they were Lawrence boys, the First Kansas was no more approving of Nute than Webber. It is no wonder Nute had a desire from the beginning to detach from the regiment and enter into service for the Sanitary Commission. There he could be continually active helping soldiers and constantly appreciated. Nute was also a teetotaler. As the enlisted men were drunk whenever they possibly could be and not in the least interested in hearing about religion, they were not grateful for the services of the chaplains and didn't seem to know why chaplains were even with the regiments.

In January, the *Chicago Tribune* published Nute's report about his work as chaplain, providing a window into where he was and what he was doing when he was absent from the regiment. He spent his time in the military field hospitals with the wounded men:

My official duties have given me daily intercourse with the sick, who have been sent thither from time to time, from the troops in the field in the southern and western part of the State. . . . Some six weeks since, between two and three hundred came in from Sedalia, Warsaw, and other points on the route between that and Springfield. Their arrival at the railroad station made one of the most distressing scenes it has ever been my lot to witness. Many of these poor fellows were in the critical stages of typhoid fevers, others worn down by hard service and long sickness, deprivation and neglect, unable to stand, and with no place to lie down but on the bare platform of the station, and almost entirely without attendance. Some tottered about delirious, unable to give any account of themselves, uttering only incoherent mutterings. One poor fellow in this condition sank down exhausted, and being taken under shelter, died that night, and was buried in a nameless grave. Those from the South had been brought in common baggage wagons, over the roughest of roads, a distance of from forty to sixty miles, and almost utterly unattended. They were filthy in the extreme and generally but half clad. Some gave shocking reports of the temporary hospitals from which they had come, at Warsaw, where hundreds had been crowded into a church without bedding, change of clothing, and for days together, without medical attendance. . . . Several days after this, business took me to Warsaw, where I spent a few hours in that hospital, and found the worst of these reports confirmed. In one small church were some twenty-five men, some wounded, some sick with fevers, and no one with the least article of bedding beyond an armful of coarse prairie hay, thrown down in a pew with the camp blanket, and at the best a knapsack for a pillow. There they lay, in the clothes in which the hard marches of weeks had been made. The effluvia of the room testified to a combination of the most sickening filths—flannels saturated to the last degree with putrid bodily excretions, vessels unemptied, or never cleansed, steam of greasy cooking; in short, a nauseous stench which made the continuance of life almost a miracle, and at best, a terrible and protracted martyrdom. The care of all these patients devolved on one young man, kind hearted, but without experience in such service. One man lay dying at sunset of typhoid pneumonia who had received no medical attendance since early morning. That night this poor neglected soldier was released from his sufferings, and before morning another followed. What must have been the condition of that room when a week before it contained nearly two hundred, with the same lack of appliances, and the like evils eight-fold intensified? . . . For the last three weeks there has been struggling into existence, against many difficulties, a large, general, hospital at Tipton, made necessary by the influx of the sick, for whom no provision was made elsewhere. Of this institution I have been a close observer. Its management has filled with daily increasing amazement and horror. The number of inmates has ranged from four hundred and fifty to six hundred. For the first ten days there were not more than fifty cots, and besides the common army blanket, absolutely no bedding. Filthiness and discomfort I will not attempt to describe. Without the utensils indispensable for keeping the rooms in cleanly conditions, with but few and inexperienced attendants, it need not be added, the distress and mortality has been appalling. I am confident that scores have died from neglect, who by a little decent nursing might have been saved. . . . At length, through much tedious formality, which had been keen torture to those on the spot, (and here, let me say, the Post Surgeons have done their part humanely and devotedly, and are beyond reproach,) this has been recognized as a general hospital and provision made for some of its most pressing needs. And yet within a few days in a state of terrible destitution. The most pressing need seems to be of good nursing. The undeniable truth is, that men are dying daily in that hospital for the want of that tender care which I believe women alone can give. At a low estimate, one hundred experienced women are today wanted there as nurses. Can it be that they are not to be had? I am loth to believe it. Let the simple facts be published and the call properly made, and ten times that number shall volunteer in this city alone before another sun shall set; or we have no civilization worthy the name, and all our talk of humanity is but empty sound. . . . In the hope that the abuses of which I now testify would be speedily remedied, and unwilling to send anguish into hundreds of homes, unless imperatively called for, I have long forborne to speak out. But with a clear conscience I can keep silent no longer.[351]

On February 23, the teenaged Sarah Brown, daughter of Unitarian minister John Stillman Brown of Lawrence, wrote to her brother Willie, describing Lawrence when the First Kansas was there. The regiment was a rough bunch, and there was animosity between it and the townspeople that threatened to erupt into violence. Sarah mentioned Nute and felt he was not a favorite of the regiment. Since Nute spoke to the troops on intemperance, and according to Private Webber's letters, they did nothing but drink, this could certainly account for his lack of popularity.

Sarah mentioned that the troops were quite proslavery and engaged in unrelenting persecution and harassment of the African-American citizens of Lawrence. This was at base the cause of the conflict with the town, which considered its African-American citizens as equals and deserving of special protection in light of territorial politics. This probably also contributed to Nute's unrelenting efforts to go into detached service from his regiment. Sarah Brown wrote,

> The Kansas First are all here now and give Lawrence quite a lively appearance but they are a rough looking and rough acting set of men. William Clark & Webber were here yesterday and they said the Lawrence people were getting up a petition to Hunter to have them removed as a nuisance, and the soldiers were quite excited about it and swore vengeance upon the leaders. . . . It is a very pro slavery regiment, not sympathizing much with Lane's policy and they are down on the darkies, will not let them walk on the side walk drive them out of the saloons and barber shops &c which rouses the Lawrence people who consider the negroes as much citizens and quite as good & peaceable citizens as the soldiers. Saturday the regs was required to cut a passage through the ice so that the Ferry boat could cross the river. Instead of doing it themselves they went around town and marched all the Negroes down at the point of the bayonet making them do it for them. Lawrence is now under martial law which makes it much more quiet than it was before yesterday and today Mr. Nute occupied Father's place, inviting the regiment to be there, but they were only called together for Sunday so many were not here and he only had about six. Today there were some fifty out to hear him which with our people made a hundred. He spoke upon intemperance and was plain and earnest and much more pointed than

he usually is. I do not think Mr. Nute is a great favorite. A few evenings ago Mary & I were downtown and we visited the Negro school . . . most of the teachers are little girls and boys twelve or fourteen years old. . . . Your letters surprise me very much. How you can take the view you do of emancipation, I can not conceive. I think history, policy, common sense all point to that as the only efficient means of subduing the rebellion, justice requires it of us, and if we had done it boldly six months ago . . . we should have been stronger and better off today. I believe if we do not proclaim emancipation . . . we shall lose the honor, glory & senses of having done our duty. You may tell me in every letter that you hate slavery and regard it as a curse, but I have heard that story too long & too often in St. Louis to put much faith in it. That is the way half of the people there talked while every one knew they were Union only because they thought slavery was safer in the Union just as the other party were secessionists because they thought slavery was safer out of the Union. I have no sympathy with either party neither do I desire to see the Union restored exactly on its former basis. I want to see the rebellion crushed and the cause of it removed. Then and not till then shall I welcome peace.[352]

In November 1862 Nute was in St. Louis trying to obtain a position with the Western Sanitary Commission, a St. Louis-based organization which rose independently of the U.S. Sanitary Commission. The Sanitary Commissions organized the medical response to soldiers in the field and supervised hospitals and soldiers' homes, as well as brought comforts to the men on the front lines.[353] Agents of the commission helped soldiers correct irregularities in their papers that prevented them from receiving pay. The commission also compiled a hospital directory that enabled families to locate their wounded loved ones in the many field and urban war hospitals that had sprung up. Support for the commission was raised by voluntary subscription and "Sanitary Fairs" in the larger cities.[354]

In May 1862, each permanent hospital was allowed to appoint a permanent chaplain, which must have appealed to Nute as a much more satisfying job than chasing a regiment that had no wish for his services and no inclination to attend them.[355] The wounded and sick from the Federal troops were initially taken to field hospitals, but soon went to larger, permanent hospitals near their own homes or in a nearby major urban area. Much of the medical work was done by both male and female nurses, assisted by hundreds of female volunteers.[356] Volunteers also garnered donations and gave clothes and food to the men. They played games with them and wrote letters home for them while they recovered.

Field hospitals were only as good as the medical personnel and supplies available to them. Soldiers might receive poor care simply because there were not enough supplies or personnel to attend to them adequately. But the larger hospitals, especially in St. Louis and Washington, were models at the time, and they must have held great appeal to any chaplain or surgeon dedicated to his work.

Nute's military record lists him as entering detached service to his regiment in November/December 1862, when he became an agent of the Western Sanitary Commission by order of General Ulysses S. Grant. Nute continued in detached service for the rest of the war. In a letter to one of the Brown daughters on November 27, 1862, Webber wrote that Nute had come back from St. Louis long enough to report that he had applied and been accepted into detached service. Webber hoped bitterly that Nute would be able to send the regiment necessary items, such as gloves, as they were all in great need.[357]

Despite Webber's complaints about Nute, Nute himself appeared to treat Webber with kindness and favor him more than others in the regiment. Decades later, in a letter from Rev. John Stillman Brown on November 26, 1892, Nute was confronted with the aspersions that Webber had cast upon Nute's character in letters to the Browns. Nute's reply corrected Brown's information from Webber about what Nute was doing when absent from the regiment.[358] Nute was not partying in St. Louis with other officers, as Webber supposed, but meeting the needs of the wounded on the front lines and engaging in a variety of clandestine efforts on behalf of the Union army.

Nute seemed unruffled by Webber, whom he characterized as a "chronic grumbler." This assessment is certainly borne out by reading Webber's complete collection of letters. Grumblers in the army were not rare. One soldier wrote home that "there are a few who are constitutional grumblers. . . . They find fault with everything. In fact, if they ever get to Heaven, they'll be finding fault with the music!"[359]

Nute mentioned in his 1892 letter to Brown that "men returning from hospitals & furloughs—had died on the levee from neglect. . . . Our ambulance was ever on hand at the arrival of a boat to take the invalids and the poor fellows who knew not where to find their camps & many of them we detained for recuperation."[360] Such was the work of the Sanitary Commission from its inception. Both the U.S. and the Western Sanitary Commission were first formed to meet the needs of the wounded in battle. As the armies progressed they devastated the countryside around them, so that nothing was available for the treatment of the wounded. Many who would have lived with treatable wounds "lie for days helpless and neglected on the battle field . . . perish by the slow oozing of their life blood, by cold, by heat, by thirst, by starvation, when the simplest succor might restore them to life and health, to the ranks, and their homes."[361]

For months the Sanitary Commission and the surgeon general had tried to push reforms on the War Department that would decrease the mortality of the wounded, to no avail. So, as the general secretary of the commission reported, they decided to add to the Sanitary Commission's legions a

> medical corps of a body of trained assistants, whose duty it shall be to gather up and remove the wounded from the battle-field, and perform for them the first necessary offices of relief; and entrusting to that department independent means of transportation and subsistence for the sick, much will be done

to economize life, prevent suffering and improve the health of the army.[362]

Field hospitals were set up in tents, taverns, and any available house. Cots were at a premium, so many of the wounded lay on the floor, in straw or blankets, when the cots were gone.[363] Battle-field casualties were numerous, nearly four times as many as first reported in the newspapers. The walking wounded got up and began to beg their way to anywhere they could get.

There were fifteen military hospitals in St. Louis alone, with the capacity to serve 5,750 patients. When large numbers of incoming casualties were expected, huge numbers of more mobile patients would be furloughed in order to make room.[364] As casualties increased, the work of the U.S. Sanitary Commission fell short, and the Western Sanitary Commission was formed.

Early on, the Sanitary Commission's attention turned to the plight of soldiers returning home on furlough, or being discharged, or returning to their regiments. They arrived in cities and travel centers without the means of paying their keep or transportation. Some, as noted in Nute's letter, might die of neglect; others might never make it to their homes or back to their regiments after falling into bad company or other distress.[365]

To address these problems, the commission established its first soldiers' home in St. Louis on March 12, 1862.[366] By the next February, the commission had opened another home in Memphis to address the same needs of discharged and invalid soldiers. The building and grounds were located in a suburb of Memphis, close to the river, on the confiscated property of a rebel officer. The large mansion and six acres held handsome lawns, beautiful shade trees, and three acres of gardens. This home was limited to discharged and invalid soldiers; those who were furloughed were sent to Fort Pickering. The superintendent of the home, the post Nute held, transported invalid soldiers between the river, the railroad depot, and the home. The superintendent helped soldiers get their papers in order, obtain their pay, and eventually continue home.[367]

The flow of wounded was so large and unrelenting that the U.S. Sanitary Commission had to set up a temporary facility near the steamboat landing, with a lodge and warehouse for storage furnished by the Western Sanitary Commission. Discharged and invalid soldiers who arrived at night would stay there until transferred to the home. The U.S. and Western Sanitary Commissions worked together to provide a meld of services.[368] An early historian of the Western Sanitary Commission reported,

> On the 16th of February, '63, the Soldiers' Home at Columbus, Ky., was opened, and has entertained many thousand soldier guests. It was at first superintended by Mr. Brown, and for a short time by Mr. Geo. E. Wyeth, when Chaplain Ephraim Nute, became superintendent in the spring of '63, and continued in charge till September of the same year, when he went to New Orleans to establish another Home for the Commission in that city. [footnote: The Soldier's Home at New Orleans was duly established in October, 1862, by Mr. Nute, acting as the agent of the Western Sanitary Commission, under a special order from Maj. Gen. Grant. He was provided with furniture, stores, and funds for this purpose, to the value of several thousand dollars, and the Home, on its first opening, was crowded with guests. Late in November it was transferred to the U.S. Commission, under whose auspices it is still continued. Rev. Mr. Nute, from the date of this transfer, ceased to be the agent of the Western Commission, and soon after returned to his regiment.][369]

From their very first opening for services in 1862 until June 1, 1863, the soldiers' homes "entertained" 25,581 soldiers, furnished 30,852 individual lodgings, and provided 73,325 meals.[370] In 1863, the Western Sanitary Commission also found itself trying to meet the relief needs of over 40,000 freedmen who had gathered along the banks of the Mississippi and were starving and dying of disease. White refugees by the thousands, often women and children, were also fleeing the battlegrounds and ended up in the care of the soldiers' homes and the U.S. and Western Sanitary Commissions.

On February 18, 1863, Nute wrote to James Yeatman, president of the Western Sanitary Commission, about the potential for violence at the home in Columbus where he was superintendent. He was still running escaped slaves North, passing them through the soldiers' home as freedmen employees, and there was trouble on the horizon. The letter read,

> The slave hunters have come down on us to day backed up with Sheriff & a civil process. They marched into our Office four of them & asked permission to search the house for their three fugitives. I refused, they have gone to the Commander of Post for permission to order me. The hunted ones have secreted themselves (I am told) & some fire arms are near them. There may be scenes in the Home. . . . I fear we must lose three of our best colored employees. One has been with the home over four months & given good satisfaction. . . . Other slaves were taken out of this town to day by consent of the Post commander who also furnished transportation for the hunter & his victim. This is hard to bear & the path of duty in my eyes is not exceeding clear. . . . Shall I pay wages to these "Chattels" for the certain benefit of their masters? Am I not bound to protect as far as in me lies these faithful servitors who claim my protection? They came early this morning asking if I would stand by them. . . . But perhaps Col. Martin by an express order will relieve me from all responsibility in the matter—though not of unspeakable grief.[371]

While Nute labored in the grand Sanitary Commission project of the Unitarians, Lawrence should have entered a period of relative peace, away from the front lines. But that was not the case, for the Unitarians who remained there came under violent assault yet again, from proslavery Border Ruffians. The bleed in Kansas was not yet stanched.

William Clarke Quantrill was originally a school teacher, first in Utah and then in Lawrence. He was a Border Ruffian sympathizer during his years in Lawrence. During the Civil War, he formed a savage and renegade Confederate fighting band and brought it back to settle old scores against James Lane's Lawrence Jayhawkers, the fierce Free-State individuals clandestinely organized to beat back the Missouri Ruffians. On August 21, 1863, Lawrence was sacked again in what became known as Quantrill's Raid. Quantrill launched a guerilla attack on the town that left almost two hundred men and boys dead and one out of four buildings burned. Although Lucy was with Nute at the Columbus soldiers' home and was not in danger, the attack would bring Nute back to Lawrence to be with those he knew and loved and to check on his own house to see if it still stood.

The incident was decried in the press as cowardly and inhumane. Quantrill, nursing his grudges from the Bleeding Kansas days, had boasted that he was going to raze Lawrence. He and his regiment systematically looted and burned their way through town, murdering all the men and boys they could find. The letters home and newspaper reports of the event are difficult to read, even now.

The women of Lawrence were no less rough and ready than in the Bleeding Kansas years and responded with courage to Quantrill's Raid. In one incident, a woman hid her husband in the cellar after seeing that Lawrence was burning. When the guerillas came to demand him, she begged them to allow her to drag out a carpet that was the only thing she had left of her father's possessions. The gents, chivalry not completely dead, allowed her to drag the carpet out, unaware that her husband scampered behind its bulk to safety.[372]

On September 1, 1863, a letter from Rev. John Stillman Brown to his friend John L. Rupin described the raid, with shocked and palpable anguish. Brown listed some of the dead, among them, of course, many Unitarians:

The Lord hath spared us—Lawrence has seen and experienced dreadful things—you have seen the lists of the dead—The Brick Walls can be built up again. But what workman can build up our dead again. . . . It was a little after sunrise when three men came galloping into our enclosure and said Quantrill has in Lawrence killing and burning. We looked towards the city which lies N.E. of us and saw very distinctly the smoke curling up. Charles took a horse and rode west to arouse the people. William took the bridle and tried to catch some of our horses—I looked up the guns and swords—we had plenty of arms but little ammunition. I went out and milked the cows, eat breakfast took a double barreled shot gun and started for town. But after going a few rods I thought how foolish it was to take a gun as I was no marksman and there bushwhackers were sharp shooters so I laid down my gun and started again for Lawrence. . . . I walked leisurely toward town and took my stand on the hill west of the city—there I could see the town—and the bushwhackers as they rode from place to place—as they went to their work of death, burning and plunder. All the business part of the city was in flames about ten o'clock the main body of the brigands had ridden out of town and formed their lines on the south East in plain sight of the place where I stood. I judged there were not over two hundred and fifty—They rode off south burning the houses as they went; we could see them push for ten miles or more by the smoke of burning buildings—after they had all got fairly away I went home—here I found some women and children—some sixty or seventy who had fled for refuge—To my surprise I found coming up from our ravine the braw Gen. James H. Lane our United States Senator and soldier—I told him the way was all clear. I had just come from town and the last guerrillas had gone. He said lots about getting a horse and pursuing them. . . . I believe he did get together a band and went after them but I hear no evidence that he was the means of shooting any. There rebels and bushwhackers, and guerillas and marauders, and murderers were a motley crew as have a set of fellows as ever rode horse—some even perfectly brutal—Some of the milder type. They came to kill and plunder. At first they shot indiscriminately every man that was seen—their object seemed at first to inspire terror—to let no men get together for concerted action—they took I judge in money not less than 150,000 dollars and destroyed in property perhaps 1500000 it may be more—then again it may be less. Probably in Lawrence and vicinity two hundred were killed—generally shot through the head. One, two, three four five balls in each. Some were killed under circumstances of the greatest atrocity—Many more burned to death. A great many houses were fired and then put out again by the inmates—Probably not one fifth of the dwelling houses in town were burned. All the stores hotels and business part of the town was destroyed there were but two or three stores left standing and these even rifled of their goods. This said took place on Friday morning about sunrise 21st of August—On Sunday night following we had an awful scare—news came that the "bushwhackers" were upon us again—that they were burning Eudora—a town six miles east, and were just coming into town—oh; what a running and shrieking—the panic was terrific—women men & children flying as for life—many crossed the river—many fled to the neighboring cornfields and staid out all night though we had a terrible thundershower between ten and eleven o'clock—I think the citizens suffered more from fear Sunday night than they did the day when the ruffians came. But we are now settling down to our former state of calmness and hopefulness. No one was prepared for such a calamity WE all thought that such a band could not enter Lawrence without our receiving some intelligence of the fact. An hours warning wont have been sufficient. We could have driven them all way if we could have had only one hours warning—we had not a moments— It came suddenly as a thunderbolt—the citizens were mostly sleeping. There had been a great Rail Road meeting the night previous and all the business men were taking an extra nap. Some twenty Negroes were killed—half of the Germans in town were shot—I mean of the voting men. . . . I understand a great many were killed—Relief in money and goods and provisions is coming in—a great many families have gone East. The shovel the saw and the hammer are again commencing to rise. We can soon recover from the loss of property. The loss of life is . . . great. The essential loss. Last Sunday we had a Union Meeting of all the churches in the city. We met at the Cordleys Church—the Congregationalists—Mr. Paddock the Methodist minister preached the sermon, a long, rambling, pointless affair—Strange how little a man can contrive to say in an hour. Mr. Nute is in town looking after his affairs. Whether we shall get together again our Congregation I cannot say—I shall try next Sunday. . . . I must go to town and visit the sick the disconsolate. Mr. Paddock saw last Sunday that there were 85 widows in town and 250 orphans made such by these.[373]

For such a small town to lose such a large part of its population, and worse yet, to brutal murder, was more than devastating. Once again, it would set the little city and its inhabitants back for years. With this tragedy added to his plate, Nute returned to his post at the soldiers' homes.

Part of Nute's duties as a supervisor was to participate in raising money for the soldiers' homes he was in charge of. In the fall of 1863, Nute sent out a letter of appeal. He had been in charge of the Columbus home for seven months. He had also moved up in the administration, and he now had charge of another soldiers' home in New Orleans and several others as well. From details in one of the few of Nute's own letters surviving from the Civil War period, it is clear that this chaplain was not sitting on his hands:

An Appeal for Support of the Soldiers' Homes of the Western Sanitary Commission. . . . The object of these institutions is to furnish a place of rest, wholesome food and social influences cheering and refining for the homeless soldier. Convalescents from the hospitals on the way to their regiments; men on sick furloughs passing to and fro between home and their fields of service; discharged men and those awaiting discharge; the soldier worn out and left behind on the march, not needing hospital treatment, but only a few days or weeks of rest, and proper nourishment to recruit his strength. . . . For the last seven months the writer of this has been in charge of the largest of these homes at Columbus, Kentucky, and is able to testify from personal observation to the great success and benefit of the institution. The number of guests has averaged about one hundred and forty, and nearly five thousand soldiers in all have been entertained. . . . Many others from the camps and regimental hospitals in the vicinity, and from regiments passing through, have shared in the benefits of our reading and writing rooms, or attended the social and religious gatherings held for months every evening at this Home. . . . In that way, at all of the Homes improving influences have been widely extended, and many doubtless restrained from evil, and kept from resorts of dissipation and vice. . . . These facts concerning the Homes are enough on which to base an appeal for their generous support which cannot be resisted by those who have the welfare of our brave soldiers at heart.[374]

In October 1863 Nute was in New Orleans looking for a site to start up another Sanitary Commission soldiers' home.[375] He reported on the property he had found to the quartermaster, who issued an order for the property to be obtained.

Nute wrote to G. W. Fox, assistant secretary at the AUA, in November 1863.[376] He had seen the recent *Monthly Journal* and bemoaned the fact that he was so cut off from contact with his colleagues in the ministry. He took the blame himself and talked about the high stress of the last eight months supervising soldiers' homes along the Mississippi and superintending the large numbers of troops who stayed at the New Orleans facility. Material he had previously requested from Fox had never arrived, and he was hoping to get back issues of the *Monthly Journal* as well as reading material appropriate for the recovering soldiers.

There follows in the record an interesting exchange concerning Nute between officers of the Western Sanitary Commission and officers of the Union army. In mid-December 1863, James E. Grotiman of the Western Sanitary Commission wrote to General Grant, whose order had put Nute in detached service with the Western Sanitary Commission. Grotiman requested that Nute be returned to his regiment after "having grossly betrayed the trust and confidence reposed in him."[377]

On January 7, 1864, there followed an order on the officer's casualty sheet that dismissed Nute from the army.[378] Soon after, on January 15, a letter from a rather horrified secretary of the Western Sanitary Commission told General Grant in no uncertain terms that they did not want Nute dismissed from the military, just returned to his regiment.[379] The secretary followed this request with the details of the debacle in which Nute, who tended to be a little too independent in his solutions to bureaucratic problems, was involved.

Nute became disgusted with the Western Sanitary Commission's inability to provide adequate supplies to run the soldiers' home, and so he negotiated with, and then transferred, the home purchased by and for the Western Sanitary Commission to the U.S. Sanitary Commission—without leave of, or notice to, the Western Sanitary Commission. When the director of the Western Sanitary Commission arrived for a site visit, he was shocked to find the U.S. Sanitary Commission flag flying over "his" home.

The secretary alleged that Nute had not effected this transfer because supplies had not been forthcoming—the secretary assured General Grant that Nute could have weathered his difficulties with "a little patience"—but because with the transfer he could put his own wife in the position of matron, and the two of them could use the residence on the grounds. From Nute's perspective, in the wake of inefficiency, he might have been perfectly justified in firing the present staff and appointing his wife as matron so he would have greater control over running the facility. This arrangement was in fact standard for married men in charge of the administration of a soldiers' home.

Oddly, the Western Sanitary Commission did nothing to reverse the transfer of the home to the U.S. Sanitary Commission. The June 15, 1864, attachment to Nute's letter of October 4, 1863, shows that the U.S. Sanitary Commission paid the Western Sanitary Commission for the building itself, and the Western Sanitary Commission honored the transfer. It would seem that if the charges against Nute by the Western Sanitary Commission were legitimate, such blatant self-serving fraud on his part would have necessitated serious legal consequences, certainly the dismissal that Grant initially issued, and a demand to return the "stolen" soldiers' home property to its rightful owner. Instead, the secretary virtually begged Grant to reverse his order to dismiss Nute from the army and simply return him to his unit, to avoid controversy. This seems to indicate that something was awry, and the Western Sanitary Commission was content to leave well enough alone rather than having the details of the matter aired publicly.

Nute's veteran record indicates that the erroneous dismissal order was subsequently revoked on January 26, 1864, and Nute's membership in the army restored. The incident ended, in the record, with an innocuous official request from the War Office in New Orleans. The transfer of the facility to the U.S. Sanitary Commission had been completed and their staff was on site to take it over. Therefore, Nute could return to his regiment because his services to the Western Sanitary Commission were no longer needed.

Nute, along with the rest of the First Kansas Regiment, was last paid on April 30, 1864, and mustered out at Fort Leavenworth, Kansas, on June 17, 1864. With the end of the war, the Bleeding Kansas era finally ended.

EPILOGUE

Following his muster out of the military, Nute's life, like many veterans, was unsettled for a period of time. If he returned to Lawrence, it was either not immediate or was temporary, as he signed on to the new AUA ministerial union in Boston on October 10, 1864. According to its records, this was a volunteer organization of Unitarian ministers, "desirous of a closer fellowship among ourselves, extending a more cordial welcome and assistance to those about entering our ministry, protecting the ministerial office from incompetent and unworthy men, promoting mutual edification, and cooperating more effectually for the diffusion of the Gospel."[380]

Nute then filled a one-year interim call at the Petersham congregation, which was his first settlement. By 1866 he was back in Lawrence as an AUA "minister at large" and the nominal owner of a ladies shop undoubtedly run by his wife, Lucy. His life from the end of the Civil War until 1871 is punctuated by a single remaining letter. In February 1871, Nute wrote to Edward Everett Hale, whom he hoped would put in a good word for him with the AUA.[381] Nute virtually begged to be appointed to another western mission, this time to the Ute Indians in Colorado. He stated that he had been unemployed for the past eighteen months. Whether he was seriously considered for the appointment cannot be discerned, but in 1873, the Lawrence city directory listed him at a residence on Indiana Street and divulged his occupation as "trav. correspondent." Nute was still working for the newspapers.

In this year, Nute's life imploded. Both Nute and Lucy were in their fifties. He sued her, his wife of thirty years, for abandonment and obtained a divorce. The dissolution papers reveal that she had refused to accompany him out of Lawrence for work purposes, or reside or sleep with him when he returned to town, or in any other way perform her duties as wife.[382]   Sadly, the witnesses were two young persons—perhaps "help" or distant relatives—who resided in the Nute household and had observed the marital decline. Under the legal system of that time, someone had to take the fall, and as the witnesses testified that Nute provided adequate support to his wife, and there was a period of estrangement, Lucy was accused of neglect of her wifely duties, according to custom.

Nute's father had died, leaving him a pocket watch and a little cash. A few weeks after his divorce became final, he married again, leaving much that could not be documented to the imagination. Mary Adelia Skinner Nute, known as Adelia, was much younger than Nute and a distant cousin of John Brown, the abolitionist. The two settled near her family in Oberlin and Cleveland, Ohio, where Nute had a fine career as an editor, writer, and translator. They had two children.

Within five years, that marriage dissolved, and Nute took his four-year-old daughter back to New England, leaving his toddler son with Adelia. A few years later, Adelia was confined in an insane asylum by her sister, and Nute's son was remanded to an orphanage. Young Tommie Nute did not find his way back to his father until he was fifteen years old.

At sixty-two, Nute married a third time, to another Unitarian woman, Catherine Ann Coffin Anderson, and acquired two stepsons. He and his third wife had two more children: a son, Ephraim Freeman, who was named for him, and a daughter, Della Gertrude, who died of meningitis at six months of age. In April 1885 Nute wrote to Oscar E. Learnard, a Lawrence Unitarian and a former officer of the First Kansas Regiment, asking for Learnard's input on his second volume of memoirs, which covered the Civil War.[383] At this time, Nute was writing for the *Boston Advertiser and*

Evening Record. He was living with his wife and four children on the outskirts of town. The four children were Mary Bancroft Nute, his daughter by Mary Adelia Skinner, aged ten or eleven; Catherine's two sons, Melvin and Charles Anderson, ages unknown (but certainly younger than Mary, given Catherine's age when she and Nute married); and little Ephraim Freeman Nute, a toddler. Nute's son Tommie from his second wife, Adelia Mary Skinner Nute, was still in Ohio in the Soldier's and Sailor's Orphan home, and it is unclear if Nute was aware of this. Nute's daughter Della Gertrude was not born until July 1885. Nute had recently published his translations of Dante in a newspaper, a common practice at that time.

By July 1891, Nute wrote to Joseph C. Halderman, his commanding general in the Civil War and the attorney handling his attempts to get his pension from the military. Nute was lonely, his thoughts turning to his broadening religious beliefs. Old friends were passing away, and he dealt with the constant frustration of trying to obtain his military pension. Despite his advanced age of seventy-two, Nute had to do manual labor—making and putting up awnings—to support his family. He continued to work on his memoirs, but life for a man in his seventies supporting a young family was fraught with uncertainty. At one point, a six-week camping trip on the beach at Plymouth Rock seems to have been a necessity to put some kind of roof over his children's heads.

Just after Thanksgiving, on November 26, 1892, Nute wrote to Rev. John Stillman Brown with details of his work during the Civil War. Brown wrote to Nute of Private Webber's disparaging remarks, probably in the context of Nute writing to Brown for information regarding his own memoirs. Nute corrected the information Brown had from Webber with an account of his work for the Sanitary Commission and a few war stories. He wrote of working on his memoirs and how his theology was changing toward a more Eastern philosophy, and yet, it was also radically Universalist, the denomination he was raised in. The letter read,

Before this you have probably come to the conclusion that I have either gone into the sleepy dotage of old age or crawled into a hole like a woodchuck at this season. For unless I am mistaken your last interesting epistle remains unanswered & then those letters of high private Webber. . . . Well, I am yet wide awake & at work on those long contemplated Reminiscences; for which I trust now a publisher stands ready to take the risk. . . . Within the last week I have again gone through the letters taking notes of things likely to interest & now I propose to return you all but a few (some 6) from which I propose to make extracts w/ incidents of the campaign of the 1st reg. principally of the scrimmages near lake Providence when I was away on detached service. . . . But what a chronic grumbler was this same good soldier [private Webber] (one of the best I ever knew)! . . . I find that he always had a sneer for the chaplain— Unprofitable servant the said chap ever was—But it happened that in every instance of his blame I was not without good excuse—of which he was ignorant & so quite uncharitably at fault. e.g. I left the reg^t not to escape duty but simply & solely because I was requested both by Genl Grant the staff officers of the reg^t & by the Western San^y Comm^{ion} to go where I could be more useful. . . . Then that I was away during the battle of Wilson's Creek was because I had been sent on a perilous service, riding over 200 miles through the enemies country to secure for the reg^t a new stand of arms (Spencer's rifles) &c. The rifles I helped to secure & used my efforts to get the reg^t mounted which was at last affected—Then, that I did not rejoin the reg^t when on their retreat to Rolla was because while making the attempt I fell into the hands of the Home Guard at Nevada Mo. from which I made my escape by the help of a slave & at imminent peril returned to Fort Scott & thence via Leavenworth went down the Missouri, was taken sick of a fever at St. Louis, rejoined the regiment at Hannibal & at Chillicothe was taken down with dysentery & came near death in my tent when I was take to a private house &c. . . . So far from running after the paymaster as he intimates I think I was only once (at Fort Riley) with the regt when it was paid off—& took my chances while in detached service of coming across a paymaster when some regiments should be paid off in my neighborhood. . . . Then—the most satisfactory service which fell to my lot while in the army was the eighteen months spent in the hospitals & soldiers homes at Columbus K^y, Vicksburg & New Orleans, especially at the last named. There I learned that men returning from hospitals & furloughs—had died on the levee from neglect. That did not happen after the establishment of the home there. Our ambulance was ever on hand at the arrival of a boat to take the invalids and the poor fellows who knew not where to find their camps & many of them we detained for recuperation. Genl Banks having given us authority to detain such until our surgeon should pronounce them fit for duty—The Kansas 1st never paid much respect to their chaplain. Perhaps it was his fault.[384]

For the next several years Nute lived with his children and struggled financially. Sometime during these years he and Catherine set up separate households, but why, how, and when is not known. While living with his daughter Mary, now a young adult and married, Nute delivered her first child himself when the rest of the family had gone to Boston. He was enraptured with grandchildren and kept writing his memoirs. When they were finished, and he had an introduction from Edward Everett Hale and a publisher, he died suddenly. On January 21, 1897, a little over a month after his last letters to General Halderman about his military pension, and Richard Hinton about his dealings with John Brown, Nute was dead at the age of seventy-nine of blood poisoning. Mary, his daughter, attributed the accident that brought it on to a horse "he should never have bought."

Ever the source of radical challenge, Nute had requested cremation, a controversial practice at that time. His request was honored at the Forest Hills Cemetery in Boston on January 22, and his ashes were scattered in the rose garden area of the cemetery on January 23. Rev. James de Normandie, author and minister of the Roxbury Unitarian congregation, preached the sermon at Nute's memorial service on January 24. Edward Everett Hale also eulogized his old friend there.

While Nute's life waned in the East, the town of Lawrence recovered slowly and began to thrive. It still sits on the ever-shrinking prairie called Kansas. It is separated from the nearest urban areas, Kansas City and Topeka, by miles of fields and a few forested river bottoms reminiscent of the glowing descriptions of verdant beauty in Nute's early letters. The landscape consists of rolling hills punctuated by trees and waterways, from which the town of Lawrence sprouts like Indian Pipe mushrooms.

Today, Lawrence's primary renown is as the home of the University of Kansas. That university grew from Amos A. Lawrence's promise of a Free-State college to cover the entire top of Mt. Oread. Now it spills down the sides, claiming the neighborhood that was home to Nute and his church for student and faculty housing. Progressive business establishments, like those that generally spring up in university towns, line the main street.

Nute's own house still stands, not far from the corner where he originally envisioned the parsonage. It is directly across from the lot that held the church, now occupied by a private residence— its importance in the history of Lawrence marked only by a small stone designating it as the site of the first free church there. Nute's home in town was later expanded with an "el" addition, but the roof line and windows of the original structure, seen in old pictures of the church, are recognizable. At this writing, the house is owned by a developer, who is restoring it according to the historic district codes of the neighborhood in which it is located, with plans to rent out its two apartments.

Lawrence is the hub for the memory of Bleeding Kansas. It holds in its libraries, museums, and historical sites that era's imprint on the ether of time. And yet, memory is short. That which was so important and so large in the national mind a little over one hundred fifty years ago, that which hundreds lived and died for, in many cases has been already forgotten by the people who conduct their daily lives in Lawrence.

"Historic Bell Again Commands Attention" proclaimed the headline of an article in the *Lawrence Journal-World* in the spring of 2004.[385] The story recounted the history of the old Lawrence Unitarian church bell that rang out for the Free-State movement so long ago. After its harrowing trip to Lawrence and its role in the history of the antislavery struggle in Lawrence, it fell into disuse with the dismantling of the old stone Unitarian church, was sold to the Lawrence school district in the 1890s, and from there disappeared into "a dark hole in the wall."[386] From there, the bell was rescued by civic-minded high school seniors, money was raised to build a display case for it, and it was installed during the Lawrence sesquicentennial celebration that year in the display case of the high school's new rotunda, with other memorabilia from the time.

That year also marked the sesquicentennial of the Lawrence Unitarian Society, begun so many years ago by Nute.[387] The society in Lawrence had barely survived the severance of the Kansas mission by the AUA in 1858, and when the original stone church building was destroyed by lightning and earthquake in 1891 (surely no surprise to the more orthodox in Lawrence!), it was abandoned. A new building was dedicated in 1893, which served the congregation until it disbanded during the Second World War. A group attempted to revive the congregation in the early 1950s, but did not succeed. The desire to revive it remained strong, though, and it finally received another charter from Boston in February 1958. Services were held on the campus of the University of Kansas for several years—an ironic switch, since the University of Kansas first met in the basement of the Unitarian church. By 1961, when the Unitarians and Universalists consolidated to form the Unitarian Universalist Association, the congregation had purchased and refurbished an old country schoolhouse for its meeting place.

In its new home, Nute's Unitarian society revived as a congregation of the UUA and continues to grow. While preserving the historic school, the congregation finished a building project in 2008 that doubled its size and worship space, freeing up the old school section as a historic meeting place. The expanded Unitarian fellowship now sits among an ever-increasing number of residential houses, just down the way from a shopping mall.

No doubt Nute would have been saddened by the disappearance, for a dozen years, of the Unitarian fellowship he struggled for, just as he was sad when the old stone church was demolished. Even more upsetting to him might have been knowing that Kansas—the state for which he nearly lost his life—became renowned for rigid conservatism before the end of the twentieth century. This more recent trend toward religious authoritarianism seemed bent on destroying the religious freedom he worked so hard for and the progressive education he advocated for during his time.

But there were also those who did not abandon the principles of freedom and liberal religion for which Nute and his congregation labored. In this he would have rejoiced: the gracious lines of the new larger wing of the Lawrence fellowship and the stalwart construction of the old building bear witness to the historic strength and resilience of the little congregation on the prairie. Reborn and thriving, it stands undaunted against a contemporary political and religious climate so much like the one Nute and his parishioners faced all those years ago.

ACKNOWLEDGMENTS

Research never happens in a vacuum, and for that reason many, many acknowledgments and thanks are in order for this book and its contents. First and foremost I would like to thank my brother Bill Groth Jr. for initiating the research on our grandfather Nute so many years ago, for putting it in my lap, and for continuing to offer his ideas, encouragement, and eBay acumen. I would like to thank Vic Cook for dreaming and scheming with Bill on how to get this important story told, and keeping him at it. I would like to thank my mother, Pat Groth, for telling us the stories of great-great-grandfather Nute and getting us excited about solving the mystery of Harper's Ferry. I would like to thank my mother and my father, Bill Groth Sr., as well as my husband, Don Lawson; sister, Dr. Charlie Groth; and again, brother Bill, for their enthusiasm, technical support, and private funding, without which this effort would never have been completed. I would like to thank Martha Harris for her unselfish fishing expeditions to Lawrence for Nute records, Bob Pfeiffer and the reference librarians at South Milwaukee Public Library and the Southwest Harbor Maine Public Library for their amazing assistance in procuring documents by inter-library loan, and Paul Steuwe of Lawrence High School for graciously including us in the rededication of Nute's church bell. I am eternally grateful to Janet Mackie and Sandy MacLean for sharing their family records and photographs with me, for helping me find the Nute family cemeteries hidden in the woods, and for introducing me to the Nute ancestral grounds in Dover. I am thankful for and in awe of Fran O'Donnell and all the other wonderful librarians, archivists, and research assistants at Harvard Divinity School; the Harvard Archives; the Massachusetts Historical Society; the libraries of the University of Kansas; the American Antiquarian Society; the Kansas State Historical Society in Topeka, Kansas; the Watkins Museum; and the public library in Lawrence, Kansas, for their remarkable expertise in support of this research. Finally, I would like to express my appreciation to Don Skinner for his encouragement and advocacy in making this book possible and to Mary Benard and Marshall Hawkins at Skinner House Books for all of their patient guidance, help, and hard work.

But Where Are Nute's Memoirs?

A call is extended to all who have heard the story of Rev. Nute to be on the lookout for his memoirs or any family letters or records that remain undiscovered. Please contact this author if something is found—no clue is too small to be important!

NOTES

A Man with a Mission

1   Descendants of James Newte (Nute) continue to reside in Dover and Portsmouth, New Hampshire, to this day.

2   Although the Nute Garrison has not survived, the family lands, including burial grounds, are now a part of the Bellamy River Wildlife Sanctuary in Dover, New Hampshire.

3   *Christian Register*, Boston, Saturday October 25, 1845, Vol. XXIV, p. 170, property of Andover-Harvard Theological Library, Andover-Harv. Theol. Mflm. Period. 4202. Used with permission.

4   Petersham Historical Society.

5   Ralph Thompson, "The Liberty Bell and Other Anti-Slavery Gift-Books," *The New England Quarterly*, Vol. 7, No. 1, March 1934, pp. 160–161.

6   Friends of Freedom, *The Liberty Bell*, Boston: National Anti-Slavery Bazaar, 1851, pp. 86–96.

7   Unitarian Universalist Association, *Singing the Living Tradition*, Boston: Beacon Press, 1993.

8   *Monthly Religious Magazine and Independent Journal*, Vol. XVIII, July 1857, No. 1, p. 161.

9   David Finkelstein and Alistair McCleery, *An Introduction to Book History*, New York: Routledge, 2005, p. 61.

10   E. Nute Jr. to H. A. Miles, November 4, 1854, property of Andover-Harvard Theological Library, *American Unitarian Association Letterbooks*, 1822–1902, bMS571/107, 10/17/1854–12/10/1854. Used with permission.

11   *The Daily Spy*, Saturday, August 12, 1854. Kansas State Historical Society, Topeka, Kansas, *Webb Scrapbook* Roll #1 Volume 1-5, LM89.

12   *Christian Register*, Boston, Saturday, October 21, 1854, p. 134, property of Andover-Harvard Theological Library, Andover-Harv. Theol. Mflm. Period. 4202. Used with permission.

13   *Christian Register*, Boston, Saturday, October 21, 1854, p. 134, property of Andover-Harvard Theological Library, Andover-Harv. Theol. Mflm. Period. 4202. Used with permission.

14   *Christian Register*, Boston, Saturday, October 21, 1854, pp. 165–167, property of Andover-Harvard Theological Library, Andover-Harv. Theol. Mflm. Period. 4202. Used with permission.

15   *Christian Register*, Boston, Saturday, October 21, 1854, pp. 165–167, property of Andover-Harvard Theological Library, Andover-Harv. Theol. Mflm. Period. 4202. Used with permission.

16   *Christian Register*, Boston, Saturday, October 21, 1854, pp. 165–167, property of Andover-Harvard Theological Library, Andover-Harv. Theol. Mflm. Period. 4202. Used with permission.

17   *Christian Register*, Boston, Saturday, October 21, 1854, pp. 165–167, property of Andover-Harvard Theological Library, Andover-Harv. Theol. Mflm. Period. 4202. Used with permission.

18   F. Tiffany to H. A. Miles, February 22, 1855, AUA Letters, January-June 1855, property of Andover-Harvard Theological Library, *American Unitarian Association Letterbooks*, 1822–1902, bMS571/108, 12/11/1854–2/16/1855.

19   *Newark Daily Advertiser*, Friday Evening, February 23, 1855, Kansas State Historical Society, Topeka, Kansas, *Webb Scrapbook* Roll #1 Volume 1–5, LM89. Used with permission.

20   E. Nute Jr. to H. A. Miles, March 5, 1855, property of Andover-Harvard Theological Library, *American Unitarian Association Letterbooks*, 1822–1902, bMS571/109, 2/16/1855–4/30/1855. Used with permission.

21   H. A. Miles to E. E. Hale, March 13, 1855, property of Andover-Harvard Theological Library, *American Unitarian Association Letterbooks*, 1822–1902, bMS571/109, 2/16/1855–4/30/1855.

22   E. Nute Jr. to H. A. Miles, March 14, 1855, property of Andover-Harvard Theological Library, *American Unitarian Association Letterbooks*, 1822–1902, bMS571/109, 2/16/1855–4/30/1855.

23   E. Nute Jr. to H. A. Miles, March 21, 1855, property of Andover-Harvard Theological Library, *American Unitarian Association Letterbooks*, 1822–1902, bMS571/109, 2/16/1855–4/30/1855.

24   E. Nute Jr. to H. A. Miles, March 24, 1855, property of Andover-Harvard Theological Library, *American Unitarian Association Letterbooks*, 1822–1902, bMS571/109, 2/16/1855–4/30/1855.

25   *Christian Register*, Boston, Saturday, April 14, 1855, Vol. XXXIV, No. 15, p. 58, property of Andover-Harvard Theological Library, Andover-Harv. Theol Mflm. Period. 4202. Used with permission.

26   *Christian Register*, Boston, Saturday, April 14, 1855, Vol. XXXIV, No. 15, p. 58, property of Andover-Harvard Theological Library, Andover-Harv. Theol Mflm. Period. 4202. Used with permission.

27   *Christian Register*, Boston, Saturday, April 14, 1855, Vol. XXXIV, No. 15, p. 58, property of Andover-Harvard Theological Library, Andover-Harv. Theol Mflm. Period. 4202. Used with permission.

Bibles and Breechloaders

28   *Milwaukee Sentinel*, April 6, 1855, Kansas State Historical Society, Topeka, Kansas, *Webb Scrapbook* Roll #1 Volume 1–5, LM89.

29   *Milwaukee Sentinel*, April 6, 1855, Kansas State Historical Society, Topeka, Kansas, *Webb Scrapbook* Roll #1 Volume 1–5, LM89.

30 *Milwaukee Sentinel*, April 6, 1855, Kansas State Historical Society, Topeka, Kansas, *Webb Scrapbook* Roll #1 Volume 1–5, LM89.

31 Theodore Parker, *The Great Battle Between Slavery and Freedom, Considered in Two Speeches Delivered Before the American Anti-slavery Society*, at New York, May 7, 1856. Boston: Benjamin H. Greene, 1856, p. 82.

32 *Daily Evening Traveller*, April 16, 1855, Kansas State Historical Society, Topeka, Kansas, *Webb Scrapbook* Roll #1 Volume 1–5, LM89.

33 *Dubuque Daily Tribune*, April 16, 1855, Kansas State Historical Society, Topeka, Kansas, *Webb Scrapbook* Roll #1 Volume 1–5, LM89.

34 *New Bedford Mercury*, *Webb Scrapbook* (book 3), p. 248, May 5, 1855, Kansas State Historical Society, Topeka, Kansas, *Webb Scrapbook* Roll #1 Volume 1–5, LM89. Used with permission.

35 Charles S. Gleed, ed., *The Kansas Memorial, a Report of the Old Settlers' Meeting Held at Bismarck Grove, Kansas, September 15th and 16th, 1879*, Ramsey, Millett & Hudson, Kansas City, Mo., 1880, pp. 184–185; Isely, W. H.: "The Sharps Rifle Episode in Kansas History," *American Historical Review*, Vol. XII, No. 3, April 1907, p. 552.

36 W. H. Isely, "The Sharps Rifle Episode in Kansas History," *American Historical Review*, Vol. XII, No. 3, April 1907, p. 560.

A Free-State Flock

37 *Christian Register*, Boston, Saturday, April 21, 1855, Vol. XXXIV, p. 1, property of Andover-Harvard Theological Library, Andover-Harv. Theol. Mflm. Period. 4202. Used with permission.

38 *Christian Register*, Boston, Saturday, July 21, 1855, Vol. XXXIV, No. 29, p. 114, property of Andover-Harvard Theological Library, Andover-Harv. Theol. Mflm. Period. 4202. Used with permission.

39   *Christian Register*, Boston, Saturday August 21, 1855, Vol. XXXIV, No. 34, pp. 134–135, property of Andover-Harvard Theological Library, Andover-Harv. Theol. Mflm. Period. 4202. Used with permission.

40   *Christian Register*, Boston, Saturday August 21, 1855, Vol. XXXIV, No. 34, pp. 134–135, property of Andover-Harvard Theological Library, Andover-Harv. Theol. Mflm. Period. 4202. Used with permission.

41   Sara T. L. Robinson, *Kansas: Its Interior and Exterior Life*, Third Edition, Boston: Crosby, Nichols and Company, 1856, pp. 59–60.

42   *The Quarterly Journal of the American Unitarian Association*, Volume II, No. 4, Boston: American Unitarian Association, July 1, 1855, Andover-Harvard Theological Library, Harvard Divinity School, Andover-Harv. Theol. Mflm. Period. 108, p. 498. Used with permission.

43   E. Nute Jr. to H. A. Miles, June 4, 1855, property of Andover-Harvard Theological Library, *American Unitarian Association Letterbooks*, 1822–1902, bMS571/110, 4/30/1855–6/22/1855. Used with permission.

44   E. Nute Jr. to H. A. Miles, June 11, 1855, property of Andover-Harvard Theological Library, *American Unitarian Association Letterbooks*, 1822–1902, bMS571/110, 4/30/1855–6/22/1855.

45   Dr. Emory Kempton Lindquist, ed., "The Letters of the Rev. Samuel Young Lum, Pioneer Kansas Missionary, 1854–1858," *The Kansas Historical Quarterly*, Spring, 1959, Topeka: Kansas State Historical Society, pp. 60–62.

46   *The Quarterly Journal of the American Unitarian Association*, Volume III, Boston: American Unitarian Association, 1856, Andover-Harvard Theological Library, Harvard Divinity School, Andover-Harv. Theol. Mflm. Period. 108, p. 54. Used with permission.

47   E. Nute Jr. to H. A. Miles, July 8, 1855, property of Andover-Harvard Theological Library, *American Unitarian Association Letterbooks*, 1822–1902, bMS571/111, 6/24/1855–8/21/1855. Used with permission.

48 *The Springfield Republican*, August 16, 1855, Kansas State Historical Society, Topeka, Kansas, *Webb Scrapbook* Roll #2, LM90. Used with permission.

49 E. Nute Jr. to H. A. Miles, August 24, 1855, property of Andover-Harvard Theological Library, *American Unitarian Association Letterbooks*, 1822–1902, bMS571/112, 8/21/1855–10/30/1855. Used with permission.

50 E. Nute Jr. to H. A. Miles, August 27, 1855, property of Andover-Harvard Theological Library, *American Unitarian Association Letterbooks*, 1822–1902, bMS571/112, 8/21/1855–10/30/1855. Used with permission.

51 List of subscribers to erect U. Church, from the old church record after 1900, pp. 16–17, Meadville/Lombard Library and Archives.

52 E. Nute Jr. to H. A. Miles, September 9, 1855, property of Andover-Harvard Theological Library, *American Unitarian Association Letterbooks*, 1822–1902, bMS571/112, 8/21/1855–10/30/1855. Used with permission.

53 E. Nute Jr. to H. A. Miles, September 9, 1855, property of Andover-Harvard Theological Library, *American Unitarian Association Letterbooks*, 1822–1902, bMS571/112, 8/21/1855–10/30/1855. Used with permission.

54 *Herald of Freedom*, September 15, 1855, microfilm Roll #1, L190, Kansas State Historical Society, Topeka, Kansas.

55 E. Nute Jr. to H. A. Miles, September 16, 1855, property of Andover-Harvard Theological Library, *American Unitarian Association Letterbooks*, 1822–1902, bMS571/112 8/21/1855–10/30/1855. Used with permission.

56 E. Nute Jr. to H. A. Miles, September 23, 1855, property of Andover-Harvard Theological Library, *American Unitarian Association Letterbooks*, 1822–1902, bMS571/112, 8/21/1855–10/30/1855. Used with permission.

57 *Christian Register*, Boston, Saturday, September 29, 1855, Vol. XXXIV, No. 39, p. 154, property of Andover-Harvard Theological Library, Andover-Harv. Theol. Mflm. Period. 4202. Used with permission.

58   E. Nute Jr. to E. E. Hale, October 3, 1855, New England Emigrant
      Aid Company Papers, Kansas State Historical Society. Used with
      permission.

59   Richard Sullivan Edes of First Parish Church of Boston.

60   E. Nute Jr. to H. A. Miles, October 7, 1855, property of Andover-
      Harvard Theological Library, *American Unitarian Association
      Letterbooks*, 1822–1902, bMS571/112, 8/21/1855–10/30/1855.
      Used with permission.

61   *The Daily Mail*, October 8, 1855, Kansas State Historical Soci-
      ety, Topeka, Kansas, *Webb Scrapbook* Roll #2, LM90. Used with
      permission. Also covered by the *Christian Register*, Boston,
      Saturday, October 13, 1855, Vol. XXXIV, No. 41, p. 163, prop-
      erty of Andover-Harvard Theological Library, Andover-Harv.
      Theol. Mflm. Period. 4202. Used with permission.

62   *Christian Register*, Boston, Saturday, October 13, 1855, Vol.
      XXXIV, Kansas State Historical Society, Topeka, Kansas, *Webb
      Scrapbook* Roll #2, LM90. Used with permission.

63   E. Nute Jr. to H. A. Miles, October 17, 1855, excerpted in *The
      Quarterly Journal of the American Unitarian Association*, Volume
      III, Boston: American Unitarian Association, 1856, Andover-
      Harvard Theological Library, Harvard Divinity School,
      Andover-Harv. Theol. Mflm. Period. 108, pp. 283–284. Used
      with permission.

64   E. Nute Jr. to H. A. Miles, October 22, 1855, property of Andover-
      Harvard Theological Library, *American Unitarian Association
      Letterbooks*, 1822–1902, bMS571/112, 8/21/1855–10/30/1855.
      Used with permission.

65   *Herald of Freedom*, October 23, 1855, microfilm, Roll #1, L190,
      Kansas State Historical Society, Topeka, Kansas. Used with per-
      mission.

66   E. Nute Jr. to H. A. Miles, October 27, 1855, property of Andover-
      Harvard Theological Library, *American Unitarian Association
      Letterbooks*, 1822–1902, bMS571/112, 8/21/1855–10/30/1855.
      Used with permission.

67   E. Nute Jr. to H. A. Miles, November 4, 1855, excerpted in *The Quarterly Journal of the American Unitarian Association*, Volume III, Boston: American Unitarian Association, 1856, Andover-Harvard Theological Library, Harvard Divinity School, Andover-Harv. Theol. Mflm. Period. 108, pp. 284–286. Used with permission.

68   Joanna L. Stratton, *Pioneer Women Voices from the Kansas Frontier*, New York: Simon and Schuster, 1981, p. 72.

69   *Christian Register*, Boston, Saturday, October 13, 1860, Vol. XXXIX, property of Andover-Harvard Theological Library, Andover-Harv. Theol. Mflm. Period. 4202, p. 18. Used with permission.

70   *Kansas Collection*, University of Kansas Libraries, 97-05-05, Box 1.

71   *New Haven Daily Palladium*, November 19, 1855, Kansas State Historical Society, Topeka, Kansas, *Webb Scrapbook* Roll #2, LM90.

72   E. Nute Jr. to H. A. Miles, November 19, 1855, excerpted in *The Quarterly Journal of the American Unitarian Association*, Volume III, Boston: American Unitarian Association, 1856, Andover-Harvard Theological Library, Harvard Divinity School, Andover-Harv. Theol. Mflm. Period. 108, pp. 433–435. Used with permission.

73   *Christian Register*, Boston, Saturday, December 8, 1855, Vol. XXXIV, property of Andover-Harvard Theological Library, Andover-Harv. Theol. Mflm. Period. 4202. Used with permission.

74   *The Quarterly Journal of the American Unitarian Association*, Volume III, Boston: American Unitarian Association, 1856, Andover-Harvard Theological Library, Harvard Divinity School, Andover-Harv. Theol. Mflm. Period. 108, pp. 435–436. Used with permission.

75   *New York Daily Tribune*, January 8, 1856, Kansas State Historical Society, Topeka, Kansas, *Webb Scrapbook* Roll #2, LM90. Used with permission.

76   *The Boston Traveller*, December 5, 1855, Kansas State Historical Society, Topeka, Kansas, *Webb Scrapbook* Roll #2, LM90.

77   C. Stearns to *The Liberator*, December 7, 1855, *The Liberator*, January 4, 1856, Kansas State Historical Society, Topeka, Kansas, *Webb Scrapbook* Roll #2, LM90. Used with permission.

78   C. Stearns to *The Liberator*, December 7, 1855, *The Liberator*, January 4, 1856, Kansas State Historical Society, Topeka, Kansas, *Webb Scrapbook* Roll #2, LM90. Used with permission.

79   Wilson Shannon was one of the "revolving door governors" of the Kansas Territory. He was commissioned in August 1855 and served until August 1856. He took the initiative to end the Wakarusa war when first in office, but he was in fact a proslavery supporter.

80   Samuel J. Jones emigrated to the Kansas Territory in 1854 and led a group of proslavery men to destroy the ballot box at Bloomington, Kansas, in 1855. This spurred proslavery territorial Governor Daniel Woodson to make him the first sheriff of Douglas County in August 1855. Jones conducted his little autocracy zealously and without regard to civil rights or federal law, making him feared and reviled by the Free-State citizens and much open to ridicule and resistance.

81   C. Stearns to *The Liberator*, December 7, 1855, *The Liberator,* January 4, 1856, Kansas State Historical Society, Topeka, Kansas, *Webb Scrapbook* Roll #2, LM90. Used with permission.

82   *The Quarterly Journal of the American Unitarian Association*, Volume III, Boston: American Unitarian Association, 1856, Andover-Harvard Theological Library, Harvard Divinity School, Andover-Harv. Theol. Mflm. Period. 108, pp. 436–438. Used with permission.

83   *Daily Advertiser*, January 7, 1856, Kansas State Historical Society, Topeka, Kansas, *Webb Scrapbook* Roll #2, LM90.

84   E. Nute Jr. to H. A. Miles, December 15, 1855, property of Andover-Harvard Theological Library, *American Unitarian Association Letterbooks*, 1822–1902, bMS571/113, 10/30/1855–1/3/1856. Used with permission.

85   *The Quarterly Journal of the American Unitarian Association*, Volume III, Boston: American Unitarian Association, 1856, Andover-Harvard Theological Library, Harvard Divinity School, Andover-Harv. Theol. Mflm. Period. 108, pp. 438–440. Used with permission.

86   *The Quarterly Journal of the American Unitarian Association*, Volume III, Boston: American Unitarian Association, 1856, Andover-Harvard Theological Library, Harvard Divinity School, Andover-Harv. Theol. Mflm. Period. 108, pp. 430–433. Used with permission.

87   E. B. Whitman to C. Clark, December 30, 1855, property of Andover-Harvard Theological Library, *American Unitarian Association Letterbooks*, 1822–1902, bMS571/113, 10/30/1855–1/3/1856. Used with permission.

Cries for Help

88   *Daily Advertiser*, January 1, 1856, Kansas State Historical Society, Topeka, Kansas, *Webb Scrapbook* Roll #2, LM90. Used with permission.

89   Richard J. Hinton, "Pens That Made Kansas Free," address before the annual meeting of the Kansas State Editorial Association at Fort Scott, January 23, 1900, *Transactions of the Kansas State Historical Society*, 1897–1900 6(1900): 371–382.

90   Richard J. Hinton, "Pens That Made Kansas Free," address before the annual meeting of the Kansas State Editorial Association at Fort Scott, January 23, 1900, *Transactions of the Kansas State Historical Society*, 1897–1900 6(1900): 376.

91   *The Herald*, January 5, 1856, Kansas State Historical Society, Topeka, Kansas, *Webb Scrapbook* Roll #2, LM90. Used with permission.

92   *The Springfield Republican*, February 4, 1856, Kansas State Historical Society, Topeka, Kansas, *Webb Scrapbook* Roll #2, LM90. Used with permission.

93   *Essex County Mercury*, February 6, 1856, Kansas State Historical Society, Topeka, Kansas, *Webb Scrapbook* Roll #2, LM90. Used with permission.

94   *The Quarterly Journal of the American Unitarian Association*, Volume III, Boston: American Unitarian Association, 1856, Andover-Harvard Theological Library, Harvard Divinity School, Andover-Harv. Theol. Mflm. Period. 108, pp. 440–445. Used with permission.

95   *Herald of Freedom*, February 2, 1856, microfilm Roll #1, LM89, Kansas State Historical Society, Topeka, Kansas.

96   *Detroit Evening Tribune*, February 26, 1856, Kansas State Historical Society, Topeka, Kansas, *Webb Scrapbook* Roll #2, LM90. Used with permission.

97   E. B. Whitman to H. A. Miles, January 27, 1856, property of Andover-Harvard Theological Library, *American Unitarian Association Letterbooks*, 1822–1902, bMS571/114, n.d. (1/1856)– 3/27/1856. Used with permission.

98   *Unity Record,* Published Monthly by the Unitarian Society, November 3, 1912, Vol. I, No. 2, *Kansas Collection,* University of Kansas Libraries, RH/MS 36:17.

99   *The Quarterly Journal of the American Unitarian Association*, Volume III, Boston: American Unitarian Association, 1856, Andover-Harvard Theological Library, Harvard Divinity School, Andover-Harv. Theol. Mflm. Period. 108, pp. 440–445. Also reported in *Herald of Freedom*, microfilm Roll #1, L190, from Kansas State Historical Society, Topeka, Kansas. Used with permission.

100   C. Baker to *Christian Register,* February 4, 1856, property of Andover-Harvard Theological Library, *American Unitarian Association Letterbooks,* 1822–1902, bMS571/114, n.d. (1/1856)– 3/27/1856. Used with permission.

101   E. B. Whitman to H. A. Miles, February 10, 1856, property of Andover-Harvard Theological Library, *American Unitarian Association Letterbooks*, 1822–1902, bMS571/114, n.d. (1/1856)– 3/27/1856. Used with permission.

102   E. Nute Jr. to H. A. Miles, February 14, 1856, property of Andover-Harvard Theological Library, *American Unitarian Association Letterbooks*, 1822–1902, bMS571/114, 1/1856–3/27/1856. Used with permission.

103   *The Springfield Republican*, March 18, 1856, Kansas State Historical Society, Topeka, Kansas, *Webb Scrapbook* Roll #2, LM90. Used with permission.

104   E. B. Whitman to H. A. Miles, March 1, 1856, property of Andover-Harvard Theological Library, *American Unitarian Association Letterbooks*, 1822–1902, bMS571/114, n.d. (1/1856)–3/27/1856. Used with permission.

105   E. Nute Jr. to H. A. Miles, March 4, 1856, property of Andover-Harvard Theological Library, *American Unitarian Association Letterbooks*, 1822–1902, bMS571/114, 1/1856–3/27/1856. Used with permission.

106   E. B. Whitman to C. Clark, March 4, 1856, property of Andover-Harvard Theological Library, *American Unitarian Association Letterbooks*, 1822–1902, bMS571/114, n.d. (1/1856)–3/27/1856. Used with permission.

107   E. Nute Jr. to H. A. Miles, March 27, 1856, property of Andover-Harvard Theological Library, *American Unitarian Association Letterbooks*, 1822–1902, bMS571/114, 1/1856–3/27/1856. Used with permission.

108   Alberta Pantle, compiled by, "Marriage Notices from Kansas Territorial Newspapers, 1854–1861," *The Kansas Historical Quarterly*, Summer 1955, Topeka: Kansas State Historical Society, pp. 445–486; Lawrence, *Herald of Freedom*, March 15, 1856, p. 484.

109   E. Nute Jr. to H. A. Miles, March 13, 1856, property of Andover-Harvard Theological Library, *American Unitarian Association Letterbooks*, 1822–1902, bMS571/114, 1/1856–3/27/1856. Used with permission.

110   E. B. Whitman to C. Clark, March 19, 1856, property of Andover-Harvard Theological Library, *American Unitarian Association Letterbooks*, 1822–1902, bMS571/114, n.d. (1/1856)–3/27/1856. Used with permission.

111   *Herald of Freedom*, March 22, 1856, Vol. II, No. 7, microfilm Roll #1, L190, Kansas State Historical Society, Topeka, Kansas. Used with permission.

112   *The Semi-Weekly Times*, April 11, 1856, Kansas State Historical Society, Topeka, Kansas, *Webb Scrapbook* Roll #3, LM91.

113   *The Semi-Weekly Times*, April 11, 1856, Kansas State Historical Society, Topeka, Kansas, *Webb Scrapbook* Roll #3, LM91. Used with permission.

114   *Gazette & Courier*, March 31, 1856, Kansas State Historical Society, Topeka, Kansas, *Webb Scrapbook* Roll #3, LM91. Used with permission.

115   *Herald of Freedom*, April 5, 1856, Vol. II, No. 6, microfilm Roll #1, L190, Kansas State Historical Society, Topeka, Kansas. Used with permission. Also *Christian Register*, Boston, Saturday, March 31, 1856, Vol. XXXV, No. 17, property of Andover-Harvard Theological Library, Andover-Harv. Theol. Mflm. Period. 4202. Used with permission.

116   *Lawrence Unitarian Society Misc 50th Anniversary*, from the old church record after 1900, pp. 1–3, Meadville Lombard Library and Archives. Also *Lawrence Journal*, October 26, 1905. Used with permission.

117   *Herald of Freedom*, April 26, 1856, Vol. II, No. 12, microfilm Roll #1, L190, Kansas State Historical Society, Topeka, Kansas. Used with permission.

118   *The Springfield Republican*, April 14, 1856, Kansas State Historical Society, Topeka, Kansas, *Webb Scrapbook* Roll #3, LM91. Used with permission.

119   Edward J. Renehan Jr., *The Secret Six: The True Tale of the Men Who Conspired with John Brown*, Columbia, S.C.: University of South Carolina Press, 1977.

120   Lawrence, Kansas, April 24, 1856 correspondence in *Chicago Daily Tribune*, May 1, 1856, Kansas State Historical Society, Topeka, Kansas, *Webb Scrapbook* Roll #3, LM91. Used with permission.

121   Sara T. L. Robinson, *Kansas: Its Interior and Exterior Life*, Third Edition, Boston: Crosby, Nichols and Company, 1856, pp. 209–211.

122 Sara T. L. Robinson, *Kansas: Its Interior and Exterior Life*, Third Edition, Boston: Crosby, Nichols and Company, 1856, p. 220.

123 *The Boston Evening Telegraph*, May 12, 1856, Kansas State Historical Society, Topeka, Kansas, *Webb Scrapbook* Roll #3, LM91. Used with permission.

124 Sara T. L. Robinson, *Kansas: Its Interior and Exterior Life*, Third Edition, Boston: Crosby, Nichols and Company, 1856, p. 221.

125 *The Boston Evening Telegraph*, June 2, 1856, Kansas State Historical Society, Topeka, Kansas, *Webb Scrapbook* Roll #3, LM91. Used with permission.

126 Springfield Republican, May 26, 1856, Kansas State Historical Society, *Webb Scrapbook* Roll #3, LM91. Used with permission.

127 *Daily Democrat*, May 23, 1856, Kansas State Historical Society, Topeka, Kansas, *Webb Scrapbook* Roll #3, LM91. Used with permission.

128 *Lexington Express Extra*, May 22, 1856, Kansas State Historical Society, Topeka, Kansas, *Webb Scrapbook* Roll #3, LM91. Used with permission.

129 *The Daily Transcript*, June 4, 1856, Kansas State Historical Society, Topeka, Kansas, *Webb Scrapbook* Roll #3, LM91. Used with permission.

130 *Christian Register*, Boston, Saturday, March 31, 1856, Vol. XXXV, No. 23, p. 1, property of Andover-Harvard Theological Library, Andover-Harv. Theol. Mflm. Period. 4202. Used with permission.

131 *Christian Register*, Boston, Saturday, March 31, 1856, Vol. XXXV, No. 23, p. 1, property of Andover-Harvard Theological Library, Andover-Harv. Theol. Mflm. Period. 4202. Used with permission.

132 *Christian Register*, Boston, Saturday, March 31, 1856, Vol. XXXV, No. 23, p. 1, property of Andover-Harvard Theological Library, Andover-Harv. Theol. Mflm. Period. 4202. Used with permission.

133   *Christian Register*, Boston, Saturday, March 31, 1856, Vol. XXXV, No. 23, p. 1, property of Andover-Harvard Theological Library, Andover-Harv. Theol. Mflm. Period. 4202. Used with permission.

134   *Christian Register*, Boston, Saturday, March 31, 1856, Vol. XXXV, No. 23, p. 1, property of Andover-Harvard Theological Library, Andover-Harv. Theol. Mflm. Period. 4202. Used with permission.

135   John Brown, Copy of a report, June 1856, of John Brown, Sr. [Browns' Station, Kansas Ter.], to Messrs. E. B. Whitman and [S. W.?] Eldridge, June 2, 1856, Ohio Historical Society Archives/ Library.

136   *Daily Chronicle*, June 4, 1856, Kansas State Historical Society, Topeka, Kansas, *Webb Scrapbook* Roll #3, LM91. Used with permission.

137   *The Atlas*, June 4, 1856, Kansas State Historical Society, Topeka, Kansas, *Webb Scrapbook* Roll #3, LM91. Used with permission.

138   *The Quarterly Journal of the American Unitarian Association*, Volume III, Boston: American Unitarian Association, 1856, Andover-Harvard Theological Library, Harvard Divinity School, Andover-Harv. Theol. Mflm. Period. 108, p. 631. Used with permission.

139   *The Quarterly Journal of the American Unitarian Association*, Volume III. Boston: American Unitarian Association, 1856, Andover-Harvard Theological Library, Harvard Divinity School, Andover-Harv. Theol. Mflm. Period. 108, p. 631. Used with permission.

140   T. Parker to L. M. Child, June 5, 1856, Theodore Parker Papers, 1826–1865, microfilm edition, 4 reels, Massachusetts Historical Society, Boston, 1978, reel 2, p. 219. Used with permission.

141   *The Boston Evening Telegraph*, June 9, 1856, Kansas State Historical Society, Topeka, Kansas, *Webb Scrapbook* Roll #3, LM91. Used with permission.

142 D. W. Wilder, *The Annals of Kansas*, 1541–1885, Topeka, Kansas: Geo. W. Martin, Kansas Publishing House, 1875, p. 119.

143 D. W. Wilder, *The Annals of Kansas*, 1541–1885, Topeka, Kansas: Geo. W. Martin, Kansas Publishing House, 1875, p. 119.

144 D. W. Wilder, *The Annals of Kansas*, 1541–1885, Topeka, Kansas: Geo. W. Martin, Kansas Publishing House, 1875, p. 119.

145 D. W. Wilder, *The Annals of Kansas*, 1541–1885, Topeka, Kansas: Geo. W. Martin, Kansas Publishing House, 1875, p. 123.

146 John Jr. Brown, Put-In-Bay, Ohio, as dictated to son-in-law T. B. Alexander, John Brown Jr. Papers 1830–1932, (microform) Ohio Historical Society. Used with permission.

147 D. W. Wilder, *The Annals of Kansas*, 1541–1885, Topeka, Kansas: Geo. W. Martin, Kansas Publishing House, 1875, p. 123.

148 E. Nute Jr. to Col. R. J. Hinton, June 4, 1893, *Richard Josiah Hinton Collection*, Box 3, Folder 60 (June 1893), Correspondence and Misc. papers, Kansas State Historical Society, Topeka, Kansas.

149 *The Quarterly Journal of the American Unitarian Association*, Volume IV, Boston: American Unitarian Association, 1857, Andover-Harvard Theological Library, Harvard Divinity School, Andover-Harv. Theol. Mflm. Period. 108, p. 211. Used with permission.

150 E. Nute Jr. to S. G. Howe, July 3, 1856, Letters Received by Samuel Gridley Howe, Massachusetts Historical Society, Boston. Used with permission.

151 *The Quarterly Journal of the American Unitarian Association*, Volume IV, Boston: American Unitarian Association, 1857, Andover-Harvard Theological Library, Harvard Divinity School, Andover-Harv. Theol. Mflm. Period. 108, pp. 94–96. Used with permission.

152 "Continued Outrages in Kansas—Testimony from Rev. E. Nute," *Hartford Daily Courant*, August 8, 1856, p. 2.

153 "Continued Outrages in Kansas—Testimony from Rev. E. Nute," *Hartford Daily Courant*, August 8, 1856, p. 2.

154 *The Quarterly Journal of the American Unitarian Association*, Volume IV, Boston: American Unitarian Association, 1857, Andover-Harvard Theological Library, Harvard Divinity School, Andover-Harv. Theol. Mflm. Period. 108, pp. 96–97. Used with permission.

155 Sara T. L. Robinson, *Kansas: Its Interior and Exterior Life*, Third Edition, Boston: Crosby, Nichols and Company, 1856, pp. 321–322.

156 Unknown, nearest date, August 31, 1856, p. 203, Vol. 16, *Webb Scrapbook* Roll #4, LM92, Kansas State Historical Society, Topeka, Kansas. Used with permission.

157 *Lawrence Daily Journal*, Holiday Number, December 25, 1890. This special Christmas edition of the *Lawrence Daily Journal* interviews Nute and reports on early Lawrence history from his perspective.

158 *Lawrence Unitarian Society Misc 50th Anniversary*, from the old church record after 1900, Meadville/Lombard Archives. Used with permission.

159 E. Nute Jr. to E. E. Hale, August 15, 1856, New England Emigrant Aid Company Papers, Kansas State Historical Society, Topeka, Kansas. Used with permission.

160 *The Kansas Weekly Herald*, Saturday, August 23, 1856, microfilm, p. 1021, Kansas State Historical Society, Topeka, Kansas. Used with permission.

161 *Christian Register*, Boston, Saturday, August 23, 1856, Vol. XXXV, p. 143, property of Andover-Harvard Theological Library, Andover-Harv. Theol. Mflm. Period. 4202. Used with permission.

162 William E. Connelley, compiler, Chapter XXXII, Bleeding Kansas, *A Standard History of Kansas and Kansans*, Chicago: Lewis, 1918. Also in *Transactions of the Kansas State Historical Society*, first and second biennial reports, together with a statement of the collections of the Society from its organization, in 1875, to

January 1881, Vols. I and II, Topeka, Kansas: Geo. W. Martin, Kansas Publishing House, 1881.

163 *The Quarterly Journal of the American Unitarian Association*, Volume IV, Boston: American Unitarian Association, 1857, Andover-Harvard Theological Library, Harvard Divinity School, Andover-Harv. Theol. Period. Mflm. Period. 108, pp. 97–100. Used with permission.

164 Colonel Titus was part of a Southern movement to expand slavery into the Kansas Territory and participated in the sack of Lawrence.

165 E. Nute Jr. to F. Tiffany, August 22, 1856, in the *Springfield Republican*, September 2, 1856, Kansas State Historical Society, Topeka, Kansas, *Webb Scrapbook* Roll #4, LM92. Used with permission.

166 E. Nute Jr. to E. E. Hale, August 24, 1856, *New England Emigrant Aid Company Papers,* Kansas State Historical Society, Topeka, Kansas. Used with permission.

167 E. Nute Jr. to H. A. Miles, August 25, 1856, *Christian Register,* Boston, Saturday, September 13, 1856, Vol. XXXV, property of Andover-Harvard Theological Library, Andover-Harv. Theol. Mflm. Period. 4202. Used with permission. Also excerpted in *The Quarterly Journal of the American Unitarian Association*, Vol. IV, Boston: American Unitarian Association, 1857, Extracts from Letters, pp. 94–100. Used with permission.

Taken Prisoner and Under Siege

168 E. B. Whitman to H. A. Miles, property of Andover-Harvard Theological Library, *American Unitarian Association Letter-books*, 1822–1902, bMS571/117, 8/9/1856–10/26/1856. Used with permission.

169 A friend of Nute and a member of his congregation.

170 Sara T. L. Robinson, *Kansas: Its Interior and Exterior Life*, Third Edition, Boston: Crosby, Nichols and Company, 1856, pp. 330–331.

171 *The Springfield Republican*, September 6, 1856, Connecticut Valley Historical Museum, Springfield, Massachusetts.

172　At the same time the meeting was being held, Nute was finally getting back to Lawrence, although it would be some time before that was known in Boston.

173　*Dean Sibley's Private Journal*, Harvard Archives, Corporation-Harvard Records Call Number UAI 5.130, 1857–1860, HUG 1791.72.10. Courtesy of the Harvard University Archives. Used with permission.

174　Notes by Edward Emerson, his son, in Ralph Waldo Emerson, *Miscellanies*, "Speech at the Kansas Relief Meeting in Cambridge, Wednesday Evening, September 10, 1856," Boston: Houghton, Mifflin and Company, The Riverside Press, Cambridge, 1893, p. 263.

175　Notes by Edward Emerson, his son, in Ralph Waldo Emerson, *Miscellanies*, "Speech at the Kansas Relief Meeting in Cambridge, Wednesday Evening, September 10, 1856," Boston: Houghton, Mifflin and Company, The Riverside Press, Cambridge, 1893, p. 263.

176　Ralph Waldo Emerson, "Speech at the Kansas Relief Meeting in Cambridge, Wednesday Evening, September 10, 1856," The Thoreau Institute, Lincoln, MA. Also in: Ralph Waldo Emerson, *Miscellanies*, "Speech at the Kansas Relief Meeting in Cambridge, Wednesday Evening, September 10, 1856," Boston: Houghton, Mifflin and Company, The Riverside Press, Cambridge, 1893, pp. 239–248.

177　Lucretia Hale was an author in her own right: *The Struggle for Life* (1861), *The Service of Sorrow* (1867), *Six of One by Half a Dozen of the Other* (1872), *The Wolf at the Door* (1877), *The Peterkin Papers* (1880), *The Last of the Peterkins with Other of Their Kin* (1886). She, like Edward Everett Hale, was the daughter of Nathan Hale, nephew of the patriot hero, and Sarah Preston Everett, also an author and sister to Edward Everett, prominent Unitarian minister and politician.

178　Mary Lesley Ames, *Life and Letters of Peter and Susan Lesley*, Volume I, New York: G. P. Putnam's Sons, The Knickerbocker Press, 1909, p. 339.

179　From Letters to Mrs. Apthorp, Frothingham, Octavius Brooks: *Theodore Parker: A Biography*, Boston: J. R. Osgood, 1874, p. 437.

180 *Christian Register*, Boston, Saturday, November 15, 1856, Vol. XXXV, p. 1(181), property of Andover-Harvard Theological Library, Andover-Harv. Theol. Mflm. Period. 4202. Used with permission.

181 *Christian Register*, Boston, Saturday, November 15, 1856, Vol. XXXV, p. 1(181), property of Andover-Harvard Theological Library, Andover-Harv. Theol. Mflm. Period. 4202. Used with permission.

182 *Christian Register*, Boston, Saturday, October 25, 1856, Vol. XXXV, p. 1(181), property of Andover-Harvard Theological Library, Andover-Harv. Theol. Mflm. Period. 4202. Used with permission.

183 *Herald of Freedom*, November 8, 1856, Vol. II, No. 16, microfilm Roll #1, L190, Kansas State Historical Society, Topeka, Kansas. Used with permission.

184 Sara T. L. Robinson, *Kansas: Its Interior and Exterior Life*, Third Edition, Boston: Crosby, Nichols and Company, 1856, pp. 338–342.

185 *Lawrence Daily Journal*, Holiday Number, December 25, 1890.

186 *The Quarterly Journal of the American Unitarian Association*, Volume IV, Boston: American Unitarian Association, 1857, Andover-Harvard Theological Library, Harvard Divinity School, Andover-Harv. Theol. Mflm. Period. 108, pp. 251–256. Used with permission.

187 *The Quarterly Journal of the American Unitarian Association*, Volume IV, Boston: American Unitarian Association, 1857, Andover-Harvard Theological Library, Harvard Divinity School, Andover-Harv. Theol. Mflm. Period. 108, pp. 251–256. Used with permission.

188 Octavius Brooks Frothingham, *Theodore Parker: A Biography*, Boston: J. R. Osgood, 1874, pp. 436–437.

189 *Daily Advertiser*, September 6, 1856, Kansas State Historical Society, Topeka, Kansas, *Webb Scrapbook* Roll #4, LM92. Used with permission.

190 *Daily Democrat,* September 25, 1856, Kansas State Historical Society, Topeka, Kansas, *Webb Scrapbook* Roll #4, LM92. Used with permission.

191 E. Nute Jr. to T. Parker, 9/14/1856, pp. 317–323 of Parker's log of letters, Massachusetts Historical Society, Boston. Used with permission.

192 Octavius Brooks Frothingham, *Theodore Parker: A Biography,* Boston: J. R. Osgood, 1874, Letters to Mrs. Apthorp, pp. 437–438.

193 Octavius Brooks Frothingham, *Theodore Parker: A Biography,* Boston: J. R. Osgood, 1874, Letters to Mrs. Apthorp, p. 438.

Scandal, Missing Funds, and a Sham Election

194 John H. Gihon, M.D., *Geary and Kansas: Governor Geary's Administration in Kansas with a Complete History of the Territory Until July 1857,* Philadelphia: Chas. C. Rhodes, 1857, p. 113.

195 Joseph Edgar Chamberlin, *The Boston Transcript: A History of Its First Hundred Years,* Boston: Houghton Mifflin, 1930, p. 121.

196 *Christian Register,* Boston, Saturday, October 25, 1856, Vol. XXXV, No. 43, pp. 169–170, property of Andover-Harvard Theological Library, Andover-Harv. Theol. Mflm. Period. 4202. Used with permission.

197 *Christian Register,* Boston, Saturday, October 25, 1856, Vol. XXXV, No. 43, pp. 169–170, property of Andover-Harvard Theological Library, Andover-Harv. Theol. Mflm. Period. 4202. Used with permission.

198 Henry Ware, D.D., Hollis Professor of Divinity at Harvard.

199 E. Nute Jr. to E. E. Hale, October 13, 1856, New England Emigrant Aid Company Papers, Kansas State Historical Society, Topeka, Kansas. Used with permission.

200 New England Emigrant Aid Company Papers, Undated, Kansas State Historical Society, Topeka, Kansas. Used with permission.

201 *Christian Register*, Boston, Saturday, October 25, 1856, Vol. XXXV, No. 43, pp. 169–170, property of Andover-Harvard Theological Library, Andover-Harv. Theol. Mflm. Period. 4202. Used with permission.

202 E. Nute Jr. to H. A. Miles, October 27, 1856, property of Andover-Harvard Theological Library, *American Unitarian Association Letterbooks*, 1822–1902, bMS571/118, 10/27/1856–1/12/1857. Used with permission.

203 *Herald of Freedom*, November 1, 1856, Vol. 2, No. 15, microfilm Roll #1, L190, Kansas State Historical Society, Topeka, Kansas. Used with permission.

204 E. Nute Jr. to H. A. Miles, November 4, 1856, property of Andover-Harvard Theological Library, *American Unitarian Association Letterbooks*, 1822–1902, bMS571/118, 10/27/1856–1/12/1857. Used with permission.

205 "Marion" to Ed., November 4, 1856, *Herald of Freedom*, November 8, 1856, Vol. 2, No. 16, microfilm Roll #1, L190, Kansas State Historical Society, Topeka, Kansas.

206 Located in Boston, Quincy Market has been a public market since 1742. At first located in Faneuil Hall, it was enlarged and moved nearby in the 1800's when a massive landmark building was erected of New England granite. The building remains a popular tourist attraction to this day.

207 E. Nute Jr. to D. H. Haskell, November 13, 1856, *Christian Register*, Boston, Saturday, October 25, 1856, Vol. XXXV, , p. (1)193, property of Andover-Harvard Theological Library, Andover-Harv. Theol. Mflm. Period. 4202. Used with permission.

208 E. Nute Jr. to E. E. Hale, November 15, 1856, New England Emigrant Aid Company Papers, Kansas State Historical Society, Topeka, Kansas. Used with permission.

209 E. Fitch to Parents, November 21, 1856, courtesy of Douglas County Historical Society, Watkins Community Museum of History.

210 *Herald of Freedom*, November 22, 1856, Vol. 2, No. 18, microfilm Roll #1, L190, Kansas State Historical Society, Topeka, Kansas. Used with permission.

211 *Christian Register*, Boston, Saturday, October 25, 1856, Vol. XXXV, property of Andover-Harvard Theological Library, Andover-Harv. Theol. Mflm. Period. 4202. Used with permission.

212 *Herald of Freedom*, November 29, 1856, Vol. 2, No. 19, microfilm Roll #1, L190, Kansas State Historical Society, Topeka, Kansas. Used with permission.

213 From remarks of Mr. C. L. Edwards, former chorister of the church and principal of the Lawrence University, in coverage of the closing of the old Unitarian Church, *Lawrence Daily Journal*, Monday, April 27, 1891.

214 *Herald of Freedom*, December 6, 1856, Vol. 2, No. 20, microfilm Roll #1, L190, Kansas State Historical Society, Topeka, Kansas. Used with permission.

215 *Herald of Freedom*, December 6, 1856, Vol. 2, No. 20, microfilm Roll #1, L190, Kansas State Historical Society, Topeka, Kansas. Used with permission.

216 *Herald of Freedom*, December 13, 1856, Vol. 2, No. 21, microfilm Roll #1, L190, Kansas State Historical Society, Topeka, Kansas. Used with permission.

217 *Herald of Freedom*, December 13, 1856, Vol. 2, No. 21, microfilm Roll #1, L190, Kansas State Historical Society, Topeka, Kansas. Used with permission.

218 William Lawrence, *Life of Amos A. Lawrence With Extracts From His Diary and Correspondence*, Boston: Houghton, Mifflin, and Company, 1899, pp. 117–118.

219 W. B. Edmonds [E. B. Whitman] to J. Brown, October, 5, 1857, Kansas State Historical Society, Topeka, Kansas; Kansas Aid Society to "Nelson Hawkins," September 14, 1857, John Brown Papers, Kansas State Historical Society; J. Brown to E. B. Whitman, October 5, 1857, Kansas State Historical Society; J. Brown to F. B. Sanborn, October 1, 1857, Stutler Collection, Middlesex County, Mass.; see also, G. L. Stearns to E. B. Whitman, Kansas State Historical Society.

220 S. Cabot to J. Blood, December 28, 1856, James Blood Collection, # 281, Box 1, Folder 1. Kansas State Historical Society, Topeka, Kansas. Used with permission.

221 E. Nute Jr. to Col. R. J. Hinton; Richard Josiah Hinton Collection, Box 3, Folder 60 (June 1893), Correspondence and Miscellaneous Papers, Kansas State Historical Society, Topeka, Kansas. Used with permission.

222 E. Nute Jr. to S. G. Howe, January 2, 1857, S. G. Howe Papers. Massachusetts Historical Society, Boston. Used with permission.

223 E. Nute Jr. to A. A. Lawrence, January 5, 1857, Amos A. Lawrence Papers, Massachusetts Historical Society, Boston. Used with permission.

224 E. Nute Jr. to T. Hyatt, January 11, 1857, Thaddeus Hyatt Papers Collection, Box/Folder Correspondence and papers of Thaddeus Hyatt, 1843–1898 (Microfilm Roll MS-571, frame 460–462), Kansas State Historical Society, Topeka, Kansas.

225 Spencer Lavan and Peter Hughes, "Carolyn Dall," *Dictionary of Unitarian and Universalist Biography*, Unitarian Universalist Historical Society, www25.uua.org/uuhs/duub/articles/caroline-dall.html.

226 Spencer Lavan and Peter Hughes, "Carolyn Dall," *Dictionary of Unitarian and Universalist Biography*, Unitarian Universalist Historical Society, www25.uua.org/uuhs/duub/articles/caroline-dall.html.

227 E. Nute Jr. to Mrs. C. W. H. Dall, February 9, 1857, Caroline H. Dall Papers, 1811–1917, microfilm edition, 45 reels (Massachusetts Historical Society, Boston, 1981), reel 2, Massachusetts Historical Society. Used with permission.

228 This house still stands in Lawrence, Kansas.

229 E. Nute Jr. to A. A. Lawrence, March 4, 1857, A. A. Lawrence Papers, Massachusetts Historical Society. Used with permission.

230 E. Nute Jr. to E. E. Hale, April 6, 1857, New England Emigrant Aid Company Papers, Kansas State Historical Society, Topeka, Kansas. Used with permission.

231   Michael W. Cluskey, ed., Postmaster of the House of Representa-
      tives of the United States, *The Political Text-book, or Encyclo-
      pedia, Containing Everything Necessary for the Reference of the
      Politicians and Statesmen of the United States*, Twelfth Edition,
      Philadelphia: Jas. B. Smith & Co., 1860, pp. 398–399.

232   *Herald of Freedom*, April 25, 1857, Vol. 2, No. 35, microfilm Roll
      #1, L190, Kansas State Historical Society, Topeka, Kansas. Used
      with permission.

233   Michael W. Cluskey, ed., Postmaster of the House of Representa-
      tives of the United States, *The Political Text-Book, or Encyclo-
      pedia, Containing Everything Necessary for the Reference of the
      Politicians and Statesmen of the United States*, Twelfth Edition,
      Philadelphia: Jas. B. Smith & Co., 1860, pp. 399–400. Additional
      Sources: *Kansas Historical Collections*, Vol. 5, 1891–1896; *Her-
      ald of Freedom*, May 16, 1857, Vol. 2, No. 38, microfilm Roll #1,
      L190, Kansas State Historical Society, Topeka, Kansas. Used with
      permission.

234   E. Nute Jr. to E. E. Hale, April 28, 1857, New England Emigrant
      Aid Company Papers, Kansas State Historical Society, Topeka,
      Kansas. Used with permission.

Deepening Rifts

235   E. Nute Jr. to H. A. Miles, May 18, 1857, property of Andover-
      Harvard Theological Library, *American Unitarian Association
      Letterbooks*, 1822–1902, bMS571/118, 10/27/1856–1/12/1857.
      Used with permission.

236   E. Nute Jr. to A. A. Lawrence, May 19, 1857, Massachusetts His-
      torical Society. Used with permission.

237   Nute, E. Jr., "The Unitarian Church," *Lawrence Daily Journal*,
      Holiday Number (insert), December 25, 1890.

238   E. Nute Jr. to H. A. Miles, June 1, 1857, *The Quarterly Journal of
      the American Unitarian Association*, Volume IV, Boston: Ameri-
      can Unitarian Association, 1857, Andover-Harvard Theological
      Library, Harvard Divinity School, Andover-Harv. Theol. Mflm.
      Period. 108, pp. 529–531. Used with permission.

239 G. Smith to J. Brown, June 4, 1859, *Herald of Freedom*, October 29, 1859, Vol. 5, No. 15, microfilm Roll #2, L191, Kansas State Historical Society, Topeka, Kansas. Used with permission.

240 E. Nute Jr. to H. A. Miles, July 1, 1857, property of Andover-Harvard Theological Library, *American Unitarian Association Letterbooks*, 1822–1902, bMS571/121, 6/18/1857–9/5/1857. Used with permission.

241 E. Nute Jr. to E. E. Hale, August 3, 1857, New England Emigrant Aid Company Papers, Kansas State Historical Society, Topeka, Kansas. Used with permission.

242 E. Nute Jr. to H. A. Miles, August 18, 1857, property of Andover-Harvard Theological Library, *American Unitarian Association Letterbooks*, 1822–1902, bMS571/121, 6/18/1857–9/5/1857. Used with permission.

243 *The Quarterly Journal of the American Unitarian Association*, Volume IV, Boston: American Unitarian Association, 1857, Andover-Harvard Theological Library, Harvard Divinity School, Andover-Harv. Theol. Mflm. Period. 108, pp. 479–480. Used with permission.

244 *The Quarterly Journal of the American Unitarian Association*, Volume V, Boston: American Unitarian Association, 1858, Andover-Harvard Theological Library, Harvard Divinity School, Andover-Harv. Theol. Mflm. Period. 108, p 112. Used with permission.

245 From remarks of Mr. C. L. Edwards, former chorister of the church and principal of the Lawrence University, in coverage of the closing of the old Unitarian Church, *Lawrence Daily Journal*, Monday, April 27, 1891, Microfilm L233, Kansas State Historical Society, Topeka, Kansas. Used with permission.

246 Dr. Emory Kempton Lindquist, ed., *The Letters of the Rev. Samuel Young Lum, Pioneer Kansas Missionary, 1854–1858, The Kansas Historical Quarterly* 25(Spring 1959): 39–67; Part II, 25 (Summer 1959), (pp. 172–196) pp. 182–183.

247 Sallie Brown to Willie Brown, September 14, 1857, John Stillman Brown Family Papers (microfilm edition, roll 1), manuscript division, Kansas State Historical Society, Topeka, Kansas. Used with permission.

248 E. Nute Jr. to H. A. Miles, September 14, 1857, property of Andover-Harvard Theological Library, *American Unitarian Association Letterbooks*, 1822–1902, bMS571/122, 9/8/1857–12/28/1857. Used with permission.

249 W. B. Edmonds (E. B. Whitman) to N. Hawkins (John Brown), October 5, 1857, John Brown Collection, Kansas State Historical Society, Topeka, Kansas. Used with permission.

250 E. B. Whitman to H. A. Miles, October 15, 1857, property of Andover-Harvard Theological Library, *American Unitarian Association Letterbooks*, 1822–1902, bMS571/122, 9/8/1857–12/28/1857. Used with permission.

251 E. Nute Jr. to J. S. Brown, December 15, 1857, Halderman Collection, Kansas State Historical Society, Topeka, Kansas. Used with permission.

252 *Herald of Freedom*, December 19, 1857, Vol. 3, No. 9, microfilm Roll #1, L190, Kansas State Historical Society, Topeka, Kansas. Used with permission.

253 E. B. Whitman to C. Clark, January 1, 1858, property of Andover-Harvard Theological Library, *American Unitarian Association Letterbooks*, 1822–1902, bMS571/123, 12/29/1857–3/23/1858 or 124, 1/1/1858–3/1858.

254 E. B. Whitman to H. A. Miles, January 5, 1858, property of Andover-Harvard Theological Library, *American Unitarian Association Letterbooks*, 1822–1902, bMS571/123, 12/29/1857–3/23/1858 or 124, 1/1/1858–3/1858. Used with permission.

255 E. B. Whitman to H. A. Miles, January 5, 1858, property of Andover Harvard Theological Library, *American Unitarian Association Letterbooks*, 1822–1902, bMS571/123 12/29/1857–3/23/1858 or 124, 1/1/1858–3/1858. Used with permission.

256 *Herald of Freedom*, January 9, 1858, Vol. 3, No. 22, microfilm Roll #1, LM89, Kansas State Historical Society, Topeka, Kansas.

257 E. B. Whitman to H. A. Miles, January 23, 1858, property of Andover-Harvard Theological Library, *American Unitarian Association Letterbooks*, 1822–1902, bMS571/123, 12/29/1857–3/23/1858 or 124, 1/1/1858–3/1858.

258 J. S. Brown to H. A. Miles, January 23, 1858, in *The Quarterly Journal of the American Unitarian Association*, Volume V, Boston: American Unitarian Association, 1858, Andover-Harvard Theological Library, Harvard Divinity School, Andover-Harv. Theol. Mflm. Period. 108, p. 358.

259 E. B. Whitman to H. A. Miles, February 18, 1858, property of Andover-Harvard Theological Library, *American Unitarian Association Letterbooks*, 1822–1902, bMS571/123, 12/29/1857–3/23/1858 or 124, 1/1/1858–3/1858.

260 E. Nute Jr. to H. A. Miles, February 22, 1858, property of Andover-Harvard Theological Library, *American Unitarian Association Letterbooks*, 1822–1902, bMS571/123, 12/29/1857–3/23/1858 or 124, 1/1/1858–3/1858.

261 J. S. Brown to E. E. Hale, May 2, 1858, New England Emigrant Aid Company Collection, #624, Box 2, Folder 2, Kansas State Historical Society, Topeka, Kansas.

262 E. Nute Jr. to E. E. Hale, May 10, 1858, New England Emigrant Aid Company Papers, MS619, Kansas State Historical Society, Topeka, Kansas.

263 E. Nute Jr. to E. E. Hale, May 10, 1858, New England Emigrant Aid Company Papers, MS619, Kansas State Historical Society, Topeka, Kansas. Used with permission.

264 Edward J. Renehan Jr., *The Secret Six: The True Tale of the Men Who Conspired with John Brown*, Columbia, S.C.: University of South Carolina Press, 1997.

265 J. S. Brown to W. Brown, June 13,1858, John Stillman Brown Collection, #300, Box 1, Folder 14, Kansas State Historical Society, Topeka, Kansas.

266 E. Nute Jr. to H. A. Miles, June 15, 1858, property of Andover-Harvard Theological Library, *American Unitarian Association Letterbooks*, 1822–1902, bMS571/126, 5/1/1858–6/30/1858. Used with permission.

267 J. Brown to "Dear Friend," June 22, 1858, Chicago; John Brown Jr. Papers 1830–1932, Ohio Historical Society Microfilm.

268 Maria Felt to Thomas W. Higginson, June 25, 1858, Kansas State Historical Society, Thomas W. Higginson Collection, #380, Box 1, Folder 7. Used with permission.

269 *Herald of Freedom*, July 3, 1858, Vol. 3, #47; Kansas State Historical Society, Miscellaneous Kansas Newspapers/*Herald of Freedom*, Microfilm Roll 1, Lab #3400. Used with permission.

270 E. Nute Jr. to A. A. Lawrence, July 24, 1858, Massachusetts Historical Society, Boston. Used with permission.

271 A. A. Lawrence to E. Nute Jr., August 5, 1858, *Kansas Collection*, University of Kansas Libraries, RH/MS/p84;B.2.

272 E. Nute Jr. to A. A. Lawrence, August 27, 1858, Massachusetts Historical Society, Boston.

273 E. Nute Jr. to A. A. Lawrence, September 1, 1858, Massachusetts Historical Society, Boston.

274 E. Nute Jr. to H. A. Miles, September 17, 1858, in the *Christian Register*, Boston, Saturday, October 30, 1858, Vol. XXXVII, property of Andover-Harvard Theological Library, Andover-Harv. Theol. Mflm. Period. 4202. Used with permission.

275 E. Nute Jr. to A. A. Lawrence, September 21, 1858, Massachusetts Historical Society, Boston. Used with permission.

276 E. Nute Jr. to H. A. Miles, October 15, 1858, property of Andover-Harvard Theological Library, *American Unitarian Association Letterbooks*, 1822–1902, bMS571/128, 10/1858–11/1858. Used with permission.

277 E. Nute Jr. to H. A. Miles, November 4, 1858, property of Andover-Harvard Theological Library, *American Unitarian Association Letterbooks*, 1822–1902, bMS571/ 128, 10/1858–11/1858.

278 E. B. Whitman to C. Clark, November 7, 1858, property of Andover-Harvard Theological Library, *American Unitarian Association Letterbooks*, 1822–1902, bMS571/128, 10/1858–11/1858.

279 E. Nute Jr. to H. A. Miles, December 21, 1858, property of Andover-Harvard Theological Library, *American Unitarian Association Letterbooks*, 1822–1902, bMS571/129, 12/1858. Used with permission.

280   E. Nute Jr. to H. A. Miles, December 25, 1858, property of Andover-Harvard Theological Library, *American Unitarian Association Letterbooks*, 1822–1902, bMS571/129, 12/1858.

281   *The Quarterly Journal of the American Unitarian Association*, Volume VI, Boston: American Unitarian Association, 1859, Andover-Harvard Theological Library, Harvard Divinity School, Andover-Harv. Theol. Mflm. Period. 108, p. 90. Used with permission.

282   *The Quarterly Journal of the American Unitarian Association*, Volume VI, Boston: American Unitarian Association, 1859, Andover-Harvard Theological Library, Harvard Divinity School, Andover-Harv. Theol. Mflm. Period. 108, p. 230. Used with permission.

283   *The Quarterly Journal of the American Unitarian Association*, Volume VI, Boston: American Unitarian Association, 1859, Andover-Harvard Theological Library, Harvard Divinity School, Andover-Harv. Theol. Mflm. Period. 108, p. 163. Used with permission.

The Underground Railroad and Harper's Ferry

284   M. A. Day Brown to W. Brown, January 30, 1859, John Stillman Brown Collection, #300, Box 1, Folder 14, Kansas State Historical Society, Topeka, Kansas. Used with permission.

285   E. Nute Jr. to unidentified recipient [Franklin Sanborn], February, 1859, John Brown Collection, #299, Box 2, Folder 2, Kansas State Historical Society, Topeka, Kansas. Used with permission.

286   E. Nute Jr. to unidentified recipient, February 14, 1859, John Brown Collection, #299, Box 2, Folder 1, Kansas State Historical Society, Topeka, Kansas. Used with permission.

287   Mary Ann Day Brown to Willie Brown, January 30, 1859, John Stillman Brown Collection; #300, Box 1, Folder 14, Kansas State Historical Society, Topeka, Kansas. Used with permission.

288   E. Nute Jr. to unidentified recipient, February 14, 1859, John Brown Collection, #299, Box 2, Folder 1, Kansas State Historical Society, Topeka, Kansas. Used with permission.

289 E. Nute Jr. to unidentified recipient [Samuel Gridley Howe], February 24, 1859, John Brown Collection, #299, Box 2, Folder 1, Kansas State Historical Society, Topeka, Kansas. Used with permission.

290 E. Nute Jr. to unidentified recipient [Samuel Gridley Howe], February 24, 1859, John Brown Collection, #299, Box 2, Folder 1, Kansas State Historical Society, Topeka, Kansas. Used with permission.

291 E. Nute Jr. to H. A. Miles, March 12, 1859, BMS 571/130, Andover-Harvard Theological Library, Manuscripts and Archives. Used with permission.

292 M. F. Conway to G. L. Stearns, March 16, 1859, John Brown Collection, #299, Box 2, Folder 2, Kansas State Historical Society, Topeka, Kansas.

293 *Herald of Freedom*, March 5, 1859, Vol. 4, No. 31, microfilm Roll #2, L191, Kansas State Historical Society, Topeka, Kansas.

294 Richard J. Hinton, "Pens That Made Kansas Free," *Transactions of the Kansas State Historical Society*, 1897–1900 6(1900): 371–382.

295 M. F. Conway to G. L. Stearns, March 16, 1859, John Brown Collection, #299, Box 2, Folder 2, Kansas State Historical Society, Topeka, Kansas.

296 E. Nute Jr. to F. B. Sanborn, March 22, 1859, John Brown Collection, #299, Box 2, Folder 2, Kansas State Historical Society, Topeka, Kansas. Used with permission.

297 E. Nute Jr. to H. A. Miles, April 17, 1859, BMS 571/131, Andover-Harvard Theological Library, Manuscripts and Archives. Used with permission.

298 E. Nute Jr. refers to the letter from C. Baker to the *Christian Register*, Boston, Saturday, February 4, 1856, property of Andover-Harvard Theological Library, *American Unitarian Association Letterbooks*, 1822–1902, bMS571/114 n.d. (1/1856)–3/27/1856. Used with permission.

299 *Herald of Freedom*, April 30, 1859, Vol. 4, No. 39, microfilm Roll #2, L191, Kansas State Historical Society, Topeka, Kansas. Used with permission.

300 E. Nute Jr. to *Christian Register*, May 9, 1859, Andover-Harvard Theological Library, Andover-Harv. Theol. Mflm. Period. 4202. Used with permission. *Christian Register*, Boston, Saturday, June 11, 1859, Vol. XXXVIII. Used with permission.

301 E. Nute Jr. to *Christian Register*, May 9, 1859, Andover-Harvard Theological Library, Andover-Harv. Theol. Mflm. Period. 4202, *Christian Register*, Boston, Saturday, June 11, 1859, Vol. XXX-VIII. Used with permission.

302 *Herald of Freedom*, June 11, 1859, Vol. 4, No. 45, microfilm Roll #2, L191, Kansas State Historical Society, Topeka, Kansas. Used with permission.

303 *Herald of Freedom*, July 16, 1859, Vol. 4, No. 50, microfilm Roll #2, L191, Kansas State Historical Society, Topeka, Kansas.

304 *Herald of Freedom*, July 30, 1859, Vol. 5, Number 2, microfilm Roll #2, L191, Kansas State Historical Society, Topeka, Kansas.

305 *Kansas Historical Collections*, Vol. 4, 1886–1890, "The Rescue of Dr. John W. Doy," paper read by Maj. James B. Abbot, of DeSoto, before the Kansas State Historical Society, at the annual meeting, January 15, 1889, pp. 312–323; *Herald of Freedom*, July 30, 1859, Vol. 5, No. 2, microfilm Roll #2, L191, Kansas State Historical Society, Topeka, Kansas.

306 *Kansas Historical Collections*, Vol. 4, 1886–1890, "The Rescue of Dr. John W. Doy," paper read by Maj. James B. Abbot, of DeSoto, before the Kansas State Historical Society, at the annual meeting, January 15, 1889, pp. 312–323; *Herald of Freedom*, July 30, 1859, Vol. 5, No. 2, microfilm Roll #2, L191, Kansas State Historical Society, Topeka, Kansas.

307 E. Nute Jr. to J. F. Clarke, August 10, 1859, property of Andover-Harvard Theological Library, *American Unitarian Association Letterbooks*, 1822–1902, bMS571/132, 6/1/1859–8/1859.

308 E. Nute Jr. to J. F. Clarke, August 10, 1859, property of Andover-Harvard Theological Library, *American Unitarian Association Letterbooks*, 1822–1902, bMS571/132, 6/1/1859–8/1859. Used with permission.

309 J. S. Brown to W. P. Tilden, September 18, 1859, property of Andover-Harvard Theological Library, *American Unitarian Association Letterbooks*, 1822–1902, bMS571/133, 9/1859–10/1859. Used with permission.

310 J. S. Brown to W. P. Tilden, September 18, 1859, property of Andover-Harvard Theological Library, *American Unitarian Association Letterbooks*, 1822–1902, bMS571/133, 9/1859–10/1859.

311 Alberta Pantle, compiled by, "Marriage Notices from Kansas Territorial Newspapers, 1854–1861," *The Kansas Historical Quarterly*, Summer 1955, Topeka: Kansas State Historical Society, pp. 445–486; *Herald of Freedom*, October 15, 1859, Vol. 5, No. 13, microfilm Roll #2, L191, Kansas State Historical Society, Topeka, Kansas.

312 J. S. Brown to W. P. Tilden, October 11, 1859, property of Andover-Harvard Theological Library, *American Unitarian Association Letterbooks*, 1822–1902, bMS571/117, 8/9/1859–10/26/1859. Used with permission.

313 J. S. Brown to G. Hosmer, October 17, 1859, property of Andover-Harvard Theological Library, *American Unitarian Association Letterbooks*, 1822–1902, bMS571/133, 9/1859–10/1859. Used with permission.

314 Edward J. Renehan Jr., *The Secret Six: The True Tale of the Men Who Conspired with John Brown*, Columbia, S.C.: University of South Carolina Press, 1977.

315 Richard Hinton, *John Brown and His Men, With Some Account of the Roads They Traveled to Reach Harper's Ferry*, New York: Funk and Wagnalls; revised ed. 1894, p. 270.

316 *New York Tribune*, December, 1859, Kansas State Historical Society, Topeka, Kansas, *Webb Scrapbook* Roll #4, LM92.

317 Frank W. Blackmar, A.M. Ph.D. *Kansas: A Cyclopedia of State History, Embracing Events, Institutions, Industries, Counties, Cities, Towns, Prominent Persons, Etc.*, Vol. II, Chicago: Standard Publishing Company, 1912, p. 552.

318 Testimony of Richard Realf, January 21, 1860, in *Senate Reports*, 36 Cong. 1 Sess., No. 278 (Serial 1040).

319   John C. Malin, *John Brown and the Legend of Fifty-six*, Philadelphia: The American Philosophical Society, 1942, p. 34. Used with permission.

320   *Herald of Freedom*, October 29, 1859, Vol. 5, No. 15, microfilm Roll #2, L191, Kansas State Historical Society, Topeka, Kansas. Used with permission.

321   John P. Cushing, ed. *Lyell's Travels in North America in 1841–42.* New York: Charles E. Merrill Co., 1909, p. 22.

322   E. Nute Jr. to Col. R. J. Hinton, April 12, 1893, Richard Josiah Hinton Collection, Box/Folder Correspondence and Misc. papers, April, 1893 (Box 3, Folder 53), Kansas State Historical Society, Topeka, Kansas; E. Nute Jr. to Col. R. J. Hinton, June 4, 1893, Richard Josiah Hinton Collection, Box/Folder Correspondence and Misc. papers, June, 1893 (Box 3, Folder 60), Kansas State Historical Society, Topeka, Kansas.

323   *Christian Register*, Boston, Saturday, October 13, 1860, property of Andover-Harvard Theological Library, Andover-Harv. Theol. Mflm. Period. 4202, p. 18. Used with permission.

324   The dungeon of Chillon was where the Genevan prior Francois Bonivard, Swiss patriot and historian, was imprisoned 1532–1536. He was memorialized in verse by George Gordon, Lord Byron.

325   *Christian Register*, Boston, Saturday, October 13, 1860, Vol. XXXIX, property of Andover-Harvard Theological Library, Andover-Harv. Theol. Mflm. Period. 4202, p. 172. Used with permission.

326   *Theodore Parker's Journals*, pp. 86–97. Property of Andover-Harvard Theological Library. Used with permission.

327   E. Nute Jr. to C. W. Slack, October 23,1860, Charles Wesley Slack Papers, 1817–1860, Kent State University Libraries, Special Collections and Archives. Used with permission.

328   J. S. Brown to J. F. Clarke, May 1, 1860, property of Andover-Harvard Theological Library, *American Unitarian Association Letterbooks*, 1822–1902, bMS571/136, 4/1860–6/1860. Used with permission.

329 J. S. Brown to J. F. Clarke, June 15, 1860, property of Andover-Harvard Theological Library, *American Unitarian Association Letterbooks,* 1822–1902, bMS571/136, 4/1860–6/1860. Used with permission.

330 E. D. Ladd to H. A. Miles, June 25, 1860, property of Andover-Harvard Theological Library, *American Unitarian Association Letterbooks,* 1822–1902, bMS571/136, 4/1860–6/1860.

331 J. S. Brown to J. F. Clarke, July 7, 1860, property of Andover-Harvard Theological Library, *American Unitarian Association Letterbooks,* 1822–1902, bMS571/137, 7/1860–8/1860. Used with permission.

332 John S. Brown to J. F. Clarke, July 7, 1860, property of Andover-Harvard Theological Library, *American Unitarian Association Letterbooks,* 1822–1902, bMS571/137, 7/1860–8/1860.

333 J. S. Brown to J. F. Clarke, August 2, 1860, property of Andover-Harvard Theological Library, *American Unitarian Association Letterbooks,* 1822–1902, bMS571/137, 7/1860–8/1860. Used with permission.

334 *Christian Register,* Boston, Saturday, October 13, 1860, Vol. XXXIX, property of Andover-Harvard Theological Library, Andover-Harv. Theol. Mflm. Period. 4202, p. 162. Used with permission.

335 *Christian Register,* Boston, Saturday, October 13, 1860, Vol. XXXIX, property of Andover-Harvard Theological Library, Andover-Harv. Theol. Mflm. Period. 4202, p. 162. Used with permission.

336 E. Nute Jr. to C. W. Slack, October 23, 1860, *Charles Wesley Slack Papers,* 1817–1860, Kent State University Libraries, Special Collections and Archives. Used with permission.

337 Edward Fitch to Mother, November 18, 1860, Peterson, John M., Kansas History, Letters of Edward and Sarah Fitch, Lawrence Kansas, 1855–1863, pp. 48–70, 78–100, Kansas State Historical Society: 1989, p. 92. Used with permission.

Civil War

338 E. Nute Jr. to G. W. Fox, April 11, 1861, property of Andover-Harvard Theological Library, *American Unitarian Association Letterbooks*, 1822–1902, bMS571/141, 3/2/1861–6/27/1861. Used with permission.

339 J. S. Brown to J. F. Clarke, April 14, 1861, property of Andover-Harvard Theological Library, *American Unitarian Association Letterbooks*, 1822–1902, bMS571/141, 3/2/1861–6/27/1861. Used with permission.

340 John W. Brinsfield, William C. Davis, Benedict Maryniak, and James I. Robertson Jr., *Faith in the Fight: Civil War Chaplains*, Mechanicsville, Pa.: Stackpole Books, A Virginia Center for Civil War Studies Book, 2003, p. 121.

341 John W. Brinsfield, William C. Davis, Benedict Maryniak, and James I. Robertson Jr., *Faith in the Fight: Civil War Chaplains*, Mechanicsville, Pa.: Stackpole Books, A Virginia Center for Civil War Studies Book, 2003, p. viii.

342 John W. Brinsfield, William C. Davis, Benedict Maryniak, and James I. Robertson Jr., *Faith in the Fight: Civil War Chaplains*, Mechanicsville, Pa.: Stackpole Books, A Virginia Center for Civil War Studies Book, 2003, p. 26.

343 John W. Brinsfield, William C. Davis, Benedict Maryniak, and James I. Robertson Jr., *Faith in the Fight: Civil War Chaplains*, Mechanicsville, Pa.: Stackpole Books, A Virginia Center for Civil War Studies Book, 2003, pp. 28–29. Used with permission.

344 John W. Brinsfield, William C. Davis, Benedict Maryniak, and James I. Robertson Jr., *Faith in the Fight: Civil War Chaplains*, Mechanicsville, Pa.: Stackpole Books, A Virginia Center for Civil War Studies Book, 2003, pp. 20–21. Used with permission.

345 John W. Brinsfield, William C. Davis, Benedict Maryniak, and James I. Robertson Jr., *Faith in the Fight: Civil War Chaplains*, Mechanicsville, Pa.: Stackpole Books, A Virginia Center for Civil War Studies Book, 2003, p. 31. Used with permission.

346 John W. Brinsfield, William C. Davis, Benedict Maryniak, and James I. Robertson Jr., *Faith in the Fight: Civil War Chaplains*,

Mechanicsville, Pa.: Stackpole Books, A Virginia Center for Civil War Studies Book, 2003, p. 45.

347 John W. Brinsfield, William C. Davis, Benedict Maryniak, and James I. Robertson Jr., *Faith in the Fight: Civil War Chaplains*, Mechanicsville, Pa.: Stackpole Books, A Virginia Center for Civil War Studies Book, 2003, pp. 43–46.

348 John W. Brinsfield, William C. Davis, Benedict Maryniak, and James I. Robertson Jr., *Faith in the Fight: Civil War Chaplains*, Mechanicsville, Pa.: Stackpole Books, A Virginia Center for Civil War Studies Book, 2003, p. 28.

349 John W. Brinsfield, William C. Davis, Benedict Maryniak, and James I. Robertson Jr., *Faith in the Fight: Civil War Chaplains*, Mechanicsville, Pa.: Stackpole Books, A Virginia Center for Civil War Studies Book, 2003, p. 28.

350 E. Nute Jr. to G. W. Fox, October 29, 1861, property of Andover-Harvard Theological Library, *American Unitarian Association Letterbooks*, 1822–1902, bMS571/142, 7/1/1861–11/30/1861. Used with permission.

351 "The Military Hospitals of Missouri—Testimony of Rev. Ephraim Nute," *Chicago Tribune,* January 9, 1862, p. 2.

352 S. Brown to W. Brown, February 23, 1862, *John Stillman Brown Family Papers* (microfilm edition roll 2), manuscript division, Kansas State Historical Society, Topeka, Kansas. Used with permission.

353 Frederick Law Olmsted, General Secretary of the Sanitary Commission, *Sanitary Commission No. 55, Reports From the Western Department*, Louisville, October 24, 1862, p. 5. Newberry Library (non-circulating) General Collections.

354 Francis A. Lord, *They Fought for the Union*, Harrisburg, Pa.: The Stackpole Company, 1960, p. 132.

355 Francis A. Lord, *They Fought for the Union*, Harrisburg, Pa.: The Stackpole Company, 1960, p. 253.

356 Francis A. Lord, *They Fought for the Union*, Harrisburg, Pa.: The Stackpole Company, 1960, p. 250.

357 L. R. Webber to Miss Brown, November 27, 1862, John Stillman Brown Family Papers, microfilm Roll #2, MS566, Kansas State Historical Society, Topeka, Kansas.

358 E. Nute Jr. to J. S. Brown, November 26, 1892, Halderman Collection, Kansas State Historical Society, Topeka, Kansas.

359 Francis A. Lord, *They Fought for the Union*, Harrisburg, Pa.: The Stackpole Company, 1960, p. 214. Used with permission.

360 E. Nute Jr. to J. S. Brown, November 26, 1892, *Halderman Collection*, Kansas State Historical Society, Topeka, Kansas. Used with permission.

361 Frederick Law Olmsted, General Secretary of the Sanitary Commission, *Sanitary Commission No. 55, Reports From the Western Department*, Louisville, October 24, 1862, pp. 1–2. Newberry Library (non-circulating) General Collections.

362 Frederick Law Olmsted, General Secretary of the Sanitary Commission, *Sanitary Commission No. 55, Reports From the Western Department*, Louisville, October 24, 1862, p. 5. Newberry Library (non-circulating) General Collections.

363 "The Military Hospitals of Missouri—Testimony of Rev. Ephraim Nute," *Chicago Tribune*, January 9, 1862, p. 2.

364 Jacob Gilbert Forman, *The Western Sanitary Commission; a sketch of its origin, history, labors for the sick and wounded of the Western armies, and aid given to freedmen and Union refugees, with incidents of hospital life*, St. Louis: R. P. Studley & Co., 1864, p. 45.

365 "The Military Hospitals of Missouri—Testimony of Rev. Ephraim Nute," *Chicago Tribune*, January 9, 1862, p. 2.

366 *Western Sanitary Commission History: Soldiers Homes*, Report of the Western Sanitary Commission ending June 1, 1863, St. Louis, Mo.: Western Sanitary Commission Rooms, 1863, p. 21. Newberry Library (non-circulating) General Collections.

367 *Western Sanitary Commission History: Soldiers Homes*, Report of the Western Sanitary Commission ending June 1, 1863, St. Louis, Mo.: Western Sanitary Commission Rooms, 1863, p. 22. Newberry Library (non-circulating) General Collections.

368   *Western Sanitary Commission History: Soldiers Homes*, Report of the Western Sanitary Commission ending June 1, 1863, St. Louis, Mo.: Western Sanitary Commission Rooms, 1863, p. 22. Newberry Library (non-circulating) General Collections.

369   Jacob Gilbert Forman, *The Western Sanitary Commission; a sketch of its origin, history, labors for the sick and wounded of the Western armies, and aid given to freedmen and Union refugees, with incidents of hospital life*, St. Louis: R. P. Studley & Co., 1864, pp. 80–83.

370   *Western Sanitary Commission History: Soldiers Homes*, Report of the Western Sanitary Commission ending June 1, 1863, St. Louis, Mo.: Western Sanitary Commission Rooms, 1863, p. 22. Newberry Library (non-circulating) General Collections.

371   Extract of a letter from E. Nute to J. Yeatman, enclosed in James E. Yeatman to Abraham Lincoln, February 23, 1863, Y-2 1863, Letters Received Irregular, RG 107 [L-122], National Archives of the United States.

372   Ann Julia Soule, in Joanna L. Stratton, *Pioneer Women Voices from the Kansas Frontier*, New York: Simon and Schuster, 1981.

373   J. S. Brown to Brother J. L. Rupin, September 1, 1863, John Stillman Brown Family Papers (microfilm edition roll 2) manuscript division, Kansas State Historical Society, Topeka, Kansas. Used with permission.

374   E. Nute Jr. to unspecified, 1863 [St. Louis?: s.n., 1863], Broadside, American Antiquarian Society. Used with permission.

375   E. Nute Jr. to Col. S. B. Holabird, October 4, 1863, MS 92-25 Box 1 FF17, Wichita State University Libraries, Special Collections, Kantor Collection of U.S. Sanitary Commission. Used with permission.

376   E. Nute Jr. to G. W. Fox, November 22, 1863, property of Andover-Harvard Theological Library, *American Unitarian Association Letterbooks, 1822–1902*, bMS571/149, 11/2/1863–12/1863. Used with permission.

377   J. E. Grotiman to Gen. U. S. Grant, December 19, 1863, National Archives Trust Fund, Washington, D.C., 20408, MWCTB, Veterans Records of Nute, Ephraim, Jr.

378 Officer's Casualty Sheet, January 7, 1864, National Archives Trust Fund, Washington, D.C., 20408, MWCTB, Veterans Records of Nute, Ephraim, Jr.

379 J. G. Foreman to U. S. Grant, January 15, 1864, National Archives Trust Fund, Washington, D.C., 20408, MWCTB, Veterans Records of Nute, Ephraim, Jr.

Epilogue

380 *Unitarian Minister's Union Records,* Andover-Harvard Theological Library. Used with permission.

381 E. Nute Jr. to E. E. Hale, February 6, 1871, property of Andover-Harvard Theological Library, *American Unitarian Association Letterbooks*, 1822–1902, bMS571/197, 8/1870–6/1871.

382 Ephraim/Lucy Nute divorce papers, 01/18/1873, 90-06-19, box 26, divorce #2448, Kenneth Spencer Research Library, University of Kansas, Lawrence, Kansas.

383 E. Nute Jr. to O. E. Learnard, April 7, 1885, Kansas Collection, University of Kansas Libraries, RH/MS/36:17.

384 E. Nute Jr. to J. S. Brown, November 26, 1892, Joseph C. Halderman Collection, Kansas State Historical Society, Topeka, Kansas. Used with permission.

385 Mike Belt, "Historic Bell Again Commands Attention," *Lawrence Journal-World*, Monday, May 10, 2004.

386 Mike Belt, "Historic Bell Again Commands Attention," *Lawrence Journal-World*, Monday, May 10, 2004.

387 Church history gathered from promotional materials provided by the Lawrence Unitarian Society for its sesquicentennial celebration.

INDEX